SHOOTING THE MESSENGER

If the Al-Qaeda terrorists who attacked the United States in 2001 wanted to weaken the West, they achieved their mission by striking a blow at the heart of democracy.

Since 9/11 governments including those of the USA, the UK, France and Australia have introduced tough, intimidating legislation to discourage the legitimate activities of a probing press, so greatly needed after the Iraq War proved that executive government could not be trusted.

Often hiding behind arguments about defending national security and fighting the war on terror, governments criminalised legitimate journalistic work, ramping up their attacks on journalists' sources, and the whistle-blowers who are so essential in keeping governments honest.

Through detailed research and analysis, this book, which includes interviews with leading figures in the field, including Edward Snowden, explains how mass surveillance and anti-terror laws are of questionable value in defeating terrorism, but have had a 'chilling effect' on one of the foundations of democracy: revelatory journalism.

Andrew Fowler is an award-winning investigative journalist and a former reporter with the Australian Broadcasting Corporation's (ABC) *Foreign Correspondent* and its premier investigative TV documentary programme, *Four Corners*. Andrew began his journalism career in the early 1970s, covering the IRA bombing campaign for the London Evening News. He first interviewed Julian Assange for *Foreign Correspondent* in early 2010 and went on to write the bestselling book *The Most Dangerous Man in the World* (Melbourne University Press, 2011), which has been translated and published in countries as diverse as China, South Korea, the USA, Russia, Indonesia, Romania and Taiwan. *The Most Dangerous Man in the World* was described by Pentagon Papers whistle-blower Daniel Ellsberg as 'a gripping thriller. By far the best account of Julian Assange's motives and the talents that make him so dangerous' and by Geoffrey Robertson QC as 'the most balanced, fair and factual account yet published of a saga much misrepresented in the media'.

His second book, *The War on Journalism* (Random House, 2015), was cited by the Australian Financial Review as one of the best books of 2015 and was a finalist in the prestigious Walkley Book Awards. Andrew's original ABC programme about Assange and WikiLeaks won the New York Festival Gold Medal. Andrew Fowler currently spends his time between Australia and France.

The Criminalization of Political Dissent
Series editor: Professor Judith Bessant, RMIT University, Melbourne, Australia

This challenging new book series explores the way governments since 9/11 from across the political spectrum intensified their efforts to criminalize both traditional and new forms of digital political dissent. The series will feature major contributions from the social sciences, law and legal studies, media studies and philosophy to document what happens when governments choose to regard activists campaigning for increased government transparency and accountability, environmental sustainability, social justice, human rights and pro-democracy as engaging in illegal activities.

The book series explores the legal, political and ethical implications when governments engage habitually in mass electronic and digital surveillance, outlaw freedom of movement, real and virtual public assembly and prosecute digital activists. The books in this series are a 'must read' for anyone interested in the future of democracy.

Series titles include:

Governing Youth Politics in the Age of Surveillance
Edited by Maria Grasso and Judith Bessant

Shooting the Messenger: Criminalising Journalism
Authored by Andrew Fowler

SHOOTING THE MESSENGER

Criminalising Journalism

Andrew Fowler

Routledge
Taylor & Francis Group

LONDON AND NEW YORK

First published 2018
by Routledge
2 Park Square, Milton Park, Abingdon, Oxon OX14 4RN

and by Routledge
711 Third Avenue, New York, NY 10017

Routledge is an imprint of the Taylor & Francis Group, an informa business

British Library Cataloguing-in-Publication Data
A catalogue record for this book is available from the British Library

Library of Congress Cataloging-in-Publication Data
A catalog record for this book has been requested

ISBN: 978-1-138-29660-2 (hbk)
ISBN: 978-1-138-29661-9 (pbk)
ISBN: 978-1-315-09992-7 (ebk)

Typeset in Goudy
by Sunrise Setting Ltd, Brixham, UK

CONTENTS

ACKNOWLEDGEMENTS

My sincerest thanks to all those who helped in the making of this book. I owe a particular debt of gratitude to my wife Pamela, who supported me throughout the venture, copy editing and providing encouragement during the process. I am also indebted to others who also gave insightful assistance, including Professor Julianne Schultz, from Griffith University, Dr Paul Lashmar (now at London City University) and Professor Judith Bessant, who had the idea for the book in the first place, and is the Routledge commissioning editor. Her support, and trust in me, was particularly valuable. Heather Forbes and Peter Cronau went out of their way to assist, as did my agent Jane Burridge, always the voice of reason, and without whom the book's brilliant cover would never have been created by Adam Yazxhi. Thanks to Sarah Harrison of the UK-based Courage Foundation and to all the journalists who encouraged me to write this book, in particular the Media Entertainment and Arts Alliance [MEAA] in Australia, which has fought hard to alert its members and the public to the extraordinary dangers posed to journalism by increasingly intrusive mass surveillance and counter terrorism laws.

INTRODUCTION

Welcome to the machine

Just half an hour's drive north-east from Washington DC, the well-paved dual highway passes a forest before a final line of trees gives way to more open ground. As the road swings round, on the left, looking like a sprawling shopping complex which has outgrown its site, the National Security Agency (NSA) appears. Its massive glass and concrete shoebox-shaped buildings dominate the skyline. The car park neatly arranged around its perimeter gives a hint at just how many thousands of people work inside. This is the headquarters of the most powerful intelligence-gathering organisation the world has ever seen.

It is the centre of a network that straddles the Earth. From the spy base at Pine Gap with its array of antennas pointing skywards against the sunset red of the Australian outback, to Menwith Hill on the green undulating farmland of Yorkshire in the north of England, the NSA is connected to satellites circling overhead, and undersea surveillance systems tapping into transcontinental telephone cables. Nearly every phone call, email or electronically created signal will at some time end up here, or in one of the data storage bases of the NSA's sister agencies in Australia, New Zealand, Canada or the UK. Known as the Five Eyes partnership, the intelligence-sharing agreement has its roots in the days of the British Empire. Now the relationship between the English-speaking nations is more equal, though new inequalities are emerging.

The NSA's impressive electronic edifice is as much a symbol of US authority as of the shifting power relationship between the individual and a state eager to control the flow of all information.

Throughout the Western liberal democracies new laws have given governments greater powers to eavesdrop on the population and the journalists whose job it is to keep them informed. Those laws which gave governments such sweeping surveillance powers were introduced ostensibly to track terrorists and reduce the number of attacks. But detailed analysis suggests the so-called anti-terror surveillance laws have not achieved what governments promised. Instead they have often been more effectively used to track down whistle-blowers and criminalise the work of journalists. So what is the NSA's true objective? It operates like a huge archival Wayback Machine, gathering detailed historical data, more suitable for plundering industrial secrets or finding targets to destroy in Cyberwars than stopping terrorists. In the hands of an unaccountable executive it is a fearsome machine, even for the citizens of the countries that run it.

The NSA was designated as the US's overseas electronic spy agency, but after the 2001 attacks on New York's Twin Towers and the Pentagon in Washington, US president George W Bush turned its awesome power inwards. He signed an executive order – of dubious legal authority and, many say, in violation of the US Constitution – lifting all restrictions to allow the NSA to spy on the US public. So concerned were the White House lawyers about the order's legality, their advice was not to seek approval from any oversight authority because it would possibly be rejected. It would be testing what one of the world's great philosophers, John Locke, called the use of 'the prerogative power' which, he explained, 'is said to be important for good order to prevail in times of exception'.[1] Locke was writing in the 17th century when monarchs claimed divine right over their subjects. Bush was drawing a long bow, but the secret leaked out.

Not far away, at the *New York Times* offices in Manhattan, two reporters discovered what President Bush and the NSA were up to. It was a scoop that any newspaper should have splashed on its front page, but the *Times* was not so sure. It contacted the White House to give Bush – who was running for re-election in 2004 – an outline of what it knew. In a lengthy exchange, he demanded the story not run because it was against the US national interest. The paper's editor Bill Keller agreed.

Yet the following year the paper did publish the report, almost unchanged from the original, apart from some information that the administration argued might 'be useful to terrorists'.[2]

The puzzling decision to delay publication certainly helped Bush avoid any embarrassing questions during the campaign and many believe it assisted him in winning the subsequent election, but it also emboldened successive administrations to clamp down on unfavourable disclosures, threatening criminal action against journalists and jailing whistle-blowers.

Forty-six years ago, when the *New York Times* published the top-secret Pentagon Papers – which revealed how successive governments had deceived the American people over the Vietnam war – it told the White House nothing. President Richard Nixon knew nothing about the story until he read it in the *New York Times*. Back in 1971 when the US was involved in a real war, the *Times* stuck to its journalistic principals. Now with a confected war on a *concept* – terrorism – the newspaper caved in. In a country where the First Amendment to the US Constitution protects journalists like nowhere else on Earth, an overly cautious media had acquiesced in what Locke had argued was the prerogative of leaders to make executive decisions which were important for order to prevail in exceptional times. Or as Richard Nixon put it more succinctly: 'When the President does it, that means it is not illegal.'[3] The fact that US phones were now being bugged without a warrant had been successfully woven into the war narrative. It was a proposition that would underpin many of the arguments advanced by the executive government to force those who disagreed with any of its operations to be silent, or suffer the consequences. It's what Professor Mark Neocleous calls 'security mongering', where any debate questioning security is closed off from discussion.[4]

Few would dispute that intelligence agencies fulfil a necessary function in tracking a state's enemies but this was very different. It showed how far the most powerful country in the world would go in bending the law on surveillance. Just as important, once given the executive nod, the NSA – without the cover of Presidential executive authority – would take the next step and break the law, illegally gathering massive amounts of metadata, detailing phone calls and email communications of millions of Americans. What was more alarming, for the rest of the world – non-members of the Five Eyes countries – there were no such 'safeguards'. If you used a telephone or the internet, nowhere on the planet was safe from the prying ears and eyes of the NSA and its sister agencies. Every mobile phone tower, every email, every payment at the supermarket, every digital trans-action added to the profile the NSA was capable of building on every person on Earth. Huge databases scattered across the world logged the digital footsteps and fingerprints of us all. Not since the concept of a public space was first identified by the German political scientist and philosopher Jurgen Habermas, as a place where ideas were debated freely and separately from the control of the state or the church, has there been such a powerful threat to public discourse in the West. As Habermas argued: 'The people themselves came to see the public sphere as a regulatory institution against the authority of the state.'[5]

Habermas's detailed assessment of the rise of the mass media in the 19th century and its use to influence and control populations by what he called the 're-feudalisation of power' is not very far removed from the view of the future which so frightened Edward Snowden, a 29-year-old computer analyst, working as a contractor for the NSA in Hawaii. In 2013 Snowden's disclosures revealed the NSA's extraordinarily intrusive capabilities: X-Key Score, Borderless Informant, Upstream . . . systems which allowed the NSA to intercept, store, categorise and assess huge amounts of strategic and personal information – and then access it at the press of a key. Snowden decided he would do all he could to prevent this kind of intrusion into people's everyday lives. He even under-stood it might cost him his life. It's not as though the world had not been warned before about the dangers of uncontrolled intelligence agencies, and the threats they posed to democratic society. The United States Senate Select Committee to Study Governmental Operations with Respect to Intelligence, chaired by Senator Frank Church, was set up in the early 1970s to investigate reports that the CIA was involved in covert assassinations and the subversion of foreign governments, and that US intelligence agencies were spying on the civilian population. On 17 August, 1975 Senator Church appeared on NBC's *Meet the Press* and without mentioning the NSA by name issued a grave warning:

> In the need to develop a capacity to know what potential enemies are doing, the United States government has perfected a technological capability that enables us to monitor the messages that go through the air. We must know, at the same time, that capability at any time could be turned around on the American people, and no American would have any privacy left: such is the capability to monitor everything—telephone conversations, telegrams, it doesn't matter. There would be no place to hide.

With the election of Donald Trump to the Presidency of the US, his words seem eerily prescient.

> If this government ever became a tyranny, if a dictator ever took charge in this country, the technological capacity that the intelligence community has given the government could enable it to impose total tyranny, and there would be no way to fight back because the most careful effort to combine together in resistance to the government, no matter how privately it was done, is within the reach of the government to know. Such is the capability of this technology. (. . .)

> I don't want to see this country ever go across [that] bridge. I know the capacity that is there to make tyranny total in America, and we must see to it that this agency and all agencies that possess this technology operate within the law and under proper supervision so that we never cross over that abyss. That is the abyss from which there is no return.[6]

Senator Church had predicted a future that Snowden wanted the world to know was real. When he decided to speak out, the *New York Times* should have been a natural choice. But Snowden strongly objected to the way the newspaper had failed to publish details of the NSA's secret surveillance programme of American citizens after the 9/11 terrorist attacks. Instead, he contacted an outsider, the lawyer turned journalist Glenn Greenwald, who had caught his attention by vigorously defending the work of WikiLeaks when it came under sustained attack from sections of the media and the US government. In 2010 WikiLeaks began releasing classified and sensitive documents which gave a glimpse into the inner workings of the State Department and the Pentagon – part of a cache of nearly three quarters of a million leaked to the organisation by US Army intelligence officer Chelsea Manning. Once again Iraq was central to the argument. The WikiLeaks files, among other things, disclosed the deception over how many civilians had been killed in the invasion. WikiLeaks worked with several traditional media outlets to produce the reports, but it was an uneasy relationship, particularly with the *New York Times*. The newspaper tried to cast Assange as a non-journalist, an argument which would strip him of his First Amendment protection, after the US administration began castigating the newspaper for running reports from WikiLeaks. There would be a price to pay for what Assange called a form of 'scientific journalism' where readers could access the original documents via the internet. The state would move against these agents of change, forcing a reassessment of what it meant to live in an open liberal democracy. As the Pentagon Papers' whistle-blower, Daniel Ellsberg, told me in 2011, instead of being more open he feared a backlash. Governments would become more secretive to protect themselves, not less.

Ellsberg's view was eerily prophetic. Despite all his calls for a relaxation of the powers of the security and intelligence agencies, and more oversight before he became president, Barack Obama presided over the largest number of prosecutions of whistle-blowers in the nation's entire history. Though Chelsea Manning's sentence was commuted by Obama she had been originally jailed for 35 years in conditions described by the UN Special Rapporteur on Torture as at 'a minimum cruel, inhuman and degrading treatment in violation of article 16 of the convention against torture'.[7] In 2017 Edward Snowden was still in Russia, under threat of arrest for charges under the US Espionage Act (1917) if he returned to the US or entered a country which might extradite him there. Julian Assange remained in the Ecuadorian Embassy in London, where he had been since 19 June, 2012. After a delay of six years the Swedish prosecutor's office finally interviewed him over allegations of rape and sexual molestation first made in 2010, which had been dealt with in a highly questionable manner by the Swedish prosecutor. In the end, all allegations against Assange were withdrawn. But there was still no agreement that Assange would not be extradited later to the US, the reason he sought political asylum in the embassy. In fact, in an extraordinary outburst, Mike Pompeo, in his first speech as director of the CIA, seemed to threaten that an attempt at extradition from the UK was a definite possibility. 'We can no longer allow Assange and his colleagues the latitude to use free speech values against us,'[8] he said indicating he believed it was possible to override First Amendment rights for foreigners. It might have been a questionable legal assertion, made more obviously dubious by the fact that Pompeo stayed clear of naming any of the big media organisations that published and broadcast WikiLeaks material, but it appeared to be a clear indication that the incoming administration wanted to crush all dissent.

How the media dealt with one of its greatest challenges in recent times – the revelations which exposed the lies and deceit of executive government – mainly divided between the political left and right. Those newspapers and organisations which had worked with WikiLeaks, *The Guardian*, the *New York Times*, *Der Spiegel*, *El Pais* and *Le Monde*, were generally in agreement about exposing as much material as possible. The right-wing media, the *Wall Street Journal*, the *Daily Mail*, the *Daily Express*, *The Australian*, *Le Figaro* and Fox News were generally opposed. Not for them the argument that the state should be held accountable, especially in areas of intelligence where there is often little competent oversight and accountability. This kind of partisanship is not unusual, but it appears to have been greatly enhanced by the argument that the West was at war – a war almost certainly without conclusion with an ill-defined enemy, terrorism. The fabricated allegations against Iraq that it had weapons of mass destruction had helped lead the first charge in this created war-on-terrorism environment, unleashing greater turmoil in the West's civil society than terrorists themselves could ever have imagined. With politicians promising total security egged on by sections of the media, the baying for greater security became deafening. There were calls for both Assange and Snowden to be executed. The Five Eyes countries, it seemed, were so bound together by common purpose in their intelligence-gathering operations that elements of nationhood itself were being redefined. To the applause of many journalists, the Australian government condemned Snowden as a traitor – even though he is an American citizen. The Australian Prime Minister, Julia Gillard, described Assange as a criminal, yet he had broken no Australian laws. It was apparently enough that his disclosures had upset the US administration and that the Justice Department was investigating his activities. In the US, the *Washington Post*, a newspaper which wrote stories based on Snowden's disclosures, called for his prosecution. The notion that the central role of journalism was to disclose secrets which powerful interests wanted kept from the public was being upended, particularly in the important area of national security.

New laws were now being shaped, both in the US and elsewhere, to make *illegal* that which had been normal journalistic practice; to make *legal* the activities of intelligence agencies which had previously been outlawed. Against sometimes hysterical claims from US politicians, other nations fell in line. In Australia sweeping laws demanded that the metadata of all phone calls should be held for two years by the telecommunications companies, on behalf of intelligence and police agencies, exposing journalists and their sources to being tracked by the very organisations it is their responsibility to hold to account. The new laws give virtually no protection to journalists – and in particular their sources. One draconian piece of legislation made it an offence punishable by up to ten years' prison in certain circumstances for a journalist to reveal what the national Australian Security Intelligence Organisation (ASIO) determined was a Special Intelligence Operation (SIO). Since ASIO would neither confirm nor deny an SIO, it was impossible to know if a journalist was about to break the law until the report was broadcast or published. In the US journalists have a degree of protection under the First Amendment of the US Constitution which guarantees the right to publication. Journalists also have strong protection from prosecution under the 1917 Espionage Act – providing they can show they were acting as journalists. In the UK, the British Parliament passed strong surveillance laws in 2016, which gave scant support for journalists attempting to hold the government to account. Called the Investigatory Powers Act (2016) or more generally the Snooper's Charter, it demands the scooping up and storing of all metadata. It gives little protection to journalists, and cuts across many European Court of Justice (ECJ) rulings guaranteeing the protection of journalists' sources. Even this safety net may disappear if Britain's withdrawal from the EU, as seems likely, is coupled with a decision to sever all connections with the ECJ. There are still further dangers ahead if a proposal from the UK's Law Commission is taken up. In a proposal contained in a consultation paper, *Protection of Official Data,* produced seemingly without much consultation with journalists, the Commission recommends a new Espionage Act which 'threatens leakers and journalists with the same extended jail sentences as foreign agents'.[9]

It is a similar story across the English Channel where journalists confronted an additional set of problems: government covert surveillance. *Le Monde*, the nation's leading paper of record, has repeatedly had its phones tapped by the forerunner of the General Directorate for Internal Security (DGSI) and newspapers have been directly threatened by the government. In Italy journalists have strong laws protecting their work, but the prosecutors ignore them, raiding newspaper offices, seizing computers and phones, and then handing them back a few months later when ordered by a court to do so. By then the prosecutors have all the information they need. As the Western liberal democracies reach further for the tools to restrain the work of journalists at home, its governments either encourage or turn a blind eye to companies selling surveillance systems to questionable regimes, such as the governments of Saudi Arabia, the United Arab Emirates (UAE), Egypt and Turkey. The sales of software systems are tricky to police, yet they can be as deadly as a missile or a tank for journalists trying to expose corrupt regimes, and laws controlling the export of spyware often lag behind fast-developing technology. Once revealed, the surveillance of journalists by foreign countries with shocking human rights records is easy to condemn, but closer to home sections of the Western media have been all too ready to turn on journalists who question state power. 'Prosecute *The Guardian* for Aiding Terrorists Via Leaks,'[10] screamed *The Sun*; 'Leftwing Paper's Leaks Caused "Greatest Damage to Western Security in History",[11] say Whitehall Insiders,' exclaimed the *Daily Mail*.[12]

These are the same newspapers who demand complete safety for the population. They castigate the intelligence agencies, and the government, when anyone is killed in a terrorist attack. In turn politicians and intelligence agencies demand greater powers, increasingly restricting the ability of journalists to hold accountable both executive government and the intelligence agencies. This is a world where some members of the media have become the cheer squad for their own destruction, propagandists for authoritarianism – the very antithesis of journalism.

Those who stand against this are faced with an uninspiring prospect; as government bends intelligence to suit its ill-conceived wars, journalists come under greater surveillance and threat. It creates a chilling effect on what they should be doing: countering the power of executive government. The *Guardian* editor Alan Rusbridger put it this way after newspapers began publishing the Snowden disclosures: 'Reporting requires a transaction between a source and a reporter, and if that transaction can't be private that's the end of investigative reporting.'[13] All this is happening as newspapers across the political spectrum have become weakened by plummeting circulation figures, their owners either unwilling or unable to stand up to governments. Journalists who see their role as telling truth to power are taking extreme steps to protect themselves and to carry out their historically designated role as the Fourth Estate – standing against the other three estates of the realm, the church, the courts and executive authority. They find themselves seeking sanctuary in far-flung places.

Notes

1 Necleous, M. 2008. *Critiques of Security*. Edinburgh University Press.
2 Risen, J. and Lichtblau, E. 16th December, 2005. *Bush Lets US Spy on Callers Without Courts*. New York Times. Available at www.nytimes.com/2005/12/16/politics/bush-lets-us-spy-on-callers-without-courts.html?_r=0 [Accessed 24 September, 2016].
3 Nixon, R. May, 1977. *Watergate Interview Frost v Nixon*. YouTube. Available at www.youtube.com/watch?v=OICmZtzAhn4 [Accessed 10 August, 2016].
4 Necleous, M. 2008. *Critiques of Security*. Edinburgh University Press.
5 Burger, T. 1989. *The Structural Transformation of the Public Sphere: An Inquiry into a Category of Bourgeois Society*. The MIT Press, Cambridge, Massachusetts.
6 Church, F. 1975. *The Intelligence Gathering Debate*. NBCUniversalArchives.com. Available at www.youtube.com/watch?v=YAG1N4a84Dk [Accessed 4 October, 2016].
7 Pilkington, E. 12th March, 2012. *Bradley Manning's Treatment Was Cruel and Inhuman, UN Torture Chief Rules*. The Guardian, London. Available at: www.theguardian.com/world/2012/mar/12/bradley-manning-cruel-inhuman-treatment-un [Accessed 5 August, 2016].
8 Pompeo, M. 13th April, 2017. *Director Pompeo Delivers Remarks at CSIS*. Central Intelligence Agency [online]. Available at www.cia.gov/news-information/speeches-testimony/2017-speeches-testimony/pompeo-delivers-remarks-at-csis.html [Accessed 23 April, 2017].
9 Campbell, D. 10th February, 2017. *Planned Espionage Act Could Jail Journos and Whistleblowers as Spies*. The Register [online]. Available at www.theregister.co.uk/2017/02/10/espionage_law_jail_journalists_as_spies/ [Accessed 1 August, 2017].
10 Newton Dunn, T. 5th April, 2016. *Prosecute Guardian for Aiding Terrorists*. The Sun, London. Available at www.thesun.co.uk/archives/politics/1058722/prosecute-guardian-for-aiding-terrorists/ [Accessed 3 January, 2017].
11 Ponsford, D. 10th October, 2013. *Leftwing Paper's Leaks Caused 'Greatest Damage to Western Security in History'*. Daily Mail, London. Available at www.pressgazette.co.uk/daily-mail-steps-its-attack-guardian-least-ralph-miliband-did-not-give-succour-our-enemies/ [Accessed 1 December, 2016].
12 Ponsford, D. 10th October, 2013. *Leftwing Paper's Leaks Caused 'Greatest Damage to Western Security in History'*. Daily Mail, London. Available at www.pressgazette.co.uk/daily-mail-steps-its-attack-guardian-least-ralph-miliband-did-not-give-succour-our-enemies/ [Accessed 1 December, 2016].
13 Rusbridger, A. 28th June, 2013. *Guardian Editors Alan Rusbridger and Janine Gibson on Edward Snowden and the NSA Leaks*. Charlie Rose. YouTube. Available at www.youtube.com/watch?v=7pdzzZB7Xgo [Accessed 1 October, 2016].

1

AN ISLAND OF HOPE

On 9 October, 1986, US President Ronald Reagan climbed aboard Air Force One for the five-hour and 20-minute flight from Andrews Air Force Base just outside Washington to the Iceland capital, Reykjavik. As the aircraft climbed into the autumn sky Reagan was already being briefed for what lay ahead. The Cold War had almost turned hot a few years earlier when the Soviet Union believed the US was about to launch a nuclear attack, and prepared to launch a counter-strike. Reagan was on his way to meet the newly elected Secretary General of the Soviet Union, Mikhail Gorbachev. Publicly it was just a meeting as a preliminary basis for discussions about nuclear arms control. But Reagan had another plan: to negotiate a nuclear arms reduction treaty, which some hoped might rid the world of atomic weapons forever. What happened during two days in October 1986 in Reykjavik did not eliminate nuclear weapons, but it did lead to negotiations which would in the end eliminate Intermediate Nuclear Forces (INF) – short range land based missiles – and, it is argued, helped thaw the frigid relations between Washington and Moscow which until then had been as dark and full of foreboding as an Icelandic winter. As Gorbachev told his foreign secretary on the flight back from Reykjavik to Moscow, before Reykjavik the 'conversation was only about limiting nuclear arms. Now it is about reduction and liquidation [of those].'[1] The choice of Reykjavik as the site of the summit was portrayed at the time as a symbolically midway point between the two nations – a place where in the event of a nuclear war the opposing missiles would cross paths not far away. However, Reykjavik was anything but neutral turf. Right next to the Keflavik airfield where President Reagan landed on that drizzly autumn day was a North Atlantic Treaty Organization (NATO) base, and not far away, a major eavesdropping facility run by the US Naval Security Group, part of the largest surveillance system in the world, the US National Security Agency (NSA). The Reykjavik base operated a program code named Classic Bullseye. Its ground-based antennas and wire fences structured in two huge circles acted as a 'range finger' to identify the location of Soviet electronic transmissions, such as radar and communications. This information – and data from undersea listening devices – helped US maritime spy planes discover the position of Russian submarines as they crossed over international telecommunications cables snaking across the ocean floor, carrying data and voice traffic from Canada, through Greenland, Iceland and on to Europe. At least some of the Soviet subs were seeking an opportunity to break into the cable to plant listening devices. They also had another mission as they made their way south-west from the Soviet port of Murmansk: eavesdropping on military and industrial communications off the coast of the US, gathering signals intelligence.

As the world increasingly embraced digital communications, Iceland was among the first to realise their incredible potential. Sitting at a mid-point between North America and Europe, the tiny island of slightly more than 330,000 people had swiftly embraced the use of high speed internet. In 2007 the town of Seltjarnarnes became the first place in the world where every member of a community had access to fibre optic communications. By 2009 Iceland was number one in the world for internet use. It was a natural place for an internet provider to set up shop. Strategically placed in a perfect time zone to serve a huge part of the world's major capitals, Iceland's cheap carbon neutral electricity, produced from natural hot springs, kept the cost of the power-hungry computer systems to a minimum. Even its cool climate made it a perfect place to maintain servers which generated a huge amount of heat. Telecommunications companies, sensing the advantage, began upgrading the links to Iceland with super high-speed fibre optic cables.

Whether or not Iceland's internet capability was aided by the presence of the US military base and its spying program is still debated. What is clear is the internet helped open up Iceland to the rest of the world and the rest of the world to Iceland. What emerged was perhaps predictable for a nation that for centuries has fought to harness its harsh natural environment. Iceland would become a major player in a battle just as demanding: support for challenging journalism, and the democracy it underpins.

The issue of self-determination runs deep in the Icelandic body politic. Not until 1944 did the country win its complete independence from Denmark, the nation that had ruled it since 1814. A binding plebiscite found that 95 per cent of voters wanted to establish an Icelandic Republic. Five years later the Cold War intervened in the fledgling nation's first steps and despite riots in the streets, in 1951 the Icelandic government signed an agreement for US troops – who had left the country seven years earlier after the Second World War – to return. It was the beginning of a prolonged period of military ping-pong. In September 2006, with the Cold War a distant memory, the foreign troops again moved out. Then, late in 2016, with Russia reasserting its presence in the world, the US government announced it again wanted to reopen its base at Keflavik. If Iceland had become an index for the earth's military pressure points it was also about to become an indicator of a completely different phenomenon, but the issue was just as dangerous.

In its 2005 annual report the Central Bank of Iceland was particularly upbeat in its assessment of the country's economic performance. Iceland had 'experienced one of the highest growth rates of GDP among OECD countries',[2] it said. In 2004 the country's GDP had risen by 6.1 per cent. The bank was positive about the country's financial system too. It was 'equipped to withstand shocks to the economy and financial markets'.[3] But all was not as it seemed. Barely two years later, when the greatest financial crisis since the Depression of the 1930s swept across the world, the economy of the smallest member of the OECD crashed with a horrific thud. This confluence of financial failure and the rise of the internet would produce an unlikely outcome.

On 1 August, 2009, Birgitta Jonsdottir settled down to watch the local 7 p.m. news in Reykjavik. Jonsdottir, an unusual mixture of computer programmer, poet and anarchist, had exchanged her street demonstration skills for parliamentary process. Just four months earlier she had been elected to the Icelandic parliament as a member of The Movement, a political party that campaigned for democratic reform 'beyond the politics of left or right'.[4] She had risen to power on a wave of public concern about how Iceland had suffered so badly during the global financial crisis. It had been hit worse than most other countries and was left close to insolvency.

One of Iceland's major savings banks had been among the first to harness the power of the internet and produce online banking. Called Icesave, it had attracted 350,000 investors in the UK and the Netherlands, with £4.5 billion of deposits. But the financial crash had destroyed its investments and now it was owned by the Icelandic government, which was keeping it afloat. With Iceland's tiny population the debts alone were enough to take the country to the brink of insolvency. As the short days of winter turned into the near never-ending days of summer, it was estimated that the local population faced the dreadful likelihood that the equivalent of every man, woman and child in the nation would have to pay up US $50,000 each to bail out the bank. With unemployment increasing and the economy in rapid decline, Iceland stood on the brink of economic collapse. Other banks had been in trouble too. Iceland's largest bank, Kaupthing, received a €700 million loan from Iceland's Central Bank, announcing that it was 'committed to working with the government to ensure regular workings of the Icelandic financial system'.[5] In other words, with all that debt, if Kaupthing failed Iceland's finances would be in tatters. Any hopes that Icelanders could be guaranteed the benefits of a stable nation state, with a strong social security net and free public health and public education programmes, were now seriously threatened. Most people understood what was at risk, but they had no idea what had actually gone on inside the secretive banking system.

Iceland had experienced a boom like none other in its history. Stefan Olafsson, an Icelandic professor called it 'probably the most rapid expansion of a banking system in the history of mankind'.[6] The country had been awash with cash.

Imported cars jammed the roads; consumer goods flooded in. Bang and Oulfsen sold more television and sound systems in Reykjavik than any other city apart from Moscow. Now, with the economy laid waste, Iceland was friendless. The US would not support its banks, neither would the Europeans, who were demanding vast amounts of money from the Icelandic Government to cover the banking debts. In what became indicative of how legislation passed in the heat of the moment could have far-reaching and unintended applications, Britain invoked anti-terrorism laws, passed after the 2001 attacks on the US, to freeze the assets of Iceland's banks in the UK.

At the local TV station, Kristinn Hrafnsson, an investigative journalist, was unusually flustered. A few weeks earlier Hrafnsson had received a tip that a then little-known website, WikiLeaks, was about to publish a document which might interest him. It involved one of the financial institutions bailed out by the Icelandic government, the Kaupthing bank. What the WikiLeaks document – the bank's 'loan book' – revealed was shocking even by the standards of the global financial crisis, which had come close to destroying the world economy. It showed that borrowings of billions of dollars made by customers of the bank were backed by virtually no security at all. The leaked documents revealed the bank had loaned billions of euros to its major shareholders, including a total of €2 billion to a company with large shareholdings in the bank and subsidiaries meaning it now owned nearly a quarter of the bank. The biggest borrowers had no collateral at all.

Working swiftly, Hrafnsson put his scoop together for that evening's news broadcast. It was a classic story of insider trading, with the public being asked to bail out the bank because it was too big to fail. But just before the TV news titles rolled the bank's lawyers intervened, managing to secure an injunction to stop the broadcast. Under legal pressure, the station pulled the story, and all its news-reader could do was point viewers to the WikiLeaks website. It was a significant moment, showing how information could bypass the old legal gatekeepers who had controlled the dissemination of information for so long.

Jonsdottir, like many Icelanders, was furious. She wondered why it took so long for the information about the bank's practices to be revealed – and why it had come from a website she'd never heard of before. Whoever had done the leaking was well informed and courageous.

There were other questions too about how it was possible for an Icelandic court to prevent the publication of information that had already been published on the internet. For although the Kaupthing bank had managed to stop Kristinn Hrafnsson, there wasn't an Icelander with even the vaguest interest in the future of their country who did not know about the contents of the WikiLeaks cable.

If the banks were friendless in Iceland, it was just the opposite for WikiLeaks. It seems that the people and WikiLeaks realised they were fighting the same battle. Despite the legal trickery which saw the Kaupthing bank story stopped at the last moment, Iceland has some of the most robust freedom of speech laws in the world. The Icelandic Constitution outlaws censorship and Reporters Without

Borders once described the country as having the freest media in the world. The Icelandic population could not have been more grateful to WikiLeaks for the revelations. The organisation was being spoken of in near reverential terms. Just a few weeks later, in late 2009 WikiLeaks founder Julian Assange and his then deputy Daniel Domscheit-Berg, were invited to be the guests of honour at a conference in Reykjavik organized by the Digital Freedom Society, an internet activist group. Assange, fond of quoting Rahm Emanuel, President Obama's former Chief of Staff – famous for saying a good crisis should never be wasted – laid out an audacious blueprint to protect WikiLeaks. He suggested embracing the systems multinational corporations, intelligence agencies and the very wealthy used to hide their activities from scrutiny:

> If you look at how multinational organisations move their tax structuring through offshore jurisdictions or just through trusts within countries like the UK, we have to do the same thing in order to protect our sources [from] malicious, vexatious lawsuits affecting our ability to continue.[7]

Assange said donations needed to be anonymized through offshore bank accounts, so that security equipment such as encrypted telephones, internet infrastructure and postal addresses could be rented, without the funds being traceable. He argued that if you wanted to publish high-level material like WikiLeaks without suffering vexatious lawsuits, there was no choice but to use trusts or international cross jurisdictional arrangements to protect the organisation. He said the issue was not evading a judicial system but preserving an organisation's ability to continue to publish while the judicial process played out. Most big organisations would drop their cases before they got to final judgement but they wanted to force publishers, like WikiLeaks, to bleed financially in the meantime. The idea of Iceland being a sanctuary for freedom of speech had first been raised at the conference exactly one year earlier by a founder of the Electronic Frontier Foundation and lyricist for the 1970s rock band the Grateful Dead, John Perry Barlow. Jonsdottir recalls Barlow took the 'essence of the mess we were in because of the lack of transparency'[8] and used the 'notion of Switzerland in a reverse way'.[9] Iceland would become 'the Switzerland of bits'.[10]

Ironically, WikiLeaks, whose motto is 'Sunlight is the best disinfectant' had chosen to launch its grand scheme just before Christmas in the depths of an Icelandic winter when the Arctic sun barely lifts above the horizon.

Impressed by their ideas, Jonsdottir, who made her speech on freedom of information and digital copyright, could see plenty of opportunities for WikiLeaks and her party to work together on the issue that united them both: whistleblowing and the protection of sources.

Over tapas at a local Spanish restaurant, Jonsdottir and her political allies discussed drawing up a shopping list to identify the best laws from tax havens and legal entities which protected freedom of speech, and adapt them to provide a safe haven, particularly for those involved in the legally hazardous business of investigative journalism. Jonsdottir wanted to make a 'legal shield'[11] for both whistle-blowers and sources. Just as important for journalists would be a guarantee that internet service providers managing the servers containing the journalists' material 'did not carry the responsibility for the content they hosted'.[12] This proposal provided a layer of legal protection which prevented material easily being erased from the internet. The new laws would guarantee 'the stories were not taken down'.[13] Once material was placed on the server in Iceland it would be illegal to remove it from the public sphere. Her party would present a bill to the Icelandic parliament to make the country, in effect, a journalistic paradise, where the right to publish and the protection of whistle-blower sources would be guaranteed by the full weight of the law.

Assistance for the cause came from an unlikely source. Jonsdottir had been invited to a cocktail party at the US Embassy and decided it would be mildly amusing to take Assange as her guest. WikiLeaks was not high on Washington's radar at that time, though it had certainly achieved enough to make partygoing at the US Embassy an interesting event. Once at the embassy Assange spent some time talking to the US Chargé d'Affaires, Sam Watson. No one thought anything of it at the time but for Assange a seemingly chance chat with Watson was either a coincidence or a deft piece of political strategy. A few weeks later, in mid-January 2010, Sam Watson began writing a routine report about Iceland's financial problems. The government was particularly concerned about how it would be possible to fund the refinancing of another Icelandic bank, Icesave, the bank that had attracted so many investors from the Netherlands and the UK, but which was now relying on support from the Icelandic government. Watson described how representatives of the government had been in talks with the embassy and wanted the US to help settle what was turning into a bitter dispute with the Netherlands and the UK. He noted that the US had said it would be neutral on the matter, a position that was to be interpreted by the Icelandic delegation as condoning the bullying of Iceland by the more powerful countries who not only wanted the government to pay the debts, but also expected a premium on top.

Watson noted that the Icelandic delegation believed that if the Icesave issue was not resolved soon and Iceland defaulted on its loans it would 'set Iceland back thirty years'.[14] When Watson pressed the send button on his embassy email, he thought that would be the last he would see of his succinct report as it winged its way electronically across the north Atlantic and into the mainframe computer of the State Department in Washington. He also copied in high-ranking officials in the National Security Council and the US Department of Defense. A few weeks later, Jonsdottir arrived at the prime minister's office ready for a meeting with the heads of government. They all trooped in to the main meeting room and prepared to sit down around the large table. On the agenda, among other matters of state, was the Icesave issue. As they waited for the final person to turn up, one of the members of the group became very focused on their mobile phone. But it wasn't a telephone call that had got their attention. They were listening to the news and with each passing second, they became more and more alarmed.

Eventually they turned and said to no one in particular: 'Oh I've never heard of such a thing. How is this possible?'[15] The news report had left nothing in doubt. Everything was there: the attempts by the Icelandic government to head off a referendum that might lead to Icelanders deciding not to pay for the millions of euros of debt incurred by Icesave. The news report also detailed the involvement of the Americans in a matter many in Iceland believed was none of their business, particularly as they appeared to be siding with the 'bullies'.[16]

Watson's classified cable was being revealed to the Icelandic people in excruciating detail. Jonsdottir believed that if Iceland had accepted the settlement being pushed by the UK and the Netherlands – and indirectly backed by the Americans – the interest payments for the bailout loan would have amounted to 70 per cent of the income taxes in Iceland. The source of the news report was, of course, WikiLeaks.

Many people believed that Assange had actually gone into the US Embassy in Reykjavik and, according to Jonsdottir, 'mysteriously sucked out the cables with some spy device or something'.[17] But it was simpler than that. The cable was one of the first sent to WikiLeaks by Chelsea (then Bradley) Manning, testing whether WikiLeaks could be trusted to deliver the maximum impact Assange promised.

The news story galvanised the Icelandic people into supporting WikiLeaks, which was only too happy to be cited as the source. Such was the anger at how Iceland was being treated and the realisation that without WikiLeaks they might not have known the facts, politicians of all persuasions supported a radical piece of legislation brought into the Parliament by Johnsdottir. Her resolution laid down firm foundations for the protection of journalists and whistle-blowers. Called the Modern Media Initiative, it pronounced that the resolution was designed to protect and promote the cornerstones of 'evolved democracy, freedom of expression and freedom of information'.

At its centre were public access to information, journalistic source protection and general communication. For the first time the Icelandic parliament deemed that all new laws should take these principles into account. Iceland, the resolution pointed out, would cherry-pick the best legislation around the world to protect journalism, and enshrine this protection in the nation's laws.

'We can create a comprehensive policy and legal framework to protect the free expression needed for investigative journalism and other politically important publishing', the resolution said. 'While some countries provide basic measures, Iceland now has an opportunity to build an internationally attractive legislative package built from the best laws of other nations.'[18]

Iceland, which already had strong protection laws, now examined a number of different models, to make the new laws even stronger:

Sweden: Source protection
It is a criminal offence in Sweden for anyone to reveal the identity of a source.

> Sweden's press freedom laws in fact not only make it a criminal offence to expose a source, but a journalist can be prosecuted for doing so.

Belgium: Communications protection
Any conversations between journalists and their sources in Belgium are not admissible as evidence in court. This also includes any electronic communications.

Norway: Freedom of information laws
Government documents in these countries are public by default. All documents, classified or not, are listed in an open directory.

New York State: Libel protection
New York will not enforce a libel verdict from a country that does not have the equivalent of America's First-Amendment right to free speech.[19]

The Swedish constitution's Press Freedom Act guarantees the protection of sources even when secret government material is involved.

Selecting the best laws from around the world was relatively simple, but getting them into legislation proved much harder. Even so, this move towards greater press protection is indicative of the strong culture of privacy protection in Iceland. As long ago as 2000, The Data Protection Act enshrined in legislation the rights of individuals to have their personal information kept secret, in all but the most exceptional circumstances. It was these kinds of protection laws which had encouraged the original whistle-blowers to leak their damaging information about the Kaupthing Bank to WikiLeaks in the first place and it is why WikiLeaks was considering making Iceland its base. It is a symbol of just how secure WikiLeaks felt that the organisation decided to operate out of Iceland during the most vulnerable time of its existence. In early 2010 Jonsdottir had met up with Assange in a Reykjavik café. As she sat down, he opened his laptop. What rolled across the screen was a classified video, shot from a US military helicopter, showing it opening fire on a crowd of people in a Baghdad square in 2007. As the bodies fell, killed by 30-millimetre cannon shells, Jonsdottir was moved to tears. Next the gunship rounded on a group of rescuers and pounded their minivan, killing those on the ground, including a still-moving Reuters journalist, and seriously wounding two children in the van. Jonsdottir and Assange both believed that if the video were released, public outrage might help end the war in Iraq sooner. But they needed to keep the fact that they had a copy of the video secret from the US military – until they were ready to go public with it.

There would be two versions of the video: a cut-down, 17-minute tape would be for general distribution, and the 38-minute uncut edition would prove that the edited material had been faithfully reproduced. As they put the final touches to the shorter version, there was still considerable debate about what it should be called, with heated discussions between senior WikiLeaks supporters across the world about naming the video 'Collateral Murder'. It was felt by some that the name was clever, but would distract from the content or be seen as propaganda. It was contrary to the philosophy that WikiLeaks so publicly supported: letting the facts tell the story. WikiLeaks could be rightfully accused of being the judge, jury and executioner without the evidence being tested. But Assange fought to keep the title:

> The promise that we make to our sources is not only will we defend them through every means that we have available, technological and legally and politically but we will try and get the maximum possible political impact for the material that they give to us.

The title had been chosen for maximum political impact.[20]

The location they chose to reveal their discoveries could not have been more pointed: the heart of the US press corps, the National Press Club, Washington. After the Collateral Murder video was shown, the US military said the gunship had mistaken a camera carried by the Reuters journalist for an RPG (rocket-propelled grenade). Reuters tried repeatedly, through freedom of information requests, to get a copy of the video, but was refused by the US military. What is more disturbing is that at least one journalist did know what had happened, but no hard questions were ever asked of the US government.

On that spring morning in April 2010 in Washington, as the world digested the power of the extraordinary gunship video, frenetic activity permeated the corridors of the Pentagon, the five-sided squat building that houses the nerve centre of America's military. Senior officials were desperately trying to discover who had leaked the video. Across town on the other side of the Potomac River there should have been fevered activity too, but inside the nondescript edifice which is home to the newspaper that produced the world's greatest exposé in the history of journalism – Watergate – it was, strangely, business as usual.

The *Washington Post* might have been famous for the toppling of President Richard Nixon nearly forty years ago, but the WikiLeaks 'Collateral Murder' exposé posed many questions about what had happened to the once mighty media institution. David Finkel, a Pulitzer Prize-winning journalist with the newspaper, was embedded with the US troops in Baghdad that day, writing a book called *The Good Soldiers*. In the book, he gives a vivid description of the killings, and quotes much of the dialogue from the video. But when Finkel's book came out, the *Washington Post* carried a story about the killings that ended with a quote from the Pentagon: 'We think the safest way to cover these operations is to be embedded with US forces.'[21] There was no follow-up investigation by the *Washington Post* on the killings of the journalists. Asked if he could say when he saw the video Finkel said, 'I can't,' and added: 'I don't need advice from WikiLeaks how to do my journalism.'[22]

Just what did the *Washington Post* know and when did they know it? This is difficult to ascertain. Assange has suggested that the *Washington Post* had a copy of the video but took no action. 'I assume they had the video, you know, close back to 2007 when these events happened. But I am sure that at least for the past year they have had it and it was not released,' he said.

The *Washington Post* has denied ever having a copy. Apart from a shocking frontline view of the war in which civilians were targeted as enemy combatants, 'Collateral Murder' also shone a bright light on the cosy relationships between journalists, journalism and the military in the US. Compounding this perception, the *Washington Post* had also alerted the CIA that it was about to publish a story which revealed it had been involved in systematically kidnapping people in foreign countries as part of the so-called war on terror. Assange was at a loss to understand how the *Washington Post* could argue that it was necessary on the grounds of national security to tip off the CIA in advance of the publication.

When WikiLeaks posted the video on its website, it ripped around the planet at viral speed. It looked like the world's media couldn't get enough of it. In the week following the release, 'WikiLeaks' was the search term with the most significant growth worldwide, as measured by Google. Yet for WikiLeaks, the overall coverage was disappointing. The international mainstream media treated it more like a video flick than a disturbing revelation about the war in Iraq. WikiLeaks would soon release the Afghan War Logs, US military field reports from Afghanistan, which made damning disclosures about how the US used assassination squads. But what was troubling the State Department concerned far more significant disclosures, what became known as Cablegate: the expected release by WikiLeaks of hundreds of thousands of classified diplomatic cables. After a crisis meeting at the State Department in Washington, Anne-Marie Slaughter, the department head of policy planning, wrote an email to Secretary Hillary Clinton which gave a hint of how far the administration was prepared to go to stop Assange. It was headed: 'Possible legal and non-legal strategies re WikiLeaks'.[23] The contents of the email, part released under freedom of information requests, did not explain what 'non-legal' strategies meant.

But Jennifer Robinson, the lawyer representing Assange, got a taste of what it might mean. After she wrote on behalf of WikiLeaks to the State Department explaining that WikiLeaks was about to publish a number of classified communiques between Washington and US embassies – seeking help to remove the names of people who might be harmed if they were published – she received a curt response. State Department lawyer Harold Hongju Koh wrote to her warning that publication of anything would put at risk the lives of countless innocent individuals, threatening ongoing military and anti-terrorism operations. For added impact, the letter – which was addressed to both Robinson and Assange, though only Robinson had written to the State Department – was leaked to the media. The impact was immediate. Robinson received death threats in 'crazy emails'.[24] The leak of the letter was designed to 'put me under pressure not to represent' Assange,[25] she said. 'This was the US Government targeting an Australian lawyer practising law in London'. It was a defining moment.

WikiLeaks had marked out a clear inflection point in modern journalism. Journalists were falling into two major divisions which did not fit the usual left/ right political classification. There were journalists who supported a kind of referential reporting, seldom challenging authority and always checking that what they wrote about sensitive national security subjects was cleared by government before it was published. They were often on the right, but could also be found in 'liberal' news media organisations. These were journalists who clung to the levers of power invested in them by the positions they held: often powerful big-name journalists in powerful big-name journals. And there was what could loosely be called the libertarian right, which carried out the more traditional roles of journalists in challenging the power of the State and in this regard were more allied to the political left in journalism. What the Iceland experience demonstrated was that the internet challenged the voice of big media. Information could not be controlled the way it had in the past. The US Embassy Icesave document written by the hapless Watson, Chargé d'affaires, had been sent to Washington, downloaded in Iraq, leaked to WikiLeaks and ended up informing the very population it was supposed to be kept secret from on the other side of the world. The first coherent shots had been fired at the establishment media, and the most powerful institutions in most powerful country in the world. And Iceland was once again centre stage in this unfolding drama which would have such a huge impact on the way in which information is gathered and disseminated.

By 2016, with its reputation as a safe hub providing secure cheap communication and storage, Iceland became host to the biggest financial scoop in the history of journalism, the Panama Papers, which disclosed wholesale tax avoidance and money laundering throughout the world. According to Jonsdottir the International Consortium of Investigative Journalists, which broke the story, chose to host at least 'some parts' of their material on Icelandic servers. But she declined to reveal any more information, saying she had gone out of her way not to know too much: 'The less we know about the data that's hosted in Iceland, the better it is for the data that's hosted in Iceland!'[26] For Iceland the decision to host Panama Papers material was an echo of events nearly a decade earlier which so clearly benefitted the country, saving it from possible bankruptcy. The WikiLeaks revelations led to the ousting of an incompetent prime minister who presided over the catastrophe. The Panama Papers produced a similar outcome, forcing another prime minister to resign after revealing he had failed to disclose a secret offshore bank account.

Iceland was marking out fresh territory for the way journalism was practised. Documents could be posted online; readers could see for themselves the raw information which formed the basis of the story. Governments were in a bind; digitisation and the internet might benefit the smooth running of an administration, but they ran counter to another priority: securing that information. Controlling who had access had become a whole lot more difficult, but the US administration in particular was ready for a fight.

Notes

1   Chernyaev, A. 1986. *Gorbachev's Thought on Reykjavik (Views Expressed on the Return Flight, and upon Arrival in Moscow)*. National Security Achieves. George Washington University, Washington. Available at http://nsarchive.gwu.edu/NSAEBB/NSAEBB203/Document19.pdf [Accessed 3 January, 2017].

2 The Central Bank of Iceland. 2005. The Economy of Iceland [online]. Iceland. Available at www.cb.is/library/Skraarsafn/Economy-of-Iceland/November%202005.pdf [Accessed 1 May, 2017].

3 The Central Bank of Iceland. 2005. The Economy of Iceland [online]. Iceland. Available at www.cb.is/library/Skraarsafn/Economy-of-Iceland/November%202005.pdf [Accessed 1 May, 2017].

4 Jonsdottir, B. September 2016. *Interview.*

5 BBC News. 7th October, 2008. Icesavers Warned on Accounts [online]. Available at http://news.bbc.co.uk/1/hi/business/7656387.stm [Accessed 1 July, 2017].

6 *Capitalist Punishment.* 10/11th December, 2016. The Financial Times. London.

7 Fowler, A. 2011. *The Most Dangerous Man in the World.* Melbourne University Press.

8 Jonsdottir, B. September, 2016. *Interview.*

9 Jonsdottir, B. September, 2016. *Interview.*

10 Jonsdottir, B. September, 2016. *Interview.*

11 Jonsdottir, B. September, 2016. *Interview.*

12 Jonsdottir, B. September, 2016. *Interview.*

13 Jonsdottir, B. September, 2016. *Interview.*

14 Fowler, A. 2011. *The Most Dangerous Man in the World.* Melbourne University Press.

15 Fowler, A. 2011. *The Most Dangerous Man in the World.* Melbourne University Press.

16 Fowler, A. 2011. *The Most Dangerous Man in the World.* Melbourne University Press.

17 Fowler, A. 2011. *Sex, Lies and Julian Assange, Four Corners,* ABC TV.

18 Immi Resolution. 2014. International Modern Media Institute [online]. Iceland. Available at https://en.immi.is/immi-resolution/ [Accessed 9 June, 2017].

19 Babbage. 17th June, 2010. *Iceland's Media Law: 'The Switzerland of Bits'.* The Economist [online] London. Available at www.economist.com/blogs/babbage/2010/06/icelands_media_law [Accessed 4 August, 2016].

20 Fowler, A. 2011. *The Most Dangerous Man in the World.* Melbourne University Press.

21 Washington Post. 15 September, 2009. *Military's Killing of Two Journalists in Iraq Detailed in New Book.*

22 Fowler, A. May, 2010. *ABC TV Foreign Correspondent Program.*

23 Clinton, H. 2010. *Possible Legal and Nonlegal Strategies Re Wikileaks.* US Department of State [online]. Washington. Available at https://foia.state.gov/Search/results.aspx?searchText=slaughter+nonlegal&beginDate=&endDate=&publishedBeginDate=&publishedEndDate=&caseNumber= [Accessed 1 September, 2016].

24 Robinson, J. August, 2016. *Interview.*

25 Robinson, J. August, 2016. *Interview.*

26 Jonsdottir, B. September, 2016. *Interview.*

2

HEART OF DARKNESS

On 12 September, 2001, with the fires still burning in the collapsed Twin Towers in downtown Manhattan, Richard A. Clark, President George W. Bush's counter-terrorism chief, slipped a .357 sidearm into his waistband and walked back out of his Arlington, Virginia home. Clark, who had worked under three previous presidents as a senior security advisor, had spent the previous 24 hours at the White House, and now after a quick shower, he was returning to help handle the biggest attack on US territory since Pearl Harbour in 1941. The Pentagon had also been hit by a hijacked plane and a fourth passenger aircraft, possibly destined for the White House, had crashed in a field not far away. His primary aim was to prevent any further attacks.

As he entered the White House, helicopter gunships hovered overhead and fighter jets streaked across the sky, completing the apocalyptic vision. Yet what he discovered inside was just as frightening.

Clark expected to go back to a round of meetings examining what the next attacks could be, what the nation's vulnerabilities were, what could be done about them in the short term. 'Instead, I walked into a series of discussions about Iraq.'[1]

At first Clarke says he was incredulous that they were talking about something other than getting al-Qaeda. Then he realised with 'almost sharp physical pain' that Secretary of Defense Donald Rumsfeld and his deputy Paul Wolfowitz were going to try and take advantage of this 'national tragedy'[2] to promote their agenda about Iraq.

Even before the administration took office they had been pressing for a war with Iraq. His friends in the Pentagon had been telling him that the word was the US would be invading Iraq sometime in 2002. Clark recognised that the Defense Department's focus was already beginning to shift from al-Qaeda even though the CIA was now explicitly stating that al-Qaeda was guilty of the attacks.

Wolfowitz was not persuaded, arguing it was too sophisticated and complicated an operation for a terrorist group to have pulled off by itself, without a state sponsor – Iraq must have been helping them.

Rumsfeld was now talking about broadening the objectives of the response and 'getting Iraq'. Secretary of State Colin Powell, according to Clarke, pushed back, urging a focus on al-Qaeda. Relieved to have some support, Clarke said he thanked Powell and his deputy, Richard Armitage. 'I thought I was missing something here', Clark says he told Powell. 'Having been attacked by Al-Qaeda, for us now to go bombing Iraq in response would be like our invading Mexico after the Japanese attacked Pearl Harbour.'[3] Clark did not know it then, but just five hours after the first plane hit the World Trade Centre, an aide to Rumsfeld had made a diary note that the White House was keen to use the attack by al-Qaeda as an excuse to hit Saddam Hussein. The aide wrote: 'Best info fast. Judge whether good enough [to] hit SH [Saddam Hussein] @ same time. Not only UBL [Usama bin Laden].'[4]

Throughout the day, deep in the basement of the White House, in an area known as the Situation Room, Clarke, generals from the Pentagon and heads of intelligence agencies worked feverishly to protect the US from further attacks, but just as important was the question: how would the US respond? At least some of the conversations took place in the Secure Video Conferencing Center – near the Situation Room in the basement of the West Wing of the White House. Built over a bowling alley created by President Harry S. Truman, the Situation Room was established at the direction of former president John F Kennedy, after the failed CIA-backed invasion of Cuba in 1961. Kennedy felt he could no longer trust the information he was receiving from the nation's defence and intelligence communities. Under orders from the then presidential security advisor, material was fed directly into the Situation Room so the White House could take a more hands-on role in the day-to-day running of US overseas operations.

While Kennedy was interested in uncovering the truth, Bush it seemed, had another problem. It was not so much a matter of trust that the intelligence agencies might not get it right that concerned him, it was more than they would not produce the 'evidence' he wanted.

As the day wore on, Clarke says he saw the president 'wandering alone'.[5] Clark said that Bush 'grabbed a few of us and closed the door to the conference room. "Look," he told us, "I know you have a lot to do and all, but I want you, as soon as you can, to go back over everything, everything. See if Saddam did this. See if he's linked in any way."'Clarke says he was 'taken aback, incredulous, and it showed. "But, Mr. President, Al Qaeda did this."[6] "'I know, I know, but – see if Saddam was involved. Just look. I want to know any shred."'[7] Clarke gave an undertaking to look again. He was, he said, 'trying to be more respectful, more responsive. "But you know, we have looked several times for state sponsorship of Al Qaeda and not found any real linkages to Iraq."'[8] Clarke maintains that he told Bush, 'Iran plays a little, as does Pakistan, and Saudi Arabia, Yemen.' But Bush was not persuaded: '"Look into Iraq, Saddam," the president said testily and left us.'[9] Lisa Gordon-Hagerty, the former director of Weapons of Mass Destruction Preparedness, according to Clarke, 'stared after him with her mouth hanging open. Paul Kurtz, a member of the White House counter-terrorism team, walked in, passing the President on the way out. Seeing our expressions, he asked, "Geeze, what just happened here?"'[10]

Those witnesses would be useful when the truth finally started to come out about how the White House had already made up its mind to invade Iraq. It was now simply a matter of finding the evidence to support that mission. They would not be disappointed.

The emergence of Rafid Ahman Alwan al-Janabi as a 'source' was exactly what the White House was looking for. It was not deemed important that al-Janabi had fled Iraq in 1999, leaving behind a trail of debts and suspected criminal activity.

What he had to say helped him jump the queue when he arrived in Germany seeking political asylum. He told the German immigration department that he once led a team of officers that equipped trucks to manufacture deadly bio-agents. Al-Janabi named six sites where Iraq might be hiding biological warfare vehicles, three of which were already operating. A farm programme to boost crop yields was cover for Iraq's new biological weapons production programme, he claimed. The immigration officers called in the Bundesnachrichtendiest (BND), Germany's foreign intelligence service, the equivalent of Britain's MI6. Perhaps somewhat prophetically, al-Janabi was given the code name Curveball. Just how he got the name is contested. 'Ball' is apparently the suffix of codenames used during the Cold War for informants dealing with information relating to weapons of mass destruction. But perhaps more appropriately in al-Janabi's case, 'curveball' is also a baseball term relating to a pitcher's ability to make a ball appear to curve in flight. There would be nothing straight about what al-Janabi would tell his BND interrogators. Whether or not he knew it, what he had to say fitted perfectly the story that Western intelligence agencies had been piecing together about Saddam Hussein's bio-weapons programme. The agencies had always been suspicious of Saddam's undertaking that Iraq had destroyed all its chemical weapons in 1991 after the first Gulf War. For al-Janabi the timing could not have been better. A few months before he defected, the CIA issued a national intelligence estimate on worldwide biological warfare (BW)programmes. It accused Iraq of 'probably continuing work to develop and produce BW agents'.[11] Ominously, it added that Iraq could restart production in six months.

As I discovered researching *The War on Journalism*, the CIA's suspicions had a reasonable basis. In mid-1995 Iraqi officials admitted that before the first Gulf War they had secretly produced 30,000 litres of anthrax, botulinum toxin, afla-toxin and other lethal bio-agents. They had also deployed hundreds of germ-filled munitions and researched other deadly diseases for military use. Al-Janabi's story to the Germans dovetailed neatly with that history and continuing CIA suspicions.

In December 2000, after a year of questioning al-Janabi, another national intelligence estimate cautiously noted that 'new intelligence' had caused US intelligence 'to adjust our assessment upward' and 'suggests Baghdad has expanded' its bio-weapons programme.

al-Janabi painted a picture of an elaborate deception created by the Iraqi government, convincing his BND handlers that the warehouses, where he had worked as an engineer, were part of Iraq's secret germ weapons programme. He claimed that mobile biochemical laboratories were hidden in a two-storey building that could be driven into from both sides.

Al-Janabi had other significant information: there were plans to build mobile biochemical factories at six sites across Iraq, from An Numaniyah in the south to Tikrit in the north.

BND reports based on al-Janabi's questioning became crucial to the CIA's estimates that Iraq 'continues to produce at least . . . three BW agents' and its mobile germ factories provide 'capabilities surpassing the pre-Gulf War era'.[12] The CIA's assertions were not based on any new intelligence about Iraq's biological weapons. Instead analysts had simply estimated what they believed would be the maximum output from seven mobile labs – only one of which Curveball said he had seen – operating nonstop for six months. They had developed a hypothesis using al-Janabi's unsubstantiated claims to produce a frightening scenario.

It is important to understand that al-Janabi had been directly assisted in building a new life in Germany by an organisation known as the Iraqi National Congress (INC), a network of Kurds, Shia and Sunnis who wanted Saddam ousted. They were closely connected to hawks in the US administration, the neocons such as Rumsfeld, Wolfowitz and the Pentagon advisor Richard Perle, known to his adversaries as the Prince of Darkness. The neocons, the so-called New Conservatives, were determined to reassert America's authority over key strategic regions of the world and in Ahmed Chalabi they had found just the person for the job.

Iraqi born but US and UK educated, Chalabi had been anointed to lead the INC by one of the most powerful men in Washington, John Rendon, whose Rendon Group gave new meaning to Noam Chomsky's seminal work, *Manufacturing Consent.* (Vintage, 1998, UK) With its US headquarters in Washington's Dupont Circle, The Rendon Group was but a few kilometres from the US Congress and the White House. In terms of political influence, though, it was even closer.

The Rendon Group prides itself on being the leader in a strategic field known as 'perception management',[13] manipulating information and the news media; in other words, spinning stories – and placing them in an often unquestioning press. The Rendon Group had been specifically hired by the CIA in 1991 to help create the conditions for the removal of Saddam Hussein from power – a demand by George H.W. Bush after the first Gulf War ended with Saddam still ruling the country.

Rendon became the de facto leader of the Iraqi Opposition. 'The INC was clueless. They needed a lot of help and didn't know where to start. That is why Rendon was brought in,' said Thomas Twetten, the CIA's former deputy director of operations. The CIA contract paid The Rendon Group extremely well – '[US] $23 million in the first year alone'.[14]

According to the author of *Flacks Americana: John Rendon's Shallow PR War on Terrorism* (New Republic, 20 May, 2002), The Rendon Group expanded dramatically. The open-ended contract gave John Rendon a free hand. The CIA officers who worked with Rendon on the INC conceded that Rendon's Langley bosses simply did not monitor his work. 'They [The Rendon Group] were broadcasting into Iraq,' said one, 'but there was no due diligence.'[15] By 1995 a new team was in charge of the CIA's Iraqi Operations Group and they severed the agency's relationship with Rendon altogether. But the period of separation did not last long. Six years later, shortly after the 9/11 attacks, Rendon was back inside the beltway with a new client: the Pentagon.

Just a few weeks after the World Trade Center attack, the Pentagon secretly awarded The Rendon Group a US$16 million contract. The mission statement: help remove Saddam Hussein from power. Rendon simply picked up where he had left off with the CIA: working with the INC and, in particular, Ahmed Chalabi. No one – publicly at least – questioned the fact Chalabi was on the run after being found guilty of embezzling millions of dollars which destroyed a Jordanian bank. The Rendon Group just wanted Chalabi, who had already delivered up Curveball, to repeat the performance. As is made clear in *The War on Journalism* (Penguin, 2015), they would not be disappointed.

The beachside town of Pattaya on the Gulf of Thailand has changed a lot since its days as a tiny fishing village and R&R haunt for US soldiers during the Vietnam War. But back in 2001 it was still home turf for the CIA, a place far enough from the capital, Bangkok, where business could be done discreetly and yet a town with its own international airport, and the possibility of a quick escape.

In December 2001 – just three months after 9/11 – a team of Defense Intelligence Agency (DIA) and CIA officers headed into town, checking in at one of Pattaya's many hotels. Though the US has 17 intelligence agencies, the rivalry between the DIA and the CIA is among the most acute. Although the CIA might focus on the great strategic plans being hatched by their political masters in the White House, it is the uniformed colleagues of the DIA who have to carry out the sharp end of operations, putting themselves in physical peril. In this case, though, the two agencies were mainly unified. Inside the hotel, they met a man in his middle forties. He sat in a padded chair while metal electrodes were attached to his ring and index fingers and a large hose was wrapped around his chest.

Wired up to the polygraph machine was Adnan Ihsan Saeed al-Haideri, who had fled his homeland in Kurdistan and was determined to do his part in bringing down Saddam Hussein. As a civil engineer, he claimed to have personally visited 20 top-secret weapons of mass destruction (WMD) sites in Iraq. The Pentagon had brought one of the CIA's best polygraph experts to confirm once and for all whether Saddam Hussein had a secret WMD stockpile. As the questioning continued, al-Haideri did not waver. He stuck to his story, insisting repeatedly that he was a civil engineer who had helped Saddam's men to secretly bury tons of biological, chemical and nuclear weapons. The illegal arms, according to al-Haideri, were buried in subterranean wells, hidden in private villas and even stashed beneath the Saddam Hussein Hospital, the largest medical facility in Baghdad.

As al-Haideri spoke, all in the room were acutely aware that if what he was telling them was true, it would make war with Iraq inevitable. After he finished the questioning, the CIA officer began the painstaking business of analysing al-Haideri's responses; his blood pressure, pulse rate, breathing rate and perspiration all produced a complex graph on the polygraph's computer screen. The scratchy lines traced how al-Haideri had reacted to every question. When he had competed his analyses the CIA officer had bad news for the Pentagon: the results indicated al-Haideri was a fabricator at best and probably a liar. His claims about Saddam's WMD programme were nonsense.

The destruction of al-Haideri's credibility as a witness should have spelled trouble for the people who had vouched for him as a reliable informant – Ahmed Chalabi and The Rendon Group. After the Pattaya meeting the CIA certainly believed he wasn't to be trusted. But at that time, the facts appeared to matter less and less. Desperate for unequivocal evidence to justify waging war with Iraq, the neocons had set up their own unit, which bypassed the intelligence agencies. Vice President Dick Cheney and Richard Perle, the policy adviser to the Secretary of Defense and a long-time supporter of Chalabi, established what was known as the Office of Special Plans (OSP). The OSP hired analysts and Middle East experts to re-examine the raw data gathered by the intelligence agencies, trying to build the case for war against Iraq. If the intelligence agencies could not provide the evidence they needed, they would find it themselves with the help of Ahmed Chalabi and the INC, according to a memorandum the diplomat sent to the office of British Prime Minister Tony Blair. When Deputy Secretary of Defense Paul Wolfowitz dined with Christopher Meyer, the British Ambassador to the US, Wolfowitz told Meyer that Chalabi 'had a record of bringing high-grade defectors out of Iraq', like Curveball. Richard Perle believed 'the most reliable person to give us advice is Chalabi'.[16] Chalabi was just the person to give the OSP what it wanted to hear. It is not the case that everyone in the Bush administration was blind to the modus operandi of the OSP. Some in the intelligence agencies believed the OSP was 'dangerous for US national security and a threat to world peace'. In an interview with the Scottish Sunday Herald, a former CIA officer, Larry C. Johnson, said the OSP lied and manipulated intelligence to further its agenda of removing Saddam. 'It's a group of ideologues with pre-determined notions of truth and reality. They take bits of intelligence to support their agenda and ignore anything contrary.'[17] Others, like W. Patrick Lang, the former chief of Middle East intelligence at the DIA, expressed outrage: 'The Pentagon has banded together to dominate the government's foreign policy, and they've pulled it off. They're running Chalabi. The DIA has been intimidated and beaten to a pulp. And there's no guts at all in the CIA.'[18] Dismissed by the CIA and now hired by the Pentagon, The Rendon Group was only too keen to wheel out the defectors the OSP believed provided the best intelligence on Iraq.

On the other side of the Atlantic, the British had their own version of the OSP, called 'Operation Rockingham', set up to 'cherry-pick'[19] intelligence proving an active Iraqi WMD programme and to ignore and quash intelligence which indicated that Saddam's stockpiles had been destroyed or wound down. Their work provided 'evidence' for British Prime Minister Tony Blair's claims that Iraq was a major threat. Blair cited the now infamous claim that Iraq could launch a WMD in 45 minutes, the so-called dodgy dossier: the document stated that Saddam's military planning allowed for some WMD to be ready within 45 minutes. While this might have been correct, what the dossier was referring to was battlefield chemical and biological weapons, not the implication that they could be loaded on to missiles capable of hitting British territory in Cyprus within 45 minutes. A recently released memo from Sir John Scarlett, chairman of the Joint Intelligence Committee, to Blair's foreign affairs advisor, unmasks the deception referring to 'the benefit of obscuring the fact that in terms of WMD Iraq is not that exceptional'.[20]

In the far distant southern hemisphere, in a low-rise utilitarian building housing Australia's senior analysis agency, the Office of National Assessments (ONA), one of the senior officers who had viewed the incoming intelligence data had come to a similar conclusion that there was nothing particularly unusual about Iraq regarding WMD. But unlike Sir John Scarlett, Andrew Wilkie, a former lieutenant colonel in the Australian Intelligence Corps, was a man of troubled conscience. He simply could not accept the WMD argument for war, and all that it entailed. A one-time member of the Liberal Party of Australia (the country's conservative party) he had trained at Canberra's elite Royal Military Academy – Duntroon. Not long after taking part in an Iraq planning meeting at 4.30 pm on 11 March, 2003, he walked out of his ONA office and resigned. That night on the Channel Nine news, on national Australian television, he told long-time political journalist Laurie Oakes that he was particularly angry that the Federal government had repeatedly linked Iraq with terrorism to justify its threats of war. 'We have not seen any hard intelligence that establishes that Iraq is actively cooperating with al-Qaeda. It is quite clear to me that the Iraq issue is totally unrelated to the war on terror,' Wilkie said. Wilkie told Oakes that although he would be 'a pariah in the public service and around the government',[21] he hoped that his speaking out would cause the government to rethink its position.

> The reason I have done what I have done – and it's obviously a very dramatic action – is that I am convinced that a war against Iraq would be wrong at this point in time and not a risk worth taking. Iraq does not pose a security threat to the US, to the UK, to Australia or any other country at this point in time. Their military is very small, their weapons of mass destruction programme is fragmented and contained, because of the way it has been managed since the last Gulf War, and there is no hard evidence for any active co-operation between Iraq and al-Qaeda.

A war is the course of action that is most likely to cause Saddam to do the things that we're trying to prevent; to make him feel cornered and force him to act recklessly, including possibly using weapons of mass destruction, possibly against his own people. It could also cause him to engineer a humanitarian disaster or to play the terrorism card and push him closer to terror organizations like al-Qaeda.[22]

While Wilkie was becoming agitated at the deception, thousands of kilometres away at Pine Gap, the joint US–Australia spy base near Alice Springs, NSA staff were also becoming uneasy about the WMD claims being made by President Bush. But unlike Wilkie, they remained silent. David Rosenberg, the author of *Inside Pine Gap: The Spy Who Came in From the Desert* (Hardie Grant, Melbourne, 2011), who worked for the NSA at Pine Gap for 18 years as an electronics intelligence signals analyst, told me that Bush's assertions, beamed in from the US on the nightly TV news, generated some spirited debates at Pine Gap about the need for war. Pine Gap had positioned its advanced Orion satellites to focus almost entirely on Iraq, probing for even the slightest shred of evidence that Saddam Hussein possessed WMDs or was developing them. Rosenberg said,

We at Pine Gap had access to a significant number of the intelligence communities' tasking messages looking for proof of Iraq's WMDs, and in the 10 years that I was looking at these messages going backwards and forwards about Iraq's WMDs nothing showed [up] that [Iraq] had them.[23]

Pine Gap had also been tasked with searching for missiles that could reach the mainland US – one of the more alarmist claims from Washington. The former official said Pine Gap had discovered 'no missile in Iraq [was] capable of hitting the US'.[24] This was the kind of intelligence Wilkie was reading as he worked at the ONA. In the battle to win the argument for war, the US, British and Australian governments simply ignored information that did not fit their agenda.

Instead the official message became amplified and relayed by radio shock jocks and newspapers like the New York Post and The Australian. The White House began turning up the pressure. In October 2001 President Bush had signed a presidential order marked 'Top Secret' and 'NoFor', meaning no foreign governments were to be told. The National Security Agency, with its network of bases around the world and a secret budget in the multiple billions of dollars, already had the right under US law to spy on any person and any government overseas, barring the promise that it would not eavesdrop on any of its Five Eyes partners. But the presidential order rewrote the rule book, granting the NSA the power to spy on US citizens at home – all in the name of national security and all done without having to seek a court warrant. Bush had bestowed fresh powers on the most powerful intelligence-gathering apparatus ever built. The president pointedly had not asked Congress to include provisions for the NSA domestic surveillance programme as part of the Patriot Act 2001, which gave authorities significantly enhanced powers of surveillance. White House lawyers had argued behind closed doors that such new laws were unnecessary; agencies already had ample power to fight terrorism. But there was another more compelling reason for secrecy about the NSA's new snooping role: seeking Congressional approval was politically risky. The White House feared that civil liberties groups would be bound to fight it – and besides, the lawyers feared they might be in breach of the Constitution. Spying on Americans on their home soil was almost certainly in breach of the Fourth Amendment, which specifically prohibits random searches of a person's private property. Originally designed to prevent the capricious abuse of government power against its citizens, it has far greater significance today in protecting a more sophisticated form of civil liberties: private electronic communications. Bush and his legal advisers believed that in the wake of the 9/11 attacks, what might have been seen as crossing the legal line before would be acceptable now in order to prevent another terrorist attack on the US. A few days after 9/11, a US Justice Department lawyer wrote an internal memorandum that argued the government might use 'electronic surveillance techniques and equipment that are more powerful and sophisticated than those available to law enforcement agencies in order to intercept telephonic communications and observe the movement of persons but without obtaining warrants for such uses'.[25] The legal advice noted that while such actions could raise constitutional issues, 'the government may be justified in taking measures which in less troubled conditions could be seen as infringements of individual liberties'.[26] By the beginning of 2003 any chance of a realistic assessment of the intelligence on Iraq had long disappeared.

On 4 February, 2003, the night before Secretary of State Colin Powell made his now infamous appeal to the United Nations Security Council for backing to invade Iraq, Tyler Drumheller, the CIA's European director – who had already passed on his concerns to the CIA director George Tenet – called the deputy head of the CIA to remind him that Curveball was a fabricator. The following day, when he turned on the television in Germany to watch Powell address the Security Council, he realised that Curveball wasn't the only person who couldn't be trusted. Despite Drumheller's warnings, Curveball's confected stories formed the main thrust of Powell's address – from the non-existent WMD sites, to the mobile facilities. Despite millions of people taking to the streets in cities around the world, in opposition to the invasion, it was too late to stop the war. The neocons had forced their argument on the world, carried along by a baying right-wing media, but also, and more surprisingly, by bastions of mainstream journalism, who either failed to comprehensively challenge the arguments for war or allowed themselves to be manipulated by confected intelligence.

Notes

1 Clarke, R. 2004. *Against All Enemies: Inside America's War on Terror*. Thorndyke Press, Waterville.
2 Clarke, R. 2004. *Against All Enemies: Inside America's War on Terror*. Thorndyke Press, Waterville.

3 Clarke, R. 2004. *Against All Enemies: Inside America's War on Terror.* Thorndyke Press, Waterville.
4 Stein, J. and Dickinson, T. September/October, 2006. Lie by Lie: A Timeline of How We Got into Iraq [online]. Available at www.motherjones.com/politics/2011/12/leadup-iraq-war-timeline/ [Accessed 29 September, 2016].
5 Clarke, R. 2004. *Against All Enemies: Inside America's War on Terror.* Thorndyke Press, Waterville.
6 Clarke, R. 2004. *Against All Enemies: Inside America's War on Terror.* Thorndyke Press, Waterville.
7 Clarke, R. 2004. *Against All Enemies: Inside America's War on Terror.* Thorndyke Press, Waterville.
8 Clarke, R. 2004. *Against All Enemies: Inside America's War on Terror.* Thorndyke Press, Waterville.
9 Clarke, R. 2004. *Against All Enemies: Inside America's War on Terror.* Thorndyke Press, Waterville.
10 Clarke, R. 2004. *Against All Enemies: Inside America's War on Terror.* Thorndyke Press, Waterville.
11 Rovner, J. 2011. *Fixing the Facts: National Security and the Politics of Intelligence.* Cornell University Press, New York.
12 Drogin, B. and Goetz, J. 20th November, 2005. Los Angeles Times [online]. Available at www.latimes.com/world/middleeast/la-na-curveball20nov20-story.html [Accessed 3 August, 2016].
13 Bamford, J. 17th November, 2005. *The Man Who Sold the War.* Rolling Stone [online]. www.twf.org/News/Y2005/1120-Propaganda.html [Accessed 21 July, 2016].
14 Fowler, A. 2015. *The War on Journalism.* Penguin Random House.
15 Foer. F. 20th May, 2002. *Flacks Americana: John Rendon's Shallow PR War on Terrorism.* New Republic [online]. Available at https://newrepublic.com/article/68667/flacks-americana [Accessed 13 August, 2016].
16 Ricks, T. 2006. *Fiasco: The American Military Adventure in Iraq.* Penguin, New York.
17 Duthel, H. 2006. *Global Secrets and Intelligence Services.* Books on Demand Norderstd, Germany.
18 Hersh, S. 12th May, 2003. *Selective Intelligence: Donald Rumsfeld Has His Own Special Sources. Are They reliable?* The New Yorker [online]. Available at www.newyorker.com/magazine/2003/05/12/selective-intelligence [Accessed 6 October, 2016].
19 Herald, S. 22nd June, 2014. *The Trial of Tony Blair.* Scotland. Available at www.heraldscotland.com/opinion/13166518.The_trial_of_Tony_Blair [Accessed 12 October, 2016].
20 Ames, C. 25th June, 2011. *Memo Reveals Intelligence Chief's Bid to Fuel Fears of Iraqi WMDs.* The Observer, London [online]. Available at www.theguardian.com/uk/2011/jun/26/intelligence-chief-iraqi-wmds [Accessed 17 May, 2016].
21 Hudson, P. and Dodson, L. 12th March, 2003. *Top Advisor Quits Over War Stance.* The Age, Melourne [online]. Available at www.theage.com.au/articles/2003/03/11/1047144972046.html [Accessed 8 August, 2016].
22 Hudson, P. and Dodson, L. 12th March, 2003. *Top Advisor Quits Over War Stance.* The Age, Melourne [online]. Available at www.theage.com.au/articles/2003/03/11/1047144972046.html [Accessed 8 August, 2016].
23 Rosenberg, D. 2014. *Interview.*
24 Rosenberg, D. 2014. *Interview.*
25 Risen, J. and Litchblau, E. 16th December, 2005. *Bush Lets US Spy on Callers Without Courts.* New York Times.
26 Risen, J. and Litchblau, E. 16th December, 2005. *Bush Lets US Spy on Callers Without Courts.* New York Times.

3

SPIN AND DECEPTION

The ancient lands of Mesopotamia, a mix of luxuriant country and arid desert encompassed in the present day by the state of Iraq, have been identified as the cradle of civilisation. They inspired some of the most important developments in history, from the wheel to the planting of cereal crops and the development of mathematics and astronomy. But these days those ancient lands are better known as a place of ongoing war, and where the greatest hoax of recent times was finally exposed. Iraq's 'Weapons of Mass Destruction' were as illusory as a desert mirage.

It is now known that the main reason for the US-led invasion was not the removal of WMD but the removal of Saddam Hussein. The Iraqi dictator had once acted as a US-friendly counterforce to Iraq's neighbour, Iran, but Saddam had overreached himself by invading Kuwait ten years earlier, and the US, once his staunchest ally, decided it wanted rid of him. As John Bolton, US Ambassador to the UN, 2005–2006, blithely wrote in 2015: 'Overthrowing Iraqi dictator Saddam Hussein in 2003 achieved important American strategic objectives.'[1] What is so remarkable is that the sham argument that Saddam threatened anyone other than his own people with WMDs was so wholeheartedly and unquestionably embraced by large sections of the world's media. Most extraordinary of all is that one of the leading supporters of the spurious claims of WMDs should be that bastion of investigative journalism, the New York Times. It was the Times which in 1971 published the Pentagon Papers, which exposed years of public deception and the truth about how the Vietnam War had been secretly expanded to include the bombing of neighbouring Laos and Cambodia. As New York Times associate editor, R. W. Apple Jnr, wrote, the Pentagon Papers 'demonstrated, among other things, that the [Lyndon]Johnson Administration had systematically lied, not only to the public but also to Congress, about a subject of transcendent national interest and significance.'[2] There had been no tip-off to the White House that the New York Times was about to publish a highly embarrassing series of reports about successive US administrations. Within hours of the newspaper hitting the streets, President Richard Nixon tried to stop further publication with a court order, a move successfully resisted by the *Times*. The marked difference between how the *Times* dealt with the Pentagon Papers publication and its coverage of the Iraq War WMD issue revealed just how deep a cultural change the newspaper had undergone over the previous three decades.

The *New York Times* would become a repository of planted stories, written by one of its most senior reporters, Judith Miller. It says much about the newspaper that Miller cited Ahmed Chalabi and the INC as one of her major sources. In a disagreement with the *New York Times* Baghdad Bureau chief she wrote that she had been 'covering Chalabi for about 10 years'; she had 'done most of the stories about him for our paper' and more importantly Chalabi had 'provided most of the front-page exclusives on WMD to our paper'.[3] It would come as no surprise that Miller was selected by the INC to write the newspaper exclusive interview with al-Haideri, the Iraqi informer who had so spectacularly failed his lie detector test in Thailand. For the worldwide broadcast rights the INC contacted Paul Moran, an Australian freelance journalist. Moran, who had worked for the ABC, was perfect for their purposes. An idealistic photojournalist, he had worked with INC spokesman Zaab Sethna on what were known as 'information operations'. According to those who worked alongside him, Moran was an unconventional journalist.

When it came to being granted visas to work in some Middle Eastern countries, he acquired a reputation for achieving what others could not. Cameramen who queried his methods or cast aspersions on the connections that got him access were accused of being jealous. In December 2001, after the INC brought al-Haideri to him, Paul Moran sat down with the Iraqi defector and conducted the most important interview of his career. Within hours of its completion the ABC had put it on air and, crucially for the INC and The Rendon Group, this ABC TV exclusive packed with disinformation and fabrication went around the world, picked up by dozens of TV stations. Unchecked, uncorroborated, the ABC broadcast a piece of pure pro-war propaganda, gratefully received by the White House.

Moran, however, would never be brought to account for his interview. By the time questions were seriously being asked, he had been killed by a car bomb in northern Iraq while working as a cameraman for the ABC.

One of the cameramen who worked alongside Moran said he believed Moran had been the subject of a 'targeted killing' because of his work supporting the Kurds. But though they might have put him in the firing line, he was killed because he was in the wrong place at the wrong time.

The 39-year-old Moran became the first international journalist to die in the Iraq War, honoured on the ABC staff memorial page set up to pay tribute to colleagues who lost their lives in the line of duty.

In the wake of the broadcast the spotlight fell on Moran, and details of his puzzling working life and Middle East connections were publicly pored over.

The ABC's then Director of News and Current Affairs, Max Uechtritz, said the ABC knew that 'Moran had obtained the interview because of his contacts with the Iraqi National Congress.' Peter Cave, who put together the ABC story from Moran's interview, put it more bluntly: 'I was conned, the ABC was conned.'[4] What has never been publicly explained is that it was common knowledge that Moran had worked for the CIA funded Rendon Group and the ABC seemed to accept it.

Moran had self-censored and failed to check the veracity of the al-Haideri story, either because he thought he was helping the Kurds or because he knew what John Rendon expected of him.

The Moran TV interview dovetailed superbly with the print version of al-Haideri's incredible story.

A confidante of I. Lewis 'Scooter' Libby, Vice President Dick Cheney's chief of staff, Judith Miller had made a name for herself writing about chemical weapons. She also had a reputation for being a ready outlet for INC propaganda.

The INC so trusted both Moran and Miller that it gave each of them access to al-Haideri in Pattaya before the CIA ran its polygraph test on him, allowing the INC to be able to get its story out before any uncomfortable truths emerged about the veracity of what he was saying. By the time al-Haideri underwent his beach-side grilling Miller was already back in New York. She later made calls to the CIA and DIA but her vaunted intelligence sources must have let her down because she claimed not to know about the results of al-Haideri's lie detector test. Instead, in her piece which appeared in the *New York Times* on 20 December, 2001, she reported that unnamed 'government experts' called his information 'reliable and significant'. Miller's story achieved the kind of exposure Rendon had been paid millions of dollars to provide. Headlined 'An Iraqi Defector Tells of Work on at Least 20 Hidden Weapons Sites', the article began by saying that this

> defector who described himself as a civil engineer said he personally worked on renovations of secret facilities for biological, chemical and nuclear weapons in underground wells, private villas and under the Saddam Hussein Hospital in Baghdad as recently as a year ago'.

If verified, added Miller, the allegations would 'provide ammunition to officials within the Bush administration [who] have been arguing that Mr. Hussein should be driven from power partly because of his unwillingness to stop making weapons of mass destruction, despite his pledges to do so'.

Newspapers and television networks around the world quickly picked up the story, reinforced by Moran's on-camera interview with al-Haideri on the ABC. It was a massive victory for John Rendon, who was on his way to helping create the first modern war built almost entirely on disinformation planted in the media. President George W. Bush increased the momentum to war in his State of the Union address of 29 January, 2002. Wearing a sombre dark suit and grey tie, he told the applauding joint sitting of the House of Representatives and Senate that

Iraq was part of an 'axis of evil'. Allied with terrorists, it posed 'a grave and growing danger' to US interests through possession of 'weapons of mass destruction'.[5] Eight months later, the *New York Times* carried another Judith Miller story. On 8 September, 2002 she wrote about 'Mr. Hussein's dogged insistence on pursuing his nuclear ambitions'. It was a bald statement of 'fact' without any attribution. She added that what defectors described in interviews as Iraq's push to improve and expand Baghdad's chemical and biological arsenals had 'brought Iraq and the United States to the brink of war.' The story, headlined 'US Says Hussein Intensified Quest for A-bomb Parts',[6] quoted not a single person by name, and relied entirely on US government sources. In the previous 14 months, Miller wrote, Iraq had tried to buy thousands of specially designed aluminium tubes, which American officials believed were intended as components of centrifuges to 'enrich uranium' to a level where it could be used to make a bomb.

Another of the 8 September, 2002 article's purported facts – again without any attribution or qualification – was that 'The attempted purchases are not the only signs of a renewed Iraqi interest in acquiring nuclear arms.'[7] Although none of this was true – not the tubes for enrichment nor the quest for atomic bomb parts; Saddam had not been 'pursuing his nuclear ambitions' – Miller and the *New York Times*, with its uncorroborated, unquestioning reporting, had provided the perfect vehicle for the White House.

Over the following 24 hours Miller's story dominated the news cycle, stirring fear of a nuclear Armageddon. On the day the story appeared, on NBC's Meet the Press, Vice President Dick Cheney cited the *New York Times* article and accused Saddam of moving aggressively to develop nuclear weapons over the past 14 months to add to his stockpile of chemical and biological arms. On CNN the same day, National Security Advisor Condoleezza Rice acknowledged that 'there will always be some uncertainty' in determining how close Iraq may be to obtaining a nuclear weapon but, in a phrase as polished as it was hollow, added: 'We don't want the smoking gun to be a mushroom cloud.'[8] On CBS President Bush said UN weapons inspectors, before they were denied access to Iraq in 1998, concluded that Saddam was 'six months away from developing a weapon'.[9] He cited satellite photos that showed 'unexplained construction' at Iraqi sites that weapons inspectors had previously searched for indications Saddam was trying to develop nuclear arms. 'I don't know what more evidence we need,'[10] Bush said. The *New York Times* now became quoted as an authoritative source. The White House 'confirmed a report in the *New York Times*' that Saddam Hussein had been attempting to get equipment to enrich uranium to produce nuclear weapons. Australian Prime Minister John Howard added to the misleading game, saying the intelligence that had come out of the US 'if accurate confirms the intelligence that we have been given'.[11] The fact is it was the same intelligence that the US had already given to Australia. Howard made great play of the possibility that 'Iraq has not abandoned her [sic] aspiration for nuclear capacity'.[12] By suggesting the *New York Times* story added yet another layer of confirmation, Howard was taking part in the Australian version of the style of journalism that Miller and the

White House specialised in: the story leaked to Judith Miller and published in the *New York Times* had been confirmed by the very people who leaked it in the first place. Iraq's nuclear ambitions were now accepted as fact. Even the BBC's prestigious Panorama programme 'The Case Against Saddam', broadcast on 23 September, 2002, supported the 'evidence', reporting that 'In the 14 last months, several shipments, a total of 1000 aluminium centrifuge tubes, have been intercepted by intelligence agencies before they actually reached Iraq', suggesting they could be used for nuclear weapons production.[13] Yet the International Atomic Energy Agency in Vienna and the senior expert at America's primary nuclear weapons research facility, Oak Ridge National Laboratory, had both informed the CIA the centrifuge tubes were no good for uranium enrichment. Like al-Janabi's 'Curveball' claims of bio-weapons and the al-Haideri stockpile of nuclear, biological and chemical weapons, the tubes for nuclear centrifuges story was pure fiction.

In April, 2003, as the US-led invasion force headed north towards Baghdad, Miller wrote an extraordinary story that a scientist who claimed to have worked for 'Iraq's chemical weapons program' had told an American military team that Iraq destroyed chemical weapons and biological warfare equipment only days before the war began. Conveying what the military officials had told her, Miller wrote that the scientist 'led Americans to a supply of material that proved to be the building blocks of illegal weapons, which he claimed to have buried as evidence of Iraq's illicit weapons programs'.[14] Just for good measure she threw in the allegation from an unnamed military source that 'Iraq was cooperating with Al Qaeda'.[15]

There was no mention of Andrew Wilkie's comprehensive first-hand rebuttal of the WMD threat six weeks earlier. Or the kind of questioning journalism epitomised by the BBC's Andrew Gilligan several weeks later that he understood the British government had 'sexed up' a dossier on WMDs to support its case for war.

In what must be one of the greatest ironic explanations in journalism, Miller wrote that US officials had asked that details of what chemicals were uncovered be deleted from her story. 'They said they feared that such information could jeopardize the scientist's safety by identifying the part of the weapons program where he worked.'[16] An alternative explanation hung in the air: that they were simply hiding the identity of someone who was gravely mistaken or a straight-out liar. Miller also wrote that she was not able to interview the scientist but only 'permitted to see him from a distance at the sites where he said that material from the arms program was buried'.[17]

The next day Miller appeared on US national television, including the PBS's prestigious NewsHour with Jim Lehrer, proclaiming that what had been discovered was 'more than a smoking gun' and was a 'silver bullet in the form of an Iraqi scientist'. She praised the Bush administration for creating a 'political atmosphere where these scientists can come forward'.[18]

The story spread quickly, repeated by conservative talk-show hosts Bill O'Reilly and Rush Limbaugh. Sent to regional newspapers via the *New York Times* wire service, it acquired even more dramatic impact. 'Illegal Material Spotted'[19] the *Rocky Mountain News* reported with a subheading that distorted even more: 'Iraqi Scientist Leads U.S. Team to Illicit Weapons Location'.[20] 'Outlawed Material Destroyed by the Iraqis Before the War' was the headline of the *Seattle Post-Intelligencer*. Out in the Iraqi desert the reporter who, more than anyone else, had produced unverified and unquestioning journalism championing the war did perhaps finally stumble across the truth: the scientist, like all the other defectors and informants who had spoken of Iraqi WMDs, simply wanted a green card or a visa – and was prepared to say anything to get it. As Miller breathlessly reported, the scientist was offering US troops information about WMDs 'and seeking their protection'.[21] Miller's stories became increasingly bizarre. If she had earlier crossed the line between journalism and public relations for the White House, she outdid herself now. She asserted that the reason the WMDs had not been found yet was possibly because 'the Pentagon-led teams, which include specialists from several Pentagon agencies, have been hampered by a lack of resources and by geography.'[22] Miller appeared to be reporting excuses rather than reasons for the failure of the US military to discover WMDs. But if anyone at the *New York Times* was challenging her about the non-existence of these weapons systems, no sense of that appeared in the stories she continued to write. Two days later Miller reported that the US military had moved on from whether or not Iraq had destroyed the WMDs and its Mobile Exploitation Team Alpha, the team dedicated to hunting for unconventional weapons in Iraq, was now focused on locating key people who worked on the programmes.

Miller wrote that she had been told, 'The paradigm has shifted. We've had a conceptual jump in how we think about, and what we look for in Iraq's program. We must look at the infrastructure, not just for the weapons.'[23]

So, what had the baseball cap-wearing Iraqi 'scientist' been pointing at on the ground? He seemed to have disappeared. The following day Miller is reporting a fresh lead: 'American-led forces have occupied a vast warehouse complex in Baghdad filled with chemicals where Iraqi scientists are suspected of having tested unconventional agents on dogs within the past year, according to military officers and weapons experts.'[24]

That also, of course, turned out to be untrue. Although Miller was one of hundreds of journalists who had been 'embedded' with military units, the veteran reporter was closer than most to the US military. She was given special clearance by the Pentagon to access information classified 'Secret'. What Miller either did not understand or did not attach importance to was that this access compromised her.

It even prevented Miller discussing with her *New York Times* editors 'some of the more sensitive information' about Iraq.

To whom did Miller give her allegiance, the Pentagon or the *New York Times*? There were many inside the newspaper who raised similar questions about Miller's relationship with the Iraqi National Congress and its leader, Ahmed Chalabi. She openly boasted of her professional relationship with Chalabi and the 'scoops' he had delivered to her.

A former CIA analyst who had observed Miller's stories and relationships for years explained to James C. Moore on the US website Salon how simple it was to manipulate the correspondent and her newspaper. 'The White House had a perfect deal with Miller,' the ex-CIA officer told Moore.

> Chalabi is providing the Bush people with the information they need to support their political objectives with Iraq, and he is supplying the same material to Judy Miller. Chalabi tips her on something and then she goes to the White House, which has already heard the same thing from Chalabi, and she gets it corroborated by some insider she always describes as a 'senior administration official.'[25]

Any newspaper, or politician, that broke ranks with this revolving door information cycle suffered savage attack. When former British Labour minister Clare Short publicly revealed that the US had been bugging the conversations of the UN Secretary General, Kofi Annan, the howls of condemnation from the right-wing press were resounding. 'Woman of Mass Destruction',[26] splashed the *Daily Mail*.

London's *Daily Telegraph* even proposed prosecuting Short under the Official Secrets Act. *The Sun* wanted Short sacked. 'What the Leftie loudmouth has done is bloody disgraceful,'[27] raged the paper. 'The fact is that all major countries spend a lot of time, money and energy spying on others. It's not necessarily sinister but is more a common-sense precaution, particularly when a war is imminent.'[28] The media did not content itself with criticising politicians. It turned on itself when it was revealed that the UN Secretary General Kofi Annan was not alone in having his phone bugged by US intelligence. I had just revealed in an ABC report the Americans were also listening in to UN weapons inspector Hans Blix during his fruitless search for WMDs and was asked by a producer at Rupert Murdoch's London-based Sky TV for an interview, which would 'give your story more oxygen'.[29] Once live on air, the presenter took a different tack. She questioned why the ABC had run the story in the first place. It was an extraordinary moment. What that brief query revealed was either that the Sky presenter did not recognise the story, in which case why carry out the interview, or alternatively how unquestioning journalists could be when expected to conform to their news' organisation's editorial line. The argument that journalism should suspend its questioning of government is a recurring issue in times of national conflict, and the War on Terror – a potentially never-ending war – is a powerful instrument for politicians and media proprietors who want to quash debate. Others in the Murdoch camp lashed out at those who had dared question the rightness of the invasion of Iraq. *The Australian*'s foreign editor, Greg Sheridan, stoked the nuclear fears. 'Hussein could invade Kuwait for a second time on his way to dominating the Persian Gulf and all its strategic oil deposits . . . [H]e could prevent the US coming to Kuwait's rescue by nuclear blackmail.'[30] When US troops reached Baghdad, *The Australian* published an

editorial, 'Coalition of the Whining Got it Wrong', which ended with unintended irony: 'Never underestimate the power of ideology and myth – in this
case anti-Americanism – to trump reality. But at least we know for sure it is not
love, but being a left-wing intellectual, that means never having to say you're
sorry.'[31] The complete absence of WMDs did not temper the belligerent assertions. Though all of Murdoch's newspapers and media outlets had championed
the war, without exception, giving the lie to the oft-repeated assertion by
Murdoch that his editors make up their own minds, it was in Australia that
some of the most unquestioning support for the war appeared. Those who stood
in the way became victims of a powerful alliance between the Murdoch papers
and the federal government. If the official leak can sometimes be a nuanced
affair, there was nothing subtle about what the government did to pay back
Andrew Wilkie. The desire for revenge appeared to consume the government
of John Howard and his Foreign Minister, Alexander Downer. As a champion
of the Iraq invasion, Downer frequently baited his political opponents with the
assertion that if they did not support removing Saddam then they must be supporting a dictator. Downer was particularly angry at Wilkie's unmasking of the
truth. It made him look foolish. In December 2002 Wilkie had written a secret
assessment of Iraq for the ONA. Sent to a restricted list of people in the government, all copies were later returned to the ONA under its strict procedures for
classified material. Six months later, on 20 June, 2003, Downer's office requested
a copy of Wilkie's report – the only such request during the six-month period.
On 23 June journalist Andrew Bolt – a darling of the right, who would later rise
to infamy when found guilty of racial discrimination – published an article
quoting extensively from Wilkie's secret document. In journalistic terms what
Bolt wrote was a smear job. In the article, which appeared in the Melbourne
Herald-Sun on 23 June, 2003, Bolt wrote that Wilkie had asserted in the ONA
report that Saddam had WMDs and Wilkie was therefore a hypocrite to speak
out against the war. A detail he failed to include was that Wilkie said those
weapons did not pose a threat to anyone, except possibly the Iraqi people. Bolt's
report was a complete distortion of Wilkie's position, but it suited the hawkish
agenda of the Murdoch media and a government increasingly embarrassed as
the likelihood of discovering WMDs dwindled. The leaking of a secret document marked AUSTEO –Australian Eyes Only – is no small matter and there
was a furore in the press.

As noted by Sydney Morning Herald journalists Tom Allard and Deborah Snow
in their 19 June, 2004 article, if indeed Downer's office leaked the report, it would
be 'a serious offence under the Crimes Act'.

If convicted the leaker could face years in prison. But nobody was ever prosecuted and the Australian Federal Police simply issued a statement saying there
was 'no direct admissible evidence to identify any of the recipients of the report
as the source of the disclosure to the journalist Andrew Bolt'. A spokesman for
Mr Downer was quoted as saying, 'We are not interested in Mr Wilkie's hysterical
claims. Speak to the AFP [Australian Federal Police].'[32]

It is unknown whether or not the Federal Police interviewed Downer or any-one in his office – such details have never been made public – but any serious investigator would have started by checking on those who benefited from the smear against Wilkie. Logic would suggest that someone in the government, probably in Downer's office, handed over Wilkie's classified report in order to settle a political score. Regardless of how it happened, whoever tried to damage Wilkie's reputation has never been called to account for their actions.

Lack of accountability for journalists who had helped create a horrific war based on lies is a major theme of the Iraq invasion.

Exactly how many Iraqis lost their lives in the war, stoked in large part by a media which failed to challenge its governments, is difficult to accurately access. What is clear is that it is a shocking figure.

One detailed study, based on a cluster of 2000 randomly selected households in the then 18 Iraqi governorates, found that the death rate rose from 2.89 per thousand in the two years prior to the invasion to 4.55 per thousand between March 2003 and June 2011. The majority of the extra deaths were violent. Thirty-five per cent were killed by Coalition forces; 32 per cent by Iraqi militias. Death by shooting was more common than death by explosion. In total, there were some 500,000 Iraqis who died as a consequence of the invasion by the US, Britain and Australia.[33]

In the US, the *New York Times* apologised, albeit grudgingly, for its flawed reporting:

> We have found ... instances of coverage that was not as rigorous as it should have been ... In some cases, the information that was controversial then, and seems questionable now, was insufficiently qualified or allowed to stand unchallenged.'[34] *New York Times* executive editor Bill Keller disputed the paper's public position, writing that he 'did not see a prima facie case for recanting or repudiating the stories. The brief against the coverage was that it was insufficiently sceptical, but that is an easier claim to make in hindsight than in context.'[35]

Perhaps one reason why Keller was so supportive of Miller was the fact that he was dealing with his own journalistic demons, which would soon be made public. Rather than scrutinise Judith Miller's work, Keller chose to base his assessment of her WMD articles on her past performances. Describing his high-profile cor-respondent as 'smart, well-sourced, industrious and fearless',[36] Keller dismissed criticisms that her work was fatally flawed. If Miller's boss had done some inves-tigative reporting of his own, he might have discovered evidence of Miller's political predisposition. The Middle East Forum, an organisation that openly advocated that the US overthrow Saddam, listed Miller as an expert speaker on its website and held a launch party for her book *God Has Ninety-Nine Names* (Touchstone, New York, 1996), which many critics have interpreted as anti-Muslim. She was represented by Benador Associates, a speakers' bureau that specialises in conservative thinkers with Middle East expertise. Asked if she supported Bush politically, Miller responded:

> My views are well known. I understood that these people . . . who hated us so much . . . that if they ever got their hands on WMD, they would use them. Do I have a belief that the WMD exist, and a fear? Yeah, I have real fear for my country.'[37]

Both Miller and Keller portray themselves as patriotic Americans doing the right thing for their country. But while it could be said of Miller than she was wilfully ignorant of the truth about Iraq, the same could not be said of Keller. In 2004, in the months leading up to the US presidential election, *New York Times* reporters James Risen and Eric Lichtblau unearthed the story of George W. Bush's decision to authorise the NSA to spy on the US public. When the White House argued that revealing this might aid terrorists, Keller made a decision not to publish the exposé. Keller says it wasn't just the issue of national security that made him hold back the story. He believed the facts needed closer checking. But the story that eventually appeared in the *New York Times* after Bush had been re-elected was not substantially different from the one that Risen had offered almost a year earlier, and the threat of terrorism had not changed.

The eventual disclosure that the NSA had been eavesdropping on billions of phone calls and intercepting data on a massive scale gave Americans an insight for the first time into the huge power of the NSA. Yet there was no contrition, in fact it could be argued that the NSA had been emboldened by Bush's executive order to spy on Americans. Whatever the reason, the NSA soon started behaving like an outlaw, without the cover of a presidential order. Not everyone inside the organisation agreed with what the NSA was doing. In Hawaii, as far away from Washington as you can go without leaving the country, a computer engineer, working as a contractor, had been watching the NSA from the inside. Perhaps unusually for someone working for the NSA, he sometimes carried with him a copy of the US Constitution. He had been concerned for some time about the organisation's extraordinary global reach into the lives of everyone on the planet and he was particularly concerned that the NSA was in breach of the Constitution's Fourth Amendment, which prohibits random searches of American citizens. Edward Snowden decided to do something about it.

Notes

1 Bolton, J. 26th February, 2013. *Overthrowing Saddam Hussein Was the Right Move for the US and Its Allies.* The Guardian [online] London. Available at www.theguardian.com/commentisfree/2013/feb/26/iraq-war-was-justified [Accessed 8 July, 2016].

2 Apple, R. W. 23rd June. *Lessons from the Pentagon Papers. New York Times* [online]. New York. Available at www.nytimes.com/books/97/04/13/reviews/papers-lessons.html [Accessed 4 August, 2016].

3 Lowenstein, A. 2004. *The New York Times Role in Promoting War on Iraq.* The Sydney Morning Herald [online]. Sydney. Available at www.smh.com.au/articles/2004/03/23/1079939624187.html [Accessed 12 February, 2017].

4 Anderson, F. and Trembath, R. 2011. *Witness to War: The History of Australian Conflict Reporting*. Melbourne University Press.

5 Bush, G. W. 29th January, 2002. State of the Union Address [online]. Washington. Available at www.smh.com.au/articles/2004/03/23/1079939624187.html [Accessed 1 October, 2016].

6 Gordon, M. and Miller, J. 8th September, 2002. *US Says Hussein Intensified Quest for A-bomb Parts*. The *New York Times* [online]. New York. Available at www.nytimes. com/2002/09/08/world/threats-responses-iraqis-us-says-hussein-intensifies-quest-for-bomb-parts.html [Accessed 10 August, 2016].

7 Gordon, M. and Miller, J. 8th September, 2002. *US Says Hussein Intensified Quest for A-bomb Parts*. The *New York Times* [online]. New York. Available at www.nytimes. com/2002/09/08/world/threats-responses-iraqis-us-says-hussein-intensifies-quest-for-bomb-parts.html [Accessed 10 August, 2016].

8 Blitzer, W. 10th January, 2003. *Search for the Smoking Gun*. CNN [online]. Washington. Available at http://edition.cnn.com/2003/US/01/10/wbr.smoking.gun/ [Accessed 10 May, 2016].

9 Milbank, D. 22nd October, 2002. *For Bush Facts are Malleable*. The *Washington Post* [online]. Available at www.washingtonpost.com/archive/politics/2002/10/22/for-bush-facts-are-malleable/9160fc58-58c8-45d2-b63a-09ed36244cde/?utm_term=. cb643d799b89 [Accessed July, 2016].

10 Milbank, D. 22nd October, 2002. *For Bush Facts are Malleable*. The *Washington Post* [online]. Available at www.washingtonpost.com/archive/politics/2002/10/22/for-bush-facts-are-malleable/9160fc58-58c8-45d2-b63a-09ed36244cde/?utm_term=. cb643d799b89 [Accessed July, 2016].

11 Fowler, A. 2015. *The War on Journalism*. William Heinemann, Australia.

12 Fowler, A. 2015. *The War on Journalism*. William Heinemann, Australia.

13 Panorama. 23rd September, 2002. *The Case Against Saddam*. BBC, London.

14 Miller, J. 21st April, 2003. *Illicit Arms Kept Till Eve of War, An Iraqi Scientist Is Said to Assert*. The New York Times [online]. Available at www.nytimes.com/2003/04/21/ world/aftereffects-prohibited-weapons-illicit-arms-kept-till-eve-war-iraqi-scientist. html [Accessed July, 2016].

15 Miller, J. 21st April, 2003. *Illicit Arms Kept Till Eve of War, An Iraqi Scientist Is Said to Assert*. The New York Times [online]. Available at www.nytimes.com/2003/04/21/ world/aftereffects-prohibited-weapons-illicit-arms-kept-till-eve-war-iraqi-scientist. html [Accessed July, 2016].

16 Miller, J. 21st April, 2003. *Illicit Arms Kept Till Eve of War, An Iraqi Scientist Is Said to Assert*. The New York Times [online]. Available at www.nytimes.com/2003/04/21/ world/aftereffects-prohibited-weapons-illicit-arms-kept-till-eve-war-iraqi-scientist. html [Accessed July, 2016].

17 Miller, J. 21st April, 2003. *Illicit Arms Kept Till Eve of War, An Iraqi Scientist Is Said to Assert*. The New York Times [online]. Available at www.nytimes.com/2003/04/21/ world/aftereffects-prohibited-weapons-illicit-arms-kept-till-eve-war-iraqi-scientist. html [Accessed July, 2016].

18 Suarez, R. 22nd April, 2003. *Search for Evidence: Judith Miller Reports*. PBS NewsHour [online]. Available at www.pbs.org/newshour/bb/middle_east-jan-june03-search_04-22/ [Accessed July, 2016].

19 Moore, J. 2004. *Bush's War for Reelection: Iraq, The White House and the People*. John Wiley & Sons, New Jersey.

20 Moore, J. 2004. *Bush's War for Reelection: Iraq, The White House and the People*. John Wiley & Sons, New Jersey.

21 Miller, J. 21st April, 2003. *Illicit Arms Kept Till Eve of War, An Iraqi Scientist Is Said to Assert*. The New York Times [online]. Available at www.nytimes.com/2003/04/21/ world/aftereffects-prohibited-weapons-illicit-arms-kept-till-eve-war-iraqi-scientist.html [Accessed July, 2016].

22 Miller, J. 21st April, 2003. *Illicit Arms Kept Till Eve of War, An Iraqi Scientist Is Said to Assert*. The New York Times [online]. Available at www.nytimes.com/2003/04/21/

world/aftereffects-prohibited-weapons-illicit-arms-kept-till-eve-war-iraqi-scientist.
html [Accessed July, 2016].

23 Miller, J. 21st April, 2003. *Illicit Arms Kept Till Eve of War, An Iraqi Scientist Is Said to Assert.* The New York Times [online]. Available at www.nytimes.com/2003/04/21/
world/aftereffects-prohibited-weapons-illicit-arms-kept-till-eve-war-iraqi-scientist.
html [Accessed July, 2016].

24 Miller, J. 21st April, 2003. *Illicit Arms Kept Till Eve of War, An Iraqi Scientist Is Said to Assert.* The New York Times [online]. Available at www.nytimes.com/2003/04/21/
world/aftereffects-prohibited-weapons-illicit-arms-kept-till-eve-war-iraqi-scientist.
html [Accessed July, 2016].

25 Moore, J. May 28, 2004. *Not Fit to Print.* Salon.com [online]. Available at www.salon.
com/2004/05/27/times_10/ [Accessed July, 2016].

26 Huges, D. 27th February, 2004. *Claire Short Plunges Tony Blair into International Spy Crisis Then Defies Him to Punish Her.* Daily Mail, London.

27 Taylor, R. 27th February, 2004. *Short Shrift.* The Guardian, London.

28 Taylor, R. 27th February, 2004. *Short Shrift.* The Guardian, London.

29 Fowler, A. 2004. *Personal Note.*

30 Manne, R. 3rd July, 2014. *The Iraq War's Coalition of the Shilling.* La Trobe University [online]. Melbourne. Available at www.latrobe.edu.au/news/articles/2014/opinion/the-iraq-wars-coalition-of-the-shilling [Accessed June, 2016].

31 Manne, R. 3rd July, 2014. *The Iraq War's Coalition of the Shilling.* La Trobe University [online]. Melbourne. Available at www.latrobe.edu.au/news/articles/2014/opinion/the-iraq-wars-coalition-of-the-shilling [Accessed June, 2016].

32 Allard, T. and Snow, D. 19th June, 2004. *Downer's Office Asked for Copy of Leaked Report.* Sydney Morning Herald [online]. Available at www.smh.com.au/news/Anti-Terror-Watch/Downers-office-asked-for-copy-of-leaked-report/2004/06/18/
1087245110202.html [Accessed July, 2016].

33 PLOS Medicine Journal. 15th October, 2013. Mortality in Iraq Associated with the 2003–2011 War [online]. Available at http://journals.plos.org/plosmedicine/article?
id=10.1371/journal.pmed.1001533 [Accessed 2 July, 2016].

34 New York Times. 26th May, 2004. From the Editors; the Times and Iraq [online].
New York. Available at www.nytimes.com/2004/05/26/world/from-the-editors-the-times-and-iraq.html?_r=0 [Accessed July 14, 2016].

35 Miller, G. 28th March, 2004. *Keller Defends Miller in Statement.* The New York Times [online]. New York. Available at www.editorandpublisher.com/news/keller-defends-judith-miller-in-statement/ [Accessed June, 2016].

36 Miller, G. 28th March, 2004. *Keller Defends Miller in Statement.* The New York Times [online]. New York. Available at www.editorandpublisher.com/news/keller-defends-judith-miller-in-statement/ [Accessed June, 2016].

37 Moore, J. 29th May, 2004. *How Chalabi and the White House Held the Front Page.* The Guardian [online]. London. Available at www.theguardian.com/world/2004/may/29/
iraq.usa1 [Accessed 20 July, 2016].

4

THE TRUTH TELLER

Edward Snowden didn't look very different from all the other young computer geeks that worked in the NSA's Hawaii base. He dressed casually, sometimes wearing a hoodie. Like many idealistic young people Snowden had wanted to make the world a better place. His father had served in the US Coast Guard and Snowden learned from him the lessons of duty and responsibility. Probably more importantly, Snowden Senior had brought his son up to be an independent thinker, and not to follow the crowd. Snowden had originally joined the CIA, but grown disenchanted at the work of deception the job demanded of him. When he started working for the NSA as a contractor, his duties seemed far more straightforward: his job as an analyst for an organisation intercepting communications would help make America stronger and thereby the population safer. It is difficult to say exactly when the disillusion set in, but he came to the conclusion that the very people he was helping the NSA spy on, themselves needed protection from that surveillance.

Yet it was the NSA itself which decided the level of protection the population could be granted. In the 1990s the US government became so concerned that the public might be given access to unbreakable encryption that it tried to ban the public from getting access to any kind of cypher that the NSA might not be able to crack.

The NSA supported a level of protection for internet users that was extremely weak. One estimate said it would be possible to crack the NSA's preferred option, the 56-bit Data Encryption Standard being proposed for all US computers, in just two minutes. Few doubted that another system developed by a supporter of the public's right to privacy, Phil Zimmermann, was the most effective tool to defeat surveillance. Zimmermann had created Pretty Good Privacy (PGP); with its 1024-bit key, it was going to be difficult and time-consuming for any intelligence agency to decipher.

In 1991, the US government took another step towards improving its capacity to gather information transmitted over the internet, calling on manufacturers of secure communications equipment to insert special 'trapdoors' in their products, so that the government could read anyone's encrypted messages. The Federal Bureau of Investigation (FBI), the NSA and the Department of Justice went so far as to demand tough laws that would mandate the public to use only government-approved encryption products or adhere to government encryption criteria. Feeling the net tightening, Zimmermann acted first, releasing his new system because he wanted cryptography to be made available to the American public before it became illegal to use it. Zimmermann became so worried he gave it away for free to increase the uptake. The result was beyond his wildest dreams. His encryption program 'spread like a prairie fire',[1] and within months it was not just net activists who were encrypting their messages. The biggest users, human rights groups, used it to encode evidence and protect the identities of witnesses. Zimmermann's system might be helping protect privacy, but it was also making the NSA's work much harder. He would never have thought that 20 years later someone working inside the NSA would become one of the world's greatest supporters of his encryption system.

Working at the top-secret NSA listening post housed in a huge tunnel – a relic of the Second World War – drilled into a rocky outcrop, Snowden held a job which described him as an infrastructure analyst. But Snowden had hidden talents. 'That kid was a genius among geniuses,' said one NSA employee who knew Snowden.[2] The fact that he did not always have security clearance for the work he was asked to do did not prevent people giving him access to some of the top levels of the NSA system so he could solve their problems. What he discovered as he worked in these areas which required high levels of security clearance made him fearful for the privacy of those the NSA was supposedly responsible for protecting. Snowden decided to do something about it. He threw what is known as a 'crypto party', an informal gathering where the technically capable teach the technically incapable how to protect their private communications. For such a daring act the location could not have been more low-key: the rear of a furniture store in Kamani Street, just a short walk from one of Honolulu's famed sandy white beaches. According to *Wired* Magazine, the grassroots crypto party movement began in 2011 with a Melbourne, Australia-based activist, Asher Wolf. The idea was to help activists, journalists, and anyone else who wanted their privacy protected to learn how to use PGP and Tor, a web browser which allows people to surf the net without being identified. Tor works by accepting connections from the public internet, encrypting the traffic and bouncing it through a winding series of relays before dumping it back on the web through any one of more than 1,000 exit relays.

Snowden was already deeply involved with Tor, running a server known as The Signal, one of the system's exit relays. According to internet freedom organisation Electronic Frontier Federation (EFF) the exit relay is the most dangerous part of the Tor network to operate. Because the Tor traffic joins the internet through these relays, the Internet Protocol (IP) address, which can identify the user, is seen by everyone using the net as the gateway for the traffic. EFF warns: 'People who run exit relays should be prepared to deal with complaints, copyright takedown notices and the possibility that their servers may attract the attention of law enforcement agencies.'[3] Technologist and writer Runa Sandvik, who co-presented with Snowden at the crypto party, said Snowden was even trying to persuade some of his co-workers working in the NSA's high security listening post to set up additional 'fast servers'. He asked Sandvik if she could send him official Tor stickers, as some 'swag might incentivize them to do it sooner rather than later.'[4]

It might be reasonable to expect that Snowden's activities would have attracted the attention of his employer, the most powerful intelligence agency in the world. For what he was quite openly doing was challenging the very principals of the organisation's activities, what it calls a 'collect it all' strategy,[5] whereas Snowden was dedicated to making sure that that did not happen.

Extraordinarily, no one took much notice. Not even, it seems, in October 2012, when Snowden says he raised his concerns with four superiors – two from the NSA's Technology Directorate and two from the NSA Threat Operations Center's regional base.

To illustrate the point that the NSA was breaking the law, Snowden says he opened a system on his computer called Boundless Informant, which used colour-coded 'heat maps' to depict the volume of data ingested by NSA taps. He showed this to his four superiors and 15 other co-workers. Snowden said his colleagues were 'astonished to learn we are collecting more in the United States on Americans than we are on Russians in Russia'.[6] Many of them were troubled, and several said they did not want to know any more.

'I asked these people, "What do you think the public would do if this was on the front page?"' he said.[7]

It is difficult to fathom how those who work at an agency whose role it is to predict and analyse threats seemingly did not understand the gravity of what Snowden was revealing. To reinforce the point he was making, Snowden kept a copy of the US Constitution, often citing the Fourth Amendment, which specifically forbids random searches of American citizens. It is a broad Constitutional pillar which defends the right to privacy – unless intelligence or police agencies specifically know what they are searching for and have reasonable suspicions that a crime has been, or is about to be committed. There is no precedent under the Constitution for the government to seize the vast amounts of data sucked up by the NSA involving innocent Americans' communications.

Such is the strength of the Fourth Amendment that in 2012 the US Supreme Court overturned a guilty finding against a cocaine trafficker because the police fixed a tracking device to the suspect's wife's car. The majority decision found that installing the device breached the Fourth Amendment which enshrines the 'right of the people to be secure in their persons, houses, papers, and effects, against unreasonable searches and seizures.'[8]

One of the most conservative members of the bench, Justice Samuel Alito, went further, supporting the ruling but also finding that the collection of data impinged on 'expectations of privacy'.[9] Putting aside all the other Snowden revelations, one of the NSA's systems, Boundless Informant – a Top Secret system that catalogued nearly 3 billion pieces of data from the US alone in one 30 day period – pointed to a possible breach of that Constitutional right. What is extraordinary is that the NSA, which has gathered more data on everyone on the planet than any other organisation in history, says it could find no record of Snowden raising any issues of illegality with its management or other members of staff. They clearly were not looking very hard. In December 2012, a full six months before he leaked his NSA cache, Snowden was publicly proselytising the benefits of encryption to anyone who would listen. By early 2013 Snowden had decided that only public disclosure of what was happening inside the NSA would be sufficient to make the organisation change. He said he was prepared to risk his life, or a life behind bars, rather than live in a world where innocent people could not go about their everyday lives without being watched and profiled by the US government. It is a world often portrayed as being like George Orwell's *Nineteen Eighty-Four* – written in 1948 and warning of the perils of communism – whose Big Brother's 'thought police' maintain surveillance of the population: 'It was even conceivable that they watched everybody all the time,' Orwell wrote,

> but at any rate they could plug in your wire whenever they wanted to. You had to live – did live, from habit that became instinct – in the assumption that every sound you made was overheard, and except in darkness, every movement scrutinised.[10]

But, as Snowden's lawyer Ben Wizner argued, Snowden was more concerned about a Kafkaesque future. This dystopian world was aptly described by Frederick R. Karl, author of a biography of Franz Kafka:

> What's Kafkaesque, is when you enter a surreal world in which all your control patterns, all your plans, the whole way in which you have configured your own behaviour, begins to fall to pieces, when you find yourself against a force that does not lend itself to the way you perceive the world . . . You don't give up; you don't lie down and die. What you do is struggle against this with all of your equipment, with whatever you have. But, of course, you don't stand a chance. That's Kafkaesque.[11]

What is called the Surveillance State seems to fulfil many of Snowden's concerns about the effect of being trapped in a place where, it is argued, no one knew who was in control and no one was accountable. Snowden's experiences at the heart of the NSA made him determined to resist, before, as it saw it, it was too late. But first Snowden had to decide how he would release the information he had been gathering for several months. Normally the *New York Times* or the *Washington*

Post would have been the first choice of any whistle-blower. The newspapers had developed a strong reputation for disclosing important information. The *Washington Post* had broken the Watergate story, which led to the removal of Richard Nixon from the White House; the *New York Times* was famous for the Pentagon Papers. Yet when Snowden planned to leave the NSA in Hawaii he did not contact either of those newspapers. In fact, he deliberately shunned the *New York Times*, citing the decision by then editor Bill Keller not to run the report exposing the NSA's spying on US citizens as the reason. Snowden bluntly asserted that if the *New York Times* had run the report it might have defeated George W. Bush, who subsequently went on to win his second term as president. 'Hiding that story changed history,' Snowden said.[12]

The new executive editor, Dean Banquet, said later that he deeply regretted that Snowden had not chosen the *New York Times*. 'I am much, much, much more sceptical of the government's entreaties not to publish today than I was ever before,' Banquet said.[13]

Banquet said the Snowden revelations yielded two key insights for American journalists: 'First off, the public wants this information. Secondly, it does not destroy everything if the information comes out.' He added: 'The government makes it sound like something really large, and in retrospect, it wasn't quite as large.'[14] The Snowden revelations published in *The Guardian* and the *Washington Post* only underscored his conviction. 'I would love to be able to tell you it wasn't good,' he said. 'But it was great. It was important, ground-breaking work. I wish we had it.'[15]

There had been a very good reason why Snowden had decided to go elsewhere and it was not just the NSA wire-tapping issue. Snowden had been closely monitoring the work of a then little-known blogger, Glenn Greenwald, contributing to the online site Salon.com.

It was a measure of what the internet had become that its ability to connect millions of people – a rich web for the NSA to monitor – also gave those who opposed surveillance the ability to connect with each other. Even though Snowden was living in Hawaii and Greenwald was operating out of Brazil, every day Snowden could read what Greenwald was writing.

What made Greenwald interesting for Snowden was the strong stand he took on challenging the US government and defending the rights of journalists to disclose information in the public interest. Of particular interest was how strongly he defended the work of WikiLeaks and its founder Julian Assange when large sections of the main stream press, particularly in the US, were condemning his work. Much of the media was acting as an unquestioning relay station for politicians who had been exposed by WikiLeaks. Vice President Joe Biden called Assange a 'high tech terrorist'.[16] Others were more direct. The Conservative website *Townhall* ran an opinion piece entitled '5 Reasons The CIA Should Have Already Killed Julian Assange'.[17] Both Rupert Murdoch's *Wall Street Journal* and former Republican Vice-Presidential candidate Sarah Palin accused WikiLeaks a non-State based group run by an Australian citizen of 'treason'. Palin also demanded Assange be 'pursued with the same urgency we pursue al Qaeda and Taliban leaders'.[18]

Even the prime minister of his own country, Australia, said he had broken the law, when the evidence was that he had not; the Australian Attorney General, threatened to take Assange's passport away, and but for the intervention of the then foreign minister, Kevin Rudd, it might have happened. The matter was under serious consideration.

Against this onslaught, the former human rights lawyer turned journalist Greenwald rallied to Assange's support. There is no doubt that WikiLeaks had made errors of judgment; publishing the names of Afghan informers certainly put lives at risk, but no one had been killed – a point made by the Pentagon after numerous assertions that Assange had blood on his hands. Just as importantly, Assange had delivered on his promise to provide maximum impact for Manning's leaks. WikiLeaks had protected Manning as a source, but in the end it was Manning herself who revealed her identity by giving details of the documents to internet activist Adrian Lamo, who turned her in to the US military.

Greenwald argued that Assange had been doing the work that other journalists had not, exposing the inside workings of government at the highest level, peeling back the lies and deception. In November 2010 Greenwald wrote that those who demanded that the US government took people's lives with no oversight or due process as though they were advocating changes in tax policy were 'morally deranged barbarians'.[19]

In May 2013, Snowden checked in sick at his NSA job in Hawaii and caught a plane to Hong Kong to meet Greenwald. Snowden had chosen the former British colony because, as he saw it, it had a 'spirited democracy' but importantly it also put him outside the clutches of both US and British security services.[20] Snowden ensconced himself in The Mira, a luxury hotel on Hong Kong's Nathan Road. It might be expensive at AU$400 a night but there were a number of attractions for a fugitive spy: reasonable security, a free smartphone to use while checked in and high-speed Wi-Fi in every room.

With the US consulate and its CIA station nearby, Snowden was only too aware of how vulnerable he was. Worried there might be spy cameras in the walls, he wore a hood which covered both his head and his laptop – a somewhat clumsy but effective protection from prying eyes when he typed passwords on the keyboard. He also barricaded the door with pillows to prevent eavesdropping devices from picking up sounds of conversations from outside. Snowden was convinced his life and those of any journalists who dealt with him were in danger. 'The US intelligence community,' he wrote later, 'will certainly kill you if they think you are the single point of failure that could stop this disclosure and make them the sole owner of this information'.[21] When Snowden met Greenwald, he told him he was willing to 'sacrifice all' because he could not in 'good conscience' allow the US government to 'destroy privacy, internet freedom and basic liberties for people around the world with this massive surveillance machine they're secretly building'.[22]

By now Greenwald, with filmmaker Laura Poitras, had teamed up with *The Guardian*, the newspaper that led the partnership with WikiLeaks to break Cablegate, the Afghan War Diaries and the Iraqi War Logs. Poitras had acted as a go-between between Greenwald and Snowden when Snowden first tried to contact him. Unable to make a connection, Snowden turned to Poitras, because he knew her work. Her films about Iraq had revealed the shocking truth about what was happening while much of the rest of the world was often accepting the official line that the war was going well. She had been stopped several times as she re-entered America and questioned about her activities. At one time as she pulled out a pen to make notes during a period of questioning, she was told to put it away because it was seen as an offensive weapon. As part of her latest film she had been filming inside the Ecuador Embassy producing a documentary about WikiLeaks. It was Poitras who received the all-important communication from Snowden by encrypted email. Greenwald had failed to install the program despite detailed prompts and even lessons from Snowden – a cyber version of his Hawaiian crypto party. As the person now entrusted with Snowden's cache of files, Poitras made a decision which would not please Greenwald: she agreed to share some of the material with the *Washington Post* reporter Bart Gellman. As Poitras navigated the labyrinthine world of activist and whistle-blower politics where trust and credibility are an often fragile commodity, the deal she struck would prove amazingly – and unexpectedly – effective. But at the time Greenwald did not see any benefits at all. He regarded the newspaper as the worst example of conservative, Establishment journalism, keen to keep onside with the US government rather than expose its wrongdoings and inclined to pump out a few stories based on a leak, pick up the journalistic awards and then move on. But Poitras remained convinced that engaging the conservative press in Washington would serve a useful purpose – blunting the inevitable attacks that would come with Snowden's disclosures. Despite their individual reservations about dealing with the mass media, both Greenwald and Poitras could see that for Snowden's stories to have maximum impact, and to meet even some of the enormous production costs involved for them personally, they would have to fully engage with at least one newspaper from the mass media. The reason they chose Britain's *Guardian* was simple. It was by far the most adventurous mainstream media outlet in the English-speaking world, Greenwald's work had been regularly published there and the paper had a track record of fearless exposure. Unavoidably there was a price to pay for dealing with *The Guardian*: the newspaper insisted on sending one of its best and most experienced journalists, Ewen MacAskill, to Hong Kong as a minder. Greenwald viewed MacAskill, who had been *The Guardian*'s defence and intelligence correspondent and was now the newspaper's Washington bureau chief, as a 'company man'. MacAskill's presence would be a constant reminder that Greenwald and Poitras were no longer totally free agents. Arrangements were made; flights booked. Four strong-minded individuals were about to meet in Hong Kong under tense circumstances.

First of all, Poitras and Greenwald had to persuade MacAskill that Snowden was an authentic whistle-blower, not merely a fantasist with a story to tell and nothing to back it up but fabricated files. They arranged a meeting in Snowden's hotel room, where MacAskill would be able to challenge Snowden to produce evidence he was not a fake. MacAskill wasted no time, pressing Snowden on details of his past, probing for any sign that his story did not add up. The robust questioning went on for over an hour. Snowden's answers were consistent and crisp. As final proof Snowden showed MacAskill his old CIA identification pass and a now disused diplomatic passport. MacAskill was convinced. With MacAskill onside – a major achievement – Greenwald and Poitras now had to persuade the formidable Alan Rusbridger. A tricky conversation ensued, using encrypted communications. Rusbridger was the quintessential newspaperman, having come up through the ranks as a reporter, and had edited *The Guardian* since 1995. Most newspapers regularly changed editors but *The Guardian* allowed an almost academic tenure for its editorial leader. It encouraged a culture of independence and allowed the editor to make big and often controversial decisions without worrying that his job was on the line. Rusbridger had long championed investigation and disclosure and thoroughly understood the cost, both emotional and financial, of taking on high-risk enterprises. Over the years fighting court cases had cost the newspaper millions of pounds. He was at the helm in 2009 through an absolute monster of a saga involving the oil trading company Trafigura and strong allegations about toxic waste it had dumped in Africa. When *The Guardian* reported it had received a demand to delete the online historical records of its reporting of the toxic oil disaster, Carter-Ruck, the defamation law firm engaged by Trafigura, said the reports were gravely defamatory and untrue. They maintained it was wrong to report that Trafigura's waste may have caused deaths and severe injury, even though, as *The Guardian* reported, Trafigura had agreed to pay compensation to its 30,000 West African victims. Within days Carter-Ruck obtained a super-injunction. It prevented *The Guardian* from revealing any information covered by the injunction, including the fact that there was an injunction at all. Even a question in the House of Commons about Carter-Ruck and Trafigura ran into problems: Carter-Ruck's injunction made the reporting of the parliamentary question a breach of the injunction. The Trafigura case was a symptom of the culture of secrecy that pervades the British legal system. In relation to Snowden's story, *The Guardian* might be protected under the First Amendment for publishing in the US but it could well fall foul of the Official Secrets Act, particularly if British interests were exposed by Snowden – as would be the case in any disclosure involving the NSA. Rusbridger would have been haunted too by the case of a whistle-blower from GCHQ who leaked a devastating memo from the NSA before the 2003 invasion of Iraq. The memo showed that the US was trying to manipulate the UN Security Council vote. After the story was published in *The Observer*, sister paper to *The Guardian*, Katharine Gun, working as a Chinese-language linguist at GCHQ, was arrested and charged under the Official Secrets Act. Rusbridger had observed the lengths the government was prepared to go to prosecute her; finally, it decided not to proceed. It is believed what saved Gun from prosecution was the fear that any court hearing would have to produce evidence which might expose the fact the government knew the argument for going to war was based on a fraud. Rusbridger was being encouraged by Greenwald and Poitras, and even *The Guardian's* own reporter, to publish as soon as possible. With the history of battle weighing heavily on Rusbridger, he was not inclined to rush his decision. If *The Guardian* was showing a sense of nervousness, the *Washington Post's* Barton Gellman was pushing for a bigger role. Gellman was in possession of at least one major scoop handed to him by Poitras and was agitating to join Greenwald and Poitras in Hong Kong; he wanted direct access to Snowden so he could produce more stories for the Post.

Meanwhile senior management at the Post seemed to be searching for reasons not to publish. Its lawyers argued that there was a chance Chinese intelligence might overhear Gellman discussing the Snowden documents, an act which could be seen as 'recklessly passing secrets to the Chinese'.[23] The lawyers warned such an action could 'result in criminal liability' for both the Post and Gellman under the Espionage Act. It is a measure of the level of fear in the United States that this advice was taken seriously by the editors of the *Washington Post*. Clearly intimidated, they prevented Gellman from boarding the plane to Hong Kong. The kind of overly cautious journalism that had lost Snowden for the *New York Times* was now being repeated at that once iconic bastion of investigative report-ing, the *Washington Post*. The Obama administration was piling on the pressure, and the *Post* had caved in. While Rusbridger continued to cogitate, over at *The Guardian's* New York office the newspaper's US editor, Janine Gibson, was already fielding the possibility of threats from the FBI. Greenwald and Gibson were in constant contact; Gibson told him, 'They're saying the FBI could come in and shut down our office and take our files.'[24]

The Guardian's lawyers thought there might be the risk of criminal expo-sure, not only for Snowden but – given the Obama administration's pursuit of journalists – for both Greenwald and Poitras as well. The Obama White House had brought charges against more whistle-blowers under the Espionage Act than all the other US governments in history. On top of that, news had just broken that the US Justice Department might charge James Rosen, head of the Fox News Washington bureau, with being a co-conspirator in a leak from the State Department. The wording of the court filings was that Rosen may have 'aided and abetted' the source's decision to leak by working closely with him to disclose classified information. The Justice Department (DOJ) was pushing back hard against the First Amendment's freedom of speech provisions.

There's a legal argument that journalists are not protected by these provisions if they take part in the process of leaking themselves – and if the DOJ could prove that Rosen had aided and abetted the source, his First Amendment protection could be in shreds. With the possible Rosen charge fresh in his mind, as the hours ticked by Greenwald became increasingly agitated. He reminded Gibson that the

Washington Post might publish its story first. Neither of them had any inkling of just how likely that would be, but the possibility did put added pressure on *The Guardian* to move ahead. Even so Gibson said she could not guarantee when the story would run. She told Greenwald *The Guardian* would be meeting its lawyers the next day, 5 June. Greenwald was itching to release one particular story about a secret court order allowing the NSA to collect information on all telephone calls handled by the US communications giant Verizon. He asked when *The Guardian* planned to run the exposé but could not get a straight answer. The 12-hour time difference between New York and Hong Kong could not have made life more difficult for *The Guardian* and Greenwald. At 3 p.m. on 5 June, Janine Gibson sat down for a meeting with lawyers in New York while Greenwald sat up at 3 a.m. wide awake in Hong Kong, waiting for the outcome. It was already 6 June in Hong Kong. Two hours later Greenwald received the answer he didn't want to hear: Gibson told him there were considerable legal questions to be addressed.

And even after that, the US government would have to be informed so that it could make its case for non-publication. According to the lawyers consulted by *The Guardian* editors, publishing classified information could be deemed a crime by the US government if it could be proved that the publication, either recklessly or with intent, damaged US national security. By alerting the intelligence agencies to sensitive information it was going to publish, a newspaper felt it could protect itself from the threat of prosecution.

Fearing *The Guardian* would give in to the US government's sustained legal threats, Greenwald began making plans to walk away and find another publisher. He made calls to both *Salon*, his old publisher for years, and *The Nation* to see if they would be happy to run the NSA stories right away. As Greenwald tells it, they offered all the support he needed, with lawyers ready to vet the articles immediately.

Just as concerning for Greenwald as having to switch publishers was the fact that the *Washington Post* was working on the Snowden material they had been given by Poitras. The possibility that they would publish first was a nightmare scenario for him, that he would be scooped on his story by one of the mainstream institutions he loathed most. After phoning his partner, David Miranda, at their home in Brazil and talking things over, Greenwald hit upon a fresh strategy. It involved both of them and Poitras opted in. If *The Guardian* dithered much longer they would set up their own website to upload the Snowden stories. With that fall-back plan in place, Greenwald's spirits lifted tremendously. From the start he believed that 'the documents presented an opportunity to shine a light not only on secret NSA spying but on the corrupting dynamics of Establishment journalism'.[25] To Greenwald, 'breaking one of the most important stories in years through a new and independent model was very important'.[26]

An energised Greenwald rang friends, lawyers and other journalists, asking for advice. They all told him it was too risky without the backing of an existing media structure.

David Miranda was adamant however that 'only releasing the stories at a newly created website could capture the intrepid spirit driving the reporting we wanted to do'. He was also convinced it would inspire people everywhere. As for Snowden, his exact words were, 'Risky, but bold. I like it.'[27]

Resolution was imminent: either *The Guardian* was going to publish or Greenwald was on the verge of making one of the greatest mistakes of his career. Self-publishing is scorned by journalists for good reason – either no one else is interested, which is a major obstacle for sales, or the risks outweigh the benefits.

On Wednesday 6 June Greenwald woke early. It was still evening the previous day in New York. He would have to wait a full 12 hours before Janine Gibson arrived at work for what he hoped would be the final day of negotiations. As soon as Greenwald saw Gibson come online he asked her what the plan was. 'Are we going to publish today?' 'I hope so,' she replied. *The Guardian* intended to contact the NSA to ask for its response. Gibson told Greenwald she would 'know our publishing schedule only once we heard back from them'.[28]

Greenwald could not understand why *The Guardian* was holding off publishing. 'For a story this clean and straightforward who cares what they think we should and shouldn't publish?'[29]

Aside from his contempt for the process – the government should not be a collaborative editorial partner with newspapers in deciding what gets published – he says he 'knew there was no plausible national security argument against our specific Verizon report, which involved a simple court order showing the systemic collection of Americans' telephone records'.[30]

The idea that terrorists would benefit from exposing the order was laughable: any terrorists capable of tying their own shoelaces already knew that the government was trying to monitor their telephone communications. Greenwald believed the people who would learn something from the article were not the terrorists but the American people. At around noon New York time Janine Gibson phoned the NSA and the White House to tell them the newspaper was planning to publish some top-secret material. The request was met with complete silence. 'Right now, they don't think they need to call us back,' Gibson wrote. 'They're going to learn quickly that they need to return my calls.'[31]

Gibson had asked to hear from the NSA 'by the end of the day'.[32]

A little over three hours later the phone rang. It was not just the NSA on the other end; there were officials from numerous agencies, including the NSA, the DOJ and the White House. What started off as an attempt to patronise Gibson by telling her she did not understand the meaning or context of the Verizon court order ended with threats. They wanted to meet her 'some-time next week'[33] to explain the sensitivity of the issues involved. Greenwald's understanding was that these callers became 'belligerent even bullying when she said she wanted to publish that day and would do so unless she heard very specific and concrete reasons not to do so'.[34]

Gibson had deftly turned the tables. The White House and the intelligence services of the US had been mercilessly trying to undermine the use of the First

Amendment, which gave journalists protection, by appealing to patriotism as a reason not to publish. They had drawn journalists into the Establishment, using the argument that the country was at war to silence its critics. Finally, a lone whistle-blower, an individual who recognised the corruption in the system, had played a different game with the powerful US media institutions, initially bypassing them, and was about to get his story told. The cosy relationships that successive administrations in Washington had so carefully tended were worthless. The internet – a system which US intelligence agencies had exploited to gather unimaginable amounts of data on billions of people – was now being used against them. It must have been wounding that *The Guardian*, a newspaper from another country, would reinvigorate the meaning of the First Amendment, freedom of speech and the right to publish – using the internet to transmit its stories across the US and across the world. The US administration was stunned. 'No normal journalistic outlet would publish this quickly without first meeting with us,' they said.[35]

Greenwald remembered thinking,

> They're probably right, that's the point. The rules in place allow the government to control and neuter the news gathering process and eliminate the adversarial relationship between press and government . . . These stories were going to be released by a different set of rules, ones that would define an independent rather than subservient press corps.[36]

Gibson now found herself being squeezed by the US administration on one side, accusing her of acting recklessly, and Greenwald on the other, suggesting she might be too weak to face up to the challenge. Extraordinarily, in the middle of one of the most difficult decisions *The Guardian* would make in its over 150-year history, the editor-in-chief, Alan Rusbridger, got on a plane for New York. With Rusbridger out of touch, and up in the air, it was Gibson who would handle the story during this critical stage.

Though Rusbridger had a demonstrable zeal for investigative journalism, he also had a barely concealed contempt for Greenwald. Explaining the perils and potential of the internet age to a Sydney audience in December 2014, Rusbridger commented that Greenwald was an activist and said he would find it hard to get a job as a journalist in the US. It was meant as a criticism but it could well have been taken as a compliment. It was an echo of the dismissive way Assange had been treated by *The Guardian* when he came to them with the WikiLeaks exposé, which until Snowden emerged had been the world's biggest scoop. Whatever was going on, Rusbridger's flying across the Atlantic at that moment placed firmly in Gibson's hands the final decision on whether to publish. Greenwald decided to pile on the pressure; first of all, he had to decide whether to stop working with *The Guardian* and go it alone, publishing the material online. David Miranda told him, 'You have no choice. If they're scared to publish, this isn't the place for you.

You can't operate by fear or you won't achieve anything. That's the lesson Snowden just showed you.'[37]

After several drafts Greenwald sent Gibson a message: 'I understand that you have your concerns and have to do what you feel is right. I'm going to go ahead now and do what needs to be done too. I'm sorry it didn't work out.' Greenwald hit 'Send'.[38]

Fifteen seconds later the phone rang in Greenwald's hotel room. It was Janine Gibson, who by now was feeling the pressure. Gibson was totally out on her own, making decisions which her immediate boss, Rusbridger – who was still out of touch – might not like. There was also the distinct possibility that a large section of the media might hate Gibson's decisions, firstly because they did not get the story but perhaps more significantly because they might accept the White House argument that the report aided terrorists. Even so, Gibson told Greenwald *The Guardian* was 'going to publish today. It will be no later than 5.30 pm'.[39] At 5.40 pm Gibson sent Greenwald an instant message: 'It's live'.[40]

The story was page one on *The Guardian* website. Headlined 'NSA Collecting Phone Records of Millions of Verizon Customers Daily', it carried that much overused but in this case deserved tag, 'Exclusive'. The National Security Agency, it reported, was currently collecting the telephone records of millions of US customers of Verizon, one of America's largest telecom providers, under a top-secret court order issued in April. The order, a copy of which has been obtained by *The Guardian*, required Verizon to give the NSA information on all telephone calls in its systems, both within the US and between the US and other countries. The document showed for the first time that under the Obama administration the communication records of millions of US citizens were being collected indiscriminately and in bulk, regardless of whether they were suspected of any wrongdoing. The impact was immediate and profound. The piece led the evening news bulletins right across the US. Greenwald appeared on CNN, MSNBC, NBC, the *Today* show and *Good Morning America*. He found the experience of being interviewed by what he called 'sympathetic reporters'[41] unusually pleasant. When he criticised the administration in his other stories he had been pilloried, but not this time. Even the *New York Times* supported the story with an editorial which said, 'Mr Obama is proving the truism that the executive branch will use any power it is given and very likely abuse it.'[42]

Snowden, sitting in his room at The Mira in Hong Kong, had watched it all. He might have sacrificed his future, even his life, but his fear that no one would care had proved unfounded, in a spectacular way. 'Everyone seemed to get it,' he told Greenwald.[43]

Snowden had every reason to feel vindicated: the course of action he had so carefully laid out had worked. Twenty-four hours later – having allowed *The Guardian* to take the first of the criticism from the White House – Gellman's *Washington Post* story appeared online. It revealed the existence of a top-secret program codenamed PRISM, which internal NSA documents showed gave the agency direct access to data held by Google, Facebook, Apple and other US internet giants. There were howls from tech companies denying that they had set up backdoor access to their systems for the US government but there was no doubt that most had been compliant in giving the NSA what it wanted. According to the New York Times, 'Twitter declined to make it easier for the government', but others developed 'technical methods to more efficiently and securely share the personal data of foreign users in response to lawful government requests'.[44]

As much of the internet media industry fell in line with the US government's demands, The Guardian began taking serious precautions against surveillance intrusion at their functional glass-clad head office near St Pancras Railway State in London. It was from here that reporter Nick Davies had taken the Eurostar to meet Julian Assange at a Brussels cafe in 2010 where they began working together on the Chelsea Manning disclosures. As we sit in a café in the genteel Sussex market town of Lewes, Davies reflects on meeting Assange and the precautions he took to protect the Brussels meeting from surveillance. Assange had flown to Brussels from Australia, changing planes in Hong Kong to lessen the possibility of being snatched during transit. Like Snowden, he chose Hong Kong because of its comparative safety from the reach of Western intelligence agencies. But Brussels could be just as dangerous for phone interception, such was the reach of GCHQ and the NSA.

'We both understood that it was highly likely that his communications were being targeted because this was about four weeks after Bradley Manning had been arrested,' Davies said.[45]

And if Assange's communications were being intercepted and he had email contact with Davies, it was conceivable, though less likely according to Davies, that Davies was also being monitored.

At one time during the six-hour conversation Davies' then girlfriend called. She knew who Davies was meeting and asked: 'How are you getting on with Julian?'[46]

Thinking quickly Davies replied: 'It's a disaster, the guy won't co-operate, it's a mess, waste of time.'[47]

The next day at dawn Davies caught the first train back to London to explain to Rusbridger in person the deal he had struck with Assange and, probably just as importantly to him, to tell the truth to his girlfriend.

Working with Assange's material, The Guardian set aside a room inside its offices, creating a secure area with some particularly journalistic touches. The office windows were pasted over with newspapers 'because it is conceivable that one of those very, very powerful cameras on a satellite could look through at the window and read something which might assist a state agency to interfere'.[48]

Davies said it might be 'a bit absurd when you get to that point and yet I think that is[it is] alright'.[49]

He said it was about 'being realistic in assessing the threat'.[50] The Guardian took other simpler precautions 'like using computers that aren't connected to the internet'.[51] Davies described these actions as 'Just being bloody careful about your electronic communications'.[52]

Three years later, again behind the newspaper-covered windows of the 'bunker', *The Guardian* team began sifting through the Snowden documents, making a choice to publish stories which would not give ammunition to the newspaper's opponents. *The Guardian* was keen to buy some time to assess the treasure trove of intelligence documents provided to it by Snowden, while at the same time beginning to publish stories, but the newspaper was wary. Davies said *The Guardian* made a conscious decision to head off attacks: 'Let us not publish anything which allows them to do the obvious thing to accuse us of helping terrorists and bad guys. That simple.'[53]

In theory, the British Official Secrets Act might cover a lot of what *The Guardian* proposed to publish, Davies said. The question was: 'Will the attorney-general use his legal power to prosecute us under the Official Secrets Act?'[54] *The Guardian* decided to position itself to put political pressure on the Attorney General or the Director of Public Prosecutions not to invoke the law against the newspaper. Though the original law, enacted in 1911, was a wide-ranging catch-all which prohibited any government information being released without authority, it was still a formidable piece of legislation specifically mentioning newspapers who publish intelligence material without authority.

Under this legislation journalists revealing what is deemed to be 'damaging information' can be charged with an offence which attracts a prison sentence of up to two years plus unlimited fines.[55]

The Guardian team, including investigations editor David Leigh, editor Alan Rusbridger and Davies earnestly discussed, 'How can we do this without getting nicked?'[56]

As Davies tells it,

> There was this image of this kind of smoke filled room in Whitehall and on one side there were the hawks who were saying 'send the police into *The Guardian* building, arrest anybody who had access to the Snowden material, seize their computers and if they don't cooperate start fining them, say a million pounds a day'. So, there would be the hawks on one side of the room and then there would be the doves saying 'hang on a moment, doesn't look great if we bust a newspaper'. So, we had to send political signals which would strengthen the hand of the doves against the hawks, so they would decide not to come after us.[57]

The Guardian decided to start by running a story that 'wasn't actually the most powerful but was politically the most helpful'.[58]

The story revealed how the NSA and GCHQ spied on foreign politicians and officials attending two G20 summit meetings in London in 2009 – and had their computers monitored and their phone calls intercepted on the instructions of their British government hosts. Some delegates were tricked into using internet cafes which had been set up by British intelligence agencies to read their email traffic. 'It was all being syphoned off by MI6,' Davies said.[59]

The revelation came as Britain prepared to host another summit a few days later – for the G8 nations, all of whom attended the 2009 meetings which were the subject of the systematic spying.

The Guardian reported: 'The G20 spying appears to have been organized for the more mundane purpose of securing an advantage in meetings. Named targets include long-standing allies such as South Africa and Turkey.'[60]

Davies told me the reason *The Guardian* started by publishing the G20 spying story first was that it hoped it would provoke the French and the Germans to say to London, 'How dare you?' If in those circumstances the British government had tried to prosecute *The Guardian* 'it would be very obvious this was a political embarrassment that was motivating them and not a genuine fear that we were helping the enemy'. Davies said *The Guardian* was 'thinking politically' to stop the law being enforced.[61]

After publishing the first story – about the Verizon phone intercepts – under heavy pressure from Glenn Greenwald to act quickly, *The Guardian* followed a voluntary process, where newspapers proposing to publish sensitive security and military information inform an independent committee which gives direction on what it believes should or should not be published. Housed in the Department of Defence, off London's Whitehall, the Defence, Press and Broadcasting Advisory Committee – known as the D-notice committee – oversees a 'voluntary code' which 'operates between the UK Government departments which have responsibilities for national security and the media'.[62] *The Guardian* consistently dealt with the D-notice committee, comprised of senior representatives of government departments like Defence and the Foreign Office, and executives from newspapers, TV stations and other media bodies. Its job is to 'prevent inadvertent public disclosure of information that would compromise UK military and intelligence operations and methods, or put at risk the safety of those involved'.[63] During the period that *The Guardian* was revealing the Snowden stories, Rusbridger estimated he had 100 meetings with Whitehall officials to discuss what it would report.

'The message that Alan conveyed,' Davies said, was

> 'We are not crazy. Don't get over excited. you know we have got this material we are not about to publish something that is going to bring the roof down on people's heads', i.e. we are not going to publish something that's going to get innocent people hurt. 'So just relax, take it easy.'[64]

If the intelligence community had been assured that there was nothing much to worry about, they were about to get a rude awakening. Cabinet Secretary Jeremy Heywood must have been well aware that he had been 'played' by *The Guardian* when he rushed to King's Place to discuss the next story the newspaper was about to publish. Exactly how much detail he knew has not been disclosed but Heywood warned the paper 'not to publish the article on the grounds that it would jeopardize national security and intelligence work against organised crime'.[65] Heywood also wanted the Snowden documents.

On 21 June, 2013, just four days after the G20 revelation, *The Guardian* splashed across its front page an incredible story which revealed the real significance of GCHQ's role in information-gathering with the NSA. In one of the most picturesque and remote areas of England, where the Atlantic Ocean laps against the south-west coast, huge cables carrying much of the data and telephone traffic from the US come ashore. Just as importantly the cables also provide a traffic link to mainland Europe, providing GCHQ with access to US-UK traffic and communications between the US and European nations. GCHQ had inserted dozens of taps on 200 of these cables, syphoning off the material – and storing it in massive computer systems. Snowden said Tempora was part of 'the largest programme of suspicion-less surveillance in human history'.[66] *The Guardian* reported that GCHQ was processing vast streams of sensitive personal information and sharing it with the NSA.

The Tempora system allowed GCHQ to store huge volumes of data drawn from the fiber-optic cables and store it for up to 30 days so that it could be sifted and analysed.

GCHQ and the NSA had access to vast quantities of communications between entirely innocent people, as well as targeted suspects. These were not just metadata, the electronic fingerprints that all users of the web leave behind. The information being sucked up by Tempora included recordings of phone calls, the content of email messages, entries on Facebook and the history of any internet user's access to websites.

GCHQ carries out much of its work under the legal protection of the 2000 Regulation of Investigatory Powers Act (RIPA), which allows communications to be tapped only with a warrant signed by the Home or Foreign Secretary.

However, paragraph four of section eight of RIPA is much looser, allowing the Foreign Secretary to issue a certificate for broad interception of categories of material relating to terrorism or organised crime, for example.[67] It appears that GCHQ was using that clause to justify its broad interception of web traffic for its own use – and sharing the spoils to allow the US government to benefit as well, circumventing its Fourth Amendment law protecting privacy. 'The US agency can get back from GCHQ the data of US persons passing along these cables without any need to comply with US law,' according to an assessment entitled 'Publishing the Snowden Secrets: *The Guardian*, the Government and the People', by Gavin Millar, QC, from Doughty Chambers. By 2010, two years after the system was first trialled, Tempora boasted it had the 'biggest internet access' of any member of the Five Eyes electronic eavesdropping alliance – the US, UK, Canada, Australia and New Zealand.

UK officials could also claim GCHQ 'produces larger amounts of metadata than NSA'.

Three hundred analysts from GCHQ, and 250 from the NSA, were assigned to sift through the flood of data.

The Americans were given guidelines for its use, but were told in legal briefings by GCHQ lawyers: 'We have a light oversight regime compared with the US.'[68]

When it came to judging the necessity and proportionality of what they were allowed to look for, would-be American users were told it was 'your call'.[69]

The Guardian reported that a total of 850,000 NSA employees and US private contractors with top-secret clearance had access to GCHQ databases. The Snowden documents revealed that by 2012 GCHQ was handling 600m 'telephone events' each day, had tapped more than 200 fibre-optic cables and was able to process data from at least 46 of them at a time.[70]

It appeared that the US was managing to circumvent the Constitution's Fourth Amendment, which protects its citizens from random search, by paying GCHQ to spy on their citizens with the looser rules which exist in the UK.

Davies described the decision to hold off on the Tempora story until later as 'an example of quite clever maneuvering to give ourselves some space which to publish information that the public need to know'.[71] *The Guardian* knew what was coming. Three weeks later Heywood returned to Kings Place. If *The Guardian* did not stop publishing the Snowden stories, it would be shut down. The government would take *The Guardian* to court. Davies said Heywood told Rusbridger: 'You've had your fun, we want the computers, we want the material.'[72] Explaining the nature of international collaborations, Rusbridger detailed to Heywood the way in which media organisations could take advantage of the most permissive legal environments – *The Guardian* did not have to do its reporting from London. But the threat was unambiguous: if *The Guardian* did not promise to stop publication it would have to destroy the files it had, or be taken to court.

Rusbridger made what appeared to be a rational decision at the time: he agreed to the destruction of the files, but it would not be a decision without consequences. On a hot Saturday morning, 20 July, 2013, two staff members from Britain's GCHQ were escorted to the basement of *The Guardian* offices not far from St Pancras railway station. Normally for jobs like this, intelligence agencies bring with them what they call 'cake mixers'. They are gadgets specifically used for destroying computers and reducing them to powder, so their drives are irretrievably damaged and all the information in them is obliterated. But this time they seemed satisfied with less conventional systems of destruction, among them electric angle grinders and a drill. Several Apple computers contained thousands of documents which formed the Snowden cache. The GCHQ staff watched as two *Guardian* staff drilled into the computer hard drives and ripped the machines to pieces. When they had finished, one of the government men joked as he swept up the remains of a MacBook Pro: 'We can call off the black helicopters.'[73]

Just why this important act was not reported immediately to the public has never been explained. It was not until the following month that Rushbridger revealed what had happened. What appeared to jolt Rusbridger into action was an act by the British police which showed how far the government was prepared to go to intimidate journalists. Their target in this case was Glenn Greenwald's partner, David Miranda.

On his way home to Brazil, Miranda was detained in the transit lounge at London's Heathrow Airport – an international no-man's land where the laws of the UK are murky to say the least. In a front-page comment piece, Rusbridger told how Miranda was kept there for nine hours under Schedule 7 of the UK's terror laws, which give enormous discretion to stop, search and question people who have no connection with 'terror' as anyone would normally understand it. Those held have no right to legal representation and may have their property confiscated for up to seven days. Under this measure – which applies specifically to places 'beyond the customs barrier' in international space – there are none of the checks and balances that apply once someone has crossed the 'frontier' into Britain. It is a complex and difficult area of operations for the police and intelligence agencies who are careful not to accuse anyone they detain of being a 'suspect', for a 'suspect' has the right to a lawyer. According to Duncan Campbell, the investigative journalist who first revealed the existence of GCHQ in the 1970s, there was

> a general agreement between Poitras, Greenwald, and *The Guardian* that they should share everything when they all left Hong Kong separately. Some parts of [Snowden's] material were with one party, some with another, so David Miranda's trip was a levelling up process.[74]

Police seized Miranda's laptop, and an encrypted external drive to search for Snowden's documents. 'As far as Miranda was concerned even if they [the police] had been found to act unlawfully subsequently which they weren't, they had got away with taking all his information'.[75] In particular, the police reported finding a written note giving the key for the memory sticks holding an index (prepared by the journalists) to all the GCHQ documents in the cache.

For Rusbridger it was a defining moment. Only now did he tell the story of the decision to allow GCHQ to destroy *The Guardian*'s copy of the Snowden files. By detaining Miranda in the Heathrow transit lounge, the security forces – in fact MI5 – had gone too far. Rusbridger wrote:

> The state that is building such a formidable apparatus of surveillance will do its best to prevent journalists from reporting on it. Most journalists can see that. But I wonder how many have truly understood the absolute threat to journalism implicit in the idea of total surveillance, when or if it comes – and, increasingly, it looks like 'when'.

He added: 'We are not there yet, but it may not be long before it will be impossible for journalists to have confidential sources. Most reporting – indeed, most human life in 2013 – leaves too much of a digital fingerprint.'[76]

For journalists like Rusbridger who stood in the way, there was a price to pay. Required to appear before the UK Parliamentary Home Affairs Committee to answer questions about the Snowden leaks, Rusbridger, who was born in Zambia, was subjected to a form of aggressive nationalism, his loyalty to the UK questioned. Rusbridger responded: 'Yes, we are patriots and one of the things we are patriotic about is the nature of a democracy and the nature of a free press.'[77] He said that the 'freedom to write and report' was 'one of the things I love about this country'.[78] The most aggressive questioning came from Michael Ellis, the Conservative MP for Northampton North, who went for the editor with all the gravitas of a prosecuting counsel, accusing Rusbridger of being a criminal. 'Mr Rusbridger, you authorised files stolen by Snowden, which contained the names of intelligence staff to be communicated elsewhere, didn't you – yes or no?' he demanded. 'Do you accept that from me that it is an offence, a criminal offence under section 58A of the Terrorism Act 2000?'[79] To the question, as pompous as the questioner, Rusbridger replied that no one had presented any evidence that any security agents had been put at risk owing to *The Guardian's* Snowden stories. *The Guardian* had published no names. The *Daily Mail*, salivating over the prospect that Guardian journalists could be jailed, headlined a story 'The Guardian May Face Terror Charges over Stolen Secrets' and 'NSA's Mission is of Great Value to the Nation'.[80]

As Rusbridger succinctly put it,

> Those colleagues who denigrate Snowden or say reporters should trust the state to know best (many of them in the UK, oddly, on the right) may one day have a cruel awakening. One day it will be their reporting, their cause, under attack.[81]

Rusbridger was asked why he had sent the Snowden material overseas to the *New York Times*. For Rusbridger the decision to do so was pragmatic: knowing that the material – which had been ground to a pulp in the basement of *The Guardian* by the 'men from Whitehall' – was still held by *the New York Times*, he had saved *The Guardian* possibly millions of pounds in court costs alone in not having to defend any legal action. Davies says he 'never quite understood why'[82] the government had deemed it necessary to destroy *The Guardian's* computers:

> Whether the London spooks were trying to send a signal to Washington [that] 'We are seriously trying to stop this happening'. Or whether they were trying to send a signal to the staff at GCHQ, [that] 'We are seriously trying to stop this happening', it was pantomime. They knew the information was no longer restricted to the computers. So, it was a pointless symbolic act.[83]

But the fact was, *The Guardian* had lost control of the information. The doubts that Davis raised earlier about whether the government – despite all the threats – would have the political strength to prosecute a newspaper reporting on matters which, though it would put *The Guardian* in a difficult position, might also raise many difficult questions for the government to answer. Prosecuting a whistle-blower was one thing, but prosecuting the editor of a significant and prestigious newspaper like *The Guardian* was another matter altogether. For whatever reason, Rusbridger had caved in. The British government 'wanted *The Guardian* to stop reporting these stories and what they did was superbly effective', according to Duncan Campbell.[84]

The Guardian had lodged safety copies of the Snowden documents under the protection of the First Amendment with the *New York Times*. 'Well what the fuck was done with them? They sit in the room in the *New York Times* office.'[85]

Campbell says that without undermining the security of the United Kingdom, it would have been 'in the public interest if *The Guardian* didn't want to publish these stories to invite others to use the material'. That would 'bring before the British public material that was pertinent to the debate',[86] as the UK Government proposed increasing the power of surveillance laws.

Dr Paul Lashmar, former UK Reporter of the Year, investigative journalist for *The Observer* and *The Independent*, and now Senior Lecturer and Journalism Lead at Sussex University, says it was 'unfortunate'[87] that Snowden gave the information to just two people, Glenn Greenwald and Laura Poitras. Lashmar, who also worked for the acclaimed British investigative TV programme *World in Action*, says that he and others feel that while Greenwald and Poitras did a good job of releasing documents responsibly in the earlier days, what was needed was 'a more systemic and speedy effort with perhaps a team of experts to assist'.[88] He added: 'They have released things when it suited them for reasons that best advantaged them and have not made them more widely available. They have certainly not utilised the expertise of a lot of leading journalists or academics.'[89] For instance, the priority had clearly been US documents and little had been released from the other Five Eyes countries' archives, which could have been extremely important in those countries.

Dr Lashmar makes the criticism that *The Intercept* used the information as its 'personal fiefdom',[90] and points out that the documents are fast losing their currency. Snowden released the documents in 2013 and 'very few of the documents are as young as that, most of the documents are older'.[91] He points out it has been estimated that are between 500,000 and 1.7 million documents. According to the authoritative website Cryptome, at the current rate of disclosure by The Intercept, it could take up to 620 years to release all the documents.

The Snowden files were indeed a gold mine for *The Intercept*; they formed the basis of its beginning and the stories have produced a sound foundation for Glenn Greenwald's challenging online journalism. They almost certainly helped propel *The Guardian*, under Rusbridger's leadership, to become the world's first truly international online newspaper, expanding with local editions in the US and Australia. Now *The Guardian* was shut out of the Snowden files – documents which had produced a wealth of stories boosting *The Guardian's* online presence and promising, in part at least, to answer the vexed question: how could newspapers survive when their incomes through classified advertisements were fast disappearing?

If *The Guardian*, funded by a trust which guaranteed its independence and allowed it to take more chances than most newspapers, couldn't hold out against the government, who could? It was a problem which afflicted other newspapers too. Just when they needed to be strong to protect vigorous, challenging journalism holding governments to account, they were transparently getting financially weaker by the day.

Notes

1 Fowler, A. 2001.*The Most Dangerous Man in the World*. Melbourne University Press.
2 Fowler, A. 2015. *The War on Journalism*. Penguin Random House.
3 Electronic Frontiers Foundation. What is Tor? [online]. Available at www.eff.org/torchallenge/what-is-tor.html [Accessed 24 November, 2016].
4 Available at www.wired.com/2014/05/snowden-cryptoparty/
5 Available at https://theintercept.com/2015/05/28/nsa-officials-privately-criticize-collect-it-all-surveillance/
6 Gellman, B. 23rd December, 2013. *Edward Snowden, After Months of Revelations Says His Mission is Accomplished*. Washington Post.
7 Gellman, B. 24th December, 2013. Mission Accomplished, Says Edward Snowden [online]. Available at www.smh.com.au/world/mission-accomplished-says-edward-snowden-20131224-hv6t0.html [Accessed 27 November].
8 Legal Information Institute. [Undated]. Fourth Amendment. Cornell Law School [online]. Available at www.law.cornell.edu/constitution/fourth_amendment [Accessed 27 October, 2016].
9 Legal Information Institute. 23rd January, 2012. *United States, Petitioner v Antoine Jones*. Cornell Law School [online]. Available at www.law.cornell.edu/supremecourt/text/10-1259#writing-10-1259_CONCUR_5 [Accessed 6 August, 2016].
10 *Nineteen Eighty-Four*. 1949. George Orwell. New American Library.
11 Edwards, I. 29th December, 1991. The Essence of 'Kafkaesque' [Online]. Available at www.nytimes.com/1991/12/29/nyregion/the-essence-of-kafkaesque.html [Accessed 12 July, 2016].
12 Greenwald, G. 2014. *No Place to Hide*. Hamish Hamilton, London.
13 Greenwald, G. 6th June, 2014. Encouraging Words of Regret from Dean Baquet and Weasel Words from James Clapper [online]. Available at https://theintercept.com/2014/06/06/encouraging-words-dean-baquet-weasel-words-james-clapper/ [Accessed 5 August, 2016].
14 Greenwald, G. 6th June, 2014. Encouraging Words of Regret from Dean Baquet and Weasel Words from James Clapper [online]. Available at https://theintercept.com/2014/06/06/encouraging-words-dean-baquet-weasel-words-james-clapper/ [Accessed 5 August, 2016].
15 Greenwald, G. 6th June, 2014. Encouraging Words of Regret from Dean Baquet and Weasel Words from James Clapper. The Intercept [online]. Available at https://theintercept.com/2014/06/06/encouraging-words-dean-baquet-weasel-words-james-clapper/ [Accessed 19 October, 2016].
16 MacAskill, E. 19th December, 2010. Julian Assange is Like a High-Tech Terrorist, Says Joe Biden [online]. Available at www.theguardian.com/media/2010/dec/19/assange-high-tech-terrorist-biden [Accessed 24 August, 2016].
17 Hawkins, J. 30th November, 2010. *5 Reasons the CIA Should Have Already Killed Julian Assange*. Available at http://townhall.com/columnists/johnhawkins/2010/11/30/5_reasons_the_cia_should_have_already_killed_julian_assange [Accessed 5 August, 2016].
18 Beckford, M. 30th November, 2010. Sarah Palin: Hunt WikiLeaks Founder Like al-Qaeda and Taliban leaders [online]. Available at www.telegraph.co.uk/news/

worldnews/wikileaks/8171269/Sarah-Palin-hunt-WikiLeaks-founder-like-al-Qaeda-and-Taliban-leaders.html [Accessed 8 August, 2016].

19 Greenwald, G. 1st December, 2010. WikiLeaks Reveals More Than Just Government Secrets [online]. Available at www.salon.com/2010/11/30/wikileaks_10/ [Accessed 1 August, 2016].

20 Fowler, A. 2015. *The War on Journalism*. Penguin Random House.

21 Gellman, B. 9th June, 2013. *Code Name Verax: Snowden in Exchange with Post Reporter Made Clear He knew the Risks*. Washington Post.

22 Gellman, B. 9th June, 2013. *Code Name Verax: Snowden in Exchange with Post Reporter Made Clear He knew the Risks*. Washington Post.

23 Greenwald, G. 2014. *No Place to Hide*. Hamish Hamilton, London.

24 Greenwald, G. 2014. *No Place to Hide*. Hamish Hamilton, London.

25 Greenwald, G. 2014. *No Place to Hide*. Hamish Hamilton, London.

26 Greenwald, G. 2014. *No Place to Hide*. Hamish Hamilton, London.

27 Greenwald, G. 2014. *No Place to Hide*. Hamish Hamilton, London.

28 Greenwald, G. 2014. *No Place to Hide*. Hamish Hamilton, London.

29 Greenwald, G. 2014. *No Place to Hide*. Hamish Hamilton, London.

30 Greenwald, G. 2014. *No Place to Hide*. Hamish Hamilton, London.

31 Greenwald, G. 2014. *No Place to Hide*. Hamish Hamilton, London.

32 Greenwald, G. 2014. *No Place to Hide*. Hamish Hamilton, London.

33 Greenwald, G. 2014. *No Place to Hide*. Hamish Hamilton, London.

34 Greenwald, G. 2014. *No Place to Hide*. Hamish Hamilton, London.

35 Greenwald, G. 2014. *No Place to Hide*. Hamish Hamilton, London.

36 Greenwald, G. 2014. *No Place to Hide*. Hamish Hamilton, London.

37 Greenwald, G. 2014. *No Place to Hide*. Hamish Hamilton, London.

38 Greenwald, G. 2014. *No Place to Hide*. Hamish Hamilton, London.

39 Greenwald, G. 2014. *No Place to Hide*. Hamish Hamilton, London.

40 Greenwald, G. 2014. *No Place to Hide*. Hamish Hamilton, London.

41 Greenwald, G. 2014. *No Place to Hide*. Hamish Hamilton, London.

42 Greenwald, G. 2014. *No Place to Hide*. Hamish Hamilton, London.

43 Greenwald, G. 2014. *No Place to Hide*. Hamish Hamilton, London.

44 Miller, C. 7th June, 2013. Tech Companies Concede to Surveillance Program [online]. Available at www.nytimes.com/2013/06/08/technology/tech-companies-bristling-concede-to-government-surveillance-efforts.html [Accessed 16 August, 2016].

45 Davies, N. August, 2016. *Interview*.

46 Davies, N. August, 2016. *Interview*.

47 Davies, N. August, 2016. *Interview*.

48 Davies, N. August, 2016. *Interview*.

49 Davies, N. August, 2016. *Interview*.

50 Davies, N. August, 2016. *Interview*.

51 Davies, N. August, 2016. *Interview*.

52 Davies, N. August, 2016. *Interview*.

53 Davies, N. August, 2016. *Interview*.

54 Davies, N. August, 2016. *Interview*.

55 UK Parliament. 2nd May, 2017. The Official Secrets Act and Official Secrecy [online]. Available at http://researchbriefings.parliament.uk/ResearchBriefing/Summary/CBP-7422 [Accessed 2 June, 2017].

56 Davies, N. August, 2016. *Interview*.

57 Davies, N. August, 2016. *Interview*.

58 Davies, N. August, 2016. *Interview*.

59 Davies, N. August, 2016. *Interview*.

60 MacAskill, E., Davies, N., Hopkins, J., Borger, J., and Ball, J. 17th June, 2013. GCHQ *Intercepted Foreign Politicians Communications at G20 Summits'*. The Guardian [online]. Available at www.theguardian.com/uk/2013/jun/16/gchq-intercepted-communications-g20-summits [Accessed 27 July, 2016].

61 Davies, N. August, 2016. *Interview*.
62 DSMA. 2017. The Defence and Security Media Advisory [DSMA] Committee [online]. Available at www.dnotice.org.uk/index.htm [Accessed 23 October, 2016].
63 DSMA. 2017. The Defence and Security Media Advisory [DSMA] Committee [online]. Available at www.dnotice.org.uk/index.htm [Accessed 23 October, 2016].
64 Davies, N. August, 2016. *Interview*.
65 Millar, G. [No date]. Publishing the Snowden Secrets, *The Guardian*, the Government and the People by Doughty Chambers, London [online]. Available at www.law.ox.ac.uk/sites/files/oxlaw/publishing_snowden_gmfinal.pdf [Accessed 8 October, 2016].
66 Available at www.theguardian.com/uk/2013/jun/21/gchq-cables-secret-world-communications-nsa
67 Available at www.legislation.gov.uk/ukpga/2000/23/contents
68 Available at www.theguardian.com/uk/2013/jun/21/gchq-cables-secret-world-communications-nsa
69 Available at www.theguardian.com/uk/2013/jun/21/gchq-cables-secret-world-communications-nsa
70 Available at www.theguardian.com/uk/2013/jun/21/gchq-cables-secret-world-communications-nsa
71 Davies, N. August, 2016. *Interview*.
72 Davies, N. August, 2016. *Interview*.
73 Rusbridger, A. 19th August, 2013. *David Miranda, Schedule 7 and the Danger that All Reporters Now Face*. The Guardian [online]. Available at www.theguardian.com/commentisfree/2013/aug/19/david-miranda-schedule7-danger-reporters [Accessed 10 August, 2016].
74 Campbell, D. October, 2016. *Interview*.
75 Campbell, D. October, 2016. *Interview*.
76 Rusbridger, A. 19th August, 2013. *David Miranda, Schedule 7 and the Danger that All Reporters Now Face*. The Guardian [online]. Available at www.theguardian.com/commentisfree/2013/aug/19/david-miranda-schedule7-danger-reporters [Accessed 10 August, 2016].
77 Rusbridger, A. 3rd December, 2013. MP's Questions to Alan Rusbridger: Do You Love this Country? The Guardian [online]. Available at www.theguardian.com/media/2013/dec/03/keith-vaz-alan-rusbridger-love-country-nsa [Accessed 28 August, 2016].
78 Rusbridger, A. 3rd December, 2013. MP's Questions to Alan Rusbridger: Do You Love this Country? The Guardian [online]. Available at www.theguardian.com/media/2013/dec/03/keith-vaz-alan-rusbridger-love-country-nsa [Accessed 28 August, 2016].
79 Burrell, I. 3rd December, 2013. MPs Question Guardian editor Alan Rusbridger's Patriotism Over Edward Snowden Leaks. The Independent [online]. Available at www.independent.co.uk/news/media/press/mps-question-guardian-editor-alan-rusbridger-s-patriotism-over-edward-snowden-leaks-8981167.html [Accessed 23 September, 2016].
80 Daily Mail reporter. 4th December, 2013. 'NSA's Mission is of Great Value to the Nation': Under Fire Spy Agency's Guide to Thanksgiving Small Talk Revealed in Leaked Memo to Employees [online]. Available at www.dailymail.co.uk/news/article-2517506/NSAs-Thanksgiving-memo-wants-employees-highlight-good-work-agency-done.html [Accessed 2 January, 2017].
81 Rusbridger, A. 19th August, 2013. David Miranda, Schedule 7 and the Danger That All Reporters Now Face. The Guardian [online]. Available at www.theguardian.com/commentisfree/2013/aug/19/david-miranda-schedule7-danger-reporters [Accessed 10 August, 2016].
82 Davies, N. August, 2016. *Interview*.
83 Davies, N. August, 2016. *Interview*.
84 Campbell, D. October, 2016. *Interview*.
85 Campbell, D. October, 2016. *Interview*.
86 Campbell, D. October, 2016. *Interview*.

87 Lashmar, P. August, 2016. *Interview.*
88 Lashmar, P. August, 2016. *Interview.*
89 Lashmar, P. August, 2016. *Interview.*
90 Lashmar, P. August, 2016. *Interview.*
91 Lashmar, P. August, 2016. *Interview.*

5

AN UNTIMELY COLLAPSE

The neo-gothic sandstone pink architecture of London's St Pancras railway station, built in the 1860s, stands in stark contrast to *The Guardian's* high-tech glass fronted headquarters nearby. Together the buildings straddle journalism's historic fault lines – from the age of steam when the printed word often only travelled as fast as the fastest locomotive, to the internet where words move at the speed of light.

Both ages have had their challenges for journalism but there is at least one overarching similarity in the way journalists throughout history have gone about their business.

Newspapers are rarely at their best when they are reporting about themselves or their rivals. The temptation to hide the truth from their readers about their own inadequacies while gleefully using a sharp eye to criticise others is perhaps also an all too human failing. There are few better examples of this phenomena than the way Alan Rusbridger's departure from the editor-in-chief's chair at *The Guardian* was reported.

The *London Evening Standard* breathlessly told its readers of the 'epic drama' of Rusbridger's time at *The Guardian* coming to a 'shocking denouement'[1] in what was an ominously numbered 'room 3.13 outside the features department'.[2]

Despite its commitment to 'open journalism',[3] The *Standard* pointed out *The Guardian* did not record 'this final act, played out' before the board of the Scott Trust, the paper's governing body. The report added that Rusbridger delivered a speech lasting around one hour, stating his case for being confirmed as the trust's chairman. The board, however, was unconvinced by the performance in which the 'normally Sphinx-like Rusbridger' displayed 'rare signs of anger'[4] that his legacy was being called into question.

The Guardian produced a slightly different report, under the headline 'Alan Rusbridger will not take over as Chair of the Scott Trust'.[5] The report quoted an email Rusbridger had sent to staff, saying it had been an 'honour' to be offered the chair of the trust – the board had apparently offered the post to him the previous September – but now it was time for a change. Rusbridger touched obliquely on the problems *The Guardian* now faced. 'All newspapers – and many media organisations beyond – have been battered by turbulent and economic forces.' Few could disagree with the observation about the 'economic forces'[6] but Rusbridger's assertion that they 'were difficult to see last summer'[7] required a great deal of faith in his reasoning. It was hardly a surprise that *The Guardian* was in financial trouble; the debts were piling up and had been doing so for years. It was the key reason the Scott Trust, whose sole purpose is to preserve *The Guardian* 'in perpetuity'[8] could not allow Rusbridger – who oversaw Guardian News and Media losses of £418 million from 2007 – to head its governance.

For the three years up to June 2012, the paper lost £100,000 a day, which prompted *The Economist* magazine's *Intelligent Life* to question 'can *The Guardian* survive?'[9]

Rusbridger's replacement as editor-in-chief, Kathryn Viner, broke the dire news of *The Guardian's* worse than expected financial plight to *Guardian* staff, who just a few weeks earlier had given Rusbridger a heady send-off, complete with a change to the masthead featuring his trademark glasses. Now the king was dead and the new queen was laying out the unvarnished truth. There would be a 20 per cent cut to the running costs of Guardian News & Media, the newspaper's publisher – a little over £50 million – in a bid to break even within three years and support future growth. The annual operating costs had reached £268 million – up 23 per cent over the five-year period, compared with a 10 per cent growth in revenues. What everyone at the meeting knew was that jobs would go, more than 300 of them.

Yet the money had not been frittered away; it had turned *The Guardian* into one of the most widely read and applauded newspapers in the world.

During 20 years as editor-in-chief Rusbridger steered *The Guardian* to a Pulitzer Prize for its revelations in the Snowden files. He directed the reporting of the WikiLeaks revelations and the UK phone-hacking scandal which held the world's most powerful media baron, Rupert Murdoch, to account and played a major role in preventing his company taking over the UK's Sky TV.

Rusbridger had initiated a major expansion of *The Guardian*, from a newspaper published in Manchester in the 1820s to one that was among the first to fully embrace the power of the internet – rather than fighting it or trying to ignore it as many of the newspaper's rivals had. Rusbridger oversaw the bold step of giving free online access to readers and moved to establish *The Guardian* as a global newspaper, setting up local editions in Australia and the US, hiring nearly 500 extra commercial and journalistic staff, to run the new ventures. It was a bold gamble, as bold as the idea conceived all those years ago in Manchester to establish a newspaper to uphold liberal values. One of its earliest editors, C.P. Scott – whose family name is enshrined in the trust – held the post for 57 years. He celebrated the newspaper's centenary by describing its founding journalistic philosophy: 'Comment is free, but facts are sacred . . . The voice of opponents no less than that of friends has a right to be heard.'[10]

As Rusbridger caught the lift down to the ground floor after accepting he had lost the chair of the Scott Trust, he might well have pondered what happened in the basement the previous year. If you accept Rusbridger's argument, one of the reasons the Snowden files had to be destroyed was the fear that a court case would be too expensive for *The Guardian* to defend. It is possible to take this at face value as a sensible commercial decision, but what we now know is that *The Guardian's* finances were in such a shocking state that the premier investigative newspaper in the Britain would sacrifice control of possibly the most significant story since the end of the Second World War because they were wary of funding a court battle against the government.

The importance of this decision for journalism's role as the Fourth Estate, holding the other estates of the realm – the church, the legislature and the courts – to account, should not be underestimated. It was not just *The Guardian* that was running up debts which would limit their ability to independently challenge the authority of the state. It seems that nobody, anywhere in the world, had managed to master the art of making newspapers pay. The 'rivers of gold', a phrase credited to Rupert Murdoch to describe the money raised by classified advertising in print newspapers, had been disappearing for years. In the preinternet age classified ads were bundled together in often bulky newspapers; wrapped around the news stories, inseparable from the news they funded. But the internet changed that arrangement, allowing classified advertising to migrate to the internet where costs were much lower; the rivers of gold dried up. As other newspapers wrestled with the issue of whether to charge for their online editions, Rusbridger and *The Guardian* locked themselves into a system which allowed readers access to the website for free. The idea was that online advertising on the website would contribute to the bottom line and *The Guardian* could always fall back on the Scott Trust to pay the bulk of the debts. It was a luxury that other newspapers, struggling to deal with the threat to their business, could not afford. As the internet grew in popularity many newspapers treated it like an extension of the marketing department, putting stories online in the hope that readers would then go out and buy the print edition. In the heart of New York City, though, one newspaper stood against the rising tide of giveaway news. It was hardly surprising that this paper, which dedicated itself to reporting business in one of the toughest cities in the world, baulked at not charging for its products. For more than a century the *Wall Street Journal* (*WSJ*), founded in a basement round the corner from the New York Stock Exchange, has made its daily duty understanding the market and sharing that knowledge, at a price. In 1995 the *WSJ* became the first daily newspaper in the US – out of nearly 15,000 others – to erect a full paywall, forcing its customers to take out a subscription to view the news online.

The decision was not purely commercial. It was also philosophical – everything had a monetary value, including the *WSJ's* journalism. It would be an argument that would play out throughout the following decades: if the net was free for everybody to use, should everything on it be free as well?

Remarkably, the *WSJ* was able to run a twin track policy: it would look to the future and charge for internet access to its newspaper, while keeping a clear view of what sustained the newspaper at that time. In its annual report to shareholders in 1997 it boasted the newspaper had just completed 'one of the most successful years in its history with news coverage sharper than ever' and 'revenue at a historic high'.[11] The *WSJ* was proudly growing circulation, readership and advertising in both its print and electronic editions. It dismissed the media analysts who heralded a digital age that consigned what it called 'dead tree editions' to history's dustbin. If the journal's heart was in the past, it was ready and equipped to embrace the electronic future. Housed today in a glittering glass tower on the Avenue of the Americas, the *WSJ* propelled itself into the internet age with enormous enthusiasm, launching itself as 'your all-day-long source of business news',[12] asking its readers to start the day with the print edition to 'understand what the news means' then to go online throughout the day for news updates – 'breaking news sent to your mobile'.[13] By February 2007 the *WSJ* was boasting that it had what appears quaint in today's language: 800,000 subscriptions, 'more than any other news site on the entire Web'.[14]

It had drawn attention to a challenge of its own making: whether its paywall policy really could produce the kind of business model which would create a profitable marriage between online and print. While newspapers around the world tracked how the *WSJ* handled the tricky balance between selling a print edition and persuading people to pay for website content, an old, nearby rival paid closer attention than most. For nearly a century, the neo-gothic *New York Times* building on 43rd Street in the centre of Manhattan was viewed as the heart of American journalism. It was here that the Pentagon Papers were published in 1971, and the newspaper's coverage of Watergate further bolstered its reputation for gutsy journalism. By 2004 the *New York Times* had won more than 100 Pulitzer Prizes, the most prestigious award in US journalism. But despite the building's grand history, three years later the paper swapped the narrow corridors and the dingy office space for a 52-storey steel and glass tower on 8th Avenue, premises far more befitting a newspaper of the modern age. Like the *WSJ*, the *New York Times* had run up an impressive level of readers on the web. In January of 2004 it had hit 1.4 million, 300,000 more than its print circulation.

But unlike the *WSJ*, The *Times* did not charge for its news coverage. The *New York Times* would not follow the *WSJ* model, which barred everyone from viewing anything on its website unless they were prepared to pay. Newspaper analyst Colby Atwood articulated the situation like this: 'A big part of the motivation for newspapers to charge for their online content is not the revenue it will generate, but the revenue it will save, by slowing the erosion of their print subscriptions.' He told the *New York Times*, 'We're in the midst of a long and painful transition.'[15] It was a masterful understatement.

The Newspaper Association of America was closely monitoring the trend. Spending on print advertising in the first three months of 2006 increased only 0.3 per cent, to US$10.5 billion, over the corresponding period of the previous year, not even keeping pace with inflation. At the same time, spending for online advertising surged 35 per cent. 'I think the handwriting is kind of on the wall that there is a large migration to the Web,' said industry analyst Colby Atwood. 'This is a transition that's taking place over several years here. It's not happening overnight, but it's definitely happening.'[16]

Those who tenaciously believed the future of newspapers would forever remain in print pointed to the small numbers involved. And it was true; most of the money was still going into print advertising. In the first quarter of 2006 online advertising for the US produced US$613 million. Although it was up from US$ 454 million in the previous year – the eighth consecutive quarter of growth – they were not making anywhere near enough money to compensate for the fall in income from print classifieds. Predictably, the price of classified ads started falling in tandem with the drop in print sales. With fewer sales, there were fewer readers and advertisers demanded a discount if they were not reaching so many people. In one six-month period, daily circulation of American newspapers had dropped 2.5 per cent, to 45.5 million. In other words, in the space of half a year, more than one million Americans had suddenly decided to stop buying the print edition of their regular newspapers. Even the relatively good news that total internet advertising revenue reached a record US$3.9 billion was tainted by the fact that the vast bulk of it had ended up on sites like Craigslist that provided a free and cut-price advertising service to its customers and reached millions of readers. Newspapers couldn't compete.

They were fast understanding that the 'rivers of gold' had lost their lustre and were making frenzied attempts to stem the tide. The *Los Angeles Times*, which had opened a paywall for its online site the previous year, shut it in 2005 just as the *New York Times* opened its version only to abandon it in 2007, passing the baton to the UK's *Financial Times*. There were no clear winners in the torturous game of paywall tag. With print advertising income and newspaper circulations continuing to drop in unison, no one knew where to run.

By 2010, with the *Financial Times* still operating a paywall while allowing readers access to a limited number of stories for free, other news publications were emboldened to try again.

There is also a danger that your brand can 'go dark'[17] if you are too restrictive. Readers are far more promiscuous than they used to be, according to John Ridding, CEO of the *Financial Times*, one of the few newspapers in the world that still makes a profit. But the *Financial Times* and the *WSJ* were both aimed at a special niche business market: people who were prepared to pay for information which in return might help them make money. The other mass circulation newspapers were different. They had a more fickle readership that could find its general news elsewhere, for free on the internet. Newspapers were in a state of full-blown panic. It is difficult to say who made the first break from the pack to try once again to find a workable formula but among the leaders were long-time French rivals *Le Figaro* – a conservative newspaper established in 1826 – and *Le Monde*, founded with the support of General Charles de Gaulle in 1944 after the liberation of Paris. As Parisians enjoyed an unusually warm spring in 2010, the country's two favourite quality newspapers finally took the plunge, erecting what are known as 'semi-paywalls' – both still allowed some of their news pages to be seen for free, but charged a hefty fee for full access. It had been a difficult choice and a long time in the making. As their print sales dropped and more people accessed their online web pages, like many other newspapers around the world *Le Figaro* and *Le Monde* faced difficult choices. They could give open access to everyone for free, thus increasing the number of hits so they could sell more online advertising at a higher rate, while keeping 'premium content' for those prepared to pay for full online access. Then there was another alternative: lock everyone out, unless they were prepared to pay for everything. That was the *WSJ* option, and as a niche business paper it seemed to be having some success, but the concept had never been tried by a mass circulation newspaper producing general news until Rupert Murdoch decided otherwise. In July 2010 Murdoch slapped a padlock on the London *Times*. There would be no more free access. The price of reading anything in 'The Thunderer', as it was known in its heyday, was a full subscription. Murdoch was leading again, and the rest of the ex-Fleet Street papers, who had followed him to Wapping, were once more looking on in amazement. It is rare for newspapers to make headlines themselves but within days of the London *Times* shutting the gate it did just that. *The Times* lost 90 per cent of the readers who read it online when it was free because they would not pay to read it online behind a paywall. Not that you would know that if you listened to the head of News Corporation's (News Corp) Digital Media Group. Speaking at a business conference at New York's Time Warner Center in December 2010, Jonathan Miller said that since the introduction of the paywall the paper's 'total economics have improved'.[18] *Forbes* magazine, best known for annually publishing the list of the 400 richest people in America, asked if Miller could possibly have meant that the paper is already making more money, in the form of subscription sales and higher ad rates, than it lost from all those hits from visits when the site was free? Not quite, said Miller. *The Times*, he insisted, was 'on an immediate path' to replacing the lost revenues, and would get there in a matter of months, not years. 'It's predictive,' he said.[19]

Three years later the joke was again on *The Times*. Not enough people were prepared to pay to read it online, even with trial subscriptions at giveaway prices. In what must be a novel first, even for the mavericks in News Corp, the chief executive of News International, Mike Darcey, began attacking a whole class of people that *The Times* had once so assiduously courted. Of the casual online reader who had failed to take up *The Times'* subscription offers he asked:

> What have we really lost? A long tail of passing trade, many from overseas, many popping in for only one article, referred by Google or a social media link, not even aware they are on a Times . . . website?'[20]

The fact that the advertisements on *The Times Online* were no longer being read by this 'passing trade' seemed not to matter to Darcey. He dismissed the former free visitors as not generating 'any meaningful revenue' and argued that pursuing them as customers 'undermines the piece of the business that does make money' – the printed edition. Taking a stand against what most other newspaper publishers in the world were doing – allowing at least some of their content to be seen free – he argued that giving digital content away undermined the print business, which was still by a long way the engine room of revenues and profits. By the end of 2014, print-at-any-cost was a difficult argument for News Corp to sustain. Like every other national daily, from the red-top tabloids to the quality newspapers, *The Times* had witnessed a considerable fall in its circulation, down from 633,000 in January 2008 to a paltry 396,000. Yet News Corp was desperate to prove the critics wrong. It was not merely ego that was at stake; if the circulation numbers fell too far, advertisers would immediately start negotiating with News Corp to cut its ad prices.

The official UK Audit Bureau of Circulations figures covering the six years between January 2008 and January 2014 reveal exactly how desperate News Corp had been to claim success for its Times paywall. At first glance it looks as though the newspaper had increased its sales between January 2014 and January 2015. But *The Times* figures include what are known as 'bulk sales' – 22,000 newspapers either given away free to every bored airline passenger, poked under every hotel bedroom door or sold at giveaway prices. Once *The Times'* circulation is measured the same way as that of its rivals the *Daily Telegraph* and *The Guardian*, which do not include bulk sales, the circulation is revealed as falling dramatically, like that of all the other UK national dailies. But late in 2016 it appeared that *The Times* had stopped the downward spiral. What had happened? It boasted that its print edition's sales were soaring, not steadily trending downwards like those of the competition. Closer examination of the sales figures, published by UK Audit Bureau, reveal what has caused this incredible turnaround. Instead of bumping the figures up with 22,000 bulk sales, *The Times* now added 79,919 bulk sales. The sales number rose to 446,164. But take off the bulk sales and the more credible circulation of the London *Times* was 367,000. *The Times* promoted its print sales as increasing whereas in truth there had been no change. There was some good news, though, for the company's bottom line. Having cut staff and production costs, Times Newspapers Limited including *The Times* and the *Sunday Times* reported a modest £10.9 million profit. Even in the cut-throat British newspaper market other newspapers focused on the profit when they reported the sales figures of the national dailies, and not how the circulation figures had been massaged. It was as though they were hoping someone, even a rival, had found the answer to newspapers' woes. One fact that emerged from the latest figures is just how much trouble *The Guardian* was in. Alone in allowing free access to its entire newspaper online, there appeared to be little reason for readers to buy the print edition, and it showed in the circulation figures. Guardian print sales fell nearly 7 per cent between December 2014 and December 2015 to 166,000, and fell another 3 per cent to 161,091 during the following year. *The Guardian* had the Scott Trust to fall back on; others were not so lucky. In 2016. *The Independent* was caught in the classic internet pincer; with revenue from print advertising collapsing as the classifieds migrated to the web, it had no alternative but to follow the advertising dollar – and operate entirely online.

It is a bleak picture for the entire industry, not just the upmarket newspapers. *The Sun*'s circulation of 1,755,331 was down 3.5 per cent, even with 95,782 bulk sales included in the total; the *Daily Mail* at 1,548,349 was down nearly 5 per cent (including 81,230 bulk sales). The *Daily Telegraph*, with sales of 496,286 (bulks 2,495), was down more than one per cent and the *Daily Express* was down 2.5 per cent with sales of 421,057.[21] Across the English Channel *Le Monde* managed to survive near bankruptcy in 2010 and then witnessed an increase in circulation after it introduced a paywall. With no free reads, many people chose to buy the print edition. Sales rose from 309,022 to 325,295 in 2011, but then resumed their downward slide. In 2015 *Le Monde* sold just 292,054 print copies of the paper.[22]

Even so in 2016 print still accounted for 80 per cent of the company's total income and 70 per cent of its advertising revenue. Louis Dreyfus, president of Groupe Le Monde, had little alternative but to pronounce: 'At Le Monde, we believe print is not dead,' because without it *Le Monde* would be in serious trouble.[23]

Oxford University's Reuters Institute for the Study of Journalism published a report in 2010 which held out some hope for plummeting circulations. Citing Germany, it argued that the country's media businesses had been 'more stable' and suggested the threat from the internet was overrated.[24]

The study held out a potentially positive view for the future of the newspaper industry 'despite the deterministic [and often fatalistic]' claims to the contrary. Unfortunately the study was slightly too optimistic. Germany was no different from all the other countries whose newspapers were suffering. Within three years of the publication of the Reuters Institute study, the highly respected German news magazine *Der Spiegel* reported in a five-part investigation: 'It came to Germany almost a decade later than America, but the newspaper crisis is sweeping the country, with plummeting circulations and revenues.'[25]

Der Spiegel summed up the problem, which applies just as much to the rest of the world:

> Making more money, developing new distribution channels, producing at a lower cost, improving quality and reinventing themselves – the survival program for German daily newspapers sounds about as cold and bold as the restructuring plan for the German steel industry decades ago. The only comfort is that German newspapers can't be written in China at rock-bottom prices.[26]

It was only in 2017 that the German Advertising Federation GIVW, responsible for auditing the circulation figures of the print media, declared that there had been 'no acceleration of the downturn'.[27]

The circulation of national newspapers in Italy was also in a downward spiral. The country's biggest newspaper, *Corriere della Sera*, had seen its circulation of

668,130 in 2006 collapse to 420,802 in 2014, while the other national dailies, *La Republica* (275,415) and *La Stampa* (188,582), were in a similar position – all heavily relying on classified advertisements to fund their journalism.[28]

Analysis by the Pew Research Centre reported that

> For newspapers, 2015 might as well have been a recession year. Weekday circulation fell 7% and Sunday circulation fell 4%, both showing their greatest declines since 2010. At the same time, advertising revenue experienced its greatest drop since 2009, falling nearly 8% from 2014 to 2015.

The US McClatchy news service saw advertising revenue fall 13 per cent (from $732 million to $637). Significantly, Pew said: 'Gains in digital ad revenue, however, have not made up for the continued decline in print revenue.'[29]

The *New York Times* is a perfect example of the problem: in 2016 the paper's profits slumped 60 per cent. In February 2017 the newspaper reported that though its 'digital advertising rose 6 per cent', correspondingly 'print advertising revenue declined by 20 per cent in 2016'.[30]

Forbes estimated that print advertising was a little over $100 million in revenue in the latest quarter, down by about $35 million or so from a year earlier. Digital ad revenue climbed by 10%, or about $7 million. So that means the *Times* is losing almost twice as much on print every quarter as it is making up in digital subscriptions and ads.[31]

However, giving new meaning to the old adage that every cloud has a silver lining, the circulation of broadsheet newspapers around the world benefitted from their coverage of the terrorist attacks in Europe in 2015, with the London *Times* editor John Witherow explaining they were in part responsible for the newspaper's lift in sales. And the election of Donald Trump in November 2016 caused a surge in online subscribers for the *New York Times*, a record 276000 in one quarter, but as Forbes pointed out, in order for digital to counter print's decline, 'the *Times* would have to add as many new subscribers this quarter as it did in the last quarter, and then do so again in the next quarter, and the one after that, and the one after that'.[32]

The fall in sales over 20 years had been catastrophic. In 1995 the *New York Times* had a daily print circulation of 1.5 million. At the last count, it was 625,000. If the highly respected media analyst Clay Shirky's is right the *New York Times* is in deep trouble. Shirky, a professor at New York University, says that a weekday circulation of 500,000 is an important psychological sticking point for advertisers. Each copy of a newspaper becomes increasingly more expensive to produce the lower the circulation. Shirky estimates that the advertising revenue from 'a print run of 500,000 would be 16 percent less than for 600,000 at best, but the costs wouldn't fall by anything like 16%'. That would substantially erode print margins and points ominously to 'some threshold, well above 100,000 copies and probably closer to 250,000, where nightly print runs stop making economic sense'.[33] By this measure, many newspaper business models are at or rapidly approaching that point. In Australia Fairfax newspapers, publishers of the *Sydney Morning Herald* and *The Age* in Melbourne, are vulnerable. Fairfax, which in 2016 made more than 100 editorial workers redundant to save on costs, witnessed a sharp slide in weekday print circulation between December 2014 and December 2015. According to the Audited Media Association of Australia, *The Age* print sales fell from 106,843 to 97,503 while the *Sydney Morning Herald* dropped from 114,634 to 104,155, once again igniting speculation that Fairfax would stop printing its daily editions and move them online. Fairfax CEO Greg Hywood denied any immediate plans to stop the weekday print editions – leaving just the classified revenue-rich weekend papers to survive in print – but pointed to a possible 'reset' at Fairfax to 'focus on the 65 per cent of advertising revenue which is generated on the weekend'. He added: 'It should surprise no one, and certainly not us, that the seven-day-a-week publishing model will eventually give way to weekend-only or more targeted printing for most publishers.'[34]

There is scant comparison between the resources of online newspapers and the traditional product, staffed by highly experienced and often well-paid journalists. When a newspaper moves online, it inevitably cuts costs – often hiring younger, less experienced journalists. For all its problems, quality journalism still remains with the traditional print media. As Douglas McCabe at the UK media research company Enders Analysis explained, 'Print newspapers may be retreating, but they remain an extraordinarily influential medium for middle-aged and older audiences.' And it was not just the influence on older people. Print newspapers still perform an extraordinarily important role in providing information for the political and economic debate in society. Many television and radio programmes rely heavily on the traditional media for their research. They very often are the main drivers of the 'story of the day'. As an investigation by Cardiff University into how the BBC covered the 2015 UK general election revealed, television agendas 'followed stories broken in the press'.[35] It is why the collapse of the traditional print media is such an important issue – and why at the moment at least, digital journalism is not the answer, only a symptom of the problem facing the Fourth Estate. While many more readers were now paying for their news, the income they produced for newspapers was tiny compared to the overheads. Those costs were still being almost entirely met by the classified ads carried in the print editions. And as print sales dropped, advertisers began looking elsewhere to place their advertising. Inevitably they also started demanding lower rates. This combination of falling readership and declining classified ad revenue created an unsustainable level of debt. As newspapers cut staff to contain costs and pay down the debt, the remaining staff were expected to pick up the workload to fill the paper. Perhaps not surprisingly, readers noticed the quality slipping. It became common practice for newspapers which operated a partial paywall to try to lure more readers in with juicy stories. But there was a downside. The demands of continually updating information to attract new viewers online, so they would stop at a 'new' story and click through, started to dominate the journalistic culture. Journalists began tailoring their stories to generate more online traffic, i.e. get more readers to click on their stories. At one of Germany's leading national newspapers, the online editors of *Suddeutsche Zeitung*, began telling their journalists how many clicks their articles received on the newspaper's website. The journalists began tailoring their stories to increase the number of hits. It was an 'experience that is gratifying and at times horrifying' to see 'how directly measurable' the response 'is to what they write', said Wolfgang Krach, deputy editor-in-chief of the print edition.[36]

At the *Washington Post*, stories were also being targeted with keywords so that they would hit the demographic target audiences that the newspapers were guaranteeing advertisers they would reach. It was a strategy being copied around the world. Search engines like Google and social network companies like Facebook – which directed surfers to the newspaper websites – cashed in on the opportunity. If newspapers needed traffic to boost their advertising revenue, they would provide it. In the end they were directing so many readers to the newspapers it was now Google and Facebook that were determining the kind of stories that were being published, because the greater the number of 'hits' online a newspaper received, the more it could charge for its advertising. But that was little compared to the super profits being made by those who contributed nothing in monetary terms to the newspapers they were feeding off.

In 2015 Google generated more than £7bn of revenues in the UK alone while, in 2014, Facebook registered £105m in revenues. Much of this income came from advertisers that once supported news publishers.

They were not just making money out of the number of visits to particular sites; both Facebook and Google were gathering data on newspaper readers. The vast amount of personal information that Google gathered when people entered newspaper websites using their search engine, if not a river of gold, was able to be transformed by Google into a solid stream of silver. Google was producing extraordinary amounts of personal information on people, from their likes and dislikes, the films they watched and their politics, to their sexual orientation. It was not only using that information to send targeted advertising to anyone who used their systems, it was also making money out of selling the information to others. A novel category of business was born: data-miners, or aggregators – companies that trawled the internet gathering all the information they could from search engines – would build comprehensive profiles of newspaper readers. They on-sold those profiles to advertising placement agencies, who consequently knew where best to place their ads. For the newspapers, this was another attack on their revenue stream, for the aggregators charged the advertisers a fraction of what newspapers used to ask for this valuable information. While News Corp, which had by now bought the *WSJ*, had become a keen advocate of full-scale paywalls to protect content, it was incensed to discover it could not keep secret from search engines like Google valuable personal information about those who entered their site. What annoyed News Corp was that aggregators were selling access to the demographic details of 75 per cent of the *WSJ*'s customers at 25 per cent of the News Corp asking price.

Google was eating the traditional media from without by stealing its news product and from within by using its analytics to undercut its advertising rates. Media lecturer Justin Schlosberg, author of the essay 'The Mission of Media in an Age of Monopoly', published by British think tank *ResPublica*, pointed out that Google 'gains traffic by using stories generated by the media but it pays nothing for the articles'.[37]

More and more people were turning to Google as a single source for their stories. Google was fast becoming, he said, the single gateway many people used to get their daily news – and some of them had no idea that news was produced by newspapers.[38]

ResPublica director Phillip Blond called for a 'a nominal levy on the revenues of large scale news intermediaries in online search and social networking, including Google and Facebook. They currently pay nothing for the news that they use.'[39]

As Alan Rusbridger, the former *Guardian* editor whose plans to 'monetise' *The Guardian*'s news pages had gone so badly awry, pointed out: 'In general news, [social media] are walking away with the money.'[40] Everything, he said, was now a media company.

Rusbridger had an unusual ally in NewsCorp chief Robert Thomson who wrote a strong complaint to the European Commission, which was investigating Google's power in Europe. He accused Google of 'undermining the business model of the content creator'.[41] Thomson argued that although the process was at a relatively early stage, it needed 'constant monitoring to ensure that abuses were halted and that there is a fair return for newspapers, publishers and other investors in original content'.[42] Not long before taking over his job in 2014, Gunther Oettinger, the EU's new Commissioner for Digital Affairs, stated his intention to reform European copyright law in 2015. Oettinger announced few details of his plans but in an interview with the German daily newspaper *Handelsblatt*, he made it clear that he wanted to tackle the profits Google made from listing European companies in search results. 'If Google takes intellectual property from the EU and works with that, then the EU can protect that property and demand Google pay for that,' he said.[43] Yet introducing this kind of Google tax will probably prove extremely difficult.

According to Julia Reda, a European parliament member from the Pirate Party who in 2015 authored a report on EU copyright law, the new proposal meant Google could be charged licensing fees merely for scraping news article content from the web and adding it to its database. But forcing Google to pay for its news media role was fraught with possible problems. When a 'news tax' was imposed on Google in Germany, Google stopped showing everything but the headlines of published articles and traffic plummeted. The publishers then granted Google a temporary free licence to use the text of the article.

'What Google would have to do [under the EU proposal] is remove the publishers from the search results altogether,' Reda told *Fortune Magazine*.

It's quite clear what's going to happen, the same thing as in Germany—publishers who want to continue to show up in Google search results will give Google a free license and [Google's smaller rivals] won't get a free license.[44]

There are perhaps even more worrying issues raised by the power of Google and Facebook, two of the biggest companies in the world who gain billions of dollars in revenue each year, and put away billions in the bank. They are also now the systems that millions of people use to get their news.

In June 2015 the US Pew Research Center reported that six in ten millennials – generally accepted to be those born between the early 1980s and the 2000s – say they get political news from Facebook every week, while only half as many adults in America say they get all their news from Facebook.[45]

The two organisations not only provide the news, they decide what is published and what is not. In 2016 Facebook censored the famous photograph of a young girl, nine-year-old Kim Phuc, badly burned in a napalm attack during the Vietnam War, on the grounds that because she was naked some people might be offended. The photograph, one of a series, was included in a post by a Norwegian journalist discussing photographs which changed the history of warfare. Understandably the ban caused an uproar.

Espen Egil Hansen, editor-in-chief and CEO of *Aftenposten*, wrote to Facebook CEO Mark Zuckerberg accusing him of thoughtlessly 'abusing your power'. Hansen said he was 'upset, disappointed – well, in fact even afraid – of what you are about to do to a mainstay of our democratic society'.[46]

Facebook eventually relented and allowed the photograph to be re-posted because 'In this case, we recognize the history and global importance of this image in documenting a particular moment in time.'[47]

Facebook made it very clear it was the company's choice whether or not to re-establish the photograph. As Martin Moore, director of the Centre for the study of Media Communication and Power in the Police Institute at King's College London, points out in his paper *Tech Giants and Civil Power*, Facebook is a powerful political tool. After terrorists shot and killed 130 people in Paris on 13 November, 2015 Facebook activated its Safety Check service. Thanks to the service, many people were able to find out if members of their family or their friends were safe and to locate them. This was the first time the service had been active after a terrorist attack, according to Moore. Previously it had only been turned on following *natural* disasters. After the Paris attacks, Facebook was confronted by a reasonable question: why had it not implemented the Safety Check system following other similar tragedies, like the ISIS (Islamic State of Iraq and Syria) bombings in Beirut the previous week? Facebook responded, saying that they would change their policy and activate the service for other serious and tragic incidents in the future. In each case it will, of course, be Facebook's decision whether to turn it on or not to turn it on. As Zeynep Tufekci, an associate professor at the School of Information and Library Science at the University of North Carolina and a self-described 'techno-sociologist' wrote, the way the Safety Check system was operated by Facebook 'demonstrates the profoundly political nature of the choices made by major internet platforms'.[48] Tufekci argued that there were no easy decisions with immediate right answers. That was because 'crisis communication'[49] was both 'incredibly valuable', and 'deeply political'. It was another moment to observe 'the intertwining of technology and politics'.[50]

It was no longer possible for social platforms to say 'we are just a platform',[51] according to Emily Bell, director of the Tow Center at Columbia University. 'It's become impossible to sustain the argument that says we have no responsibility to people who upload content, and we have no responsibility to people who are affected by it.'[52] News spaces were no longer owned by newsmakers. 'The press is no longer in charge of the free press and has lost control of the main conduits through which stories reach audiences.'[53]

As all communications systems collapse onto a single internet pathway, the concentration of power into the hands of the huge American corporations Facebook and Google has made them the biggest monopolies the world has ever seen. They dwarf by far the dominance of Standard Oil, the original company ordered to be broken up in 1911 under US antitrust laws that deemed the company to be a monopoly and therefore detrimental to competition. Yet there has been no suggestion in the US that Google and Facebook should be broken up. They are treated very differently from their predecessors like AT&T, the huge telecommunications giant which fell foul of anti-competition laws, and was ordered to be dismantled. Google, on the other hand, remains intact, unchallenged by a government that both polices their activities and also directly benefits from their services. In 2003 Google secured a US $2,070,000 million contract to outfit the NSA with a Google system capable of 'searching 15 million documents in twenty-four languages'.[54] At the same time that Google was working with the NSA it was also forging links with two other US intelligence agencies – the National Geospatial-Intelligence Agency, which provides live satellite imagery to US military battlefield operations, and the CIA.

Google denies that it is a willing partner in providing personal data to the US intelligence agencies, but as Snowden revealed under the PRISM program, the NSA has front-door access to Google user accounts through a court-approved process and it has been revealed that Google's servers have been secretly tapped by the NSA and Britain's GCHQ.

This type of collaboration, of democratic states working closely with corporations that have such detailed knowledge of the minutiae of our political and social lives, raises a rather frightening prospect that neither George Orwell or Aldous Huxley fully imagined. A world in which governments have access to all our digital information and communication, and therefore almost complete knowledge of who we are, who we communicate with, and how we engage with politics – not only via their own systems but via those run by the information intermediaries. And as the means of surveillance and control are outsourced, there are few democratic mechanisms of transparency or accountability.

It seems that little can stop Google in particular from devouring the 'free' news it makes so much money from, although in 2016 Europe's competition watchdog launched a new round of antitrust charges against the company – the third set since early 2015 – claiming that some of the company's advertising products had restricted consumer choice.

Even if this and other actions against the search engine are successful it appears not much can be done to reduce the perverse power of Google as the world's electronic editor-in-chief: it is killing off the very product that provides its news source – newspapers. Google turns over about US$70 billion a year, but very little of that money goes to the traditional media which provides so much of the content that helps make Google the world's most used search engine.

According to the UK *Press Gazette*, in 2016 online comprised more than half of the entire UK advertising market with total sales of £10.3bn, according to the Internet Advertising Bureau. 'By Press Gazette's reckoning well over half of that £10.3bn went to Google and Facebook,'[55] the magazine reported. 'The market grew by 17 per cent year on year and more than 80 per cent of that new money went to Google and Facebook.'[56]

UK Press Gazette reported that over the last decade 'well in excess of £2bn a year has been taken out of the journalism industry and most of that money is now going to Google and Facebook',[57] money which previously went 'towards paying journalists' wages and providing us with democratic accountability'.[58] It added: 'Payment appears to have gone from the creators of content to those who aggregate it and provide a platform for others to share it.'[59] Accelerating the decay, in an industry which has such a special role in democratic society, could not have come at a more difficult time.

Notes

1 Burrel, I. 17th May, 2016. *Everything You Need to Know About the Guardian's Giant Bust Up*. Evening Standard [online]. Available at www.standard.co.uk/lifestyle/london-life/fueding-and-financial-meltdown-everything-you-need-to-know-about-the-guardian-s-giant-bustup-a3249961.html [Accessed 30 August, 2016].
2 Burrel, I. 17th May, 2016. *Everything You Need to Know About the Guardian's Giant Bust Up*. Evening Standard [online]. Available at www.standard.co.uk/lifestyle/london-life/fueding-and-financial-meltdown-everything-you-need-to-know-about-the-guardian-s-giant-bustup-a3249961.html [Accessed 30 August, 2016].
3 Burrel, I. 17th May, 2016. *Everything You Need to Know About the Guardian's Giant Bust Up*. Evening Standard [online]. Available at www.standard.co.uk/lifestyle/london-life/fueding-and-financial-meltdown-everything-you-need-to-know-about-the-guardian-s-giant-bustup-a3249961.html [Accessed 30 August, 2016].
4 Burrel, I. 17th May, 2016. *Everything You Need to Know About the Guardian's Giant Bust Up*. Evening Standard [online]. Available at www.standard.co.uk/lifestyle/london-life/fueding-and-financial-meltdown-everything-you-need-to-know-about-the-guardian-s-giant-bustup-a3249961.html [Accessed 30 August, 2016].
5 Sweney, M. 13th May, 2016. *Alan Rusbridger Will Not Take Up Role As Chair of the Scott Trust*. The Guardian [online]. Available at www.theguardian.com/media/2016/may/13/alan-rusbridger-scott-trust-guardian [Accessed 28 August, 2016].
6 Sweeney, M. 13th May, 2016. *Alan Rusbridger Will Not Take Up Role As Chair of the Scott Trust*. The Guardian [online]. Available at www.theguardian.com/media/2016/may/13/alan-rusbridger-scott-trust-guardian [Accessed 30 August, 2016].

7 Sweeney, M. 13th May, 2016. *Alan Rusbridger Will Not Take Up Role As Chair of the Scott Trust*. The Guardian [online]. Available at www.theguardian.com/media/2016/may/13/alan-rusbridger-scott-trust-guardian [Accessed 30 August, 2016].

8 *The Scott Trust: Values and History*. The Guardian [online]. Available at www.theguardian.com/the-scott-trust/2015/jul/26/the-scott-trust [Accessed 23 December, 2016].

9 De Lisle, T. 2012. *Can the Guardian Survive?* The Economist [online]. Available at www.1843magazine.com/content/ideas/tim-de-lisle/can-guardian-survive [Accessed 30 August, 2016].

10 *The Scott Trust: Values and History*. [online]. Available at www.theguardian.com/the-scott-trust/2015/jul/26/the-scott-trust [Accessed 23 December, 2016].

11 The Wall Street Journal. 8th January, 1997. A Report to the Wall Street Journal's Readers [online]. Available at www.WSJ.com/articles/SB852688850493222500 [Accessed 25 August, 2016].

12 Doctor, K. 5th January, 2007. *Wall Street Journal Redesign Ups Stakes in War for Business Readers*. Newsonomics [online]. Available at http://newsonomics.com/wall-street-journal-redesign-ups-stakes-in-war-for-business-readers/ [Accessed 10 November, 2016].

13 The Wall Street Journal. 8th January, 1997. A Report to the Wall Street Journal's Readers [online]. Available at www.WSJ.com/articles/SB852688850493222500 [Accessed 25 August, 2016].

14 The Wall Street Journal. 8th January, 1997. A Report to the Wall Street Journal's Readers [online]. Available at www.WSJ.com/articles/SB852688850493222500 [Accessed 25 August, 2016].

15 Seelye, K. 14th March, 2005. *Can Papers End the Free Ride Online?* The New York Times [online]. Available at www.nytimes.com/2005/03/14/business/media/can-papers-end-the-free-ride-online.html?_r=0 [Accessed 8 December, 2016].

16 Bosman, J. 6th June, 2006. *Online Newspaper Ads Gaining Ground on Print*. The New York Times [online]. Available at www.nytimes.com/2006/06/06/business/media/06adco.html [Accessed 19 October, 2016].

17 Ridding, J. 2015. *Response to Author Questions*. Financial Times, London.

18 Bercovici, J. 3rd December, 2010. *Times of London Paywall Paying off Already!* Forbes Magazine [online]. Available at www.forbes.com/sites/jeffbercovici/2010/12/03/times-of-london-paywall-paying-off-already/#27c90b9534fc [Accessed 30 November, 2016].

19 Bercovici, J. 3rd December, 2010. *Times of London Paywall Paying off Already!* Forbes Magazine [online]. Available at www.forbes.com/sites/jeffbercovici/2010/12/03/times-of-london-paywall-paying-off-already/#27c90b9534fc [Accessed 30 November, 2016].

20 Sinclair, L. 4th July, 2013. *Paid Sales of The Times Up on 2010 as Digital Subscriptions Hit 140,000*. The Australian [online]. Available at www.theaustralian.com.au/business/paid-sales-of-the-times-up-on-2010-as-digital-subscriptions-hit-140000/news-story/fb59f2a12d2dce6d30ba7f21fd721059 [Accessed 9 November, 2016].

21 Ponsford, D. 21st July 2016. *ABC Figures: National Press Sees June Brexit Vote Boost in Print and Online*. UK Press Gazette [online]. Available at www.pressgazette.co.uk/abc-figures-national-press-sees-june-brexit-vote-boost-in-print-and-online/ [Accessed 3 July, 2016].

22 Statista. 2016. Circulation of Le Monde from 1999 to 2016 [online]. Available at www.statista.com/statistics/304642/le-monde-circulation/ [Accessed 10 November, 2016].

23 Scott, C. 14th June, 2016. How Le Monde Transformed Its Business Model to Become a Profitable News Publisher [online]. Available at www.journalism.co.uk/news/how-le-monde-transformed-its-business-model-to-become-a-profitable-news-publisher/s2/a646756/ [Accessed 10 November, 2016].

24 Reuters Institute. [No date]. The Changing Business of Journalism and Its Implications for Democracy [online]. Available at http://reutersinstitute.politics.ox.ac.uk/publication/changing-business-journalism-and-its-implications-democracy [Accessed 27 October, 2016].

25 Schnibben, C. 13th August, 2013. *Newspaper Crisis Hits Germany.* Der Spiegel [online]. Available at www.spiegel.de/international/germany/circulation-declines-hit-german-papers-a-decade-after-america-a-915574.html.

26 Schnibben, C. 13th August, 2013. *Newspaper Crisis Hits Germany.* Der Spiegel [online]. Available at www.spiegel.de/international/germany/circulation-declines-hit-german-papers-a-decade-after-america-a-915574.html.

27 Scott, C. 14th June, 2016. *How Le Monde Transformed Its Business Model to Become a Profitable News Publisher.* Journalism.co.uk [online]. Available at www.journalism.co.uk/news/how-le-monde-transformed-its-business-model-to-become-a-profitable-news-publisher/s2/a646756/ [Accessed 12 August, 2016].

28 Federazione Italiana Editori Giornali. 2017. ADS: TIRATURE E DIFFUSIONI DI QUOTIDIANI, SETTIMANALI (March 2017) E MENSILI (February 2017) [online]. Available at www.fieg.it/documenti_item.asp?page=1&doc_id=350 [Accessed 21 April, 2017].

29 Barthel, M. 15th June, 2016. *Newspapers: Fact Sheet.* Pew Research Center [online] Available at www.journalism.org/2016/06/15/newspapers-fact-sheet/?mobiright-demo= anchor,anchor [Accessed 16 November].

30 Ember, S. 2nd February, 2017. New York Times [online] Available at www.nytimes.com/2017/02/02/business/media/new-york-times-q4-earnings.html [Accessed 10 February, 2017].

31 Ingram, M. 3rd February, 2017. Donald Trump is Helping, But the New York Times is Still Struggling [online] Available at http://fortune.com/2017/02/02/nyt-earnings/ [Accessed 5 February, 2017].

32 Ingram, M. 3rd February, 2017. Donald Trump Is Helping, But the New York Times Is Still Struggling [online]. Available at http://fortune.com/2017/02/02/nyt-earnings/ [Accessed 5 February, 2017].

33 Sullivan, M. 10th April, 2015. A *'Darker Narrative' of Print's Future from Clay Shirky.* The New York Times [online]. Available at https://publiceditor.blogs.nytimes.com/2015/04/10/a-darker-narrative-of-prints-future-from-clay-shirky/.

34 White, D. and Mason, M. 6th May, 2016. *Greg Hywood Flags Future Print Changes as Fairfax Embraces 24/7 Digital.* The Sydney Morning Herald [online]. Available at www.smh.com.au/business/media-and-marketing/greg-hywood-flags-weekendonly-print-editions-as-fairfax-embraces-247-digital-20160505-gonp18.html [Accessed 10 July, 2016].

35 Cardiff University. 2015. TV News Coverage of the 2015 UK General Election Campaign [online]. Available at www.cardiff.ac.uk/research/explore/find-a-project/view/188437-2015-uk-general-election-campaign [Accessed 21 July, 2017].

36 Schnibben, C. 13th August, 2013. *Newspaper Crisis Hits Germany.* Der Spiegel [online] Available at www.spiegel.de/international/germany/circulation-declines-hit-german-papers-a-decade-after-america-a-915574.html.

37 Schlosberg, J. May 2016. *The Mission of the Media in an Age of Monopoly.* ResPublica [online]. Available at www.respublica.org.uk/wp-content/uploads/2016/05/The-Mission-of-Media.pdf [Accessed 6 October, 2016].

38 Greenslade, R. 26th May, 2016. *Make Google and Facebook Pay Levy to Support Journalism.* The Guardian [online]. Available at www.theguardian.com/media/greenslade/2016/may/26/make-google-and-facebook-pay-levy-to-support-journalism-academic [Accessed 28 July, 2016].

39 Greenslade, R. 26th May, 2016. *Make Google and Facebook Pay Levy to Support Journalism.* The Guardian [online]. Available at www.theguardian.com/media/greenslade/2016/may/26/make-google-and-facebook-pay-levy-to-support-journalism-academic [Accessed 28 July, 2016].

40 Burrel, I. 17th May, 2016. *Everything You Need to Know About the Guardian's Giant Bust Up*. Evening Standard [online]. Available at www.standard.co.uk/lifestyle/london-life/fueding-and-financial-meltdown-everything-you-need-to-know-about-the-guardians-giant-bustup-a3249961.html [Accessed 30 August, 2016].

41 Williams, C. 18th September, 2014. *Murdoch Renews Hostilities with Google Over 'Contempt' for Copyright*. London Daily Telegraph [online]. Available at www.telegraph.co.uk/finance/newsbysector/mediatechnologyandtelecoms/digital-media/11103767/Murdoch-renews-hostilities-with-Google-over-contempt-for-copyright.html?fb [Accessed 14 November, 2016].

42 Williams, C. 18th September, 2014. *Murdoch Renews Hostilities with Google over 'Contempt' for Copyright*. London Daily Telegraph [online]. Available at www.telegraph.co.uk/finance/newsbysector/mediatechnologyandtelecoms/digital-media/11103767/Murdoch-renews-hostilities-with-Google-over-contempt-for-copyright.html?fb [Accessed 14 November, 2016].

43 Stupp, C. 2nd December, 2014. *The Fight to Get Google to Pay for News Continues in Europe*. NiemanLab [online]. Available at www.niemanlab.org/2014/12/the-fight-to-get-google-to-pay-for-news-continues-in-europe/ [Accessed 2 January, 2017].

44 Meyer, D. 31st August, 2016. *EU Lawmakers Are About to Try Making Google Pay for Google News*. Fortune [online]. Available at http://fortune.com/2016/08/31/eu-google-ancillary-copyright/ [Accessed 10 October, 2016].

45 Mitchell, A., Gottfried, J. and Matsa, K. 1st June, 2015. *Millennials and Political News*. Pew Research Center [online]. Available at www.journalism.org/2015/06/01/millennials-political-news/ [Accessed 30 December, 2016].

46 Levin, S., Wong, J. and Harding, L. *Facebook Backs Down from 'Napalm Girl' Censorship and Reinstates Photo*. The Guardian [online]. Available at www.theguardian.com/technology/2016/sep/09/facebook-reinstates-napalm-girl-photo [Accessed 31 December, 2016].

47 Levin, S., Wong, J. and Harding, L. *Facebook Backs Down from 'Napalm Girl' Censorship and Reinstates Photo*. The Guardian [online]. Available at www.theguardian.com/technology/2016/sep/09/facebook-reinstates-napalm-girl-photo [Accessed 31 December, 2016].

48 Tufekci, Z. 24th November, 2015. *The Politics of Empathy and the Politics of Technology*. The Message [online]. Available at https://medium.com/message/the-politics-of-empathy-and-the-politics-technology-664437b6427#.lcdup775a [Accessed 31 January, 2017].

49 Tufekci, Z. 24th November, 2015. *The Politics of Empathy and the Politics of Technology*. The Message [online]. Available at https://medium.com/message/the-politics-of-empathy-and-the-politics-technology-664437b6427#.lcdup775a [Accessed 31 January, 2017].

50 Tufekci, Z. 24th November, 2015. *The Politics of Empathy and the Politics of Technology*. The Message [online]. Available at https://medium.com/message/the-politics-of-empathy-and-the-politics-technology-664437b6427#.lcdup775a [Accessed 31 January, 2017].

51 Bell, E. 21st November, 2014. *Silicon Valley and Journalism: Make Up or Break up?* Reuters Institute [online]. Available at http://reutersinstitute.politics.ox.ac.uk/news/silicon-valley-and-journalism-make-or-break [Accessed 7 November, 2016].

52 Bell, E. 21st November, 2014. *Silicon Valley and Journalism: Make Up or Break up?* Reuters Institute [online]. Available at http://reutersinstitute.politics.ox.ac.uk/news/silicon-valley-and-journalism-make-or-break [Accessed 7 November, 2016].

53 Bell, E. 21st November, 2014. *Silicon Valley and Journalism: Make Up or Break up?* Reuters Institute [online]. Available at http://reutersinstitute.politics.ox.ac.uk/news/silicon-valley-and-journalism-make-or-break [Accessed 7 November, 2016].

54 Fowler, A. 2015. *The War on Journalism*. Penguin Random House.

55 Ponsford, D. 12th April, 2017. UK Digital Ad Market Growing 17.3 Per Cent to £10.3bn – Google and Facebook Take Nearly all the Money [online]. Available at

www.pressgazette.co.uk/uk-digital-ad-market-grows-17-3-per-cent-to-10-3bn-google-and-facebook-take-nearly-all-the-extra-money/ [Accessed 2 May, 2017].

56 Ponsford, D. 12 April, 2017. UK Digital Ad Market Growing 17.3 Per Cent to £10.3bn – Google and Facebook Take Nearly all the Money [online]. Available at www.pressgazette.co.uk/uk-digital-ad-market-grows-17-3-per-cent-to-10-3bn-google-and-facebook-take-nearly-all-the-extra-money/ [Accessed 2 May, 2017].

57 Ponsford, D. 12th April, 2017. UK Digital Ad Market Growing 17.3 Per Cent to £10.3bn – Google and Facebook Take Nearly All the Money [online]. Available at www.pressgazette.co.uk/uk-digital-ad-market-grows-17-3-per-cent-to-10-3bn-google-and-facebook-take-nearly-all-the-extra-money/ [Accessed 2 May, 2017].

58 Ponsford, D. 12th April, 2017. UK Digital Ad Market Growing 17.3 Per Cent to £10.3bn – Google and Facebook Take Nearly all the Money [online]. Available at www.pressgazette.co.uk/uk-digital-ad-market-grows-17-3-per-cent-to-10-3bn-google-and-facebook-take-nearly-all-the-extra-money/ [Accessed 2 May, 2017].

59 Ponsford, D. 12th April, 2017. UK Digital Ad Market Growing 17.3 Per Cent to £10.3bn – Google and Facebook Take Nearly all the Money [online]. Available at www.pressgazette.co.uk/uk-digital-ad-market-grows-17-3-per-cent-to-10-3bn-google-and-facebook-take-nearly-all-the-extra-money/ [Accessed 2 May, 2017].

6

SHIELDING THE SOURCE

Six days after he was inaugurated as the 45th president of the US, Donald Trump reached for his mobile phone. He had a habit of tweeting in the early hours of the morning, but this was a more reasonable hour, just gone ten o'clock at night. Why the leader of the 'free' world felt his observations could not have waited until the next day is unclear. He had already made it known that he was very unimpressed that the outgoing president Barak Obama had reduced the sentence of Chelsea Manning from 35 to seven years, using the power ceded to presidents in the US Constitution – ironically part of the royal prerogative used by King George III, which so angered the early Americans and in part led to the split from Britain. What seemed to annoy Trump was that Manning had written a newspaper column explaining what she believed Obama might have done to be a better president. In a mixture of questionable high dudgeon and apparent faux concern Trump tweeted: 'Ungrateful TRAITOR Chelsea Manning, who should never have been released from prison, is now calling President Obama a weak leader. Terrible!'[1] If the tweet was designed to engender publicity for the commander in chief, it achieved its goal. Trump would get immediate satisfaction watching 'Breaking News' crawl across the bottom of the screen on CNN or Fox. But it seems Trump missed the more significant event in Obama's decision to cut Manning's sentence.

As Obama prepared to leave the White House in a few hours' time on that cold January day in 2017 he would have been acutely aware of the kind of administration that would be moving in: a president who would bring an unusual style of blunt and at times brutal subjugation of all who stood in his way. It was perhaps at this moment that Obama, who entered the White House showing sympathy for whistle-blowers – and concern about the rising power of the state – reverted to his true self. Cutting the sentence of a transgender person being held in an all-male military prison under the control of a commander in chief like Trump, showed his humanity. It was not just that the sentence of 35 years was much longer than a penalty imposed for commensurate crimes. Manning had been found by the UN rapporteur on torture to have been held in conditions which were 'cruel, inhuman and degrading'[2] during her pre-trial incarceration.

The UN special rapporteur concluded that imposing 'seriously punitive conditions of detention on someone who has not been found guilty of any crime is a violation of his right to physical and psychological integrity as well as of his presumption of innocence'.[3]

It could be argued that what was contained in the WikiLeaks cables was anything but surprising. History tells us about the duplicity, underhandedness and secrecy of governments and the military, but much material is often revealed decades after the event, when circumstances have changed and the participants have moved on. In this case the information was current, and the public could become privy to the inner thinking of the administration in near 'real' time, allowing it to make better informed political decisions. It was one of the prime reasons that Manning said she decided to release the data to WikiLeaks. 'It was not until I was in Iraq and reading secret military reports on a daily basis that I started to question the morality of what we were doing,'[4] she wrote in a letter to President Obama.

> It was at this time I realized that (in) our efforts to meet the risk posed to us by the enemy, we have forgotten our humanity. We consciously elected to devalue human life both in Iraq and Afghanistan. When we engaged those that we perceived were the enemy, we sometimes killed innocent civilians. Whenever we killed innocent civilians, instead of accepting responsibility for our conduct, we elected to hide behind the veil of national security and classified information in order to avoid any public accountability.[5]

Manning added: 'It was never my intent to hurt anyone. I only wanted to help people. When I chose to disclose classified information, I did so out of a love for my country and a sense of duty to others.'[6]

The way the US administration responded to Manning's leaks said much about how the truth becomes a tradeable commodity when those who have much to lose from full disclosure are cornered. In 2010, shortly after the Cablegate leaks, US Secretary of State Hillary Clinton publicly castigated WikiLeaks and Manning: 'The United States strongly condemns the illegal disclosure of classified information. It puts people's lives in danger, threatens our national security, and undermines our efforts to work with other countries to solve shared problems.'[7]

Clinton's attempt to divert attention from the administration's shortcomings exposed in the documents, had grave consequences for Manning. It gave political cover to the military court-marshal which accused her of 'aiding the enemy' – a section of the Espionage Act (1917) which carries the death penalty. Although eventually thrown out by the military judge who heard the case, it set the tenor of the proceedings. Instead of this being a case of illegal disclosure of information, the military charged Manning with being a traitor, putting her on trial for her life. Harvard Law Professor Yochai Benkler, who testified in Private Manning's defence, criticised 'the prosecution's effort to launch the most dangerous assault on investigative journalism and the free press in the area of national security that we have seen in decades'.[8]

Just what was the calibre of the information she received which so threatened the security of the US? All the documents released to WikiLeaks were either Secret, Confidential or unclassified and though Secret may sound significant it is not a particularly high classification used by the military and intelligence communities. Yet Clinton was only too keen to give the impression that Manning had run off with extremely high-grade military intelligence.

It was another matter entirely in 2016 when Clinton herself was under investigation by the FBI for using an insecure server to send and receive classified State Department and White House emails. The whole question of the security of classified information suddenly seemed not so important. Questioned by the FBI about an email she had sent shortly after the release of the Cablegate documents, Clinton told the FBI she recalled the time period of the WikiLeaks disclosures because it was a 'difficult time for [the] State'[Department]. She said she had spent long hours on the phone with foreign diplomats addressing the WikiLeaks disclosures and ensuring 'no one was in danger as a result of the disclosures'.[9]

It was a distinct and meaningful change in Clinton's language: lives were no longer in danger because she was ensuring that. It placed her much closer to the sentiments of Defense Secretary Robert Gates who at the time of the disclosures in 2010, while Clinton was warning of the damage, played down the impact of Manning's leaks:

> I've heard the impact of these releases on our foreign policy described as a meltdown, as a game-changer, and so on. I think those descriptions are fairly significantly overwrought. Is this embarrassing? Yes. Is it awkward? Yes. Consequences for U.S. foreign policy? I think fairly modest.[10]

Since Manning worked in a branch of military security in the organisation which Gates headed, it is perhaps understandable he would make light of the leaks. But others, with less to lose, had a similar view: Brigadier General Robert Carr, a senior counter-intelligence officer who headed the Information Review Task Force that investigated the impact of WikiLeaks disclosures on behalf of the Defense Department, told Manning's court hearing that they had uncovered no specific examples of anyone who had lost his or her life in reprisals that followed the publication of the disclosures on the internet. To understand why Manning was given such a long jail sentence it is important to take into account that she was tried by a military court. A Congressional Research Service report 'Military Justice: Courts-Martial, an Overview', points out the essential difference: In the civil criminal system 'some basic objectives are to discover the truth, acquit the innocent without unnecessary delay or expense, punish the guilty proportionately with their crimes, and prevent and deter further crime, thereby providing for the public order'. The report points out that although 'Military justice shares these objectives in part' there was one important difference, it 'also serves to enhance discipline throughout the armed forces', which it said served the overall objective of providing an 'effective national defense'.[11]

As Fred Kaplan, author of *Dark Territory: The Secret History of Cyber War*, pointed out, 'By that standard, a member of the U.S. armed forces who violates military law is to be punished to the max, regardless of its consequences.'[12]

In the final news conference of his presidency Obama cut across that military legal doctrine to address his decision to commute Manning's sentence: 'Let's be clear: Chelsea Manning has served a tough prison sentence,' he said. It made sense to commute – and not pardon – her sentence. Obama said he felt very comfortable that justice had been served and that 'a message [had] still been sent'.[13] Few would disagree that the reduction in sentence from 35 years to seven has sent a message; the question is: what exactly was that message?

The House speaker Paul Ryan, a Republican, railed against the decision: 'President Obama now leaves in place a dangerous precedent that those who compromise our national security won't be held accountable for their crimes.'[14]

The chairman of the Senate Armed Service Committee, Republican Senator John McCain said he was 'stunned'.

'President Obama's commutation of Chelsea Manning's sentence is a grave mistake that I fear will encourage further acts of espionage . . .'[15]

Exactly what form that 'espionage' would take was never debated. Perhaps Obama, fearful of what the incoming administration would attempt to do to human rights and freedom of speech, had reverted to his pre-presidential self when he spoke passionately against overly intrusive surveillance, and believed the state needed to be transparent and held to account. As far back as 2003, as a senate candidate, he called the Patriot Act, which gave far reaching powers to the intelligence agencies to gather personal information on US citizens, 'shoddy and dangerous'.[16]

In 2008, Senator Barack Obama promised that, if elected president, he would run the most transparent administration in history and would champion the cause of whistle-blowers. 'Such acts of courage and patriotism . . . should be encouraged rather than stifled' Obama said.[17] Obama was particularly opposed to the power of the intelligence agencies to act without sufficient oversight.

Whatever the truth of that, Obama had certainly blunted the military's harsh sentence and sent a clear signal to whistle-blowers that he believed if you act in all good conscience and admit your crimes, you will not be overly punished just because you were serving your country at the time, though seven years in jail is hardly an incentive. But Obama's decision went further than that. It also gave legitimacy to WikiLeaks, which had led the campaign for Manning to be released, and strengthened the political and moral arguments of every whistle-blower. The contradiction in Obama's position is that he did not pardon Edward Snowden, who had done more than any whistle-blower to expose the wrongdoing of the intelligence agencies and caused a change in US laws. The decision to release Manning was a political call; so too was the decision to abandon Snowden. In an effort to describe why Snowden was being treated differently, Obama and his Attorney General at the time, Eric Holder, were reduced to doing legal hand-stands. Holder made this extraordinary admission while being interviewed by David Axelrod, Obama's former chief of staff, on 'The Axe Files', a podcast produced by CNN and the University of Chicago Institute of Politics, 'We can certainly argue about the way in which Snowden did what he did, but I think that he actually performed a public service by raising the debate that we engaged in and by the changes that we made.'[18]

And he went further: 'I think in deciding what an appropriate sentence should be, I think a judge could take into account the usefulness of having had that national debate.'[19]

But Holder was either not thinking, or at best being disingenuous as he spoke to the mainly young audience:

> I think that he's got to make a decision. He's broken the law in my view. He needs to get lawyers, come on back, and decide, see what he wants to do: Go to trial, try to cut a deal. I think there has to be a consequence for what he has done.' Snowden has always said he would return to the United States to put his case if he could be guaranteed a 'fair trial'. But as he pointed out: 'The Espionage Act does not permit a public interest defense. You're not allowed to speak the word "whistle-blower" at trial.'[20]

Even so, this reversion to a more engaged policy on whistle-blowers, despite its obvious shortcomings, did signal a shift back, at least in public thinking, to the more open and democratic policy which had helped sweep Obama to power in 2008. The orthodox view is that in office, Obama, ever the conciliator and pragmatist, seems to have buckled under the awesome responsibility of protecting the US from another 9/11. The turning point, it has been widely reported, came in December 2009.

On a cold Christmas eve Umar Farouk Abdulmutallab, a 25-year-old engineer, changed planes at Amsterdam's Shimpol Airport. He had travelled from Nigeria and was still dressed for warmer weather, but the transit lounge air conditioning shielded him from the near-zero temperature outside as he boarded Norwest Airlines Flight 253 headed for Detroit. Once on board he spent more time than the others watching the flight path map as the aircraft made its way across the North Atlantic Ocean. Following orders he had been given in Yemen by Al-Qaeda, he waited until the aircraft passed into US airspace before heading for the toilet. There he mixed up an explosive device he had smuggled on board in his hand luggage. He strapped it to his inner thigh and returned to his seat. As the plane prepared to descend passengers heard a pop and smelt smoke; some saw fire emerging from under the blanket which Abdulmutallab had draped across his lap.

He had tried to blow up the aircraft. If the bomb had exploded properly it could have ripped a hole in the side of the aircraft, dooming all on board and doing immeasurable damage below. What the 'underwear' bomber, as he became known, had exposed was not just lax airport security, but a huge hole in the security intelligence network which is supposed to pick up likely terrorists and stop them from boarding aircraft. Just a few weeks earlier Abdulmutallab 's father had received a phone call from his son saying it would be the last time they would talk. The father, fearing his son, who was calling from Yemen, had been radicalised, called the US Embassy in the Nigerian capital, Abuja. According to ABC America News, the Embassy brought him in to meet the CIA station chief. The information was duly passed on and incorporated to the Terrorist Identities Datamart Environment (TIDE), which contains about 550,000 individuals and is maintained by the Office of the Director of National Intelligence at the National Counterterrorism Center. TIDE is a catch-all list into which all terrorist-related information is sent. Some, but not all, information from TIDE is transferred to the FBI-maintained Terrorist Screening Data Base (TSDB), from which airline watch lists are drawn. The Transportation Security Administration has a 'no-fly' list of about 4,000 people who are prohibited from boarding any domestic or U.S.-bound aircraft.

Umar Farouk Abdulmutallab's name never made it past the TIDE database. A TIDE record on Abdulmutallab was created in November 2009, one US administration official said, but 'there was insufficient information available on the subject at that time to include him in the TSDB or its "no fly" lists'.[21]

The issue of vital information from highly reliable sources (in this case the bomber's father) not being adequately dealt with by the existing counter-terrorism agencies in the West, has been a recurring theme ever since 9/11: credible intelligence warned the US to expect an attack but it was not taken seriously. Obama described the failure to stop Umar Farouk Abdulmutallab as a 'systemic failure'.[22] These kind of intelligence oversights, where warnings and even evidence were ignored, became a regular occurrence as acts of terrorism began to dominate the public debate. Less than one year into his presidency, Obama appeared to be rattled. According to Ryan Lizza, writing in the New Yorker, many intelligence officials believed that the underwear bomber marked a turning point for Obama on whistle-blowing and surveillance. 'The White House people felt it in their gut with a visceralness that they did not before,' Michael Leiter, who was then the director of the National Counterterrorism Center, said. The Center was sharply criticised for not detecting the attack. 'It's not that they thought terrorism was over and it was done with' Lizza quoted Leiter as saying, 'but until you experience your first concrete attack on the homeland, not to mention one that becomes a huge political firestorm – that changes your outlook really quickly'.[23]

Under attack for being weak on security, from this point on Obama abandoned his long-held opposition to mass surveillance which had helped forge such a strong relationship with Oregon's Senator Ron Wyden, a long-time member of the Senate select committee on intelligence and long-time critic of security agency over-reach. Obama did still increase whistle-blower protection for some government employees, but left those in the intelligence agencies out in the cold. They were prohibited from going to the media with their grievances, even as a last resort. The secret world would remain locked away from public view, a policy reinforced by the failure of the security agencies to properly identify Umar Farouk Abdulmutallab as a serious threat to the US. Abdulmutallab was a significant example of what could go wrong. Even in its first year of office it was embarrassing for a political party to be accused, perhaps wrongly but nevertheless repeatedly, of being weak on security. As the administration cast about to find an example which would prove their robust commitment to national security, they came up with a perfect target. It sent a strong signal to one of their most hated media outlets.

Like any Washington-based representative of a major news outlet in the US, James Rosen of Rupert Murdoch's Fox News has a small cubicle office in the Department of State building – the Harry S. Truman Building. This kind of arrangement is mutually beneficial: the government has the journalists on hand to feed them information, and the journalists have the chance to question the government.

But the journalists there, James Rosen included, understood the real business was not the press briefings, which are available to all, but the extra information they can garner from others – especially the public officials who speak on behalf of the State Department before the cameras and then afterwards brief off-the-record to their favoured reporters. The State Department's press office is also keen to help, putting reporters in touch with the right people.

As a way of explaining government policy on containing North Korea the press office decided to put one of the best nuclear arms experts in the world, Stephen Jin-Woo Kim, in contact with a member of the press pool. Kim worked in the Bureau of Verification, Compliance, and Implementation (VCI), which monitors the development of all WMDs, including nuclear. Here the best and the brightest scientists that the State Department can assemble are gathered together to provide highly classified analysis and advice to the secretary of state and assistant secretaries whose job it is to deal with policy detail. Banks of terminals access documents from the NSA, the CIA and a myriad of other intelligence agencies, classified beyond Top Secret to Sensitive Compartmented Information (SCI) – information restricted on a need-to-know basis. Material so sensitive even those with a Top-Secret clearance may be refused access.

The person chosen to be background briefed by Kim was Fox News' James Rosen. By the middle of 2009 events on the Korean peninsula were increasingly demanding the attention of the State Department. Two journalists working for Current TV – former Democrat presidential contender Al Gore's media company – were on trial in North Korea for crossing into the country without a visa; stiff penalties were likely for the pair. The North had just conducted a nuclear test and the UN Security Council was deciding whether or not to introduce sanctions against the regime of Kim Jong-Il. Rosen decided to gather information for a story, but this time he would by-pass the State Department press office. Instead he would go straight to Kim, setting up a covert system of communication. It is difficult to understand how someone like Rosen, who had written a book on Watergate, could have made so many basic errors in handling a source but, as became apparent, he did.

He described a system of codes to be used so the two could communicate. An email containing one asterisk would indicate a need to contact the other person 'or that previously agreed plans for communication are to proceed as agreed'; two asterisks meant 'the opposite': no contact should be made and any other arrangements which had been made were now cancelled.[24]

When he later created a secret email account to contact Kim, Rosen looked to the players in the Watergate saga for a false name. What's intriguing is that where most journalists might appropriate the mantle of Bernstein or his fellow Watergate reporter, Bob Woodward, as an alias, Rosen chose the name of Nixon's deputy assistant, Alexander Butterfield, and signed his emails 'Alex'. Forty years ago, Butterfield recorded all of Nixon's Oval Office discussions, using technology that now seems incredibly outmoded. These days people with surveillance tools document far more than just conversations. But all this seemed to be beyond Rosen as he wrote to 'Leo', the alias Kim used.

Rosen bluntly states his case: 'What I am interested in, as you might expect, is breaking news ahead of my competitors.'[25] He says he wants to report authoritatively on new initiatives or shifts in US policy and events on the ground in North Korea, 'what intelligence is picking up, etc'.[26] He also would like to know 'maybe on the basis of internal memos'[27] what action the US is planning for North Korea. Playing to Kim's genuine concern to alert the American public to the perils of a nuclear-armed North Korea, which so clearly threatened the country of his birth, Rosen wrote urging action.

> In short, let's break some news and expose muddle-headed policy when we see it – or force the administration's hand to go in the right direction, if possible. The only way to do this is to EXPOSE the policy, or what the North Korea is up to, and the only way to do that authoritatively is with EVIDENCE.[28]

The fact that Rosen was playing on what he assessed as Kim's desire to expose the North was blatant. Understanding what motivates a source to reveal information can often be used as a key to extract more. For example, the reason why the deputy director of the FBI Mark Felt, later revealed by Bob Woodward as his Deep Throat informant, decided to reveal such damaging information about President Richard Nixon may well have been because he saw a crooked president who needed to be brought to account. It may equally well have been because Felt was angered that Nixon had passed him over to take over as head of the FBI when Edgar Hoover died. Whatever the reason, the way that Rosen dealt with his source was very different from the caution used by Woodward.

On 9 June, 2009 at about 10.15 am Rosen called Kim's phone in the high-security area of the VCI and left a message. At 10.17 am Kim called Rosen and the two spoke for approximately 11 minutes. Within minutes of the release of an intelligence report on North Korea to members of the intelligence community, classified in the special compartmentalised category beyond Top Secret, Kim called Rosen: at 11.18 am. They spoke for four minutes. At 11.24 am Kim called Rosen again. The call lasted 18 seconds. Two and a half minutes later Kim logged on to his secure computer and accessed the intelligence report at 11.27 am. At 11.37 am, with Kim again logged in to the intelligence report, he called Rosen on his desk phone, where he apparently left a message before calling Rosen's cell-phone. Rosen and Kim could not have left a clearer set of electronic fingerprints. At a little after midday they compounded the problem. When Kim walked through the security door of the entrance to the State Department on 2201 C Street in the north-west of Washington, his identity card automatically registered him leaving. The time was 12.02. One minute later James Rosen left the building through the same door. Like Kim's, his exact time of departure was recorded. At 12.26 pm Kim walked back into the building. Four minutes later he was joined by Rosen. Later that afternoon James Rosen gave Fox News what it wanted - an exclusive story on North Korea:

> U.S. intelligence officials have warned President Obama and other senior American officials that North Korea intends to respond to the passage of a UN Security Council resolution this week – condemning the communist country for its recent nuclear and ballistic missile tests – with another nuclear test.[29]

It was hardly an earth-shattering revelation and few, if any other news organisations followed the Fox story. North Korea had in the past responded to action against it by detonating nuclear weapons. It would have been more of a story – news in the real sense – if the North had decided to do nothing in response to planned UN sanctions. It was Rosen's attempt to boost this mediocre story with details about the source which caused so much damage.

In the second paragraph Rosen revealed 'the Central Intelligence Agency has learned, through sources inside North Korea'[30] about the planned nuclear response. The problem with the story wasn't that it should not have been published but that by specifically identifying the CIA as a source of the information on North Korea, it pointed the finger at the people who had access to the above top-secret intelligence report, which had just been released. By a process of elimination, the FBI established that of the 95 people who had accessed the intelligence report on the day that Rosen's story appeared, only Kim had had contact with Rosen. Matched with the electronic fingerprints that Rosen and Kim had left behind with their frequent contact, it was only a matter of time before the FBI came knocking on the door.

After piecing together Kim's phone records as well as his access to the computer and his contact with Rosen, the FBI was sure that it had its suspected leaker.

But instead of stopping there, the Department of Justice (DOJ) – which was directing the investigation – wanted to send a powerful warning to journalists: when it came to security leaks, they were not necessarily protected by the First Amendment. The Obama administration was ramping up its assault on leakers by attacking those who benefited from the leaks: journalists.

With this new focus on leaking, the hunt took the FBI to previously uncharted territory for a security investigation: a journalist's personal email account. The search warrant, served on Google's high-tech showpiece headquarters overlooking San Francisco Bay, demanded access to information the FBI knew lay hidden in far less prosaic surroundings, the large shed-like structures that are home to Google's servers, dotted across the US. The affidavit lodged with the US District Court in Washington wanted 'subscriber information records and the contents of limited wire and electronic communications pertaining to the account'.[31] The FBI – working under the instruction of the DOJ – wanted to leave no doubt it believed that Rosen had acted like a spy. It argued that Rosen had behaved 'much like an intelligence officer would run a clandestine intelligence source'.[32] It said that 'From the beginning of their relationship, the Reporter asked, solicited and encouraged Mr. Kim to disclose sensitive United States internal documents and intelligence information . . .'[33] By framing the request in this way, the FBI was arguing that Rosen was no longer protected by the First Amendment. Now Rosen could be prosecuted under the Espionage Act. He had committed a crime, and evidence that he was a 'conspirator and/or aider and abettor'[34] was likely to be contained within his Gmail correspondence. The FBI argued that the Gmail account fell squarely within the exemption, permitting searches of media-related work product materials, even when possessed by a national news reporter, because there is 'probable cause to believe that the person possessing such materials has committed or is committing the criminal offense to which the materials relate'.[35] Once the FBI had Rosen in its sights, public sympathy was with the reporter. Glossed over – at least for the time being – was the question of the responsibility that reporters have not only to protect their sources but to protect their sources from themselves. What happened shifted the ground in the long-established procedures governing reporter–source relationships, built up over decades in the US. It is a side effect of the protection under the First Amendment afforded to reporters that – at least until the Kim case – only the source could be in danger of being prosecuted under the Espionage Act. It could make journalists lazy about source protection, since their lives or careers were seldom in danger.

James Rosen, who had used flattery, charm, and the potential promise of a glamorous role in a think tank to entice an émigré who had worked tirelessly for the US, had written a story which warned the despotic regime of North Korea that it had possibly been penetrated by the CIA. As is often the case, the highest principles are frequently fought for using the worst example. Rosen would become the poster boy of press freedom. For the first time, it appeared that a journalist might be charged under the Espionage Act. So, what had made the Obama White House – and the DOJ – so angry and fearful about leaking?

Just 24 hours earlier, on 27 May, at Forward Operating Base Hammer, east of Baghdad, US Military Police had arrested Chelsea (Bradley) Manning and it had dawned on the administration that the leaking of the source material of Collateral Murder – the shocking video of the gunship killing – was not a one-off event. As they rifled through Manning's computer, the US military discovered evidence that a cache of information had also been copied. It would soon be published as the Afghan War Diary and Iraq War Logs, along with hundreds of thousands of State Department Cablegate communications.

While Kim was arrested, tried and jailed for 13 months, his career in ruins, the state of outrage across the political spectrum, from the New York Times to News Corporation, stopped the case against Rosen. He managed to escape prosecution because the offence was relatively minor, but while the government retreated on one front, it continued pursuing a much bigger journalistic quarry: James Risen. Although he might have a similar name to the Fox News presenter, that's where the similarity ends. Whereas James Rosen worked for the Murdoch organisation, James Risen was a star reporter with the New York Times. Risen is best remembered as the reporter who had two of his exposés blocked from publication at the behest of the George W. Bush White House – on national security grounds. The first story – of how the NSA spied on Americans – was eventually published by the paper, but Risen's second story, which was equally sensitive – about how the CIA became involved in sending blueprints for a nuclear bomb to Iran – never graced the pages of the New York Times. The story was killed after then National Security Advisor Condoleezza Rice told the newspaper's editors disclosure of the mission threatened US national security. It was not until 2006 that Risen managed to get the story out; it was included in his book about the Bush administration titled State of War: The Secret History of the CIA and the Bush Administration (Simon & Schuster, New York). State of War takes the reader through a plot by the CIA to plant fake blueprints for a nuclear bomb with the Iranian government. If it came off it would dramatically set back any plans by Tehran to put together a nuclear weapon. As though playing out a modern-day version of the Cold War classic, The Third Man, the CIA decided to run their operation in the world's most notorious spy capital, Vienna. To add a further dash of drama, they used a Russian scientist who had recently defected to the West to be the courier for the bomb plans. The problem was the scientist was smarter than the CIA thought. When he saw the blueprints he noticed that they contained a major and obvious flaw which would stop the bomb working properly. What the CIA did not know at the time was that the scientist, in an effort to protect himself from any Iranian revenge, opened the envelope containing the blueprints and slipped a handwritten note inside pointing out that they were faulty. So, it seems the Iranians – and their intelligence agencies – knew they had been given a dud; the Russian knew it; the CIA knew it. The only people who were kept in the dark about the CIA's incompetence were the American public.

The source of Risen's information was almost certainly former CIA officer Jeffrey Sterling, an African American, found guilty in January 2015 of breaches of the 1917 Espionage Act. Sterling worked as a CIA officer in the Far East and South Asia section of the agency and later took up a position recruiting Iranian nationals to work for the agency to gather information on Iran's weapons capabilities. Sterling had left the CIA complaining bitterly he had been passed over for promotion because of his colour. Risen then wrote a story for the *New York Times* about Sterling's claim. Later, as explained in *The War on Journalism* (Penguin Random House, 2015) he gathered information about the Iranian bomb hoax; the two of them left a string of electronic markers across the Washington telephone and email networks which revealed dozens of conversations over the years.

Many legal commentators believe there was more than enough electronic evidence to bring Sterling to court and convict him of being the source. Unlike Rosen, who was not prosecuted and was not called to give evidence at Kim's trial, the DOJ subpoenaed Risen. They ordered him to appear before the court to be questioned on whether Sterling was his source. If Risen would not reveal who gave him the information he ran the risk of being jailed for contempt of court.

The DOJ had found another way to attack journalists who disclosed sensitive information about the government. They did not need to be directly charged under the Espionage Act.

The US government had sent an unequivocal message to whistle-blowers and journalists that there was no place to hide from electronic surveillance: every phone call, every mobile phone tower, every electronic tag and every email could be used to track their movements. Snowden had yet to reveal the extent of the state's intrusive powers but to all but the casual observer the Risen and Rosen cases produced stark examples of how electronic surveillance made any form of investigative journalism a harrowing and dangerous pursuit. The very system that allowed gigabytes of information to be downloaded could be turned against the leaker – and those who published that information. In this post 9/11 world it was not just the US administration that was clamping down on journalists and their sources. Across the Atlantic in the UK, where BBC reporter Andrew Gilligan had exposed the fraudulent claim that Britain could be under attack in 45 minutes from Saddam Hussein's missiles, the government understood that prosecuting a journalist might not be too politically popular; outing the whistle-blower who told him would be just as effective in attacking opposition to the Iraq war.

Dr David Kelly, a British government expert in biological warfare and WMD, told the government he had spoken to Gilligan – something well within his normal sphere of activities in backgrounding journalists. As a Parliamentary House of Commons Committee began investigating the details of the Iraqi WMD's so-called 'sexed up' dossier which contained the 45 minute warning, Tony Blair's media manager, Alistair Campbell, made a diary entry that he needed to 'open up a flank on the BBC' to distract attention from his difficulties over the dossier.[36]

Just why he chose the BBC to attack is explained by Paul Lashmar, who was working for the *Independent on Sunday* newspaper and producing similar reports to Gilligan's, questioning the dossier's authenticity. 'We were saying . . . it's politicised. They're up to no good.' But Campbell went after the BBC because it was a target and importantly 'it was definitive', Lashmar said. It paved the way for other reporters to be able to say 'that's why they wanted a war with the BBC'.[37]

Campbell, a former journalist, knew more than most about how sources could be used, and abused.

The way in which the government dealt with Kelly was, perhaps not surprisingly, inconsistent with the way it dealt with the source that provided the twisted information which supported its argument for war. Whereas it kept secret the source of its misinformation which deceived the public into believing the UK was under direct threat, it lured a truthful source into a trap. Kelly had identified himself to his supervisors at the Ministry of Defence as having spoken to Gilligan but he told them he could not have been his only source. When the Ministry of Defence (MoD) press officers announced that a source had come forward, they began handing out 'clues allowing journalists to guess who he was'.[38] They confirmed Kelly's name to any reporter who guessed right. According to Gilligan, one newspaper was allowed to put more than 20 names to the MoD before it got to Dr Kelly's.

Once outed, Kelly became the victim of a sustained attack by the foreign secretary, Jack Straw. Called before the Foreign Affairs Committee, he was questioned about which journalists he had met. A few days later Kelly walked out of his Oxfordshire home and would never return. His body was discovered the next morning in the nearby woods. A corner found that he committed suicide by ingesting 29 analgesic tablets and slashing his left wrist.

In the delicate relationship between journalists, governments and their sources, the case of Kelly raised many questions. Much of the criticism of Gilligan was that Kelly had not used the words 'sexed up', but had simply agreed to the description. And who had actually sexed up the document in the first place? What we do know is that Campbell repeatedly demanded the intelligence assessments be changed to better reflect the case for war and that the 45-minute warning was not seen as credible by the intelligence agencies. Yet by the end of the affair, the BBC Director General had resigned after an early investigation chaired by Lord Hutton had found against the organisation in what many saw as a whitewash of government policy on Iraq, Gilligan had left the BBC and the person who blew the whistle on the fraudulent 'evidence' had been humiliated and killed himself. Clear and unambiguous protection for whistle-blowers acting in the public interest could not have been more clearly shown to be a necessary brake on the overpowering authority of the executive. As Jennifer Robinson, the WikiLeaks lawyer, remarked, 'We think we live under the rule of law, but when push comes to shove, the hypocrisy of the West when it comes to certain standards when it suits them, is quite breath-taking'.[39]

Unlike Britain and America, in Europe, especially in France, journalists have long accepted the inevitability of state intrusion into their work. At *Le Monde* Yves Eudes, one of the first journalists to recognise the significance of WikiLeaks and interview Assange, told me: 'I never assumed that my communication on the internet or the good old telephone were safe.'[40]

On 4 January, 2010, the French National Assembly met to discuss a law which would go some way to calm the fears of Eudes and other journalists who daily speak to sources who prefer to remain anonymous. On that cold winter's day with the temperature outside never above freezing, the deputies decided to create a greater distinction between the church, the state, the judiciary and the fourth estate. They passed into law an amendment which guaranteed freedom of the press, bringing France into line with the ruling of the European Court of Human Rights (ECHR), which regularly condemned attempts to compel journalists to disclose their sources. The ECHR systematically relied on the right to 'freedom to receive or impart information or ideas without interference by public authorities', as stipulated in Article Ten of the Convention on the Rights of Man. The French law went even further.

Supported by President Nicholas Sarkozy and his prime minister, Francois Fillon, it stated: 'Le secret des sources des journalistes est protégé dans l'exercice de leur mission d'information du public.' ['The confidentiality of journalists' sources is protected in the exercise of their mission of informing the public.']⁴¹

The law did not provide complete protection, though. For example, the secrecy of sources could be directly or indirectly over-ridden if there was an 'un impératif prépondérant d'intérêt public' ['overriding imperative in the public interest'.]⁴² No matter which way that part of the law was interpreted, it would be thin ground for a defence of what happened nine months later. There would be no public interest, only personal gain for the President of the Republic, Nicholas Sarkozy and his political party.

On 7 July, 2010, the French news site, Mediapart, published astonishing details about France's richest woman, Lilliane Bettencourt, heiress to the L'Oreal company. Her former accountant told Mediapart that Conservative MPs had been regular visitors to the Bettencourt villa in the swish 15ᵗʰ arrondissement on the western side of Paris where they had been given envelopes stuffed with cash. The money had been paid in €10,000, €20,000, €50,000 and even €100,000 bundles. But what was even more sensational was the claim that Sarkozy had been one of the regular visitors. 'Sarkozy got his envelopes too,'⁴³ Mediapart quoted the accountant as saying. The Elysée Palace denied the claim as 'a libel that aims only to smear without the slightest basis in reality'.⁴⁴ According to Mediapart founder Edwy Plenel, the Mediapart journalists who first unearthed the scandal surrounding Bettencourt – allegations of tax evasion as well as political donations – had for months been under surveillance in an operation controlled by the Elysée Palace. Plenel also said agents from France's domestic intelligence service (DCRI) had even analysed the mobile phone records of two of his journalists to precisely map out their network of contacts and tracked their movements, pinpointing their whereabouts by using GPS coordinates provided by their mobile phones.

The fact that Plenel backed the report gave it added credibility. He has a long and distinguished record as an investigative journalist. At Le Monde in the 1980s he exposed state terrorism: the bombing of the Greenpeace Rainbow Warrior in

New Zealand's Auckland Harbour by French intelligence agents. Earlier he had been a target of a special team assigned by former president Francois Mitterrand to tap his phone after he exposed how the police had framed terrorist suspects known as the Irish of Vincennes.

The publication by Mediapart, with its influential online circulation, was a major irritation for Sarkozy, but a few days later on 17 July, 2010, Le Monde journalist Gerard Davet produced a report which gave the material a mainstream profile. It also added significant details about the relationship between Bettencourt's wealth manager, and Eric Woerth, the former Minister of Labour and treasurer of Sarkozy's political party, the UMP.

Within hours of the newspaper publishing the story, the head of French counterintelligence, Direction centrale du reseignement intérieur (DCRI), the equivalent of MI5 or the FBI, received a phone call. Getting ready to attend a wedding, Bernard Squarcini was relaxing in the Corsican village where he was born, when the director general of the National Police told him of Le Monde's report.

Within minutes Squarcini called his deputy in Paris and they hatched a plan to catch the leaker, but instead of going through the normal channels and asking permission from the National Commission of the Interceptions of Security (NCIS), they targeted Davet directly and unknown to him, demanded copies of his telephone bills for the previous four days from the telecommunications provider, Orange. Armed with the information the police began trawling through the list of people Davet had spoken to, using his mobile phone to track his movements. It was not long before their suspicion fell on a senior advisor to the Justice Ministry, whose name was on the list of phone numbers contacted by Davet. Though David Senat denied being the source, within six weeks of the story appearing he had moved from the inner sanctum of the Justice Department to take up a new job on the outskirts of Paris administering a court in one of France's far-flung territories, Guiana on the south American east coast. And though Senat has never been officially identified as the source, within weeks of his demotion Le Monde filed an action against the head of the agency, Squarcini, a close confidant of Sarkozy. Le Monde accused Squarcini of breaking the law which protected journalists' source. The interception, which was used to identify the source inside the Justice Ministry was 'a reckless violation of the law on the secrecy of sources that had been solemnly adopted in January 2010 by the National Assembly'.[45]

French authorities denied any involvement in spying. The former minister of the interior, Brice Hortefeux, joked that the DCRI 'was not the Stasi'.[46] Claude Guéant, a close Sarkozy associate and minister of the interior, even sued the independent website Mediapart after it accused him of ordering the interception of the Monde journalist's phone records. The complaint was discreetly dropped on 30 June, 2011, Le Monde reported.

For his part, Squarcini denied breaking the law, saying the target was not the press but the civil servant who was guilty of giving information to the reporter and possibly posed a threat to national security. But he admitted that his organisation had demanded and received Davet's telephone records directly from

Orange – bypassing the normal procedure of seeking the approval of the National Advisory Committee on Security Intercepts (CNCIS).

Squarcini argued that the agency's actions were legal, covered by a law which allowed it to intercept electromagnetic communications, – and that mobile phone calls fell into that category. A key piece of incriminating evidence involved the fact that Davet's phone records had not been swept up as part of the inquiry to find the leaker. In fact the Monde journalist had been deliberately targeted in an attempt to find his source. The court ruled that Squarcini was guilty of 'illegally collecting data and violating the confidentiality'[47] of sources and ordered to e pay an €8000 fine. By the time the court ruling was handed down France had a new government, Squarcini had resigned – and socialist President Francois Hollande was promising that under the new regime France could expect the rule of law to prevail. Few journalists in France believed it would last for long, given the history of French governments' use of electronic interception to track journalists.

At Le Monde's glass-walled headquarters on the Boulevard Auguste-Blanqui on the fringe of the Parisian Latin quarter, quiet celebrations marked the victory over the intelligence agency. The guilty verdict convinced even those who had frowned on the idea that journalists needed to treat security seriously to protect both themselves and their informants. Now they embraced the concept that the type of systems used by the state to spy on them could be turned around and used to protect both journalist and whistle-blower. According to Eudes French journalists were very 'sceptical of encryption devices and encryption software, [but] now they are beginning to learn'.[48] Le Monde had appointed a special employee whose job it is to 'evangelise'[49] the issue of journalistic and source security. 'This is what's changing and the journalists are coming round. and people are starting to understand.'[50] It was Eudes idea to set up a secure drop box, so that whistle-blowers could directly and anonymously connect to Le Monde journalists. These systems had long been in use in the US and the UK, but in France and much of Europe the notion of anonymising contact with informants is only now being fully embraced The Fadettes [itemised telephone bill] case, as it became known, seemed to change that, invigorating the French media as they came to terms with an even tougher working environment. The vexed issue confronting Le Monde was: how could the newspaper provide simple and effective security for both the whistle-blower and the journalist? There was little room for error which could damage the newspaper's reputation. Fresh in the minds of Le Monde's management was the spectacular failure of the Wall Street Journal's SafeHouse site, which had security issues allowing third parties to intercept submissions. Within hours of its launch it was described by one encryption analyst as a 'total anonymity failure' that could compromise the security of whistle-blowers.[51] Jacob Appelbaum, a developer of Tor, described the Journal as 'negligent'.[52]

Media organisations had great trouble in bringing their technology divisions and editorial staff together to solve common problems. For the computer experts, it was a usual procedure to run a trial Beta version – as the Wall Street Journal had done – to sort out the bugs, but it is clear little thought was given to what might happen to the whistle-blower if those 'bugs' caused a leak of information from the site. Laws specifically protecting sources, like those in France and Iceland for example, could help, but a secure drop box, run by an individual news site, was an attractive option. The problem of how to create an off-the-shelf drop box was finally solved by an until recently little known organisation, GlobaLeaks. Developed by the Hermes Centre for Transparency and Digital Human rights, an Italian-based not-for-profit organisation supporting freedom of speech online, GlobaLeaks provides secure source protection for journalists and non-government workers. Sitting at a small restaurant in a bustling square in the centre of Rome, Fabio Pietrosanti, who conceived the original idea, told me that he created GlobaLeaks to counter the problems that he saw with WikiLeaks, a centralised system operating mainly in English, and other systems which had vulnerable security. GlobaLeaks, he pointed out, was designed to help journalists who did not have advanced computer skills, but who needed a secure platform to protect their sources. 'WikiLeaks showcased the "power of digital whistleblowing activism, bringing technology activism and journalism together,"'Pietrosanti said.[53] As the late Gavin MacFadyen, founder-director of both the London's Centre for Investigative Journalism and the Courage Foundation, which supports whistle-blowers including Snowden, said, 'J.A. [Julian Assange] opened the door'[54] by creating a submissions system which was adapted by others. What GlobaLeaks aimed to do was to take that concept and allow individual journalists, newspapers and television stations to have their own secure drop boxes. Unlike WikiLeaks it would be decentralised. Anyone could download the technology and set up a site. Though there was always the possibility of fake news sites being established, dealing with established media names or known organisations would come as near to guaranteeing anonymity as was possible. There were other important issues for whistle-blowers to be aware of. Though GlobaLeaks recommend the anonymiser Tor as a first step before connecting and sending in a submission, that too could have its problems in a country where communication systems were poor and most people were forced to use internet cafes. In that case, as Pietrosante points out, it would be 'highly suspicious if you start using an anonymised tool in an internet café'.[55] One of the great benefits of the GlobaLeaks system was the openness of its developers to dealing with potential problems. They have recently been developing an education system where whistle-blowers will be given individual advice on the protective steps they can take, depending on where and in which country they are about to make their submission. Within months of being released GlobaLeaks had spread across the world, spawning a network of safer havens for journalists, activists and whistleblowers from Source Sûre in Europe, the site shared by Le Monde, Radio Telecom Switzerland (RTS), the news magazine L'OBS and a French language newspaper in Belgium, Le Soir, to Croatia, Africa, Mexico, South America, the Philippines and Amnesty International in Saudi Arabia. When Pietrosanti embarked on the programme in 2010 he could have had no idea how important anti-surveillance procedures would become for journalists. They would be under greater threat than ever before.

Notes

1 Trump, D. 26th January, 2017. *Twitter*. Available at https://twitter.com/realdonaldtrump/status/824573698774601729?lang=en [Accessed 1 February, 2017].
2 Zetter, K. 3rd December, 2012. *UN Torture Chief: Bradley Manning Treatment Cruel, Inhuman*. Wired [online]. Available at www.wired.com/2012/03/manning-treatment-inhuman/ [Accessed 31 July, 2016].
3 Zetter, K. 3rd December, 2012. *UN Torture Chief: Bradley Manning Treatment Cruel, Inhuman*. Wired [online]. Available at www.wired.com/2012/03/manning-treatment-inhuman/] [Accessed 20 August, 2016].
4 Manning, B. 1st March, 2013. *Bradley Manning's Statement to Court Marshall. Full Text*. The Guardian [online]. London. Available at www.theguardian.com/world/2013/mar/01/bradley-manning-wikileaks-statement-full-text [Accessed 22 August, 2016].
5 Manning, B. 1st March, 2013. *Bradley Manning's Statement to Court Marshall. Full Text*. The Guardian [online]. London. Available at www.theguardian.com/world/2013/mar/01/bradley-manning-wikileaks-statement-full-text [Accessed 22 August, 2016].
6 The Guardian [online]. London. Available at www.theguardian.com/world/2013/mar/01/bradley-manning-wikileaks-statement-full-text [Accessed 22 August, 2016].
7 Staff Reporters. 29th November, 2010. *Clinton Condemns Leak as Attack on International Community*. CNN [online]. Available at http://edition.cnn.com/2010/US/11/29/wikileaks/ [Accessed 30 August, 2016].
8 Savage, C. 30th July. *Manning in Acquitted of Aiding the Enemy*. The Washington Post [online]. Washington. Available at www.nytimes.com/2013/07/31/us/bradley-manning-verdict.html [Accessed 30 August, 2016].
9 Archive.Org. *Hilary R Clinton – Full FBI Emails from her Private Illegal Server*. Available at https://archive.org/stream/HillaryClintonFBIemails/1353814-0%20-%20HRC%20302%20-V2_djvu.txt [Accessed 29 August, 2016].
10 Bumiller, B. 1st December, 2010. *On Disclosures Yates Takes the Long View*. The New York Times [online]. New York. Available at http://query.nytimes.com/gst/fullpage.html?res=9C04E5D71E3CF932A35751C1A9669D8B63 [Accessed 26 June, 2016].
11 Mason, R. 12th August, 2013. *Military Justice: Courts-Martial, an Overview*. Library of Congress Washington DC Congressional Research Service [online]. Washington. Available at http://oai.dtic.mil/oai/oai?verb=getRecord&metadataPrefix=html&identifier=ADA584682 [Accessed 25 August, 2016].
12 Kaplan, F. 20th January, 2017. *Obama Was Right to Commute Chelsea Manning's Sentence*. Slate [online]. Available at www.slate.com/articles/news_and_politics/war_stories/2017/01/why_president_obama_was_right_to_grant_chelsea_manning_clemency.html [Accessed 28 June, 2016].
13 Kaplan, F. 20th January, 2017. *Obama Was Right to Commute Chelsea Manning's Sentence*. Slate [online]. Available at www.slate.com/articles/news_and_politics/war_stories/2017/01/why_president_obama_was_right_to_grant_chelsea_manning_clemency.html [Accessed 28 June, 2016].
14 Gerstein, J. and Wheaton, S. 17th January, 2017. *Obama Commutes Chelsea Manning's sentence*. Politico [online]. Available at www.politico.com/story/2017/01/obama-commutes-chelsea-mannings-sentence-233722 [Accessed 10 March, 2017].
15 Gerstein, J. and Wheaton, S. 17th January, 2017. *Obama Commutes Chelsea Manning's sentence*. Politico [online]. Available at www.politico.com/story/2017/01/obama-commutes-chelsea-mannings-sentence-233722 [Accessed 10 March, 2017].
16 Lizza, R. 16th December, 2013. *State of Deception*. The New Yorker [online]. New York. Available at www.newyorker.com/magazine/2013/12/16/state-of-deception [Accessed 10 October, 2016].
17 Press, E. 7th December, 2016. *Obama Leaves Trump a Mixed Legacy on Whistle-Blowers*. The New Yorker [online]. New York. Available at www.newyorker.com/news/daily-comment/obama-leaves-trump-a-mixed-legacy-on-whistle-blowers [Accessed 4 January, 2017].

18 Jaffre, M. 31st May, 2016. *Eric Holder Says Edeward Snowden Performed a 'Public Service'.* CNN [online]. Available at http://edition.cnn.com/2016/05/30/politics/axe-files-axelrod-eric-holder/ [Accessed 30 October, 2016].

19 Jaffre, M. 31st May, 2016. *Eric Holder Says Edward Snowden Performed a 'Public Service'.* CNN [online]. Available at http://edition.cnn.com/2016/05/30/politics/axe-files-axelrod-eric-holder/ [Accessed 30 October, 2016].

20 Jaffre, M. 31st May, 2016. *Eric Holder Says Edward Snowden Performed a 'Public Service'.* CNN [online]. Available at http://edition.cnn.com/2016/05/30/politics/axe-files-axelrod-eric-holder/ [Accessed 30 October, 2016].

21 Eggen, D., De Young, K., and Hsu, S. *Plane Suspect Was Listed in Terror Database After Father Alerted U.S. Officials.* The Washington Post. Available at www.washingtonpost.com/wp-dyn/content/article/2009/12/25/AR2009122501355_2.html?sid=ST2009122601151 [Accessed 28 March, 2017].

22 Hughes, D. and Radia, K. 31st December 2009. *Underwear Bomber's' Alarming Last Phone Call.* ABC News America [online]. Available at http://abcnews.go.com/WN/bombers-phone-call-father/story?id=9457361 [Accessed 10 February, 2017].

23 Lizza, R. 16th December, 2013. *State of Deception.* The New Yorker [online]. New York. Available at www.newyorker.com/magazine/2013/12/16/state-of-deception [Accessed 10 October, 2016].

24 The United States District Court for the District of Columbia. 2010. *Affidavit in Support of Application for Search Warrant 10-291-M-01. Copy held by Fowler, A.*

25 The United States District Court for the District of Columbia. 2010. *Affidavit in Support of Application for Search Warrant 10-291-M-01. Copy held by Fowler, A.*

26 The United States District Court for the District of Columbia. 2010. *Affidavit in Support of Application for Search Warrant 10-291-M-01. Copy held by Fowler, A.*

27 The United States District Court for the District of Columbia. 2010. *Affidavit in Support of Application for Search Warrant 10-291-M-01. Copy held by Fowler, A.*

28 The United States District Court for the District of Columbia. 2010. *Affidavit in Support of Application for Search Warrant 10-291-M-01. Copy held by Fowler, A.*

29 Rosen, J. 11th June, 2009. *NK's Post UN Sanctions Plans, Revealed.* Fox News [online]. Available at www.foxnews.com/politics/2009/06/11/nk-post-un-sanctions-plans-revealed [Accessed 26 August, 2016].

30 Rosen, J. 11th June, 2009. *NK's Post UN Sanctions Plans, Revealed.* Fox News [online]. Available at www.foxnews.com/politics/2009/06/11/nk-post-un-sanctions-plans-revealed [Accessed 26 August, 2016].

31 The United States District Court for the District of Columbia. 2010. *Affidavit in Support of Application for Search Warrant 10-291-M-01. Copy held by Fowler, A.*

32 The United States District Court for the District of Columbia. 2010. *Affidavit in Support of Application for Search Warrant 10-291-M-01. Copy held by Fowler, A.*

33 The United States District Court for the District of Columbia. 2010. *Affidavit in Support of Application for Search Warrant 10-291-M-01. Copy held by Fowler, A.*

34 The United States District Court for the District of Columbia. 2010. *Affidavit in Support of Application for Search Warrant 10-291-M-01. Copy held by Fowler, A.*

35 The United States District Court for the District of Columbia. 2010. *Affidavit in Support of Application for Search Warrant 10-291-M-01. Copy held by Fowler, A.*

36 Gilligan, A. 2nd July 2013. *The Betrayal of Dr David Kelly, 10 Years on.* Daily Telegraph [online]. London. Available at www.telegraph.co.uk/news/politics/10192271/The-betrayal-of-Dr-David-Kelly-10-years-on.html [Accessed 17 June, 2016].

37 Lashmar, P. August, 2016. *Interview.*

38 Gilligan, A. 2nd July 2013. *The Betrayal of Dr David Kelly, 10 Years on.* Daily Telegraph [online]. London. Available at www.telegraph.co.uk/news/politics/10192271/The-betrayal-of-Dr-David-Kelly-10-years-on.html [Accessed 17 June, 2016].

39 Robinson, J. August 2016. *Interview.*

40 Fowler, A. January, 2017. *Interview.*

41 L'Assemblee nationale et le Senat. 2010. *LOI n° 2010-1 du 4 janvier 2010 relative à la protection du secret des sources des journalistes*. Available at www.legifrance.gouv.fr/affichTexte.do?cidTexte=JORFTEXT000021601325&categorieLien=id [Accessed 12 November, 2016].

42 L'Assemblee nationale et le Senat. 2010. *LOI n° 2010-1 du 4 janvier 2010 relative à la protection du secret des sources des journalistes*. Available at www.legifrance.gouv.fr/affichTexte.do?cidTexte=JORFTEXT000021601325&categorieLien=id [Accessed 12 November, 2016].

43 Staff, S. 7th July, 2010. *L'Oreal Affair Reaches Sarkozy*. Der Spiegel [online]. Available at www.spiegel.de/international/europe/a-growing-scandal-in-france-l-oreal-affair-reaches-sarkozy-a-704885.html [Accessed 18 June, 2016].

44 Staff, S. 7th July, 2010. *L'Oreal Affair Reaches Sarkozy*. Der Spiegel [online]. Available at www.spiegel.de/international/europe/a-growing-scandal-in-france-l-oreal-affair-reaches-sarkozy-a-704885.html [Accessed 18 June, 2016].

45 Marthoz, J. 3rd September, 2011. *Spying on Media Exposes French government's Dark Side*. Committee to Protect Journalists [online]. Available at https://cpj.org/blog/2011/09/spying-on-media-exposes-french-governments-dark-si.php [Accessed 10 September, 2016].

46 Samuel, H. 2nd September, 2011. *French Intelligence Chief 'Under Pressure to Resign' After Spies Targeted Journalist to Protect Nicolas Sarkozy*. Daily Telegraph [online]. London. Available at www.telegraph.co.uk/news/worldnews/nicolas-sarkozy/8738060/French-intelligence-chief-under-pressure-to-resign-after-spies-targeted-journalist-to-protect-Nicolas-Sarkozy.html [Accessed 12 July, 2016].

47 Freedom House. 2012. Freedom of the Press 2012: Breakthroughs and Pushback in the Middle East [online]. Available at https://freedomhouse.org/sites/default/files/FOTP%202012%20Final%20Full%20Report.pdf [Accessed 1 August, 2016].

48 Eudes, Y. January, 2017. *Interview*.

49 Eudes, Y. January, 2017. *Interview*.

50 Eudes, Y. January, 2017. *Interview*.

51 Halliday, J. 6th May, 2011. *Wall Street Journal Faces Backlash Over WikiLeaks Rival*. The Guardian [online]. Available at www.theguardian.com/media/2011/may/06/wall-street-journal-wikileaks-safehouse [Accessed August, 2016].

52 Halliday, J. 6th May, 2011. *Wall Street Journal Faces Backlash Over WikiLeaks Rival*. The Guardian [online]. Available at www.theguardian.com/media/2011/may/06/wall-street-journal-wikileaks-safehouse [Accessed August, 2016].

53 Pietrosant, F. 2016. *Interview*.

54 MacFadyen, G. 2016. *Interview*.

55 Pietrosant, F. 2016. *Interview*.

7

SPIES, LIES AND US INDUSTRIES

In 1972 when the *Washington Post*'s Bob Woodward met the man known at the time simply as Deep Throat for a briefing on what to look for next in his Watergate investigation of President Richard Nixon, he took the kind of precautions which kept the identity of his source secret for 30 years. The famous rendezvous between Woodward and the deputy director of the FBI, Mark Felt, took place close enough to the centre of Washington to be accessible, without being somewhere they might easily be seen by people they knew. Felt and Woodward took simple precautions to keep their meetings secret. They would head there separately, meeting up at 2 a.m. in Arlington, just across the Potomac River from the scene of the famous break-in at the Watergate complex. The prearranged spot, in a North Nash Street carpark, was as deserted a place as you would find: space 32D, where they talked away the hours, as far away as possible from the entrance ramp, and in the event of being seen by early morning visitors was also close to a side door for a quick exit into the street.

Woodward says that whenever he wanted to contact Felt, he made a prearranged signal – moving a flowerpot containing a red flag on the windowsill of his apartment, and then heading off to the car park that night. When Felt wanted a meeting he circled the number of page 20 of the *New York Times* and drew a clock face indicating the time he wanted to see Woodward. Even in those days, they did not trust the phone to make contact to arrange their meetings.

The fact that for two years Woodward and Felt managed to maintain their clandestine relationship without discovery is perhaps testimony to their professional capabilities. As deputy chief of the FBI – America's counter-intelligence agency whose job it is to catch foreign spies – it might be expected that Felt would be used to living in the shadows and remaining anonymous. Woodward too had no doubt learned skills in the US Navy, where he had top-secret security clearances in cryptography before turning to journalism.

Forty years on and they would not even be confident that they could drive down the street without being highly visible, and potentially even audible. On his way to meet Felt in Arlington, the drive from Woodward's apartment (No. 617, housed in a plain brick block at 1718 P Street North West Washington DC) would take him past several of the 33 permanent CCTV street cameras in the city and many of the 354 Federal Communications Commission registered antenna towers. Whether his phone was on or off it would automatically send out a tiny electronic signal to each mobile phone tower he passed along the route, allowing his precise location to be triangulated and thus calculated during his five-kilometre journey across town to Arlington, where he would be met by another 134 antenna towers and 180 traffic cameras. It was no longer possible to hide in plain sight, even in a high street store or a hotel lobby.

In March, 2017 WikiLeaks revealed that the CIA had developed, in cooperation with the UK's MI5, a system called Weeping Angel which turned Samsung Smart TVs into surveillance tools. The TV could be used to record any conversations nearby, relaying them to a covert CIA server, even if the TV was turned off. WikiLeaks also reported that in October 2014 the CIA was examining the possibility of interfering with the computerised control systems on cars and trucks.

It is this interlocking web which is a central part of modern-day surveillance capabilities. Communications systems, including internet browser use, banking, toll-way use, speed cameras, licence plate identification cameras, and even the landline telephone, add to the capability of intelligence agencies to conduct surveillance and track the movements of anybody, making the job of gathering information and dealing with sources in 2017 so much more difficult than it was in the 1970s.

Journalists have been caught between twin forces, the so-called war on terrorism with its intrusive gathering of mass data and the desire by executive government to keep secret the systems used to gather that information and to control the content of the information itself. There is little new about the desire of prime ministers and presidents – or intelligence and law enforcement agencies – to restrict information to those who are sympathetic. It is a tried and tested way to attempt to shape public opinion. The Iraq War 'sexed-up' dossier – a piece of pure propaganda – is but one of the most recent examples, coupled with the *New York Times* reporting on weapons of mass destruction by Judith Miller. But there are many others, hidden from public view in the world's democracies. The UK government set up an entire organisation, housed as a separate unit in the British Foreign Office. Called, innocuously, the Information Research Department (IRD) it was in fact an arm of British propaganda.

Established after the Second World War in Central London's Carlton House Terrace, just off Horse Guards Parade, it shared the building with an MI6 Russian translation unit before moving to larger accommodation just down the road from MI5 and across the River Thames from MI6, which moved from St James to Lambeth in 1964. For 30 years, it pumped out slanted material mainly to foreign journalists to counter what they saw as Soviet propaganda. But many mainstream

UK media organisation were also on the mailing list of the IRD. Like any good disinformation service, it also provided a lot of accurate information, some of it about places in the Cold War where it was impossible for a British journalist to visit. Dr Paul Lashmar, whose book *Britain's Secret Propaganda War, 1948–1977* (Sutton Publishing Ltd, May 1999) gives a detailed insight into the workings of the IRD, explained that many journalists were given briefings 'which enabled them to write about the inside of the Soviet Union when nobody could get into the Soviet Union at that point'.[1] For many journalists information provided by the IRD was career-enhancing, and the temptation was not to write a critical story.

Though the IRD was shut down in the 1970s, another version emerged. During the military battle to defeat the Irish Republican Army (IRA) in Northern Ireland in the 1970s, the UK's domestic security service, MI5, worked closely with an organisation called the Information Policy Unit – part of the British Army press office in Belfast. Like the IRD's, its work included routine public relations. And like the IRD, its primary objective was to place stories based on disinformation in the press as part of a psychological warfare operation. A black propaganda task force called 'Clockwork Orange' was set up to spread fake stories about the Provisional IRA, questioning their competence and effectiveness. Once again, the stories were published, sometimes without question, by journalists such as Chapman Pincher of the UK's *Daily Express*. Under the byline 'Chapman Pincher: The Man Who Gives You Tomorrow's News – Today', Pincher reported that the IRA was recruiting ex-Vietnam veterans in the US to fight in Ireland. With the Vietnam War unpopular in the United Kingdom it was an attempt to blacken the name of the IRA. If the Vietnam vets ever ended up in Northern Ireland they were the quietest Americans in history. No one has ever heard of them since. Another planted fake story given to Pincher portrayed the IRA as incompetents. It involved claims in a supposed internal IRA memo that the British had intercepted weapons and bombs being imported by the IRA and had tinkered with them to make them misfire or prematurely explode. Pincher explained that the IRA had deliberately concocted this document and then leaked this 'false information' in the hope of 'showing that the British will stoop to any devilry'.[2] Pincher explained to his readers that it was all a hoax. 'My inquiries have established this memo is a fake,' he wrote.[3] Pincher was absolutely right about that: it was a fake. What he did not understand was who had faked it. The document had not been written by the IRA, but by the Clockwork Orange group. They had concocted the fake IRA document and 'leaked' it in an attempt to sow doubt and confusion in the IRA's ranks.

Over the following 30 years not much changed in the attempt to mould public opinion; if anything it possibly became more institutionalised. As the US Defense Department tried to spin stories of success in Iraq, it fell back on the well-trodden path of bribery and deception. While President Bush was announcing victory in Iraq, the government ran a covert operation to counter media reports which questioned that assertion. Few people had a better understanding of what happened in the Pentagon than Rosa Brooks, Professor of International Law at Georgetown University. She served as counsel for the Under-Secretary of Defense for Policy and led a major overhaul of the Defense Department's Department of Strategic Communications and Infrastructure.

'All sorts of things happened under the rubric of communication at the Pentagon, particularly during the first years after the 9–11 attacks,'[4] Professor Brooks told 'Spycast', the online radio station of Washington DC's International Spy Museum. 'Planting fake stories in foreign press outlets, things they should not have been doing. Dumb, Dumb, and ineffective,'[5] she said. The administration 'got up to some pretty crazy stuff, some of which had to be repudiated when it got leaked to the press',[6] including paying for stories to be planted in Iraqi media.

The Pentagon 'crazy stuff'[7] was but one example of the strategy of the neocon philosophy which defined the entire US population as either combatants or potential victims in the war on terror.

Brooks explains that 'Once, war was a temporary state of affairs'[8] – a violent but brief interlude between times of peace. But today 'America's wars are everywhere and forever. America's enemies change constantly and rarely wear uniforms, and virtually anything can become a weapon.'[9] As the definition of war expanded, so too did the role of the US military. 'Today, military personnel don't just "kill people and break stuff".[10] Instead, they analyse computer code, train Afghan judges, build Ebola isolation wards, eavesdrop on electronic communications, develop soap operas, and patrol for pirates. You name it, the military does it.'[11] As Brooks argues in her book *How Everything Became War and the Military Became Everything* (Simon and Schuster, New York, 2016), the blurring of the line between war and peace has had serious repercussions. 'As war rules trickle down into our ordinary life, they are beginning to change everything,'[12] she said.

Her experiences led her to an urgent warning: 'When the boundaries around war disappear, we risk destroying America's founding values and the laws and institutions we've built – and undermining the international rules and organizations that keep our world from sliding towards chaos.'[13] Her findings have an eerie echo in the findings of a detailed study by the Chicago Law School which questioned American exceptionalism and raised the possibility of a drift away from democracy to authoritarianism. The study, citing the Trump administration, warns that one of the danger signals of an anti-democratic drift from the principles of the US Constitution has been the use of 'aggressive misinformation by the White House' on what it calls 'matters of signal national concern'.[14]

The White House of George W. Bush might have been just as culpable in the use of disinformation, particularly as it fought to win public support for the Iraq invasion, but Trump's outright lies and fearmongering about refugees and terrorism has created a dangerous coupling: even less respect for the office of the president and greater reliance on militaristic action. The posing of a threat from without, bound up with a threat from within, has created heightened levels of anxiety and pushed sections of the population into supporting a non-democratic solution to America's problems. Consciously or not, many people appear to be turning more and more to the very organisations which pose the biggest threat to its democratic process, what Republican US President Dwight Eisenhower presciently warned about in 1961. In his farewell address as he stepped down from office, Eisenhower – a former commander of NATO and US Five-Star General – coined a chilling phrase denoting the perils of a powerful military linked to big business and a compliant political class:

> In the councils of government, we must guard against the acquisition of unwarranted influence, whether sought or unsought, by the military industrial complex. The potential for the disastrous rise of misplaced power exists and will persist. We must never let the weight of this combination endanger our liberties or democratic processes. We should take nothing for granted. Only an alert and knowledgeable citizenry can compel the proper meshing of the huge industrial and military machinery of defense with our peaceful methods and goals, so that security and liberty may prosper together.[15]

Fifty-four years later in 2015, a Gallup poll suggested his warnings had not been heeded. The poll revealed that 72 per cent of American expressed 'a great deal' or 'quite a lot'[16] of confidence in the military, compared to 33 percent expressing confidence in the presidency. And only eight per cent expressed any confidence in Congress. The Chicago Law School analysis points out that over the past three decades, the proportion of U.S. citizens who believe it would be a 'good'[17] or a 'very good'[18] thing for the 'army to rule'[19] has spiked from one in sixteen to one in six. Among the cohort of 'rich young Americans'[20] the proportion of those who look favourably on military rule is more than one in three.[21] It is a view partly explained by the fact that 'the U.S. defense industry remains well-funded and has become one of 'the best places for new college graduates to turn to for employment'.[22]

Successive US governments have poured billions of dollars into military and intelligence institutions. It is estimated that during the Cold War, spending on intelligence alone peaked at US$71 billion (in 2013 dollars), surging to US$75 billion in 2013. Since the attacks on the World Trade Center and the Pentagon in September 2001 the US has spent an estimated US$500 billion on intelligence, according to a secret report[23] given to the *Washington Post* by Edward Snowden.

For all the public affirmation that the increases were about fighting terrorism, much of the evidence points to the contrary. Having worked as a CIA operative and been employed as an analyst with access to some of the most highly classified inner workings of the NSA, Snowden says the US intelligence agencies have a completely different agenda.

'These programs were never about terrorism; they're about economic spying, social control, and diplomatic manipulation. They're about power.'[24]

It seemed like an obvious comment, since the intelligence agencies had been operating well before terrorism became such a significant political issue.

The question is: what have the intelligence agencies really been doing with the money which has poured into their coffers? If it were not for Edward Snowden we might have believed the extra income was being spent protecting the Five Eyes countries' citizens from terrorism. But Snowden's claims that the real work covers other areas of national interest, such as trade and strategic power, are compelling. Every four years the head of US national intelligence publishes the *Quadrennial Intelligence Community Review*. In April, 2009 the report, classified Secret, outlined projected future plans for the Intelligence Community (IC) for the next 10–15 years. Many of these plans reveal just how closely the IC works with corporate America. Significantly in the 32-page, 7600-word document there is only one oblique mention of terrorism. The document gives an example of 'transnational interest group[s]'[25] who question limiting 'human enhancement' to the 'wealthy few'[26] There was an 'extremist sub-current'[27] which the intelligence community was concerned could lead to 'medical terrorism',[28] the document adds, without explaining further. As an oblique example, it could be moulded to fit other kinds of terrorism too, but it appears as a passing mention in a long and densely-written forecast of how the intelligence community should prepare for the future. The threat of rampaging terrorism as a huge threat is nowhere to be found. Instead the review reads like a handbook for how to keep US industry as the predominant force in the world, focussing on a situation where the country's 'innovative edge slips'.[29] Under one scenario, a bloc of states actively seeking to undermine US geostrategic leadership could deny access to key emerging technologies. Another example raises the possibility that the technological capacity of foreign multinational corporations could outstrip that of US corporations.

The review says the intelligence community would be challenged to understand technological innovation outside its traditional competencies (e.g., weapons systems) and in domains where it traditionally has focused less effort (e.g., commercial research and development (R&D). It warns that United States industry could become left behind putting the US at 'a growing – and potentially permanent – disadvantage in crucial areas such as energy, nanotechnology, medicine, and information technology'.[30]

To deal with this potential loss of leadership the US would need to use what the report called a 'multi-pronged systemic effort'[31] to gather both open-source information and material through what it calls physical and cyber means, in other words old-fashioned break-ins and the planting of listening devices and other forms of surveillance. How the intelligence community might go about this work is explained in a secret section which includes 'cooperating U.S. students, professors, and researchers'[32] to help the intelligence community 'continue to advance U.S. scientific progress'.[33] Another Secret section deals with 'direct penetration'[34] for 'more restrictive environments'[35] which might involve sending in intelligence officers to directly download sensitive material. The US was particularly focused on implanting bugs to spy on 'software and hardware used by foreign researchers and manufacturers, and by conducting computer- network exploitation of foreign R&D intranets'.[36] The intelligence community should also prepare itself for 'possible loss of access'[37] to what it calls reliable financial and economic data 'by penetrating corporations, foreign finance ministries, central banks, and market participants'.[38]

As a blunt statement of mission the review could not be clearer: 'As the United States struggles to maintain its world standing amidst competing and insular blocs, the IC is predominantly focused on economics and commercial science and technology (S&T) missions.'[39]

In what are called illustrative examples in another section marked [S/REL] meaning Secret only to be released to the Five Eyes countries, the review puts forward two scenarios:

1. (S//REL) India and Russia are pursuing high- temperature superconductivity, which would yield a significant economic advantage to the first adopter. But four separate streams of intelligence, when put together, yield a new insight – the two countries are working together.
2. (S//REL) Sustained reporting from open and clandestine sources enables a team of experts from the IC, academia, and industry to assess the likelihood, either moderate or high, of a breakthrough by India and Russia. Counterintelligence reporting suggests the two countries are not very interested in U.S. superconductivity efforts, which may indicate they believe they have a secure lead.

The report suggests that after sifting the evidence, the intelligence community would secretly try to break up the partnership by 'conducting cyber operations against research facilities in the two countries',[40] as well as the intellectual 'supply chain'[41] supporting these facilities. Finally, it would assess whether and how its findings 'would be useful to U.S. industry'.[42]

If those examples were designed to show how the US intelligence community was preparing to deal with a threat to the country's industrial supremacy, there was nothing hypothetical about the action the NSA took against Brazil. While many embassies are protected by guards and razor wire, Brazil's in Washington DC stands in stark contrast. The country's mission at 3006 Massachusetts Avenue, Washington, DC is open to surrounding land, its large, lofty glass walls given shade by towering deciduous trees. It would appear to have been an easy target for what the NSA calls 'Close Access domestic collection'.[43] Documents released by Snowden show that in September 2010 the embassy – plus its representative at the UN in New York – were singled out for special attention. While other embassies and diplomatic missions were being removed from a long list of targets, Brazil became one of the most heavily surveilled foreign missions in the US. Using code names such as LIFESAVER, HIGHLANDS AND VAGRANT, the NSA collected information from 'implants',[44] surveillance devices planted in the embassy, 'screen shots 'or 'mirroring',[45] copying the entire hard drive of computers used by Brazil's diplomatic service. The NSA, however, did not confine its attention to Washington. As WikiLeaks revealed, the NSA also selected a list of 29 key

Brazilian government phone numbers for intensive interception. WikiLeaks said the documents, classified Top Secret, proved that not only Brazilian President Dilma Rousseff was targeted but also her assistant, her secretary, her chief of staff, her Palace office and even the phone in her presidential jet. Documents show the US focused on not only those closest to the president, but waged a broad 'economic espionage campaign against Brazil',[46] spying on those responsible for managing Brazil's economy, including the head of its Central Bank and diplomats, targeting the phones of its Foreign Minister and its ambassadors to Germany, France, the EU, the US and Geneva.

The key areas of surveillance included the country's Finance Ministers and even a senior member of the Central Bank of Brazil: Cabinet Minister Nelson Henrique Barbosa Filho, who served as Executive Secretary at Brazil's Ministry of Finance from 2011 to 2013 and who was now Minister of Planning, Budget and Management.

This whole-of-government attack could possibly be explained by Brazil's rise as a leader in a part of the world the US has long considered its area of influence. As a part of the so-called BRICS group – Brazil, Russia, India, China and South Africa – of developing nations on the rise, Brazil had also recently signed an agreement with France to buy four nuclear-powered submarines, giving its already impressive navy a huge reach throughout the south Atlantic and even further afield. It had become the only nuclear-powered navy in South America. If the NSA documents had simply revealed a list of names and targeted phone numbers, the spying could possibly be explained away as keeping an eye on an emerging power in the neighbourhood. Strategically it would be important for the US to understand the position that Brazil would take on any given issue. But as a subsequent release of Snowden documents disclosed, there was a very specific target for the NSA's surveillance programme. It fitted perfectly with the Secret Quadrennial Intelligence Report which outlined the US intelligence community's priorities. What the state-owned Brazilian petroleum company Petrobras had managed to do very much interested the US. For decades petrol companies had been searching the nearby seabeds in the hope of discovering what geological surveys suggested might be huge oil reserves. In 10 years Petrobas spent about $350 billion on expanding the company's In May 2010 the effort and the gamble paid off: the country discovered huge gas and oil fields in the pre-salt substrata of the ocean off the coasts of San Paulo and Rio de Janeiro. The pre-salt oil is found in high seas, at depths of two thousand metres – below a layer of rocky salt, four kilometres underneath the ocean floor. Reaching this oil requires a lot of technology, and Petrobras is a world leader in deep-sea oil extraction.

Adriano Pires, a specialist in infrastructure, considers many countries would be interested in ocean-floor exploration technology. 'Petrobras is the world's number one in drilling for oil at sea. Pre-salt layers exist all around the world – there's a pre-salt in Africa, in the Gulf of Mexico, in the North Sea. If I have this technology I can drill anywhere I want,' he said.[47] This kind of information would be extremely useful to oil companies grappling with the problem of how to extract oil from fields, not only out in deep water, but also far below the ocean floor. Sometimes the oil could be several kilometres under the crust of the earth and the best oil, a particularly light grade in the case of Brazil, could be found even deeper, four kilometres below a two-kilometre thick layer of salt laid down when the earth was first forming. In ten years Petrobas spent about $350 billion on expansion, a period during which it made some of the world's largest ever offshore oil finds. In May 2010, the country discovered huge gas and oil fields in the pre-salt substrata of the ocean off the coasts of San Paulo and Rio de Janeiro. The Brazilian oil company had achieved some incredible, and enviable, results. Petrobras bragged that the average time to build an offshore well in the Santos Basin had been slashed from 310 days to 89 days using 'advanced technologies',[48] – a 71 per cent reduction.

The savings were staggering. Petrobras reported that 'due to technological innovation' the costs had fallen consistently from US $9.1 per barrel of oil equivalent (oil plus gas), in 2014, to $8.3 in 2015, and to less than $8 per barrel in the first quarter of 2016. It was just the kind of R&D expertise which US intelligence highlighted as important to acquire from countries like Brazil. The government guarded the information carefully, using virtual private networks (VPNs) – not part of the national communications grid – to communicate, reducing the chance that data transmissions involving vital information might be intercepted. They were also concerned about protecting the details of exactly where new oil fields – some of the world's largest ever off shore discoveries – were located.

It was just four months after the oil discovery that the NSA document showed the Brazilian Embassy in Washington being bugged by the NSA's Sigads program to gather signals intelligence. Exactly why they had targeted the Brazilians was not clear at the time, but the circumstantial evidence suggested that there might be a connection between Brazil's new oil wealth and the technology it was using to extract it. If there was doubt about what the NSA was up to before, there is no doubt that the NSA had made up its mind by the southern autumn of 2012.

A Top-Secret document dated May 2012 reveals that the NSA was training its officers to spy on private computer systems. The internal networks of companies, governments, and financial institutions, sometimes called VPNs, are designed for maximum security to protect highly important information. The documents reveal how the NSA set about breaking into those systems. High on the list under the headline 'Many Targets Use Private Networks' appears the name of Brazil's state-owned petrochemical giant and largest company, Petrobras.

Other targets included French diplomats – with access to the private network of the Ministry of Foreign Affairs of France – and the SWIFT network, the security system that unites over 10,000 banks in 212 countries and provides communications that enable international financial transactions.

The name Petrobras appeared on several slides, as the training explained how data from the target companies could be monitored and stored. Individual folders were created for each target, containing the intercepted communications and IP addresses – the identification of each computer on the network. The Brazilian newspaper *Fantastico* broke the story, working with Glenn Greenwald, who discovered the document among the trove handed to him by Edward Snowden; *Fantastico* asked Paulo Pagliusi, an author with a PhD in information security, to analyse whether or not the documents were merely examples for training purposes. Pagliusi pointed out that the networks in the presentation all belonged to real companies.

'These are not made-up situations,'[49] he said. Some details of telephone numbers were blacked out. 'Why would they be blacked out if they weren't real?'[50] he asked. The NSA instructors did not want the trainees to see details of the documents which revealed a programme of systematic spying. 'You don't obtain all of this in a single run,' he said. 'From what I see, this is a very consistent system that yields powerful results; it's a very efficient form of spying.'[51]

Much of the data held by Petrobras, including seismic research which evaluated oil reserves from samples collected at sea, was stored on two supercomputers – used mainly for seismic research. They were vital for the company's mapping of the pre-salt layer, which revealed the largest discovery of new oil reserves in the world in recent years.

There is no information on the extent of the spying, nor on whether it managed to access the data contained in the company's computers. It is clear Petrobras was a target, but no documents show exactly what information the NSA searched for. What we do know is that Petrobras's computerised records contained information about deals involving billions of dollars, including the Libra Field, in the Bay of Santos, part of the pre-salt bonanza.

Former Petrobras Director Roberto Villa pointed out the sensitivity of the information held by Petrobras: everybody knew where the oil fields were, the question was which ones were the richest. Only Petrobas knew, he asserted. 'Petrobras knows. And I hope only they know.'[52] In an act of understatement, he said that anyone who managed to discover that information will 'know where to invest and where not to. It's a handy little secret.' Another former Petrobras director, Antonio Menezes, said that commercially and internationally, the Brazilian oil business was now a 'game with marked cards'.[53]

The NSA presentation contains documents prepared by GCHQ, the British spying organisation, revealing how two spy programs operate together. Known as 'Flying Pig' and 'Hush Puppy',[54] they monitor private networks which carry secure information.

The presentation also gives an indication how the NSA intercepted the data, through an attack known as 'Man in the Middle'.[55] In this case, data is rerouted to the NSA central server, and then relayed to its destination, without either end noticing.

A few pages later, the document asks, 'Results – what do we find?' . . . 'Foreign government networks', 'airlines', 'energy companies – like Petrobras – and 'financial organisations'.[56]

How the NSA responded to being caught engaging in industrial espionage would be in keeping with the assurances James Clapper, the US director of

National Intelligence, gave to Senator Ron Wyden when questioned during an open congressional hearing about surveillance of US citizens: 'We don't hold data on US citizens' and 'the story that we have dossiers on millions or hundreds of millions of people is absolutely false'.[57] Wyden publicly accused Clapper of a 'deliberate decision to lie to the American people about what their government was doing'.[58]

In the case of the Petrobras revelations, Clapper declared that the agency collected information in order to give the US and their allies early warning of international financial crises which could negatively impact the global economy and also to provide insight into other countries' economic policy or behaviour which could affect global markets.

The statement also stressed that the collected intelligence was not used 'to steal the trade secrets of foreign companies on behalf of – or give intelligence we collect to – US companies to enhance their international competitiveness or increase their bottom line'.[59]

The fact is that according to much of the available evidence, stealing trade secrets and helping the US economy to beat competition from foreign companies is exactly where the US intelligence community expends much of its effort. The massive data collection and the billions of dollars spent gathering every scrap of information and storing it in huge depots the size of several football fields around the world, it seems, is primarily focused on supporting the economies of the English speaking Five Eyes countries.

It is hardly a new concept. Nations have been spying on each other for commercial and trade advantage for centuries, but what is different now is the scale of the espionage and the public denial of the agencies' real purpose. The fear of terrorism is being used to deceive a susceptible public into squandering untold billions – often paid in secret – to publicly unaccountable agencies, while at the same time building a global intelligence network with terrifying power.

The hysterical response to terrorism has been supported and encouraged by many politicians who genuinely fear the consequences of an attack – and at the same time play to those fears for political gain. As Duncan Campbell told me: 'Just as there is a blurring of the lines between military and civilian activities in the US, there is a vagueness about what it is a legitimate target and what is not'[60] The notion expounded by the NSA to 'collect it all' has produced the largest concentration of personal information ever assembled. The question is: what is it for? And how effective is it in helping an intelligence agency to do its job?

One person who has first-hand experience of how the system works is Bill Binney, a former senior NSA analyst. As he tells it, he had been working on a system called ThinThread which would correlate data from financial transactions, travel records, Web searches, and other inputs that might identify the 'bad guys'.[61] Binney says that by 2000 he had set up a computer network that could construct a 'social network' picture of people in real time: where they travelled, who they met and sometimes even what they said. According to Jane Mayer writing in the New Yorker 'it also turned the NSA's data collection paradigm upside down'[62] Instead of vacuuming up information around the world and then sending it all back to headquarters for analysis, ThinThread processed information as it was collected – discarding useless material on the spot and avoiding the overload problem that plagued centralised systems. Binney explained that

> ThinThread [was] designed to be able to look into massive amounts of data and only pull out things that were relevant to spot individuals engaged in criminal activities, like terrorism or drug smuggling or money laundering. That was a very selected, targeted and focused programme.[63]

Pilot tests of ThinThread proved almost too successful, according to a former intelligence expert who analysed it. 'It was nearly perfect,' the official said.[64] Though ThinThread was intended to intercept foreign communications, it continued documenting signals when a trail crossed into the U.S. This was a big problem: federal law forbade the monitoring of domestic communications without a court warrant. And a warrant could not be issued without probable cause and a known suspect. In order to comply with the law, Binney installed privacy controls and added an 'anonymizing feature'[65] so that all American communications would be encrypted until a warrant was issued.

Binney said the material was encrypted, so the NSA 'couldn't tell who it was',[66] yet it was still possible to see the networks and if granted a court order the agency could unscramble the coded messages and examine the social connections. The system was so sophisticated it would alert NSA officers when a pattern looked suspicious enough to justify a warrant, according to Binney.

Binney says his team at the NSA proposed deploying ThinThread to 18 sites that were 'producing information on terrorism'.[67] It was, he said, comparatively easy to install. Using a simple software download it would have taken about a day to become operational and would have been comparatively easy for NSA analysts to isolate the 9–11 hi-jackers before they struck. 'They couldn't have done anything this system wouldn't have picked up,'[68] he said.

Frustrated at a lack of progress, Binney tried to argue with his superiors at the NSA that ThinThread was much more effective than another system they had poured billions into, and at US$9.5 million, a fraction of the price, but they ignored him. In theory, there was a system he might have been able to use. Known as the Whistleblower Protection Act (1989,) it covers 'disclosures of illegality' in all areas of government, including intelligence agencies. But as many have discovered before, it is a flawed piece of legislation. All references to possible wrongdoing are first investigated internally by the very organisation against which the complaint has been made. After that the only credible recourse for grievances rests with the Senate Select Committee on Intelligence – responsible for oversight of the FBI, the CIA and the NSA.

Binney, who had worked at the agency for more than 30 years, went to the committee soon after the 2001 terrorist attacks. The story he told them bore a striking resemblance to what Snowden would reveal more than a decade later: the NSA was gathering information on American citizens using a system that he said was not only unconstitutional but also ineffective. He explained that, even more unsettlingly, the NSA had rejected an interception system which allowed the NSA to sift information on targets in real time, only collecting the material it needed.

Binney says that the September 11 attacks 'brought a complete change in the approach of the NSA toward doing its job'.[69] He said that the FISA (Foreign Intelligence Surveillance Act) court 'ceased to be an operative concern, and the individual liberties preserved in the U.S. Constitution were no longer a consideration'.[70] It was at that time that the NSA began to implement the group of intelligence activities now known as the President's Surveillance Program (PSP), turning the NSA to spy on the US population under presidential direction. It seemed that because of its extraordinary capability parts of the ThinThread program were now co-opted into the domestic surveillance programme without any of the privacy protections. Binney was not alone in trying to sound the alarm with congressional committees. Others attempted to work within the system. Computer expert Thomas Drake, who also worked on ThinThread, thought blowing the whistle on what he considered unconstitutional NSA programs would lead to an investigation and changes in the organisation, but that is not what happened. In the end the only person who was investigated, prosecuted, charged in secret, then indicted, and who faced a trial and 35 years in prison was Drake.

Like Binney, Drake had taken his case both to the NSA and to Congress. After concluding his complaints were going nowhere, he showed unclassified information from the NSA to a newspaper reporter. For that he was charged with violating the Espionage Act of 1917. The FBI raided his home. Four months earlier the FBI had raided Binney's home after he publicly criticised the NSA. As is so frequently the case with whistleblowers, both Drake and Binney suffered the consequences of challenging the system. 'Your life's never the same,'[71] said Drake. 'All your colleagues and people you used to work with all disappear. You're persona non grata, you're radioactive.'[72] Though charges were brought against both Binney and Drake the Justice Department did not pursue them through the courts. No explanation was given but the administration may have been fearful of what might have transpired during any hearing, although much of it would have been in secret. Certainly, it is possible any court case would have addressed the actions of the NSA and its director General Michael Hayden who turned down ThinThread for the 'collect it all' system known as Trailblazer, which was finally abandoned after costing in excess of US$1 billion.

Binney is convinced that the NSA systems which gather so much information are 'doomed to fail, because they are locked into the concept that they have to collect everything, and that just makes it impossible'.[73] Binney said the NSA was 'very good at collecting data, but they haven't made any improvements at all in trying to figure out what they have in the data they've collected'.[74]

Even industrial espionage on a grand scale would require some form of focus, but there's another possibility. Describing Edward Snowden as an infrastructure analyst is curious. Snowden isn't saying exactly what he did, but he was assigned to a contract called Signals Development Support (SDS2), part of a Booz Allen team, within the NSA. Snowden's role, it appears, involved analysing what are known as digital infrastructures: entire computer systems of nations. He was not directly involved in the interception of data and telephone transmissions. While the other parts of the NSA were working to 'collect it all', Snowden's job would be important in tracking down the source of a cyber aggressor, or seeking out an adversary's weakness. What the NSA had created was a kind of surveillance time machine, with information stored in the purpose-built compounds scattered around the world in Five Eyes countries. In one 30-day period between December 2012 and January 2013, one collection program, Muscular, jointly run by GCHQ and the NSA, scooped up more than 14 billion records. The information, which can include voice recordings, is normally held for only seven to ten days because of the amount of storage space required. Other collection systems, which archive only snippets of the identifying material such as email addresses, use less space and can thus be stored for much longer, possibly up to three months. If the NSA decide the information is important enough it can be held for five years.

One possibility is that the NSA used this huge archival collection to identify the hackers of the Democratic National Committee emails, including Hilary Clinton's, during the 2016 US election campaign. 'You didn't know it was coming,'[75] I was told by a former NSA employee who asked not to be named.

> You don't know who did it but you get notification that it happened within that period where you still have the internet buffer. You can go back in time and see exactly what happened. It is like a security camera for the entire internet.'[76] It was possible that the material, which would identify the hackers, had 'rolled out of the buffer' but, if not, the source believed the 'NSA could plausibly know who is behind these attacks'.[77]

It may explain the certainty with which all the US security organisations pointed to Russia as being the culprit for the hack. It was a powerful weapon the US, in particular, was disinclined to put down.

The UN Special Rapporteur on the right to privacy (SRP), Professor Joe Cannataci, whose job it was to investigate the possibility of controlling surveillance in cyber space, said without naming the countries involved, that 'a tiny minority of states'[78] had tried to discourage him from attempting to find solutions to privacy issues. 'Approximately 15–25 states treat the Internet as their own playground over which they can squabble for spoils,'[79] he said.

But as a Rapporteur it was his duty to report back that these seemed to be the only people who did not wish to have internationally enforceable safeguards and remedies on the internet. Civil society and large corporations were in favour, he said. By not taking action, Snowden believed the large industrial nations were 'setting off an arms race in the context of the violation of human rights and mass surveillance',[80] which might prove to be unstoppable.

The vacuuming up of vast amounts of information might have been an understandable knee-jerk reaction for the US post 9/11; none of the intelligence agencies wanted to miss anything, even if it meant breaking the law. But did this action catch terrorists? And if the 'catch it all' mantra of the NSA was not about catching terrorists it might explain why Binney's ThinThread system, which specifically targeted individuals and did not gather and store masses of information, was of little use to the agency. While the NSA argued it was not breaking the law and that everything had been legally scrubbed down by the White House lawyers, we now know that the NSA did in fact break the law, over a prolonged period until the Snowden revelations and even now there are doubts that what the NSA is doing is legal. Left to themselves, as we saw earlier with the lies told by the NSA's James Clapper, there is often little they will not do, if they can get away with it. Sussex University's Paul Lashmar, who spent much of his life reporting on intelligence matters for Britain's *Observer* newspaper, told me:

> Having watched intelligence agencies for 40 years and know them historically, I know that on every occasion when they are left to themselves they have abused their power, because no one has come up with a really effective means of accountability.[81]

And any journalists trying to hold them to account, or to expose their wrongdoing, should prepare themselves to be treated like criminals. There is a long history of governments using national security as a pretext for attempting to silence journalists.

Notes

1 Lashmar, P. 2016. *Interview.*
2 Lobster Magazine. 1988. Wallace Clippings Planted on Chapman Pincher [online]. Available at www.lobster-magazine.co.uk/intro/search.cgi?zoom_query=pincher [Accessed 15 November, 2016].
3 Lobster Magazine. 1988. Wallace Clippings Planted on Chapman Pincher [online]. Available at www.lobster-magazine.co.uk/intro/search.cgi?zoom_query=pincher [Accessed 15 November, 2016].
4 Brooks, R. 9th August, 2016. *Blurred Lines: An Interview with Georgetown International Law Professor Rosa Brooks.* Spy Museum, Washington, DC [online]. Available at www.spymuseum.org/multimedia/spycast/episode/blurred-lines-an-interview-with-georgetown-international-law-professor-rosa-brooks/ [Accessed 30 January, 2017].
5 Brooks, R. 9th August, 2016. *Blurred Lines: An Interview with Georgetown International Law Professor Rosa Brooks.* Spy Museum, Washington, DC [online]. Available at www.spymuseum.org/multimedia/spycast/episode/blurred-lines-an-interview-with-georgetown-international-law-professor-rosa-brooks/ [Accessed 30 January, 2017].
6 Brooks, R. 9th August, 2016. *Blurred Lines: An Interview with Georgetown International Law Professor Rosa Brooks.* Spy Museum, Washington, DC [online]. Available at www.spymuseum.org/multimedia/spycast/episode/blurred-lines-an-interview-with-georgetown-international-law-professor-rosa-brooks/ [Accessed 30 January, 2017].
7 Brooks, R. 9th August, 2016. *Blurred Lines: An Interview with Georgetown International Law Professor Rosa Brooks.* Spy Museum, Washington, DC [online]. Available at

www.spymuseum.org/multimedia/spycast/episode/blurred-lines-an-interview-with-georgetown-international-law-professor-rosa-brooks/ [Accessed 30 January, 2017].

8   Brooks, R. 9th August, 2016. *Blurred Lines: An Interview with Georgetown International Law Professor Rosa Brooks*. Spy Museum, Washington, DC [online]. Available at www.spymuseum.org/multimedia/spycast/episode/blurred-lines-an-interview-with-georgetown-international-law-professor-rosa-brooks/ [Accessed 30 January, 2017].

9   Brooks, R. 9th August, 2016. *Blurred Lines: An Interview with Georgetown International Law Professor Rosa Brooks*. Spy Museum, Washington, DC [online]. Available at www.spymuseum.org/multimedia/spycast/episode/blurred-lines-an-interview-with-georgetown-international-law-professor-rosa-brooks/ [Accessed 30 January, 2017].

10   Brooks, R. 9th August, 2016. *Blurred Lines: An Interview with Georgetown International Law Professor Rosa Brooks*. Spy Museum, Washington, DC [online]. Available at www.spymuseum.org/multimedia/spycast/episode/blurred-lines-an-interview-with-georgetown-international-law-professor-rosa-brooks/ [Accessed 30 January, 2017].

11   Brooks, R. 9th August, 2016. *Blurred Lines: An Interview with Georgetown International Law Professor Rosa Brooks*. Spy Museum, Washington, DC [online]. Available at www.spymuseum.org/multimedia/spycast/episode/blurred-lines-an-interview-with-georgetown-international-law-professor-rosa-brooks/ [Accessed 30 January, 2017].

12   Brooks, R. 2016. *How Everything Became War and the Military Became Everything*. Simon & Schuster, New York, New York.

13   Brooks, R. 2016. *How Everything Became War and the Military Became Everything*. Simon & Schuster, New York, New York.

14   Huq, A. and Ginsburg, T. 20th January, 2017. *How to Lose Constitutional Democracy*. Chicago Law School [online]. Available at https://papers.ssrn.com/sol3/papers.cfm?abstract_id=2901776 [Accessed 21 July, 2017].

15   Eisenhower, D. 17th January, 1961. *Farewell Address*. The Eisenhower Project [online]. Available at http://eisenhowerproject.org [Accessed 20 September, 2016].

16   Huq, A. and Ginsburg, T. 20th January, 2017. *How to Lose Constitutional Democracy*. Chicago Law School [online]. Available at https://papers.ssrn.com/sol3/papers.cfm?abstract_id=2901776 [Accessed 21 July, 2017].

17   Huq, A. and Ginsburg, T. 20th January, 2017. *How to Lose Constitutional Democracy*. Chicago Law School [online]. Available at https://papers.ssrn.com/sol3/papers.cfm?abstract_id=2901776 [Accessed 21 July, 2017].

18   Huq, A. and Ginsburg, T. 20th January, 2017. *How to Lose Constitutional Democracy*. Chicago Law School [online]. Available at https://papers.ssrn.com/sol3/papers.cfm?abstract_id=2901776 [Accessed 21 July, 2017].

19   Huq, A. and Ginsburg, T. 20th January, 2017. *How to Lose Constitutional Democracy*. Chicago Law School [online]. Available at https://papers.ssrn.com/sol3/papers.cfm?abstract_id=2901776 [Accessed 21 July, 2017].

20   Huq, A. and Ginsburg, T. 20th January, 2017. *How to Lose Constitutional Democracy*. Chicago Law School [online]. Available at https://papers.ssrn.com/sol3/papers.cfm?abstract_id=2901776 [Accessed 21 July, 2017].

21   Huq, A. and Ginsburg, T. 20th January, 2017. *How to Lose Constitutional Democracy*. Chicago Law School [online]. Available at https://papers.ssrn.com/sol3/papers.cfm?abstract_id=2901776 [Accessed 21 July, 2017].

22   Office of the Director of National Intelligence. 22nd January, 2009. Alternative Futures the IC Could Face [online]. Available at https://fas.org/irp/dni/qicr.pdf [Accessed 26 October, 2016].

23   Gellman, B. and Miller, G. 29th August, 2013. *Black Budget Summary Details US Spy Network's Successes, Failures and Objectives*. Washington Post [online]. Available at www.washingtonpost.com/world/national-security/black-budget-summary-details-us-spy-networks-successes-failures-and-objectives/2013/08/29/7e57bb78-10ab-11e3-8cdd-bcdc09410972_story.html?utm_term=.c32a0513882d [Accessed 25 October, 2016].

24 Snowden, E. 17th, December, 2013. *Snowden's Open Letter to Brazil. Read the Text* [online]. Available at www.washingtonpost.com/world/national-security/snowdens-open-letter-to-brazil-read-the-text/2013/12/17/9bf1342a-6727-11e3-8b5b-a77187b716a3_ story. html?utm_term=.783b2273910a [Accessed 12 July, 2016].

25 Office of the Director of National Intelligence. 22nd January, 2009. Alternative Futures the IC Could Face [online]. Available at https://cryptome.org/2014/09/dni-qicr-2009-the-intercept-14-0905.pdf [Accessed 26 October, 2016].

26 Office of the Director of National Intelligence. 22nd January, 2009. Alternative Futures the IC Could Face [online]. Available at https://cryptome.org/2014/09/dni-qicr-2009-the-intercept-14-0905.pdf [Accessed 26 October, 2016].

27 Office of the Director of National Intelligence. 22nd January, 2009. Alternative Futures the IC Could Face [online]. Available at https://cryptome.org/2014/09/dni-qicr-2009-the-intercept-14-0905.pdf https://fas.org/irp/dni/qicr.pdf [Accessed 26 October, 2016].

28 Office of the Director of National Intelligence. 22nd January, 2009. Alternative Futures the IC Could Face [online]. Available at https://fas.org/irp/dni/qicr.pdf [Accessed 26 October, 2016].

29 Office of the Director of National Intelligence. 22nd January, 2009. Alternative Futures the IC Could Face [online]. Available at https://fas.org/irp/dni/qicr.pdf [Accessed 26 October, 2016].

30 Office of the Director of National Intelligence. 22nd January, 2009. Alternative Futures the IC Could Face [online]. Available at https://fas.org/irp/dni/qicr.pdf [Accessed 26 October, 2016].

31 Office of the Director of National Intelligence. 22nd January, 2009. Alternative Futures the IC Could Face [online]. Available at https://fas.org/irp/dni/qicr.pdf [Accessed 26 October, 2016].

32 Office of the Director of National Intelligence. 22nd January, 2009. Alternative Futures the IC Could Face [online]. Available at https://fas.org/irp/dni/qicr.pdf [Accessed 26 October, 2016].

33 Office of the Director of National Intelligence. 22nd January, 2009. Alternative Futures the IC Could Face [online]. Available at https://fas.org/irp/dni/qicr.pdf [Accessed 26 October, 2016].

34 Office of the Director of National Intelligence. 22nd January, 2009. Alternative Futures the IC Could Face [online]. Available at https://cryptome.org/2014/09/dni-qicr-2009-the-intercept-14-0905.pdf [Accessed 26 October, 2016].

35 Office of the Director of National Intelligence. 22nd January, 2009. Alternative Futures the IC Could Face [online]. Available at https://cryptome.org/2014/09/dni-qicr-2009-the-intercept-14-0905.pdf [Accessed 26 October, 2016].

36 Office of the Director of National Intelligence. 22nd January, 2009. Alternative Futures the IC Could Face [online]. Available at https://cryptome.org/2014/09/dni-qicr-2009-the-intercept-14-0905.pdf [Accessed 26 October, 2016].

37 Office of the Director of National Intelligence. 22nd January, 2009. Alternative Futures the IC Could Face [online]. Available at https://cryptome.org/2014/09/dni-qicr-2009-the-intercept-14-0905.pdf [Accessed 26 October, 2016].

38 Office of the Director of National Intelligence. 22nd January, 2009. Alternative Futures the IC Could Face [online]. Available at https://cryptome.org/2014/09/dni-qicr-2009-the-intercept-14-0905.pdf [Accessed 26 October, 2016].

39 Office of the Director of National Intelligence. 22nd January, 2009. Alternative Futures the IC Could Face [online]. Available at https://cryptome.org/2014/09/dni-qicr-2009-the-intercept-14-0905.pdf [Accessed 26 October, 2016].

40 Office of the Director of National Intelligence. 22nd January, 2009. Alternative Futures the IC Could Face [online]. Available at https://cryptome.org/2014/09/dni-qicr-2009-the-intercept-14-0905.pdf [Accessed 26 October, 2016].

41 Office of the Director of National Intelligence. 22nd January, 2009. Alternative Futures the IC Could Face [online]. Available at https://cryptome.org/2014/09/dni-qicr-2009-the-intercept-14-0905.pdf [Accessed 26 October, 2016].

42 Office of the Director of National Intelligence. 22nd January, 2009. Alternative Futures the IC Could Face [online]. Available at https://cryptome.org/2014/09/dni-qicr-2009-the-intercept-14-0905.pdf [Accessed 26 October, 2016].

43 Snowden Archives. 10th September 2010. Close Access Sigads [online]. Available at https://snowdenarchive.cjfe.org/greenstone/collect/snowden1/index/assoc/HASH01da/d86eda87.dir/doc.pdf [Accessed 30 November, 2016].

44 Snowden Archives. 10th September 2010. Close Access Sigads [online]. Available at https://snowdenarchive.cjfe.org/greenstone/collect/snowden1/index/assoc/HASH01da/d86eda87.dir/doc.pdf [Accessed 30 November, 2016].

45 Snowden Archives. 10th September 2010. Close Access Sigads [online]. Available at https://snowdenarchive.cjfe.org/greenstone/collect/snowden1/index/assoc/HASH01da/d86eda87.dir/doc.pdf [Accessed 30 November, 2016].

46 WikiLeaks. 4th, July, 2015. Bugging Brazil [online]. Available at https://wikileaks.org/nsa-brazil/ [Accessed 4 July, 2016].

47 Fantastico, Brazil. 8th September, 2013. NSA Documents Show United States Spied [on] Brazilian Oil Giant [online]. Available at http://g1.globo.com/fantastico/noticia/2013/09/nsa-documents-show-united-states-spied-brazilian-oil-giant.html [Accessed 12 June, 2016].

48 Petrobras. [No date]. Important Achievements [online]. Available at www.petrobras.com.br/en/our-activities/performance-areas/oil-and-gas-exploration-and-production/pre-salt/ [Accessed 27 October, 2016].

49 Fantastico, Brazil. 8th September, 2013. NSA Documents Show United States Spied [on] Brazilian Oil Giant [online]. Available at http://g1.globo.com/fantastico/noticia/2013/09/nsa-documents-show-united-states-spied-brazilian-oil-giant.html [Accessed 12 June, 2016].

50 Fantastico, Brazil. 8th September, 2013. NSA Documents Show United States Spied [on] Brazilian Oil Giant [online]. Available at http://g1.globo.com/fantastico/noticia/2013/09/nsa-documents-show-united-states-spied-brazilian-oil-giant.html [Accessed 12 June, 2016].

51 Fantastico, Brazil. 8th September, 2013. NSA Documents Show United States Spied [on] Brazilian Oil Giant [online]. Available at http://g1.globo.com/fantastico/noticia/2013/09/nsa-documents-show-united-states-spied-brazilian-oil-giant.html [Accessed 12 June, 2016].

52 Fantastico, Brazil. 8th September, 2013. NSA Documents Show United States Spied [on] Brazilian Oil Giant [online]. Available at http://g1.globo.com/fantastico/noticia/2013/09/nsa-documents-show-united-states-spied-brazilian-oil-giant.html [Accessed 12 June, 2016].

53 Fantastico, Brazil. 8th September, 2013. NSA Documents Show United States Spied [on] Brazilian Oil Giant [online]. Available at http://g1.globo.com/fantastico/noticia/2013/09/nsa-documents-show-united-states-spied-brazilian-oil-giant.html [Accessed 12 June, 2016].

54 Fantastico, Brazil. 8th September, 2013. NSA Documents Show United States Spied [on] Brazilian Oil Giant [online]. Available at http://g1.globo.com/fantastico/noticia/2013/09/nsa-documents-show-united-states-spied-brazilian-oil-giant.html [Accessed 12 June, 2016].

55 Fantastico, Brazil. 8th September, 2013. NSA Documents Show United States Spied [on] Brazilian Oil Giant [online]. Available at http://g1.globo.com/fantastico/noticia/2013/09/nsa-documents-show-united-states-spied-brazilian-oil-giant.html [Accessed 12 June, 2016].

56 Fantastico, Brazil. 8th September, 2013. NSA Documents Show United States Spied [on] Brazilian Oil Giant [online]. Available at http://g1.globo.com/fantastico/noticia/2013/09/nsa-documents-show-united-states-spied-brazilian-oil-giant.html [Accessed 12 June, 2016].

57 Ackerman, S. 13th June, 2013. *Senators Challenge NSA's Claims to Have Foiled 'Dozens' of Terror Attacks*. The Guardian [online]. Available at www.theguardian.com/world/2013/jun/13/senators-challenge-nsa-surveillance-terrorism [Accessed 28 October, 2016].

58 Wyden, R. 17th November, 2016. *Wyden Statement on Director Clapper's Resignation* [online]. Available at www.wyden.senate.gov/news/press-releases/-wyden-statement-on-director-clappers-resignation [Accessed 24 December, 2016].

59 Fantastico, Brazil. 8th September, 2013. NSA Documents Show United States Spied [on] Brazilian Oil Giant [online]. Available at http://g1.globo.com/fantastico/noticia/2013/09/nsa-documents-show-united-states-spied-brazilian-oil-giant.html [Accessed 12 June, 2016].

60 Campbell, D. October, 2016. *Interview.*

61 Mayer, J. 23rd May, 2011. *The Secret Sharer.* The New Yorker [online]. Available at www.newyorker.com/magazine/2011/05/23/the-secret-sharer [Accessed 12 June, 2016].

62 Mayer, J. 23rd May, 2011. *The Secret Sharer.* The New Yorker [online]. Available at www.newyorker.com/magazine/2011/05/23/the-secret-sharer [Accessed 12 June, 2016].

63 Mayer, J. 23rd May, 2011. *The Secret Sharer.* The New Yorker [online]. Available at www.newyorker.com/magazine/2011/05/23/the-secret-sharer [Accessed 12 June, 2016].

64 Mayer, J. 23rd May, 2011. *The Secret Sharer.* The New Yorker [online]. Available at www.newyorker.com/magazine/2011/05/23/the-secret-sharer [Accessed 12 June, 2016].

65 Mayer, J. 23rd May, 2011. *The Secret Sharer.* The New Yorker [online]. Available at www.newyorker.com/magazine/2011/05/23/the-secret-sharer [Accessed 12 June, 2016].

66 Mayer, J. 23rd May, 2011. *The Secret Sharer.* The New Yorker [online]. Available at www.newyorker.com/magazine/2011/05/23/the-secret-sharer [Accessed 12 June, 2016].

67 Mayer, J. 23rd May, 2011. *The Secret Sharer.* The New Yorker [online]. Available at www.newyorker.com/magazine/2011/05/23/the-secret-sharer [Accessed 12 June, 2016].

68 Mayer, J. 23rd May, 2011. *The Secret Sharer.* The New Yorker [online]. Available at www.newyorker.com/magazine/2011/05/23/the-secret-sharer [Accessed 12 June, 2016].

69 US District Court. 28th September, 2012. *Declaration of William E. Binney in Support of Plaintiffs' Motion for Partial Summary Judgment Rejecting the Government Defendants' Secret Defense* [online]. Available at https://info.publicintelligence.net/NSA-WilliamBinneyDeclaration.pdf [Accessed 24 January, 2017].

70 US District Court. 28th September, 2012. *Declaration of William E. Binney in Support of Plaintiffs' Motion for Partial Summary Judgment Rejecting the Government Defendants' Secret Defense* [online]. Available at https://info.publicintelligence.net/NSA-William BinneyDeclaration.pdf [Accessed 24 January, 2017].

71 Welna, D. 22nd July, 2014. Before Snowden: *The Whistleblowers Who Tried to Lift the Veil.* NPR [online]. Available at www.npr.org/2014/07/22/333741495/before-snowden-the-whistleblowers-who-tried-to-lift-the-veil [Accessed 30 June, 2016].

72 Welna, D. 22nd July, 2014. Before Snowden: *The Whistleblowers Who Tried to Lift the Veil.* NPR [online]. Available at www.npr.org/2014/07/22/333741495/before-snowden-the-whistleblowers-who-tried-to-lift-the-veil [Accessed 30 June, 2016].

73 Maurizi, S. 11th February, 2017. *NSA Bill Binney: 'Things Won't Change Until We Put These People in Jail'.* Repubblica [online]. Available at www.repubblica.it/esteri/2017/02/11/news/usa_nsa_bill_binney_integrale_eng-158062766/ [Accessed 7 December, 2016].

74 Maurizi, S. 11th February, 2017. NSA Bill Binney: 'Things Won't Change Until We Put These People in Jail' Repubblica [online]. Available at www.repubblica.it/esteri/2017/02/11/news/usa_nsa_bill_binney_integrale_eng-158062766/ [Accessed 7 December, 2016].

75 Anonymous source. 2017. *Interview.*

76 Anonymous source. 2017. *Interview.*

77 Snowden, E. 2017. *Interview*.
78 Cannataci, J. 27th February, 2017. *(Advanced United Version) Report of the Special Rapporteur on the Right to Privacy, Jospeh A. Cannataci*. United Nations Human Rights Council. [Copy held by author].
79 Cannataci, J. 27th February, 2017. *(Advanced United Version) Report of the Special Rapporteur on the Right to Privacy, Jospeh A. Cannataci*. United Nations Human Rights Council. [Copy held by author].
80 Snowden, E. 2017. *Interview*.
81 Lashmar, P. August, 2016. *Interview*.

8

TRUTH TO POWER

The Ministry of Defence (MoD) in central London, not far from the Palace of Westminster, the Houses of Parliament, is not famous for providing top cuisine in its canteen. It serves staple fare, from fish and chips to spaghetti bolognaise with the possibility of a glass of rosé to wash it down. These are hardly facts that need to be kept under lock and key, but until a few years ago, that is exactly how the MoD treated them – even the canteen menu, as an internal MoD publication, was a state secret. Anyone publishing it, according to the letter of the law, would be in breach of Section 2 of the Official Secrets Act (1911). As an act of publicity for its launch, as much as its desire to draw attention to the all-encompassing nature of Britain's secrecy laws, the first edition of the *News on Sunday*, in 1989, reproduced a copy of the MoD canteen menu under the headline: 'This Newspaper Is Dangerous. If You Read Page 11 You Are Liable to Two Years in Prison.'[1]

Had the *News on Sunday* published the menu from the Ministry of Agriculture, the same rules of secrecy would have applied, but it might not have been as promotable from the newspaper: 'You are technically breaking the law and could go to prison for reading *News on Sunday*.'[2] While most, though possibly not all journalists would be untroubled by Section 1 of the Official Secrets Act which deals with spying, it was Section 2 that was a much greater problem. This part of the Act made it an offence to publish *any* government material without the express permission of the minister concerned.[3]

The broadening of the UK's first Official Secrets Act (1889) to include Section 2 had its roots in the early 1900s – a time when large sections of the population believed Britain was under threat of an imminent invasion. Their fear was fed by what was known as 'invasion scare' fiction: books that conjured up visions of French and Russian forces capturing British military charts and codes, and in one celebrated case carrying out the murder of a military officer. The main perpetrator of this scaremongering was author William Le Queux, a journalist with a flair for creative writing, the ability to blend fact and fiction and the aptitude to pass off fiction as fact. He prefaced one of his books, *Spies of the Kaiser*, with the statement that the book pointed to the 'important lesson' underlying it: 'the French are laughing at us, the Russians presume to imitate us and the Day of Reckoning is hourly advancing,'[4] he wrote. *Spies of the Kaiser*, published in early 1909, was a bestseller and, according to author Philip Knightly, it soon became clear that the book's thousands of readers considered it 'as they had every right to do in view of Le Queux's ambiguous presentation of the book as fact in fictional form – as being totally true'.[5] Other books by Le Queux offered a similar narrative: the German army, invading on a Sunday morning, had been helped by their agents who severed the telegraph links between East Anglia and London.

Stirring up the fear of foreigners, the *Daily Mail* cashed in on what was fast developing into a national psychosis. Le Queux worked closely with his friend Alfred Harmsworth, later Lord Northcliffe, owner of the *Daily Mail*, who not only shared his views about the perils of a fifth column of German informants living in Britain, but also agreed to serialise his books. Le Queux repaid the favour by tailoring the stories of treacherous German activity to the areas where most *Daily Mail* readers lived, maximising their impact and sending both book sales and the circulation of the *Daily Mail* soaring. To promote the serialisation Northcliffe sent an army of men into the streets dressed as German military, complete with spiked helmets and billboards warning of the Kaiser's spies. The newspaper enlisted the support of its readers: 'Refuse to be served by a German waiter', the *Daily Mail* advised. 'If your waiter says he is Swiss, ask to see his passport.'[6]

As a revolving-door form of feedback, spy fever spread across Britain. Readers inundated Le Queux with letters telling alarming stories of a nation filled with Germans: they worked in the post office, they were barbers, waiters, even army officers. When Le Queux sent the letters to a House of Commons sub-committee investigating state security, they played a direct role in the creation of Section 2, the 'tightening of the Official Secrets Act', according to Knightly.[7] Such was the xenophobia enhanced by the *Daily Mail's* campaign that many cite it as one of the reasons that the commons sub-committee went on to recommend the 'formation of the Secret Service Bureau' – the forerunner of MI5.[8] Whether or not it was that clear-cut is difficult to tell but there is no doubt that the first task of the Secret Service Bureau was to investigate the 'spy scare stories' of Le Queux and other authors.[9] As MI5's current website explains, 'Most of the "spies" who persuaded Whitehall that it was faced with 'an extensive system of German espionage' in Britain were figments of the media and popular imaginations'.[10]

'Next to the Kaiser', wrote social rights campaigner and journalist A.G. Gardiner, 'Lord Northcliffe has done more than any other living man to bring about the war.'[11] He had also assisted in the creation of a new section of the Official Secrets Act which would severely hamper the work of journalists for decades to come.

On 11 January, 1970, the *Sunday Telegraph* published extracts from a confidential report on a civil war which was raging in Nigeria. Written by Colonel Robert

E. Scott, defence adviser to the British High Commission in the Nigerian capital, Lagos, the report was embarrassing for Britain's Labour government. It revealed that Britain had been secretly helping the Nigerian government in its attempts to recapture the secessionist state of Biafra. What was most worrying for the government, the report revealed that the British Government was sending a huge amount of arms and equipment to help the Biafran secessionists, well in excess of what ministers had acknowledged in Parliament. The *Sunday Telegraph's* editor, Brian Roberts, had been given a copy of the report by Jonathan Aitken, a successful journalist and supporter of Biafran self-determination. Aitken in turn had acquired a copy of the report from Major General Henry Templer Alexander, a British representative on the International Military Observer Team and the father of one of Aitken's girlfriends. According to author Christopher R. Moran, Alexander had given Aitken the report after he had questioned his assertion 'during a postprandial drinking session'[12] that the war was nearing its end. Delighted to have in his possession evidence that government spokesmen had been misleading the public, Aitken made two copies of the report. The one that went to Roberts was used as the basis for an article in the *Sunday Telegraph*; the other went to Hugh Fraser, a Conservative MP who supported the Biafra cause.

When the story broke, Prime Minister Harold Wilson ordered an immediate investigation. Leaks from his government had already caused great embarrassment, and Wilson wanted them stopped. In the past leakers had been charged, but not journalists. This time the government changed course. Aitken was charged under Section 2 of the Official Secrets Act with illegally receiving classified government documents.

Though journalists have been known to celebrate the misfortune of their rival colleagues in the combative world of British newspapers, the trial which began on 12 January, 1971 united Fleet Street. The sight of a journalist in the dock at Court Number 1 at the Old Bailey they found deeply worrying, possibly concerned that they could be next. Curiously missing from the charge sheet was Major General Alexander, who had leaked the material.

In his summing up, before acquitting Aitken and ordering the prosecution to pay full costs, Justice Caulfield pointed to a glaring error in the prosecution's case: without Alexander being tried too, it was impossible to determine what the intention had been in publishing the details of the report. Justice Caulfield attacked the notion that once an official document was stamped 'Secret' anyone handling that document was breaking the law. In the interests of freedom of speech, Caulfield concluded, Section 2, which was nearing its 60th birthday, had reached retirement age and should be 'pensioned off'.

What was needed,[13] he continued, was a section that would enable men like Aitken and Roberts 'and other editors . . . to determine without any great difficulty whether a communication is going to put them in peril of . . . facing a criminal charge'.[14] Resistance to change in Whitehall could be summed up by the comments of Cabinet Secretary Burke Trend. Committed to defending the status quo, he reminded Prime Minister Wilson that the Official Secrets Act had a 'remarkably stabilising effect', not unlike the 'cane in the best type of orthodox school'.[15] American allies, he said, were extremely envious of Section 2 for its inhibiting effect on the behaviour of journalists. There were no irksome problems like the First Amendment with its implications for freedom of the press.[16] The case caused such a degree of concern among both journalists and the judiciary that when Wilson's government was re-elected – after losing the election in 1970 – it made a specific undertaking in 1974 that Section 2 would be repealed and the mere receipt of information would no longer be an offence.

But just as the American intelligence agencies might be envious of Section 2, British journalists were equally highly enamoured with the First Amendment provisions of the US Constitution. In the 1970s Duncan Campbell turned his analytical capabilities as a physicist to journalism. He joined *Time Out*, a magazine which published lists of events mixed with often revelatory journalism. Campbell's work would return the essential elements of freedom of speech to the country of its birth, Britain, where John Milton is widely lauded for his argument for free speech and an eloquent campaign to stop Parliament regulating printing presses in the 17th century.

In 1976, Campbell revealed one of the most closely held secrets in British intelligence, the existence of GCHQ. Entitled 'The Eavesdroppers', Campbell's report, published on May 21st 1976, in *Time Out*, told how

> from two modern office blocks on the outskirts of Cheltenham, the directors of GCHQ manage a world-wide network of listening posts. They have directed aircraft and ships into foreign air and sea space to obtain information on their communications and defences.'[17]

The article said that the 'listening posts are often found in the most remote places – Cyprus, Hong Kong, Singapore, Oman, Belize, St Helena, the Ascension Islands and Botswana'.[18] It also told how 'another base was recently identified in Australia when after a typhoon hit Darwin large numbers of RAF personnel were discovered on a nearby off-shore island'.[19] By today's standards the report might seem quite innocuous, but in the 1970s, when the existence of GCHQ was hidden, even from Parliament, it was explosive.

Campbell's report was in part based on information provided by Perry Fellwock, a former NSA analyst who, like Daniel Ellsberg, had first-hand knowledge that the US public was being lied to about the Vietnam War. 'Daniel Ellsberg's releasing the Pentagon Papers made me want to talk,' Fellwock said in an interview.[20] 'We must take steps to insure there are no more Vietnams,'[21] he told an assembled crowd shortly after his interview was published in *Ramparts*, an influential radical magazine which had already made a name for itself publishing details of covert CIA funding of student university groups. 'I believe I have taken such a step. I have done it for neither money nor glory, but to bring to the American people knowledge which they have a need to know.'[22]

Just why Fellwock, who used the name Winslow Peck, was not prosecuted under the Espionage Act (1913) was not explained at the time but James Bamford in his ground breaking book about the NSA, *The Puzzle Palace* (Penguin, 1983), wrote: 'Prosecution they must have reasoned, would only serve to confirm all that Fellwock had said.'[23] Before publication Ramparts had received similar advice from Ellsberg's lawyers that the government would not risk exposing more secrets by publicly pursuing them exposing the NSA's activities.

The NSA simply hoped the storm would pass, but on the other side of the Atlantic, Campbell, who had keenly read the *Ramparts* article, arranged to interview Fellwock when he visited London in 1976. Here Campbell benefitted from the freedom of speech provisions in the US Constitution while he carried out his work. For while investigating such a secret organisation as GCHQ by speaking to UK citizens might be against the law, US citizens could not be prosecuted under the Official Secrets Act. Further, anything told to him by a US citizen was effectively covered by the First Amendment. Thus, using information publicly available in the UK and the US, piecing together what Fellwock told him, Campbell was able to reveal the existence of GCHQ, and its activities.

The fact that Fellwock had not been prosecuted in the US under the Espionage Act only added to the extraordinary nature of the unfolding events. The NSA and GCHQ might have mastered the art of transnational spying; now transjurisdictional laws were being used against them.

In the best traditions of traditional journalism, after he had completed his report Campbell phoned GCHQ for a comment. Campbell asked to be put through to the press office. To put it mildly, his call took the most secret intelligence agency in the UK totally by surprise. 'After the operator picked up the phone again after thinking about it I was referred to the librarian at GCHQ to whom I gave questions.'[24] Campbell did not have to wait long for the reply. 'The response two days later was to tap my phone and to follow me around intensively, they put the top people in the security service on to me,' he said.[25]

'They knew who I had talked to. There was nothing they could do. There was no legal means for attacking me for publishing that article because I hadn't broken any British law,' not even Section 2 of the Official Secrets Act. Campbell said from that moment on he became 'a marked person . . . they just launched a campaign to bring this kind of journalism to an end,'[26] he said.

The reaction from GCHQ was palpable. One overseas local head of GCHQ had been sent a copy of Campbell's article before a weekly local intelligence meeting. 'He was incoherent, his world had been torn apart',[27] Campbell said.

> My source recalls him almost frothing at the mouth in his incoherence to explain the appalling situation from Britain that he had just learned about that GCHQ had been written about by a journalist. It was secret. And I had just broken their first canon. Told people they existed.[28]

As Campbell spoke to me at his home on Britain's South Coast, I asked him why in particular he thought it was important to reveal the existence of GCHQ.

Campbell: Because this was the largest intelligence organisation in the country. The political significance of what they did and the dangers of what they commanded. Their interventions in political and public affairs were of huge public interest. The Russians – our strategic enemy – knew everything about them because of a litany of agents who were inside and every time these cases would come up they would use the D-notice system to stop anybody finding out what the Russians knew because the matters concerned were about Russian agents. So from about 1956 onwards GCHQ was penetrated again and again. So there was no counter veiling interest not to put these particulars out there. And reasons for concern. These guys could have started wars at some stages by getting aircraft to overfly just so they could collect some more signals.

Q: And there was no oversight at that time?

CAMPBELL: It didn't exist. They weren't avowed. Most Cabinet ministers were not allowed to know. They weren't listed in government directories, you couldn't ask about them in parliament. There were no signs outside buildings saying what they did. They were anonymous buildings with anonymous people. The names of everyone who worked for them was secret, what they did was secret.

Q: How were they funded?

CAMPBELL: By the government with the 'Secret Vote' money.

Q: Why wasn't that publicly made available?

CAMPBELL: Because it was then sacred in Britain never to ask about intelligence. It would be unpatriotic and deeply wrong. I speak of the 70s. The funding was secret, staffing was secret, the roles were secret, and it was prohibited to even ask questions about them in parliament. The answer was: 'It is the policy of the government not to comment on intelligence or security matters, full stop.'[29]

But neither the intelligence agencies nor the government had finished with Campbell. They targeted the person who had shared the 'Eavesdroppers' byline, another US citizen, Mark Hosenball. The British Government announced that both Hosenball and former CIA officer Phillip Agee, whose CIA Diary (Penguin Books, 1975) revealing many of the agency's more unsavoury activities in South America had become a best seller, were to be deported as posing threats to British national security. Many people believed that the expulsions were a result of 'kow-towing' to the Americans, but Campbell believed the action against Hosenball was a substitute for punishing him. He joined a campaign to have the deportation revoked. If the British security forces had taken the lead from the US government's treatment of Peck, the story might have faded from public view. But instead the row over Hosenball and press freedom had an unintended consequence. If it was meant to engender fear and stifle debate, it did just the opposite.

In a suburban home in the north of London it captured the attention of a former British intelligence corporal, John Berry. He had served in one of GCHQ's listening posts, the 9th Signal Regiment in Cyprus. Berry had read 'The Eavesdroppers' and wanted to know what he could do to help Agee and Hosenball.

Berry wrote a letter to the 'Agee-Hosenball Defence Committee', care of the National Council for Civil Liberties (NCCL). He identified himself as a former member of 'an organisation spending vast amounts of money in total absence of public control' who would 'like to know of any medium through which these concerns could be published'.[30] Several days later Berry went to the NCCL headquarters in King's Cross and typed out a statement in which he wrote:

> It appears to me that secrecy is one of the most important keys to power and the existence of an organization capable of spending vast sums of money in the total absence of public control should do much to dispel any illusion about the democratic nature of our government.[31]

The NCCL passed the letter to *Time Out*, the only underground newspaper which might be prepared to defy the D-notice that excluded any reporting of GCHQ. The letter ended up on the desk of the environmental reporter Crispin Aubrey, an unlikely recipient since he knew little about electronic eavesdropping. Aubrey turned to the acknowledged expert, Campbell, to help him interview Berry 'to decide whether he's a bull-shitter'.[32]

On a foggy Friday evening, 18 February, 1977, Campbell and Aubrey travelled to Muswell Hill in North London to meet Berry. They suspected they were under surveillance; we know now that MI5 not only tapped Campbell's phone and the NCCL's but the intelligence agency's director general had singled Campbell out as 'a person of greatest interest'.[33]

There, over a bottle of Chianti in Berry's basement flat, they spoke for three hours, the entire conversation recorded by Aubrey's tape recorder. At 10 p.m. when the tape ran out they decided to call it a night. But as Campbell and Aubrey headed for home they were confronted by 13 police from Special Branch, who arrested them on suspicion of offences against Section 2 of the Official Secrets Act – legislation that the government in its election manifesto had promised to remove from the statute book. Campbell and the others had every reason to be surprised and angry. Just three months earlier, in a testy Parliamentary debate about Section 2 the Home Secretary Merlyn Rees had announced that the 'mere receipt of unauthorised information should no longer be an offence'.[34]

Yet what the Home Secretary said publicly and what the government and the intelligence agencies did privately, differed greatly. In the 1970s, at the height of the Cold War, Labour – concerned about being seen as soft on communism and security – would be ruthlessly hard on journalism. Campbell and Aubrey were charged under section 2 with 'unauthorised receipt of classified information' and Berry was charged with 'communicating classified information to unauthorised persons'. Yet this was, as the police said, a 'holding charge': justification, as their lawyer Geoffrey Robertson pointed out tongue in cheek, 'for holding 'dangerous men in custody until more serious charges were formulated'.[35] Within the next few hours police raided Campbell's home and took away vast amounts of paper and 400 books, including the novels of Ernest Hemingway and Graham Greene, and according to Robertson a book listed in the trial exhibits as The Female Unok [sic]. Subsequently, Campbell, Aubrey and Berry were charged with one of the most serious offences a state can allege: espionage.

Under Section 1 of the Official Secrets Act they were accused of obtaining or publishing information 'intended to be directly or indirectly useful to an enemy'. It carried a possible sentence of 14 years' imprisonment.

Within six weeks, Campbell was indicted on another Section 1 espionage charge which amounted to simply collecting too much information. Even today as he sits in his study surrounded by some of the files that were seized, Bob Dylan songs playing gently in the background, Campbell is still aghast at the additional charge under Section 1.

The files were packed with 'public source information, defence magazines, official publications and unpublished information, and none of it secret,' he said. 'So, journalism was espionage.'[36]

The ABC case, as it became known, after the initials of Aubrey, Berry and Campbell, was designed with one major objective, to stop Duncan Campbell's journalism. It wanted Campbell put away 'for a very long time',[37] as the prosecutor candidly told Robertson. The Crown's determination to get the result it wanted led to some overly zealous activity, or at least activity which no one at the time thought would ever be revealed. The court clerk disclosed to Jeremy Hutchinson, the senior counsel, that the prosecution had vetted the jury, several of whom worked for government departments and had signed the Official Secrets Act, and one, a former SAS soldier, was almost certainly hostile to the activities of the defendants. All this might have remained secret but for a note being passed to the judge that some members of the jury were worried that by even listening to the evidence, they might be breaking the Official Secrets Act. When news inevitably leaked out publicly that the prosecution had vetted the jury, the judge abandoned the trial. It was an appropriate end to a hearing which had bordered on farce. Barrister Jeremy Hutchinson, a doyen of the English criminal bar who defended such differing cases as the publication by Penguin of Lady Chatterley's Lover and the trial of Great Train Robber Charlie Wilson, had ridiculed and demolished the prosecution, exposing the fact that the supposedly secret information which was such a danger to Britain's security was publicly available. One of the star witnesses, whose identity was so secret he could only be referred to by a code, was in fact a minor military celebrity. His identity had been readily published in a regimental magazine, where he had been described as 'the don of the communications underworld'.[38] Other Crown witnesses found themselves acting out the idiocy of the Crown's secrecy claims.

Jeremy Hutchinson: [showing the witness a photograph of a sign at the entrance to a particular base]: Is that the name of your unit?

WITNESS: I cannot answer that question, that is a secret.
JEREMY: Is that the board that is up outside the door of your unit?
WITNESS: yes.
JEREMY: Read it out to the jury.
WITNESS: I cannot do that, that is a secret.[39]

Though a second trial was ordered, the prosecution was in disarray; Aubrey, Berry and Campbell were found to have breached Section 2 but received non-custodial sentences. The Section 1 charges against Campbell were dropped completely, though he remains the first and only British journalist in the UK to face trial for espionage, an accusation based on the fact that he had too much information stored in his home.

If, as is highly probable, the case against him was, as Campbell contends, pay-back for the 'Eavesdroppers' article, it creates a significant connection which over the decades has bound dissidents together. Just as Snowden and Manning were motivated to leak because of government deception, Perry Fellwock became motivated to blow the whistle on the NSA's activities – and through Campbell the surveillance and wiretapping by GCHQ – because of government deceit about the Vietnam War. In recent history, it has been these hegemonic wars, and the deception surrounding them, which have either encouraged or facilitated journalists and whistle-blowers to acts of dissent – even when it meant breaking the law. Aspects of the persecution of Duncan Campbell can be seen in the attacks on Snowden and Manning: the severity of Manning's 35-year sentence; the decision by the US government not to allow Snowden to receive an open trial where he could argue a public interest defence; and the ABC case using Section 2, which was widely discredited as a piece of law and would soon be removed from the statute book. Holding surveillance agencies to account for their covert actions is dangerous and difficult work, particularly when challenging the very powerful institutions which will do all they can to defend and protect their secrecy. As Jeremy Hutchinson remembered,

> The public became aware at last of what our potential enemies had known for years, that GCHQ at Cheltenham was the centre of a surveillance and intelligence organisation with a global network of listening posts. From that moment, it became clear that this institution could be misused and could give rise to the dangers of the 'surveillance state', with ever increasing power of intrusion into our private lives.[40]

Others may have been chastened by the repercussions of confronting the full power of the state. Yet barely out of the court room at the end of his trial, Campbell set about producing another revelatory report, this time for the *New Statesman* which disclosed for the first time the existence of a secret telephone-tapping operation being run by the government in central London. Campbell pointed out that it was a legitimate concern that there was no oversight or accountability over who the government or its agencies tapped and on what grounds they carried out this intrusive surveillance. It is hardly surprising that declassified records reveal that the government of Margaret Thatcher, elected six months after the trial ended, became fixated on Campbell's work. The Cabinet Secretary, Sir Robert Armstrong, ordered a close watch be kept on the BBC's documentary programme *Panorama,* which in the wake of the trial verdict had begun working on the possibility of doing a report on Britain's security intelligence agencies. A message to the prime minister, marked at the top and bottom of the page TOP SECRET AND PERSONAL, laid out what could be called a Campbell containment policy. 'The activities of Duncan Campbell, and the interest and activity they are generating (particularly in circles whose political motivation is suspect) have some effect on the morale and effectiveness of the intelligence services,' the prime minister was told. 'So long as all this is confined to the columns of the *New Statesman,* the *Leveller* and left-wing papers of that kind and to a small group of left-wing MPs, the damage is containable.'[41]

What concerned the government was that Campbell's arguments about accountability and transparency might be picked up by mainstream media, particularly the BBC. The memo continued: 'A BBC Panorama programme is a different kettle of fish. It would give respectability to the activities of Campbell; it would spark a much wider curiosity about the intelligence services'.[42]

Other MPs and other newspapers would feel obliged to 'jump on the bandwagon'[43] and the resulting damage to the morale and effectiveness of the Service could be 'very serious indeed'.[44] The Top-Secret message added: 'That of course is what Campbell and other are aiming at.' It ended somewhat ominously: 'It is very much in the national interest they should not succeed.'[45]

What the government failed to grasp was that while Campbell might have been talking to journalists at the BBC, Panorama did not need to be told by anyone that British security intelligence – and the laws protecting it from accountability – was an important area of investigation. The ABC trial had put on public display the shortcomings of the law, and the bungled attempts at protecting the identities of witnesses in the case verged on high farce. The programme that *Panorama* was working on was a natural extension of that: journalism designed to hold the intelligence agencies to account. The *Panorama* team was working on a programme which would disclose how a former agent claimed to have arranged hundreds of illegal telephone taps, provide fresh information about the notorious Profumo Affair, where the Conservative Cabinet Minister became potentially compromised by model and showgirl Christine Keeler, and reveal MI6 plots to liquidate Iran's Prime Minister Mossadeq and Egypt's Colonel Nassar.

Though at the time neither Thatcher nor other members of the Conservative government knew the details of what the Panorama programme might contain, Armstrong became increasingly anxious, putting pressure on Sir Ian Trethowan, the BBC's Director General, to discover exactly what would be in the programme.[46]

The government reasoning, that disclosure of unpleasant activities by the intelligence agencies might weaken Britain's security, hid a more obvious concern.

The future Labour Foreign Secretary, Robin Cook, believed that the intelligence agencies – which were still not publicly acknowledged – needed to be more accountable, and was pressing for the laws to be changed. The last thing the Thatcher government needed was huge amounts of credible evidence on one of Britain's most trusted programmes supporting the actions of their political opponents.

In another Top-Secret briefing paper Armstrong gave Thatcher an insight into how the BBC Director General might deal with the matter. 'Trethowan at first thought that when the production team had put their material together and made a film, he should see the film, together with one or two members of the editorial and production teams,' he wrote. Armstrong wrote that Trethowan also thought he might bring along MI5's Bernard Sheldon, the agency's legal advisor but 'later on he decided that that would be too difficult, since the role of Mr Sheldon would be liable to leak'.[47]

Instead, Sir Ian decided that 'he and Mr Sheldon should watch the film privately together, and that thereafter having heard Mr Sheldon's comments, he should take his own responsibility for deciding whether certain portions of the programme should be omitted'.[48]

On 13 January, Sir Ian Trethowan and MI5's Sheldon settled down to watch the Panorama programme 'MI5/MI6: The Need to Know'.

As Armstrong later reported to Thatcher, 'Sir Ian Trethowan has now put the programme in the hands of Mr Richard Francis, Director of News and Current Affairs.'[49] He reminded the prime minister that Francis was a member of the Defence, Press and Broadcasting Committee responsible for D-notices, so he would know what to do. Armstrong wrote that Francis had 'been asked to reduce'[50] the programme to 50 minutes – cutting it in half – taking into account the 'various comments made and deletions suggested by Sir Ian Trethowan'.[51] And just in case the prime minister was having a slow morning and thought the director-general might have been acting independently at the BBC he pointed out that the deletions were being made 'following Mr Sheldon's comments'.[52]

The public, meanwhile, would continue to be lied to about the involvement of the government in pressuring and threatening to muzzle the BBC. 'Sir Ian Trethowan has told the Press that no-one (from the Government) has seen the film and that there has been no pressure from the Government on the BBC,'[53] Armstrong wrote to Thatcher. He added that in the newspaper reports which speculated on government involvement 'the main attack is on him; and he is content to take it'.[54]

Even so Armstrong was not completely sure 'that all the [agreed] comments [for the program] will be followed'. But he did not think there was 'any more we can do, short of an outright veto; and it remains my view that cure would be worse than the disease'.[55]

The Panorama reporter, Tom Mangold, put it more succinctly, telling the BBC's *PM* current affairs show: 'It wasn't the greatest program but it was the best we could do at the time.'[56] *Panorama* may not have got exactly what it wanted but it did manage to point to problems of accountability in the intelligence establishment. What the No 10 documents suggest is that Cabinet secretary Sir Robert Armstrong and Prime Minister Thatcher were more concerned about the political problems the *Panorama* program might raise; the issue of national security was barely mentioned. The failings of MI6 – hidden from the British public until decades later when some of its files were declassified – confronted Thatcher on 2 April, 1981, when Argentina invaded the Falkland Islands. Britain was caught completely unawares. MI6 missed it. The MI6 chief at the time Colin McColl later admitted the failure to warn the government, with the oblique comment: 'We were clearly seen to be too thin.'[57]

Programs like *Panorama*'s 'MI5/MI6: The Need to Know', and the work of journalists like Duncan Campbell, tenacious and forensically committed to accountability, were advancing journalism at a time when the fear of a real world-ending nuclear holocaust was very strong. When governments invoked the possibility of a threat to national security it could cause real dread, and they used it time and again to silence critics and control their opponents. At the time, even the official existence of state spying organisations GCHQ and MI5 were not publicly recognised. Similarly, in Australia, the existence of the Australian Security Intelligence Agency (ASIO) and the Australian Secret Intelligence Service (ASIS) were still secret and in France there was no official confirmation of the General Directorate for External Security (DGSE) or the Directorate of Territorial Security (DST). Governments in the West wielded an almost unassailable power. But the journalistic enlightenment which came with the release of Pentagon Papers, the Church Committee investigation into CIA assassination programs, and Watergate was emerging as a force which affected not only the way journalists went about their jobs, but even what they thought their jobs were. This form of investigative journalism, digging deep into government wrongdoing, had seen many incarnations down the ages, but a newly educated post-war generation would use it to challenge the status quo with extraordinary political effect. Journalists would begin holding the state to account.

Slightly more than a year after *Panorama* had managed to wrestle its programme to air, across the English Channel a reporter who shies away from being called an investigative journalist, because he argues all good journalism involves investigation, began unearthing government wrongdoing which took on all the dimensions of a French Watergate.

Unlike Watergate, though, which began with a seemingly humble break-in at a Washington office complex, the French version took off with gusto. On 9 August, 1982, two gunmen threw a grenade into a Jewish restaurant on the Rue des Rosiers in central Paris, and opened fire on passers-by. The attack killed six people and wounded 22. With Paris under regular assault from terrorist shootings and bombings the rue des Rosiers attack gave French President Francois Mitterrand the opportunity to set up what would become his own covert Pretorian guard. Within hours he had directed Christian Prouteau, head of the elite National Gendarmerie Intervention Group [Groupe d' Intervention de la Gendarmerie Nationale – CIGN] to establish a 'Mission of Coordination, information and action against terrorism'.[58] Unlike normal procedure, where a crime fighting unit would be part of police and security services under the control of the Minister of the Interior, this group would operate in secret and to report directly to the president. When the anti-terror group discovered three members of the Irish Republican Socialist Party, which had a paramilitary wing, the Irish National Liberation Army, in Paris it was enough for the anti-terrorist group; all they needed was the evidence.

When police raided the homes of the Irish nationalists in the Rue Diderot in the suburb of Vincennes in the east of Paris they found three handguns and some explosives. But an examining magistrate ruled that the police had broken the rules of evidence, as the suspects had not been present when the search was made. The 'Irish of Vincennes' as they became known, were set free, the charges annulled. At *Le Monde* Edwy Plenel began digging into the case and published an article on 31 October, 1985 alleging that one of the police officers, Captain Paul Barril, had supplied incriminating evidence in the Vincennes case. Plenel had seen information gathered by the DST which revealed that the guns and explosives had been given to Barril to plant on the 'Irish of Vincennes'. Suspicious that there was more to the story, Plenel began investigating. On 21 March 1991, *Le Monde* published a lengthy follow-up article entitled 'Irlandais de Vincennes: les cachoteries de l'Elysée' (The Irishmen in Vincennes: an Elysée cover-up), which claimed that executive members of the government had withheld documents from the courts.

Plenel was right, but what no one knew then was that many of the documents were thousands of pages of transcripts of telephone conversations recorded by the anti-terrorist group using illegal intercepts on the orders of the French president. In a windowless room at the Elysée Palace the anti-terrorism team had set up a secret listening post, with 'gleaming banks of tape-recorders' and a 'large functional table in the centre of a polished, tiled floor'.[59]

All the illegally recorded conversations would bypass the normal intelligence and surveillance apparatus and be relayed directly to the Elysée, where they would be transcribed. Like US President Richard Nixon, President Mitterrand had ordered a covert spying campaign.

Yet it would be three more years before the truth started to be revealed. In 1993 the newspaper *Liberation* published a report that the anti-terrorism team had been secretly recording Plenel's phone calls for two months between 1985 and 1986, and published 16 pages of transcripts. What had clearly concerned the anti-terrorism team was that Plenel himself was about to disclose an act of terrorism that the President of France wanted kept secret. Plenel had been investigating the mysterious sinking of the Greenpeace Ship *Rainbow Warrior* in New Zealand's Auckland Harbour on 10 July, 1985. The ship had been on its way to protest French nuclear tests on the tiny French atoll of Mururoa,

1200 kilometres south east of Tahiti. Though the story of the attack on the *Rainbow Warrior* by French military and intelligence officers was first revealed by the Australian Broadcasting Corporation's *Four Corners* programme, in September 1985 Plenel's report in *Le Monde* disclosed the extent of French intelligence involvement in the bombing, codenamed Operation Satanique, which killed Portuguese photographer Fernando Pereira.

In March 1993 – just four days after *Liberation*'s report – Plenel successfully sought a judicial investigation. But Jean-Paul Valat, the investigating magistrate, immediately ran into huge obstacles. First he was prevented from gaining access to a secret internal government report, then the police officer responsible for guarding the telephone intercept data was found hanged.

During the following year, with the investigation floundering, Valat benefitted from an unexpected find. A 'brunette dressed in black'[60] – a person who remains anonymous – gave the magistrate five computer disks containing 5,000 pages of transcripts of the bugged phone calls. The disks showed the unit eavesdropped on a bewildering array of prominent people from 1983 to 1986, recording more than 3000 conversations involving 150 people from lawyers to rival politicians and journalists. Mitterrand's personal assistant Gilles Manage personally handed over transcripts of the conversations from Plenel's phones to Mitterrand. As the President of France perused the transcripts he wrote the word 'Seen'[61] on them in his distinctive handwriting.

The investigation was also greatly helped when five metal trunks of documents detailing the wire-taps were seized from a garage rented by the head of the CIGN, Christian Prouteau. But before the metal trunks were handed over to authorities, according to the *Le Canard Enchaîné*, one of the few French newspapers which embraced investigative journalism, Alain Juppé's conservative government confiscated documents relating to the 1986–88 government led by fellow party member and former president Jacques Chirac. The newspaper said the government did not want to admit the illegal recordings took place while conservatives were in power.

It was an action consistent with the unconstrained exercise of executive authority: a political system in which it was possible for the head of state to establish a team to break the law to protect not the state of France, but the political power and personal secrets of the French president. It was not just the *Rainbow Warrior* affair Mitterrand was concerned about; he wanted the French public kept unaware of his extramarital affair with historian and museum curator Anne Pingeot, that produced their daughter, Mazarine, the head of the CIGN anti-terrorism group, Christian Prouteau, explained what was expected. 'The President called me into his office,' he reportedly told investigators:

> He opened the newspaper and showed me an article. He was extremely angry. He said the article contained information known only to him and the interior minister. He suspected his rooms may have been bugged, but they hadn't. He said he wanted the journalist's phone tapped. So we did.[62]

On another occasion Mitterrand directed Prouteau to spy on Plennel.

'I spoke to [Defence Minister Charles] Hernu, and they gave me access to the phones, that's all it needed,'[63] Prouteau said. To avoid arousing suspicion, the anti-terrorism group sought permission to eavesdrop not directly on Plenel but on his girlfriend, who lived with him. To create a level of cover for the surveillance request they described her as an arms trafficker, though she worked as a secretary.

In an echo of President Nixon's behaviour one person close to the inquiry was quoted as saying: 'It seems Mitterrand just became more and more paranoid. Anyone and everyone who looked like posing a threat to his public image had their phones tapped, against the law.'[64]

But it is here that the comparison with the US, and the form of inquiring journalism which became so disruptive to the old power relationships, part company. Only a few journalists in France followed the lead of Plenel in challenging government authority. Thirty years after the sinking of the *Rainbow Warrior*, Plenel reflected on the state of French journalism and its journalists which, with few exceptions, avoided confronting the powerful and instead accused Plenel of being a 'vigilante not a journalist'.[65]

Even now in France, Plenel says, his 'conception of the role of the journalist is not yet accepted'.[66] He 'believed in a journalism of inquiry, of challenge, of holding to account'.[67] Many of his colleagues seemed to prefer a' kind of sitting down journalism ... a journalism of commentary, that seeks to explain and justify rather than to challenge government'.[68]

The fact that the anti-terrorism spy case dragged on for more than a decade raised important questions about the efficacy of the French political and judicial systems, and the role of the Fourth Estate in holding them to account. The problem is they have a close financial relationship.

In a political culture where the practice of étatisme plays a key role, there are few places where this is more obvious than in the subsidies the government has given to the French press. In 1993 the then prime minister, Edouard Balladur produced a 200 million French franc (approximately €31 million) government rescue plan for the print media, regarded as vital by many observers to foster a market shaken by an economic downturn in advertising, under-capitalisation of companies, escalating production costs, and plummeting circulations.

The state-sponsored subsidy measures were aimed at offering access to information for all citizens 'in order to stimulate their participation in public life'.[69]

The former director of the French Press Institute, Pierre Albert, pointed out that the role of the state, in France, was the 'exact opposite of its Anglo-Saxon counterpart'.[70] In the US or in England, freedom of expression was considered the natural sequel to 'laissez faire',[71] which meant that the market ruled the world of information, and that any regulatory restriction was considered intolerable. But in France with the 'tradition of the Roman law',[72] the press asked for

> the law to guarantee its freedom in the name of the necessary protection of pluralism against the eventual excesses of the powers of money: the media cannot be treated as ordinary products or goods for the simple reason that they perform a public service.[73]

Albert argued that 'while certain State subsidies are, for us, considered as a natural contribution of the collectivity to safeguard the press' pluralism',[74] across the Channel – and 'even more so, across the Atlantic'[75] – they were 'considered as a soft-core form of corruption of the paper's independence'.[76]

Whatever the reason for the investigatory failure of the French media, the Elysée Palace spying scandal raised questions about the fundamental freedoms in the French state. 'We are a long, long way from what a democracy should expect after such a monumental violation of people's rights,'[77] said Antoine Comte, one of several lawyers who were the victims of eavesdropping. 'In America, an affair like this would – and did – lead to the resignation of the president.'[78]

In all 12 staff from senior levels of the French government were charged, from private secretaries to executive officers of the DST. It was perhaps fitting that the hearings took place in the 17e Chambre du Tribunal du Grand Instance de Paris, the court whose magistrates deal with issues relating to freedom of the press. Cases involving *Charlie Hebdo* and *Mediapart* have often been heard here beneath the light panelled wood and the cracked floors, part of the Palace of Justice which dates back to the 13th Century. When the court handed down its decision, it gave a rare insight into a political culture which accepted dictates from the executive seemingly without question. The orders from Mitterrand were 'relayed without any reservations'[79] by the government, the court ruled. Pierre Mauroy, the prime minister between 1982 and 1984, had what the court described as 'full conscience'[80] of the illegality of the intercepts. The protests of ignorance of his successor, Laurent Fabius, appeared to the court 'surprising'[81] and the magistrates mocked 'the defective memory'[82] of Paul Quilès, then minister of defence. Yet none of these politicians were punished for the illegalities they had been directly involved in, or knew about but did nothing. It was those who worked for the politicians who were held to account. And even they received only minimal punishment although they faced the possibility of a year in jail and a fine of €45,000.

Christian Prouteau received the heaviest sentence – eight months suspended and a €5,000 fine even though the court noted, that he 'lied, either directly or through omission',[83] something it found 'obviously a disconcerting attitude for a person from an elite corps (the gendarmerie)'.[84]

General Jean-Louis Esquivié, number two of the cell, who told the tribunal 'lies'[85] and acted in 'bad faith',[86] was sentenced to a four months suspended sentence and fined €3,000. Pierre-Yves Gilleron, commissioner of the Surveillance of the Territory (DST), criticised for using secrecy as a defence, was sentenced to three months in prison and fined €2,000.

Gilles Ménage was the victim of 'a form of submission to the presidential will',[87] even if it did not exempt him 'from his own criminal responsibility'.[88] He received a six-month suspended sentence and was fined €5,000.

All the secretaries who worked under Christian Prouteau 'lied under oath without any hesitation'. And the behaviour of Jacques Fournet, a director of the DST, meant that his testimony had to be taken 'with great reserve'.[89]

But the court saved its severest criticism for the man who would never have been present. It was he who 'was personally responsible for the creation of the Elysée cell',[90] he was 'the highest placed political leader'[91] and the person who most benefitted from the illegal spying, the court said. Yet even if he had lived, it is unlikely that President Mitterrand, who died in 1996, would have been held to account. Under the French constitution, representatives of the National Assembly would have been called to investigate his wrongdoings, something they were not inclined to do. For although Mitterrand had been caught out, he almost certainly was not alone. Other presidents too had been suspected of spying on their political opponents. Any investigation would be dangerous political territory for the National Assembly. Despite the obvious failings of the French system – by the time the appeals had been heard, and rejected, it was 20 years since the first intercepted phone calls – the court case did achieve one remarkable outcome: a finding of guilt against senior members of the French intelligence and security agencies. They had been brought to court to publicly answer for their crimes and held to account for their actions. Even though Plenel had revealed state secrets, he did not face the prospect of prosecution in France. Plenel, like all French journalists, was protected by both statutory law, which in all but the most extreme cases guarantees freedom of expression, and decisions of both the European Court of Human Rights and the European Court of Justice, which have repeatedly made findings guaranteeing the rights of journalists to protect their sources from disclosure.

While investigators in France had been gathering evidence which would condemn state spying on journalists, and implicitly support their role to expose state secrets for the national benefit, on the other side of the world an intriguingly different situation was unfolding.

In Australia, under the Crimes Act (1914) the all-encompassing laws matched much of Britain's Official Secrets Act. A Commonwealth government employee who communicated 'a prescribed sketch, plan, photograph, model, cipher, note, document or article, or prescribed information, to a person' with intent to damage the security of Australia could be charged with committing an indictable offence and be jailed for seven years.

But in the 1980s, unlike in the UK, the onus was on the government to keep its secrets. The receipt of classified or 'non-ministerial approved' information itself was not illegal. Even though, like the UK, Australia operated a D-notice system, where media organisations self-censored about a list of 'banned' subjects, it was a voluntary code. Significantly, not everyone agreed with the D-notice, or abided by it.

In 1988 when journalists Brian Toohey and William Pinwell began writing a book on Australia's overseas spy agency, the Australian Secret Intelligence Service, (ASIS), they found themselves entering a cross between what former CIA head of counterintelligence chief James Jesus Angleton called 'the Wilderness of Mirrors' and 'Alice in Wonderland'. Angleton was talking about how the world was often different from how it appeared; Toohey and Pinwill were about to discover how bizarre it could be. As Toohey, who was also the editor of *The Eye*, a monthly independent journal which specialised in breaking hard-edged political stories, worked on his book, *Oyster*, he received an unexpected leak: thousands of pages of highly classified documents apparently from Australian foreign minister Bill Hayden's office. Hayden had just been appointed Governor General of Australia, and the material arrived shortly after he had cleared out his desk in the Parliamentary offices, ready for the move to Government House.

The documents produced a plethora of stories to fill *The Eye*'s pages. They exposed details about how in 1984 the Australian government had been forced to back down over whether US nuclear warships could enter Sydney harbour. *The Eye* revealed how the Foreign Affairs Department had followed nearly word for word a press release written by US Secretary of State George Shultz's department, and issued it in the name of the Australian government.

In another embarrassment for the government, Hayden had written scathing notes in the margins of some of the documents. 'There is no doubt about it, the Indonesians are erratic, hostile people to deal with, with an added sententious-ness which makes them difficult neighbours,'[92] Hayden wrote.

In other notes Hayden also referred to the 'oafish behaviour' of the Malaysian Foreign Minister, Ghazalie Shafie; to the Japanese as 'hypocritical' and 'self-effacing'; and to Papua New Guineans as having 'limited maturity' and 'clumsy bluff', which might lead them 'deeper and deeper into a quagmire of confusion and incompetence'.[93]

Another cable revealed that the Defence Signals Directorate, now the Australian Signals Directorate, the electronic eavesdropping arm of the Australian intelligence services, was spying on Indonesian troops, using a naval vessel under the guise of monitoring illegal fishing.

Within hours of *The Eye* appearing on the streets, the government lodged an immediate action with the Australian High Court, seeking an interim injunction on the grounds that public disclosure of the contents of the documents would endanger national security. The fact that Toohey had broken no laws and had merely ignored the voluntary D-notice process left the government with few options but to take action in the highest court in Australia, if it wanted to stop further publication of the Hayden documents. Toohey's tactics of publishing first had wrong footed the government and made its actions appear extreme. It allowed Toohey to say – with tongue perhaps planted firmly in cheek – he could not com-prehend how any government would seek to prevent him from writing about defence and foreign affairs issues, but more genuinely to add: 'I will obviously contest vigorously any attempt to suppress information which the public needs to judge policies of politicians and Governments.'[94]

As in the UK, the government appeared uncomfortable and at times unable to deal with the kind of journalism which had lived on the fringes of the main-stream, but in the wake of the Watergate disclosures had grown in power and influence. The government's counsel, Stephen Charles, accused Toohey of pub-lishing information to obtain a 'journalistic scoop for profit'.[95] It was a difficult argument to run against a magazine that barely made any money. What seemed even more difficult to sustain was that in quoting directly from the documents Toohey had been 'deliberately unfair, misrepresented the views of Hayden'.[96]

Far more damaging to the government was that *The Eye* had in fact faithfully reported what Hayden had written. It is unlikely that what was published came as any great surprise to the countries involved, since they routinely carried out what are known as 'technical operations' – surveillance – against visiting diplomatic delegations and made a point of targeting communications traffic into and out of Australian embassies. But the defence minister, Kim Beazley, argued that revealing a specific intelligence-gathering activity against Indonesian armed forces who occupied East Timor after invading the country in 1975 would damage Australia's international relations. It could be equally argued that publicly revealing the fact that Australia was spying would at least remind Indonesian troops that they were being watched as they carried out countless atrocities in East Timor, which lost an estimated 200,000 people during the Indonesian invasion and occupation of their country.

The fact that, as with most journalistic endeavours, the most significant information had been published first, seemed to escape the government's attention. Still it pressed on, demanding that all the Hayden documents, including those which had not been published, should be returned. Much to the government's dismay, Toohey pointed out that he had already destroyed them, so consequently there would be no more reports based on the Hayden papers.

And there the matter might have rested, but for a train of events which is still not fully explained.

As Toohey tells it, during the editing process of *Oyster* he sent a couple of chapters to the publisher by mail. It should have been safe to assume that once in the care of the Australian Post Office, the material would be safe. But that wasn't the case. The book didn't arrive. Instead, Toohey says he was told: 'someone found it on a grass verge by the side of the road and gave it to a local television station [Channel 10] because its contents looked interesting'.[97] The TV station, in Sydney, thinking they might have a scoop on their hands, arranged for the material to be sent to its office at Parliament House, Canberra, for its political reporters to examine. From there the mystery deepened. Whether it ever turned up or not is not clear, but what is known is the minister responsible for Australia's counter intelligence agency, ASIO, the attorney general, got a tip off that Toohey was writing a book on ASIS. Part of the 'unfinished manuscript fell into the government's hands', Toohey wrote.[98] From there the situation turned from absurd to farcical. A little over a month after the government had secured its limited victory over Toohey, they were all back at the High Court. Following a meeting of senior ministers on the Cabinet Security Committee, the Attorney General, with a team of senior counsel, wanted another injunction. They feared that Toohey was about to publish material about Australia's overseas spy agency, not in *Oyster* which so clearly had not yet been finished, but in *The Eye*. Toohey had a long record of producing high-quality journalism as editor of the *National Times*, a newspaper which dominated the Australian political agenda for much of the 1980s, but had become disenchanted and moved on to set up *The Eye*, similar to Edwy Plenel's French news site *Mediapart*.

At the High Court, as dusk was falling on 31 October, 1988, the attorney-general's team told Mr. Justice Deane that Toohey's magazine might contain the kind of information about ASIS which would be damaging to national security. They sought a temporary injunction to stop *The Eye* being published.

Had the attorney-general's team stopped off at parliament on their way to the High Court their concerns might have been assuaged. For though the magazine wasn't due to be published until later, there were many advance copies circulating among some of *The Eye*'s most avid readers, Australian politicians. There was nothing in the current issue about ASIS.

It seems that Toohey's sources were better than those of Senator Gareth Evans, who later told Parliament that two days earlier he had received information that material about ASIS was likely to appear in the magazine. It could have been that publication had been intended in the following issue. The government would not apologise for acting in the national interest.

Evans, who made the switch from attorney general to Foreign Minister when Hayden left office, said he believed Toohey was going to publish an article outlining ASIS operations outside Australia, disclosing the identity of an ASIS officer. He believed publication of the material would prejudice national security. It would, he said, adversely affect 'the further utility to ASIS' of an officer or agent whose identity had been disclosed. The officer, their family and property could all be endangered, Evans argued. The fact was that Toohey had no intention of naming the ASIS officer – something that Evans later accepted – and the people he wanted to name were long gone from the service.

Australia, like other Western liberal democracies, had found itself struggling to deal with a newly assertive media, particularly in the form of journalists who did not play by the rules which governed much of journalism until the 1970s. In earlier days merely the threat of a D-notice was enough to tame the media. Both the *National Times* and *The Eye* broke out of this conformity, and without other laws to prevent publication of state secrets, the government had been repeatedly forced back on to the legal provisions provided even by interim injunctions seeking 'prior restraint'.[99] The problem for the government was that if it won the case, by the time the court demanded there should be no further publication, it was too late.

It was not the first time that the Australian government had found itself outmanoeuvred by a newly inquisitive press. In 1983 it had successfully applied for a High Court injunction against the *National Times* as the newspaper began to publish a series of secret defence and Foreign Affairs documents called the AUSTEO Papers – top secret documents marked for Australian Eyes Only. Once again, by the time the case got to court the main thrust of the story had already been revealed.

After the ASIS case had been settled Evans told the Australian Senate that the principles guiding the government's actions were those enunciated by Mr Justice Mason in another case of prior restraint.

The Court will not prevent the publication of information which merely thrown light on the past workings of government, even if it be not public property, so long as it does not prejudice the community in other respects. Then disclosure will itself serve the public interest in keeping the community informed and in promoting discussion of public affairs. If, however, it appears that disclosure will inimical to the public interest because national security, relations with foreign countries, or the ordinary business of government will be prejudiced, disclosure will be restrained.[100]

Toohey and Pinwill said that 'while the concept of prior restraint was 'repugnant and contrary to the democratic right of freedom of expression', they had no choice but to accept the court's decision and submit 'every word of the completed manuscript to Canberra', though they added the amendments and 're-phrasing which resulted from our negotiations have not impaired the overall integrity of the book'.[101]

Evans appeared to have gone part way to allowing the large part of the book to be published, untouched.

There is much in the manuscript that ASIS and the Government itself, would ideally prefer not to see published or re-published, but, recognising the importance of principles of free expression and freedom of information [there is] very little that we will actually seek to delete.[102]

Nearly 30 years later in November 2016, he reflected on the way the government had dealt with protecting state secrets. Shortly after a memorial ceremony for an Australian strategic analyst, Professor Des Ball, whose work helped journalists better understand complex military intelligence issues and at the same time made him a target of ASIO (Australian Security Intelligence Organisation) surveillance, Evans told me: 'In terms of the great policy issues the military secrets so called, the secrets of the [US] Alliance, the diplomatic secrets that people like to keep, 95 per cent of it is wildly exaggerated'.[103] He said it kept everybody 'a lot more honest, a lot more disciplined and a lot more focused on sensible policy making if a lot of this stuff was in the open'.[104]

He said he had 'never got into so much trouble politically'[105] than when he took seriously the advice that he was given by the security agencies, whether it was ASIO or ASIS. To rush out in the 'national interest'[106] to stop information being released which ASIO or ASIS thought should not be in the public domain,'by and large all those efforts to keep it out of the public domain proved absolutely fruitless'.[107] In retrospect there was 'very little, of that secrecy that I felt was totally justified'.[108]

Evans, who as attorney general was responsible for ASIO and later as Foreign Minister for the activities of ASIS, said that in his 13 years in Cabinet 'very little of any of the stuff that was . . . gleaned [by ASIO or ASIS]' added 'much value to our understanding of what was going on, let alone our vital security interests'.[109] He thought the benefit from the intelligence agencies had been 'pretty marginal'.[110]

Evans, a civil libertarian lawyer before he entered politics, might have been out of step with many of his contemporaries in other members of the Western Alliance with these views, but he would change his mind, after an event in the US in September. 'I take a different view . . . regarding the counter terrorism stuff',[111] he said. He was not alone among politicians.

Notes

1 Herman, A. 26th April, 1987. *Left-Wing Tabloid Joins Newspaper War*. UPI [online]. Available at www.upi.com/Archives/1987/04/26/Left-wing-tabloid-joins-newspaper-war/6773546408000/ [Accessed 12 March, 2017].
2 Herman, A. 26th April, 1987. *Left-Wing Tabloid Joins Newspaper War*. UPI [online]. Available at www.upi.com/Archives/1987/04/26/Left-wing-tabloid-joins-newspaper-war/6773546408000/ [Accessed 12 March, 2017].
3 Legilsation.gov.uk. 1981. Contempt of Court Act, 1981 [online]. Available at www.legislation.gov.uk/ukpga/1981/49/contents [Accessed 1 July, 2017].
4 Le Queux, W. 1909. *Spies of the Kaiser*. Hurst & Blackett Ltd, UK.
5 Knightly, P. 1987. *The Second Oldest Profession: Spies and Spying in the Twentieth Century*. W. W. Norton & Company, New York.
6 MI5. 2017. The Establishment of the Secret Service Bureau [online]. Available at www.mi5.gov.uk/the-establishment-of-the-secret-service-bureau [Accessed 10 January, 2017].
7 Knightly, P. 1987. *The Second Oldest Profession: Spies and Spying in the Twentieth Century*. W. W. Norton & Company, New York.
8 Cambridge University Library. 2017. Under Covers: Documenting Spies [online]. Available at www.lib.cam.ac.uk/exhibitions/Spies/captions.html [Accessed 10 January, 2017].
9 Cambridge University Library. 2017. Under Covers: Documenting Spies [online]. Available at www.lib.cam.ac.uk/exhibitions/Spies/captions.html [Accessed 10 January, 2017].
10 MI5. 2017. The Establishment of the Secret Service Bureau [online]. Available at www.mi5.gov.uk/the-establishment-of-the-secret-service-bureau [Accessed 10 January, 2017].
11 Jackson, P. and de Castella T. 14th July, 2011. *Clash of the Press Titans*. BBC News [online]. Available at www.bbc.com/news/magazine-14136044 [Accessed 10 January, 2017].
12 Moran, C. 2013. *Classified: Secrecy and the State in Modern Britain*. Cambridge University Press.
13 Moran, C. 2013. *Classified: Secrecy and the State in Modern Britain*. Cambridge University Press.
14 Moran, C. 2013. *Classified: Secrecy and the State in Modern Britain*. Cambridge University Press.
15 Moran, C. 2013. *Classified: Secrecy and the State in Modern Britain*. Cambridge University Press.
16 Moran, C. 2013. *Classified: Secrecy and the State in Modern Britain*. Cambridge University Press.
17 Campbell, D. 1976. *The Eavesdroppers*. Time Out [online]. Available at www.duncancampbell.org/PDF/1976-may-time-out-the-eavesdroppers.pdf [Accessed 27 August, 2016].

18 Campbell, D. 1976. *The Eavesdroppers*. Time Out [online]. Available at www.duncancampbell.org/PDF/1976-may-time-out-the-eavesdroppers.pdf   [Accessed 27 August, 2016].

19 Campbell, D. 1976. *The Eavesdroppers*. Time Out [online]. Available at www.duncancampbell.org/PDF/1976-may-time-out-the-eavesdroppers.pdf [Accessed 27 August, 2016].

20 Cryptome. 1998. U.S. Electronic Espionage: A Memoir [online]. Available at https://cryptome.org/jya/nsa-elint.htm [Accessed 10 August, 2016].

21 Chen, A. 12th November, 2013. *After 30 Years of Silence, the Original Whistle-blower Looks Back*. Gawker [online]. Available at http://gawker.com/after-30-years-of-silence-the-original-nsa-whistleblow-1454865018 [Accessed 12 August, 2016].

22 Chen, A. 12th November, 2013. *After 30 Years of Silence, the Original Whistleblower Looks Back*. Gawker [online]. Available at http://gawker.com/after-30-years-of-silence-the-original-nsa-whistleblow-1454865018 [Accessed 12 August, 2016].

23 Bamford, J. 1983. *The Puzzle Palace*. Penguin, US.

24 Campbell, D. October, 2016. *Interview*.

25 Campbell, D. October, 2016. *Interview*.

26 Campbell, D. October, 2016. *Interview*.

27 Campbell, D. October, 2016. *Interview*.

28 Campbell, D. October, 2016. *Interview*.

29 Campbell, D. October, 2016. *Interview*.

30 Robertson, G. 1999. *The Justice Game*. Vintage, London.

31 Aubrey, C.1981. *Who's Watching You: Britain's Security Services and the Official Secrets Act*. Penguin, London.

32 Robertson, G. 1999. *The Justice Game*. Vintage, London.

33 Aldrich, R. 2010. *GCHQ: The Uncensored Story of Britain's Most Secret Intelligence Agency*. Harper Press, London.

34 Rees, M. 22nd November, 1976. Official Secrets Act 1911 [online]. Available at http://hansard.millbanksystems.com/commons/1976/nov/22/official-secrets-act-1911 [Accessed 24 July, 2017].

35 Robertson, G. 1999. *The Justice Game*. Vintage, London.

36 Campbell, D. October, 2016. *Interview*.

37 Robertson, G. 1999. *The Justice Game*. Vintage, London.

38 Hutchinson, J. 2015. *Jeremy Hutchinson's Case Histories: From Lady Chatterley's Lover to Howard Marks*. Hachette, UK.

39 Hutchinson, J. 2015. *Jeremy Hutchinson's Case Histories: From Lady Chatterley's Lover to Howard Marks*. Hachette, UK.

40 Hutchinson, J. 2015. *Jeremy Hutchinson's Case Histories: From Lady Chatterley's Lover to Howard Marks*. Hachette, UK.

41 National Archives, Kew. 2017. Catalogue Reference PREM.19/587.

42 National Archives, Kew. 2017. Catalogue Reference PREM.19/587.

43 National Archives, Kew. 2017. Catalogue Reference PREM.19/587.

44 National Archives, Kew. 2017. Catalogue Reference PREM.19/587.

45 National Archives, Kew. 2017. Catalogue Reference PREM.19/587.

46 National Archives, Kew. 2017. Catalogue Reference PREM.19/587.

47 National Archives, Kew. 2017. Catalogue Reference PREM.19/587.

48 National Archives, Kew. 2017. Catalogue Reference PREM.19/587.

49 National Archives, Kew. 2017. Catalogue Reference PREM.19/587.

50 National Archives, Kew. 2017. Catalogue Reference PREM.19/587.

51 National Archives, Kew. 2017. Catalogue Reference PREM.19/587.

52 National Archives, Kew. 2017. Catalogue Reference PREM.19/587.

53 National Archives, Kew. 2017. Catalogue Reference PREM.19/587.

54 National Archives, Kew. 2017. Catalogue Reference PREM.19/587.

55 National Archives, Kew. 2017. Catalogue Reference PREM.19/587.

56 BBC. 30th December, 2011. Panorama Reporter Recalls BBC Censorship [online]. Available at www.bbc.com/news/av/uk-16369440/panorama-reporter-recalls-bbc-censorship [Accessed 30 December, 2016].

57 Dorril, Stephen. 2000. MI6: *Inside the Covert World of Her Majesty' Secret Intelligence Service*. Fourth Estate, UK.

58 Beigbeder, Y. 2011. *Judging War Crimes and Torture: French Justice and International Criminal Tribunals and Commissions (1940–2005)*. Palgrave MacMillan, UK.

59 Field, C. 1st December, 2004. *Private Spy Unit Kept Tabs on French President's Foes*. New Zealand Herald [online]. Available at www.nzherald.co.nz/world/news/article. cfm?c_id=2&objectid=9001267 [Accessed 13 October, 2016].

60 The Age, Melbourne. 16th November, 2004. *Mitterrand Terror Unit Hid Affair, Love Child* [online]. Available at www.theage.com.au/news/World/Mitterrand-terror-unit-hid-affair-love-child/2004/11/15/1100384496445.html [Accessed 12 November, 2016].

61 The Age, Melbourne. 16th November, 2004. *Mitterrand Terror Unit Hid Affair, Love Child* [online]. Available at www.theage.com.au/news/World/Mitterrand-terror-unit-hid-affair-love-child/2004/11/15/1100384496445.html [Accessed 12 November, 2016].

62 Henley, J. 9th August, 2002. *Bugging Scandal Lands Mitterand Allies in Court*. The Guardian [online]. Available at www.theguardian.com/world/2002/aug/09/france. jonhenley [Accessed 30 April, 2016].

63 Field, C. 1st December, 2004. *Private Spy Unit Kept Tabs on French President's Foes*. New Zealand Herald [online]. Available at www.nzherald.co.nz/world/news/article. cfm?c_id=2&objectid=9001267 [Accessed 13 October, 2016].

64 Henley, J. 9th August, 2002. *Bugging Scandal Lands Mitterand Allies in Court*. The Guardian [online]. Available at www.theguardian.com/world/2002/aug/09/france. jonhenley [Accessed 30 April, 2016].

65 Lichfield, J. 25th April, 2013. *Edwy Plenel: Is the Journalist Detested by Politicians and Colleagues Alike the Most Hated Man in France?* Independent, London [online]. Available at www.independent.co.uk/news/world/europe/edwy-plenel-is-the-journalist-detested-by-politicians-and-colleagues-alike-the-most-hated-man-in-8588747.html [Accessed 4 October, 2016].

66 Lichfield, J. 25th April, 2013. *Edwy Plenel: Is the Journalist Detested by Politicians and Colleagues Alike the Most Hated Man in France?* Independent, London [online]. Available at www.independent.co.uk/news/world/europe/edwy-plenel-is-the-journalist-detested-by-politicians-and-colleagues-alike-the-most-hated-man-in-8588747.html.

67 Lichfield, J. 25th April, 2013. *Edwy Plenel: Is the Journalist Detested by Politicians and Colleagues Alike the Most Hated Man in France?* Independent, London [online]. Available at www.independent.co.uk/news/world/europe/edwy-plenel-is-the-journalist-detested-by-politicians-and-colleagues-alike-the-most-hated-man-in-8588747.html.

68 Lichfield, J. 25th April, 2013. *Edwy Plenel: Is the Journalist Detested by Politicians and Colleagues Alike the Most Hated Man in France?* Independent, London [online]. Available at www.independent.co.uk/news/world/europe/edwy-plenel-is-the-journalist-detested-by-politicians-and-colleagues-alike-the-most-hated-man-in-8588747.html.

69 Lardeau, M. and Le Floch, P. [No date]. *France: Press Subsidies – Inefficient but Enduring*. Researchgate.net [online]. Available at www.researchgate.net/publication/265122807_France_Press_Subsidies_-_Inefficient_but_Enduring#pf12 [Accessed 28 July, 2016].

70 Lardeau, M. and Le Floch, P. [No date]. *France: Press Subsidies – Inefficient but Enduring*. Researchgate.net [online]. Available at www.researchgate.net/publication/265122807_France_Press_Subsidies_-_Inefficient_but_Enduring#pf12 [Accessed 28 July, 2016].

71 Lardeau, M. and Le Floch, P. [No date]. *France: Press Subsidies – Inefficient but Enduring*. Researchgate.net [online]. Available at www.researchgate.net/publication/265122807_France_Press_Subsidies_-_Inefficient_but_Enduring#pf12 [Accessed 28 July, 2016].

72 Lardeau, M. and Le Floch, P. [No date]. *France: Press Subsidies – Inefficient but Enduring*. Researchgate.net [online]. Available at www.researchgate.net/publication/265122807_France_Press_Subsidies_-_Inefficient_but_Enduring#pf12 [Accessed 28 July, 2016].

73 Lardeau, M. and Le Floch, P. [No date]. *France: Press Subsidies – Inefficient but Enduring*. Researchgate.net [online]. Available at www.researchgate.net/publication/265122807_France_Press_Subsidies_-_Inefficient_but_Enduring#pf12 [Accessed 28 July, 2016].

74 Lardeau, M. and Le Floch, P. [No date]. *France: Press Subsidies – Inefficient but Enduring*. Researchgate.net [online]. Available at www.researchgate.net/publication/265122807_France_Press_Subsidies_-_Inefficient_but_Enduring#pf12 [Accessed 28 July, 2016].

75 Lardeau, M. and Le Floch, P. [No date]. *France: Press Subsidies – Inefficient but Enduring*. Researchgate.net [online]. Available at www.researchgate.net/publication/265122807_France_Press_Subsidies_-_Inefficient_but_Enduring#pf12 [Accessed 28 July, 2016].

76 Lardeau, M. and Le Floch, P. [No date]. *France: Press Subsidies – Inefficient but Enduring*. Researchgate.net [online]. Available at www.researchgate.net/publication/265122807_France_Press_Subsidies_-_Inefficient_but_Enduring#pf12 [Accessed 28 July, 2016].

77 Lardeau, M. and Le Floch, P. [No date]. *France: Press Subsidies – Inefficient but Enduring*. Researchgate.net [online]. Available at www.researchgate.net/publication/265122807_France_Press_Subsidies_-_Inefficient_but_Enduring#pf12 [Accessed 28 July, 2016].

78 Henley, J. 9th August, 2002. *Bugging Scandal Lands Mitterand Allies in Court.* The Guardian [online]. Available at www.theguardian.com/world/2002/aug/09/france.jonhenley [Accessed 30 April, 2016].

79 Johannes, F. 20th November, 2005. *Le tribunal juge Mitterrand responsable des ecoutes.* Le Monde [online]. Available at www.lemonde.fr/societe/article/2005/11/10/le-tribunal-juge-mitterrand-responsable-des-ecoutes_708806_3224.html [Accessed 27 September, 2016].

80 Johannes, F. 20th November, 2005. *Le tribunal juge Mitterrand responsable des ecoutes.* Le Monde [online]. Available at www.lemonde.fr/societe/article/2005/11/10/le-tribunal-juge-mitterrand-responsable-des-ecoutes_708806_3224.html [Accessed 27 September, 2016].

81 Johannes, F. 20th November, 2005. *Le tribunal juge Mitterrand responsable des ecoutes.* Le Monde [online]. Available at www.lemonde.fr/societe/article/2005/11/10/le-tribunal-juge-mitterrand-responsable-des-ecoutes_708806_3224.html [Accessed 27 September, 2016].

82 Johannes, F. 20th November, 2005. *Le tribunal juge Mitterrand responsable des ecoutes.* Le Monde [online]. Available at www.lemonde.fr/societe/article/2005/11/10/le-tribunal-juge-mitterrand-responsable-des-ecoutes_708806_3224.html [Accessed 27 September, 2016].

83 Johannes, F. 20th, November, 2005. *Le tribunal juge Mitterrand responsable des ecoutes.* Le Monde [online]. Available at www.lemonde.fr/societe/article/2005/11/10/le-tribunal-juge-mitterrand-responsable-des-ecoutes_708806_3224.html [Accessed 27 September, 2016].

84 Johannes, F. 20th November, 2005. *Le tribunal juge Mitterrand responsable des ecoutes.* Le Monde [online]. Available at www.lemonde.fr/societe/article/2005/11/10/le-tribunal-juge-mitterrand-responsable-des-ecoutes_708806_3224.html [Accessed 27 September, 2016].

85 Johannes, F. 20th November, 2005. *Le tribunal juge Mitterrand responsable des ecoutes.* Le Monde [online]. Available at www.lemonde.fr/societe/article/2005/11/10/le-tribunal-juge-mitterrand-responsable-des-ecoutes_708806_3224.html [Accessed 27 September, 2016].

86 Johannes, F. 20th November, 2005. *Le tribunal juge Mitterrand responsable des ecoutes.* Le Monde [online]. Available at www.lemonde.fr/societe/article/2005/11/10/le-tribunal-juge-mitterrand-responsable-des-ecoutes_708806_3224.html [Accessed 27 September, 2016].

87 Johannes, F. 20th November, 2005. *Le tribunal juge Mitterrand responsable des ecoutes.* Le Monde [online]. Available at www.lemonde.fr/societe/article/2005/11/10/le-tribunal-juge-mitterrand-responsable-des-ecoutes_708806_3224.html [Accessed 27 September, 2016].

88 Johannes, F. 20th November, 2005. *Le tribunal juge Mitterrand responsable des ecoutes.* Le Monde [online]. Available at www.lemonde.fr/societe/article/2005/11/10/le-tribunal-juge-mitterrand-responsable-des-ecoutes_708806_3224.html [Accessed 27 September, 2016].

89 Johannes, F. 20th November, 2005. *Le tribunal juge Mitterrand responsable des ecoutes.* Le Monde [online]. Available at www.lemonde.fr/societe/article/2005/11/10/le-tribunal-juge-mitterrand-responsable-des-ecoutes_708806_3224.html [Accessed 27 September, 2016].

90 Johannes, F. 20th November, 2005. *Le tribunal juge Mitterrand responsable des ecoutes.* Le Monde [online]. Available at www.lemonde.fr/societe/article/2005/11/10/le-tribunal-juge-mitterrand-responsable-des-ecoutes_708806_3224.html [Accessed 27 September, 2016].

91 Johannes, F. 20th November, 2005. *Le tribunal juge Mitterrand responsable des ecoutes.* Le Monde [online]. Available at www.lemonde.fr/societe/article/2005/11/10/le-tribunal-juge-mitterrand-responsable-des-ecoutes_708806_3224.html [Accessed 27 September, 2016].

92 Toohey, B. and Pinwill, W. 1st September, 1988. *Secrets: Govt to Appeal to Court.* The Sydney Morning Herald [online]. Available at www.newspapers.com/newspage/120466787/ [Accessed 17 June, 2016].

93 Toohey, B. and Pinwill, W. 1st September, 1988. *Secrets: Govt to Appeal to Court.* The Sydney Morning Herald [online]. Available at www.newspapers.com/newspage/120466787/ [Accessed 17 June, 2016].

94 Toohey, B. and Pinwill, W. 1st September, 1988. *Secrets: Govt to Appeal to Court.* The Sydney Morning Herald [online]. Available at www.newspapers.com/newspage/120466787/ [Accessed 17 June, 2016].

95 Scott, K. and Campbell, R. 2nd September, 1988. *Court Orders Toohey to Hand Over Papers.* The Canberra Times [online]. Available at http://trove.nla.gov.au/newspaper/article/102067182/11017386 [Accessed 25 June, 2016].

96 Scott, K. and Campbell, R. 2nd September, 1988. *Court Orders Toohey to Hand Over Papers.* The Canberra Times [online]. Available at http://trove.nla.gov.au/newspaper/article/102067182/11017386 [Accessed 25 June, 2016].

97 Toohey, B. April, 2017. *Interview.*

98 Toohey, B. and Pinwill, W. 1989. *Oyster.* Heinemann, Australia.

99 Toohey, B. and Pinwill, W. 1989. *Oyster.* Heinemann, Australia.

100 Toohey, B. and Pinwill, W. 1989. *Oyster.* Heinemann, Australia.

101 Toohey, B. and Pinwill, W. 1989. *Oyster.* Heinemann, Australia.

102 Toohey, B. and Pinwill, W. 1989. *Oyster.* Heinemann, Australia.

103 Evans, G. November, 2016. *Interview.*

104 Evans, G. November, 2016. *Interview.*

105 Evans, G. November, 2016. *Interview.*

106 Evans, G. November, 2016. *Interview.*

107 Evans, G. November, 2016. *Interview.*

108 Evans, G. November, 2016. *Interview.*

109 Evans, G. November, 2016. *Interview.*

110 Evans, G. November, 2016. *Interview.*

111 Evans, G. November, 2016. *Interview.*

9

THE CLAMPDOWN

On 11 September 2001, NBC News presenter Tom Brokaw told his audience, 'There has been a declaration of war by terrorists on the United States'.[1] The next day President George W. Bush turned the phrase around, declaring that the US was now fighting a war on terror, thereby elevating himself to the position of wartime president. What Bush did not make clear was that much of the war would be fought in the US based on questionable legality. Such was the revulsion and fear generated by the attack on the mainland of the US that many in Congress seemed to give up defending the basic tenets of the Constitution, and one of the bastions of the Fourth Estate, the *New York Times*, abrogated its responsibility to report to its readers what it knew about the NSA spying on them.

Unaware that the *New York Times* would eventually disclose the NSA domestic spying programme, the Bush administration went looking for legal cover for the actions which had already started: the wholesale surveillance of American citizens.

Just 45 days after the 9/11 attacks, Congress passed an Act which, according to the American Civil Liberties Union (ACLU), simply 'made it easier for the government to spy on ordinary Americans'.[2] Known as the Patriot Act, it seemed the acronym PATRIOT stood for the most important part of the clumsily named 'Uniting and Strengthening America by Providing Appropriate Tools Required to Intercept and Obstruct Terrorism Act of 2001'.

According to the ACLU, the Patriot Act would cut across two of the fundamental provisions of the US Constitution: the First Amendment giving the right to free speech and the Fourth Amendment preventing unreasonable searches and seizure of personal property. The government's plan appeared designed to give intelligence and police authorities greater powers to counter terrorism. However, the real failure to stop the 9/11 terrorists lay in the fact that information was not shared between law enforcement and intelligence agencies, as well as the failure of the Bush administration to take action after a specific warning from the CIA that the US was about to be attacked by al-Qaeda; as the 9/11 Commission of Inquiry pointed out, there were 'failures of imagination' that something like a massive attack on the US could happen.[3] The Patriot Act was not simply designed to change the law, it was also an attempt to shut down any criticism of the administrations' actions. Even the name Patriot could be used to mute the opposition – by definition those who opposed it were in danger of having their patriotism challenged. Despite some spirited debate arguing that the Act struck at the heart of the constitutional protections of free speech and privacy, it passed through Congress, and was signed into law by President Bush on 26 October, 2001. With the government increasing the powers of the police and the intelligence agencies, many US journalists, like the country's politicians, failed in their primary responsibilities, wrapping themselves even more securely in the flag. Silvio Waisbord's analysis, 'Journalism, Risk and Patriotism', described the post 9/11 US as having 'a social climate in which patriotism rapidly suffused the public sphere, mainstream journalism opted to ignore dissent and avoided questioning the dangers of exuberant patriotism'.[4] As Herbert Gans argued, Americanism is a bedrock value of US journalism. 'When the news is tragic or traumatic, it becomes the nation-cum-individual whose character and moral strength are tested', he wrote.[5]

The Act expanded the government's authority to monitor phone and email communications, collect reporting records and track internet use. Using a system known as National Security Letters (NSLs) FBI agents can obtain personal information without a judge's approval, including phone records, computer records, credit and banking history. The ACLU pointed out that between 2003 and 2006 the FBI used 192,499 NSLs which led to 'one terror-related conviction' which 'would have occurred even without the Patriot Act'.[6] At least 34,000 law enforcement and intelligence personnel had access to phone records collected through these NSLs. The ACLU said that in response to nine requests for NSLs – cases the FBI was working on – 11,100 US telephone accounts were handed over between 2003 and 2005. As a result of those 143 NSLs the FBI made 53 reported criminal referrals to prosecutors; of those 17 were for money laundering, 17 related to immigration, and 19 for fraud. Absolutely none were for terrorism.

The Patriot Act also allowed for what were known as 'sneak and peek' searches, where federal law enforcement agencies delayed giving notice when they would conduct secret searches of US homes and offices, what the ACLU described as a 'fundamental change to Fourth Amendment privacy protection and search warrants'.[7] Government agents were allowed to enter a house, an apartment or an office with a search warrant while an occupant was away, search through their property, take photographs – and in some cases, seize property and electronic communications – and not tell the owner until later. Of the 3,970 'Sneak and Peeks' in 2010, 76 per cent were drug related, 24 per cent related to 'other matters' and just 1 per cent were terrorism related.[8] The case of Brandon Mayfield is a good example of what happened when an individual challenged what he saw as unconstitutional action by the state.

During early 2004 the FBI secretly put Mayfield, a Muslim convert, under 24-hour surveillance, listened to his phone calls and covertly searched his home and office. In May, 2004, the FBI took him into custody because they said a fingerprint found on a detonator at the scene of the Madrid train bombing on 11 March, 2004, which killed 191 people, matched his. He spent two weeks in jail before the FBI released him. They had made a mistake. It wasn't his fingerprint. A Justice Department review said federal prosecutors and FBI agents had made inaccurate and ambiguous statements to a federal judge to get arrest and criminal search warrants against Mayfield.

When Mayfield took the FBI to court seeking compensation in 2007 US District Court Judge, Anne Aiken, punched a constitutional legal hole in the Patriot Act. The Foreign Intelligence Surveillance Act, as amended by the Patriot Act 'now permits the executive branch of government to conduct surveillance and searches of American citizens without satisfying the probable cause requirements of the Fourth Amendment,'[9] she wrote. The federal government, it seemed at the time, could not have chosen a worse case to prosecute, or a better one for civil liberties advocates to defend.

Justice Aitken said in her judgement: 'For over 200 years, this Nation has adhered to the rule of law – with unparalleled success. A shift to a Nation based on extra-constitutional authority is prohibited, as well as ill-advised.'[10]

The federal government apologised and settled part of the lawsuit for $2 million, allowing Mayfield to keep his right to challenge parts of the Patriot Act.

In 2009, Mayfield opened up his constitutional challenge in Oregon, based on the Fourth Amendment. His case claimed that several provisions of the Foreign Intelligence Surveillance Act (FISA), as amended by the Patriot Act, were unconstitutional. Mayfield's case rested on the fact that the government used the new laws to conduct covert surveillance, search the family's private quarters, and seize the family's private materials. Mayfield also said that because the government obtained the materials unlawfully the continued retention of any, what he called derivative material was also unlawful. But Mayfield's argument that the court should rule that his Fourth Amendment rights had been breached rested on thin ground. Under existing law, the government was not obliged to hand back any material to Mayfield. The court ruled that since his previous hearing had been settled with an apology and a compensation payment, Mayfield did not have a case. It seemed that in taking the money Mayfield had been outmanoeuvred by the government lawyers.

The court ruled, because his 'injuries had already been substantially redressed' by the multi-million dollar payout anything the judiciary decided would not serve to further benefit him or his family.[11] The judges were unable to make a ruling on whether Mayfield's Fourth Amendment rights had been infringed. The ACLU put it more succinctly:

'While most Americans think [the Patriot Act] was created to catch terrorists' the Act 'turned regular citizens into suspects'.[12] And then, it could be argued, tricked its victims into a sophisticated legal maze.

Across the Atlantic in the UK the Stars and Stripes became replaced with the Union Jack as many journalists put scepticism aside and rallied round the flag, unquestioningly accepting whatever law enforcement agencies said, particularly when terrorism cases were involved. Ten days after 9–11 an Algerian-born British resident, pilot Lotfi Raissi was arrested at his home near London's Heathrow Airport. The prime facie case looked strong.

The FBI and British authorities alleged that Raissi had trained some of the 9/11 pilots. According to the *Atlantic's* Raymond Bonner, 'The evidence seemed compelling – pages missing from his flight log – and few journalists expressed scepticism.' Bonner includes himself in this: 'I must ashamedly plead guilty.'[13]

As the world subsequently learned, the pages were 'missing' due to the negligence of Scotland Yard. After nearly five months of being held in London's notorious Belmarsh Prison, along with other terrorism suspects, Raissi was released. Even so it was not until 2010 that the British government entertained any question of compensation for Raissi's ruined life, and then only after being ordered to consider it by a British Appeal Court ruling saying he had been the victim of the 'heightened emotional atmosphere'[14] at the end of 2001.

Journalism and politics it seemed were coexisting in a relationship defined by hate and fear.

In 2003, US Attorney General John Ashcroft gave testimony to a congressional committee that a mosque in Brooklyn was sending money to al-Qaeda. In *Bush's Law: The Remaking of American Justice*, (Knopf Doubleday, 2009) *New York Times* correspondent Eric Lichtblau told how he wrote a story that ran on the front page of the *New York Times*, even though the *Times* reporter in Brooklyn warned him that Ashcroft could be wrong. As Lichtblau points out in his book, the reporter was right. 'We in the media were no doubt swept up in that same national mood of fear and outrage,'[15] Lichtblau wrote.

In the aftermath of the 9/11 attacks the Patriot Act led the way, as governments around the world were forced to deal with the consequences of the attack on the US. Drawn together mainly by their shared intelligence arrangements, the Five Eyes countries in particular began either changing old legislation or introducing new laws. In the United Kingdom, there had been a harbinger of what was to come with the introduction of the Regulation of Investigatory Powers Act, 2000, known as RIPA. Largely seen as a catch-up to deal with the emergence of the internet age, it already gave the state wide-ranging surveillance powers. Defence and intelligence agencies like GCHQ could legally intercept communications with a warrant from the Home Secretary or the Cabinet Secretary for Justice; others, gathering their own information through bugging, such as the prisons service or Customs, only needed permission from the senior member of their organisation. What is significant is that the judiciary was not involved in the decision-making process. There would be no legal argument about whether the surveillance should take place, or whether it was necessary to protect national security, or prevent a crime. By locking the judiciary out of the process, who would and would not be bugged became a political decision as much as matter of national security.

Thirty-eight days after the Twin Towers attack the British government rushed the UK Anti-Terrorist Crime and Security (ATCS) Bill into Parliament. Like the Patriot Act, the big shift was from targeting individuals to blanket surveillance of the entire population.

Under RIPA law enforcement and intelligence agencies already had extensive powers to intercept communications carried by telephone and internet companies. The ATCS Act gave government agencies the authority to compel telephone and internet companies to stockpile traffic data on all their customers in case they were required to provide information retrospectively to law enforcement agencies. Anyone who had a computer, used a mobile telephone, paid with a credit card, or withdrew cash from an ATM was caught in the surveillance net. Caspar Bowden, director of the Foundation for Information Policy Research, a non-profit think-tank for internet policy in the UK and Europe, pointed out the dangers of such surveillance: It 'reveals the sequence and pattern of thought of individuals using the internet – and could be described as closed-circuit television for the inside of your head'.[16]

Though the focus of the bill was terrorism, it was clearly much more than that, involving:

Traffic Analysis: Trawling the net to log who spoke to whom, by phone or email.

Location: Where people travelled. The mobile phones we all use send out a unique identifying number to every phone tower, whether the phone is on or off. The signal allows authorities to estimate within a few metres not only the phone's location, but the location of mobile phones nearby. With this simple data it is possible to discover who met whom and for how long.

Web Browsing history: Held by the communications companies, it gives a clear picture of which internet sites are visited and for how long.

Internet and telephone companies are required to stockpile all this data on the entire population for long periods, what Bowden described as 'the penultimate step towards a national "traffic data warehouse,"'[17] Of similar concern, a police superintendent or someone of equivalent rank could authorise access to data of a single person or millions of people, without any judicial or executive warrant. In other words, police or intelligence agencies could go on 'fishing expeditions'[18] to gather information on any individual they felt might be of interest at some time in the future. And they would never have to explain why.

Though the Act was presented as a counter-terrorism measure by the Labour Government of Tony Blair, the surveillance elements of the legislation could also be used for a wide range of possible offences, from health to public order. No one was safe from this dragnet. It placed the work of journalists and the whistle-blowers they spoke to in an extraordinarily vulnerable position. When questions were raised about the intrusive nature of the Bill weeks before it was passed, the director of the powerful National Criminal Intelligence Service (NCIS), John Abbott, wrote a letter to *The Guardian* complaining that 'conspiracy theorists must not be allowed to get away with the ridiculous notion that law enforcement would or even could monitor all emails'. The intelligence agencies, he said, 'have neither the inclination nor the resources, nor the legal ability to monitor the massive amounts of electronic communications that flow through the UK every day'. Abbott wrote that 'it does not happen with letters or telephones and it will not with emails'.[19]

Yet at that very time NCIS was calling on the Home Office for the creation of a national 'traffic data warehouse' covering the entire population. One year of records would be kept online in an enormous database, and at least three years, possibly six, held in archive. The document, first published in *The Observer*, was remarkable in that MI5, MI6, GCHQ ACPO (The Association of Chief Police Officers) and Customs and Excise were prominently named as jointly supporting the proposals, including a plan to deceive the British population. 'It may be less politically sensitive to set up data warehouses operated by . . . sub-contractors,' the report said. 'This could avoid suggestions over the Government's collection of personal data.'[20]

All along it seemed the security agencies understood there would be stiff opposition to their desire to 'collect it all', something that Abbott went to so far as to publicly deny. After 911 there would be no need for subterfuge.

In December 2001, the UK Anti-Terrorism Crime and Security Act received Royal Assent and became law, giving the intelligence and security organisations the legal capability to do much of what Abbott said was not possible and not needed. This tiny window into the publicly exposed deceptive behaviour of the security and intelligence agencies, which now had the capability to comb through the data of everyone in the UK whenever they wanted, did not bode well for the future. Across the English Channel the French government were posting similar laws.

On 15 November, 2001, the French Parliament introduced the 'Law on Everyday Security', which mirrored much of the US Patriot Act and the UK Anti-Terrorism and Crime Act and in the area of electronic intelligence-gathering. It extended the period for which records of internet activity and email traffic needed to be held by internet service providers. In other ways, the French law went further. It not only directed the storage of digital meta data by the telecommunications companies for a year but also required that the government have access to encryption keys and 'put restrictions on encryption software use'[21]

All the major western democracies were falling into line. But not all countries were that speedy. In Australia, after 9/11 four bills were rushed into Parliament, including one which would give the police the power to snoop on messages stored on phones or computers. They already had the authority to intercept messages, but were restricted from accessing data which had been stored, or not been read by the recipient: for example, an email or an SMS which had not been opened. There had been strong resistance in the community to the intrusion of the state into individual privacy. A plan to introduce a national identity card had been firmly rejected in a vote by the Australian people. The attack on Australia's military ally changed the public's attitude. Without a history of anti-terrorism legislation, the bills were quickly drawn up and introduced into Parliament after the summer recess on 12 March. They were passed by the lower house the next day. According to Australian historian Jenny Hocking they were sent on 'a rushed and heavily criticised trajectory during which the government gagged the debate which lasted barely a few hours'.[22]

The government introduced amendments to the Australian Security Intelligence Organisation Act (1979) which gave the domestic spy agency widespread powers: anyone suspected of being linked with terrorism could be held without charge for seven days. Even those subjected to abuse by ASIO would not be allowed to reveal what happened until long after the event. And any journalist who revealed anything about the case, or identified the person involved, could face five years in prison.

In a 2005 report the MEAA (Media, Entertainment and Arts Alliance) identified the ASIO Legislation Amendment Act 2003 as the law of main concern to journalists because of its effective limits on any media exposure of any active operation by the national security force under warrant for up to two years, 'even if the operation is in violation of international human rights conventions'.[23] The Act lists two offences for individuals who disclose 'operational information' designed to stop those questioned talking to other terrorists; as the MEAA points out, it also 'stops those who have been questioned by ASIO and/or their lawyers from talking to the media'.[24]

Other items of anti-terrorism legislation of concern to media advocates were:

- Criminal Code Amendment (Terrorist Organisations) Bill 2003 and the Anti-Terrorism Bill (no. 2) 2004; prohibiting 'association' with terrorist organisations. This has the potential to impede journalists trying to report on such groups, the report said.
- Amendments to the Telecommunications (Interception) Act 1979, enacted in 2004 and 2006; allowing enforcement agencies to obtain warrants to access stored communications such as SMS, MMS, email and voicemail messages held by journalists. This might jeopardise the identity of their confidential sources.

In its 2006 report, the MEAA suggested journalists now needed to assume that their conversations with sources on terrorism stories would be intercepted, as one of the 2006 amendments allowed phone tapping of third parties to suspected terrorist plots.

Those journalists who did contact terror suspects for a story might have their phone tapped, giving authorities access not only to conversations with the suspect but those of other innocent sources. At any time police could be listening, obliterating any professional right the journalist had to protect the confidentiality of their source, the MEAA report warned.

Australia, which had no anti-terrorism laws on the federal statute before 9/11, was playing catch-up. Over the following decade Australia made up for lost time, becoming the country that introduced the biggest number of anti-terror laws in the world – 54 separate pieces of legislation.

Two years later, after the London's 7/7 bombings, the Madrid train attack and the deaths of nearly 100 Australians in successive attacks on the island resort of Bali, the government again added new laws. Introduced into Parliament as 'The Anti-Terrorism (No. 2) Bill (2005), it left a publisher who had reported on ASIO's activities liable to an offence of 'reckless disclosure'. This law effectively marooned journalists without proper defences against the government's attempt to censor publishers through anti-terrorism-related laws. As the MEAA noted, 'there is nothing in the [Anti-Terrorism (No. 2) Bill 2005) to suggest that publishing "operational information" that is in the public interest is defensible against the definition of "reckless" disclosure'.[25]

The MEAA also said:

> It is simply unacceptable that any journalist be threatened with imprisonment for publishing something in the public interest – especially in Australia, where the right to inform and be informed is a cornerstone of our democracy. If a journalist did violate the laws, it is entirely possible that, under the very same laws, their arrest could be withheld from public debate.[26]

One of the biggest problems for Australia was that it had no Bill of Rights, and therefore no protection from large swathes of government intrusion on crucial rights like privacy, freedom of speech and procedural fairness. British journalists, on the other hand have been shielded to some extent by the European human rights laws, mirrored in British legislation through its membership of the Council of Europe and its submission to the European Court of Human Rights jurisdiction. The US journalists receive protection through the First Amendment which protects publishers. The laws that were passed in Australia in the decade after 9/11 faced none of those legal hurdles. There was no guaranteed freedom of speech, no protection against random search, as there is in the US, and while Australia is a signatory to the Universal Declaration of Human Rights, which in Article 19 guarantees 'freedom of expression',[27] the declaration is not mirrored in Australian legislation and is therefore not binding. Freedom of expression in Australia is only protected in very limited circumstances. The High Court has developed an 'implied right' through a holistic reading of the Australian Constitution. Known as the 'Lange Test', this implied right is limited to freedom of political expression.

According to George Williams, a noted Australian constitutional lawyer, Australia needed new anti-terror laws, but, he argues, the laws actually enacted reflected major problems of process and political judgement. To a large extent, this was a result of many of the laws being enacted as a reaction to catastrophic attacks overseas, especially 9/11 and the 2005 London attack. 'Too many of Australia's laws were passed in response to those and other events with inordinate haste and insufficient parliamentary scrutiny', he wrote.[28]

Australia has exceeded the UK, the US and Canada in the sheer number of new anti-terrorism laws that it has enacted since 9/11. As Kent Roach, Professor of law at Toronto University, wrote,

> this degree of legislative activism is striking compared even to the United Kingdom's active agenda and much greater than the pace of legislation in the United States or Canada. Australia's hyper-legislation strained the ability of the parliamentary opposition and civil society to keep up, let alone provide effective opposition to, the relentless legislative output.[29]

What no one knew at the time was that the legislative output was only part of the picture, obscuring what was really happening. In the US, the NSA continued to spy on American citizens under the President's Surveillance Program (PSP), which operated under the code name Stellar Wind. Just as importantly, the NSA was able to intercept all communications which crossed the country from outside its borders. Global companies like Google, Facebook and Microsoft, based in the US, control a huge slice of the world's data traffic which travels through the US, making it extremely vulnerable to this kind of interception. According to a classified NSA document the US is also the world's most significant 'choke point' for international telephone calls.

> The United States is a major crossroads for international switched telephone traffic. For example, in 2003, circuit switches worldwide carried approximately 180 billion minutes of telephone communications. Twenty percent of this amount, over 37 billion minutes, either originated or terminated in the United States, and another thirteen percent, over 23 billion minutes, transited the United States (neither originating nor terminating here) [NSA is authorised under Executive Order 12333 to acquire transiting telephone calls.][30]

The NSA was supposedly only allowed to intercept communications that entered the US from non-US citizens under strict rules which required a warrant issued by the secret FISA court. But armed with dubious legal advice, Bush expanded the programme – and ignored the necessity of a warrant. The NSA would be able to spy on anybody – collecting both the metadata and the content of telephone calls in some cases. Significantly the 'NSA was also allowed to retain, process, analyse and disseminate intelligence from the communications acquired under the authority'[31] of the president.

'They didn't know even in the most generous sense whether if there were genuine al Qaeda cells in the United States – there weren't – but they wiretapped the entire country to find out,' Snowden told me.[32] 'This goes on for months and months months and months, months grow to years.'[33]

At one time the then acting Attorney General James Comey refused to authorise Bush's continued use of Stellar Wind, but Comey was bypassed and the then head of the NSA Michael Hayden signed off on the programme on the president's say-so. Much of the Stellar Wind operation would be kept secret from both the Department of Justice and members of congressional oversight committees.

By 2005, with the NSA becoming increasingly anxious that it still relied on dubious legal opinion furnished by the White House that the organisation was not breaking the law, an attempt began to legitimise the 'warrantless wiretapping'. But it was not until 2007 that the Department of Justice instructed the NSA to 'find a legal basis' to 'collect bulk internet metadata'.[34] There were questions about whether or not the Protect America Act (2007) which supposedly legitimised Stellar Wind – and various amendments to the FISA (1978) – made the surveillance constitutional. At issue was the US Constitution's Fourth Amendment, which outlawed the search and seizure of property without due cause. With the NSA effectively rifling through the internet files of thousands of Americans on the off-chance they may be linked to al-Qaeda, they were already operating in a murky legal environment. Under the law the NSA was only allowed to intercept foreign communications, to and from people outside the US, but that was becoming increasingly difficult. The original Act which established FISA had been written in the pre-digital age when communications were transmitted by radio waves. These were analogue laws regulating digital behaviour. But now much of the world's information was sent digitally by fibre-optic cable. The agency was given permission to plug in to overseas communications cables when they landed on US soil. In 2012 William Binney, the former NSA cryptographer, broke a small hole in the security blanket which quarantined Stellar Wind from scrutiny. Binney explained that the agency could have installed its tapping gear at the nation's cable landing stations – the more than two dozen sites on the periphery of the US where fibre-optic cables come ashore. If it had taken that route, the NSA would have been able to limit its eavesdropping to just international communications, which at the time was all that was allowed under US law. Instead the NSA chose to put the wiretapping rooms at key junction points throughout the country – large, windowless buildings known as switches – thus gaining access not just to international communications but also to most of the domestic traffic flowing through the US. The network of intercept stations went far beyond the single room in an AT&T building in San Francisco exposed by a whistle-blower in 2006. 'I think there's 10 to 20 of them,' Binney says. 'That's not just San Francisco; they have them in the middle of the country and also on the East Coast.'[35]

Even the calls that are sent by satellite are sucked up. To capture satellite communications in and out of the US, the agency also monitors AT&T's powerful earth stations, satellite receivers. In rural Catawissa, Pennsylvania, three 105-foot dishes handle much of the country's communications to and from Europe and the Middle East. In remote Arbuckle, California, three similar dishes at the company's Salt Creek station service the Pacific Rim and Asia. The network switches of the communications giants systematically sift all cross-border international internet traffic, sending it to the NSA; messages containing not only the email address of the targeted person, but the communications data of others who simply mentioned them in a message.

Binney was not the only person too concerned about Stellar Wind. Edward Snowden had discovered a copy of a top-secret draft report by the NSA Office of the Inspector General into the operation of Stellar Wind between 2001 and 2007. It laid bare the entire story of deception and unaccountable behaviour of the US government and NSA.

'It unsettled me,' Snowden said as we spoke by video link between Sydney and Moscow.[36] 'I was shocked to see everything that was going on.' He said the US had a system of laws and regulations which meant that an organisation like the NSA was supposed to be kept in check. Snowden described the memo as the 'smoking gun'. This was a 'black letter classified document from the NSA itself'.[37]

The report – marked Top Secret – gave a significant insight into how the senior members of the intelligence establishment and the Bush administration were prepared to flout the law. According to the report at one time General Hayden said 'his personal standard was so high that there would be no problem getting a FISC order for domestic collection' of US phone calls and other data.[38]

The report also said it 'found the secrecy surrounding the legal rationale to be odd'. The Inspector General said that it was 'strange that NSA was told to execute a secret programme that everyone knew presented legal questions, without being told the underpinning legal theory'.[39] Anecdotal evidence suggests that government officials feared the public debate surrounding any change to the FISA.[40]

'This is where secrecy truly corrupts' Snowden said.

> This was a program that they knew from the get go (i.e. the beginning) was not legally authorised. They knew it was potentially unconstitutional, no one has seen or got a copy of the legal justification for it. And when the department of justice, the Attorney General says 'Look you guys need to change the law', the response from the executive is not to change the law but to say: 'Is there a backdoor, can we go to the NSA director personally and say will you do this anyway and we will keep it quiet?' and they said 'Yes!' And what horrifies me about this and everything else is that if they are willing to do this on something that is this spread around, that is we'll known, the DoJ knows about it, Congress, members of the intelligence committees, what is happening with the things that are quiet?[41]

One year later in June 2013 Snowden's explosive revelations spilled across the front pages of world's newspapers and dominated the online media.

One week later President Obama launched a whole-hearted defence of the NSA and its work, dismissing Snowden's revelations and the media reports that no one's private life was safe from NSA intrusion. 'What I can say unequivocally is that if you are a U.S. person, the NSA cannot listen to your telephone calls, and the NSA cannot target your emails . . . and have not,'[42] Obama told PBS interviewer Charlie Rose.

Seven months later, in January 2014, Obama's attitude had shifted. The Department of Justice staff who filed through the ornate doors on department's Pennsylvania Avenue home, with the message engraved above: A Place of Justice is a Hallowed Place, would hear Obama spell out some concerns. He talked of providing greater oversight of the NSA's activities and introducing a higher level of transparency of the FISA Court decisions. Without referencing Snowden, he said he now believed that the 'critics are right' about bulk collection of electronic data by the NSA. 'Without proper safeguards, this type of program could be used to yield more information about our private lives and open the door to more intrusive bulk collection programs in the future,' he said.[43]

He proposed a plan to end bulk collection and 'establish a mechanism that preserves the capabilities we need without the government holding this bulk data'.[44]

The reason for his change of mind was not difficult to discover. He had just been handed a review of the NSA's Stellar Wind operation The review said that the NSA's storage of phone data 'creates potential risks to public trust, personal privacy, and civil liberty' and that as a general rule, 'the government should not be permitted to collect and store mass, undigested, non-public personal information' about Americans to be mined for foreign intelligence purposes.[45]

Though the panel included a range of intelligence experts including a former director of the CIA, Michael Morell, some in the intelligence community warned against accepting all the recommendations: 'If adopted in bulk, the panel's recommendations would put us back before 9/11 again', said Joel F. Brenner, a former NSA Inspector General.[46] But the panel headed off that criticism that restricting access to the data would create an open door for terrorists. 'Our review suggests that the information contributed to terrorist investigations by the use of . . . telephony metadata [but] was not essential to preventing attacks and could readily have been obtained in a timely manner using conventional [court] orders',[47] it said.

It might have been a deft political move, in an attempt to take the sting out of Snowden's revelations, but it was no more than shifting the 'ownership' of the stored data from the NSA to the telecommunications companies. There would still be massive data collection which could be tapped into by the NSA, although under the new proposal the agency would now need a warrant. Six months after Snowden's first leak which exposed the wiretapping of US citizens connected to Verizon telephone network, and six years after Obama's election, only now was the agency coming under public scrutiny. A rare glimpse into how the NSA operated was provided when the *New York Times* used the Freedom of Information Act to access the findings of one of the hearings. The heavily redacted file revealed how the NSA misled the court as it used a warrantless system to scoop up data ostensibly targeting overseas suspects. 'The court previously understood that NSA's technical measures would prevent the acquisition of 'any communication as to which the sender and all intended recipients were located in the United States' ('wholly domestic communication') except for 'theoretically possible' cases,' the court said.[48] In other words, the NSA would not pick up the communications of US citizens if it was targeting a foreign terrorist suspect. But that is not what happened. 'If the certification and procedures now before the Court are approved, [the NSA] will continue to acquire, tens of thousands of wholly domestic communications,'[49] Judge John D Bates wrote.

Under one aspect of the warrantless surveillance programme, which Congress legalised with the FISA Amendments Act of 2008, telecommunications companies like AT&T and Verizon give the NSA copies of internet messages that cross the international border and contain a search term that identifies foreigners overseas the government has targeted for surveillance; email addresses are one example. The agency called this 'upstream' collection which included communications like email addresses phone numbers, IP addresses, WhatsApp addresses and screenshots of US citizens on the basis that the material had been inadvertently obtained.

But by 2011, with privacy groups concerned about possible breaches of the Fourth Amendment, FISA began taking a closer look at how the NSA was operating.

> The record before this court establishes that NSA's acquisition of Internet transactions likely results in NSA acquiring annually tens of thousands of wholly domestic communications, and tens of thousands of non-target communications of persons who have little or no relationship to the target but [should be] protected under the Fourth Amendment.[50]

The information involving American citizens, it seems, had not been caught up inadvertently in the NSA dragnet. The court ruled that the NSA had been 'intentionally'[51] collecting communications – while supposedly targeting an overseas suspect – 'with the knowledge that there are tens of thousands of wholly domestic communications' contained within that material. The court pointedly reminded the NSA that its 'targeting procedures must be reasonably designed to prevent intentional acquisition of 'any communication as to which the sender and all the intended recipients are known at the time of acquisition to be located in the United States'.[52]

The court accused the NSA of doing exactly the opposite of its legal obligation not to spy on Americans. It added that rather than attempting to identify and segregate information 'not relevant to the authorized purpose of the acquisition' or to 'destroy such information promptly'[53] after it had been gathered, NSA's proposed system for handling this information tended to 'maximize the retention of such information, including information of or concerning United States persons with no direct connection to any target'. Much of this information would be stored for up to five years, 'despite the fact that they have no direct connection to a targeted selector and therefore are unlikely to contain foreign intelligence information'.[54]

The court ruled that 'the government has failed to demonstrate that it has struck a reasonable balance between its foreign intelligence needs and the requirement that information concerning United States persons be protected'.[55] The NSA's proposals tended to 'enhance the risk'[56] that the communications could be 'disseminated' to other agencies like the FBI, or the CIA. The court found that the NSA's overseas surveillance system, which also picked up US domestic traffic, was in breach of the US Constitution's Fourth Amendment.

As the court sifted through the NSA's litany of what the court described as intentional breaches of the Constitution, Ed Snowden had witnessed first-hand the breaches of the Fourth Amendment. When he raised these issues with superiors it was hardly surprising they ignored him. It appeared they were ignoring the FISA court too.

Only after Snowden's revelations were any of the until then top-secret findings of the court made public. By 2017, the FISA court was growing frustrated by the NSA and what can only be described as its deceitful prevarications. The Presiding FISA Court Judge Rosemary Collyer refused to reauthorise the NSA spying programme. She pointed out that in 2016, the FISA court asked the NSA to prove that the system involving the collection involving Americans was legal under the Fourth Amendment. The court also asked the US government for internal reviews about the programme, which it did not initially disclose. 'The Court ascribed the government's failure to disclose those reviews at the 4 October, 2016 hearing to an institutional "lack of candour" on NSA's part and emphasized that "this is a very serious Fourth Amendment issue,"' Judge Collyer wrote.[57]

Judge Collyer demanded that by no later than 16 June, 2017 the NSA should report to the court on 'whether there have been additional cases in which the FBI improperly afforded non-FBI personnel access to raw FISA-acquired information'.[58]

It was Snowden who first revealed that the National Counterterrorism Center, a clearinghouse of terrorism threat information, had been given access to 'raw FISA information' in early 2012.[59] Aware that the top-secret FISA court was about to blow the whistle on their anti-constitutional activities, the NSA admitted to 'inadvertent compliance lapses' and said it would abandon its terrorism targeting system which – without a warrant – swept up data produced by American citizens. It would also erase the huge cache of data that it had built and was now storing.[60]

Given the scathing comments by two FISA judges about the NSA's track record on compliance, the views on these changes held by privacy advocates is perhaps understandable. 'This decision doesn't reduce that need for legislative reform, it highlights the need', according to Robyn Greene, policy counsel at the Open Technology Institute.[61]

If the court overseeing the legality of the NSA's surveillance programme could be misled and deceived over such vital programs there were serious questions about how they handled more mundane, but significant matters of privacy. The US with its constitutional safeguards was clearly having trouble controlling its intelligence-gathering organisations. As Danny O'Brien of Electronic Frontiers pointed out in a well-argued article published in September 2015:

> The US makes an improper division between surveillance conducted on residents of the US and the surveillance that is conducted with almost no restraint upon the rest of the world. This double standard has proved poisonous to the rights of Americans and non-Americans alike. In theory, Americans enjoy better protections. In practice there are no magical sets of servers and internet connections that carry only American conversations. To violate the privacy of everyone else in the world, the U.S. inevitably scoops up its own citizens' data. Establishing nationality as a basis for discrimination also encourages intelligence agencies to make the obvious end-run: spying on each other's citizens, and then sharing that data. Treating two sets of innocent targets differently is already a violation of international human rights law. In reality, it reduces everyone to the same, lower standard.[62]

In Australia, the federal seat of government, Parliament House, with its barracks-style square windows, looks as though it would fit easily into a Washington streetscape, but appearances can often be misleading in assessing the inner workings. Although the layout of the surrounding city of Canberra was designed by an American (Walter Burley Griffin), Australian law, and the legislators who make it, often find themselves sitting uneasily between Washington and London. Without the US guarantee of freedom of speech and publication, or the European Court of Human Rights rulings supporting the right to protect the identity of sources, Australia is marooned mid-way in a legal version of a choppy Atlantic Ocean. The country might have produced some of the most outspoken proponents of libertarian free speech in Rupert Murdoch and Julian Assange but Australian laws restricting expression are some of the most draconian in the world. French philosopher Michel Foucault, writing in the early 1970s, talked of a 'permanent test' without a final point, 'An inquiry before any offence'.[63] He could well have been writing about Australia in 2012. In September the then Attorney General, Labour's Nicola Roxon, proposed the introduction of the Telecommunications [Interception and Access] Amendment [Data Retention] law to mirror the UK's Investigatory Powers Act (2015), which was by then in various guises beginning its arduous course through the British Parliamentary system.

At around the same time the Telecommunications [interception and Access] Amendment [Data Retention Act (2015) passed through the Australian Parliament. Telecommunications companies would be forced to store metadata on all Australians for two years. Though Australia's Parliamentary system is based on that of the UK, for Australian journalists there were none of the protections afforded by the European Court of Human Rights. In an attempt to assuage journalists' fears that their sources were vulnerable to exposure, the government offered what it suggested was a compromise: to get access to journalists' data, security and police agencies would need a Journalist Information Warrant, signed off by a judge. But it would be no normal court: any hearing would be held in secret and the journalist would be kept unware of the request to look through their meta data. They would be represented, without their knowledge, in the secret court by an advocate appointed by the government. In the event that the journalist became aware they were under investigation, there was another twist to the law. Public disclosure of the existence of a warrant would be punishable by two years' imprisonment. In the event the application of a Journalists Information Warrant came from ASIO, not one of the other 20 authorities which had the right to see the data, there would be no judge, or public advocate potentially standing in the way, representing the journalist. The signature of the Attorney General would be sufficient to give the domestic spy agency access to any journalist's metadata. The CEO of the Media and Arts Alliance, Paul Murphy, described the Journalist Information Warrant as 'a threat to journalism'. It was clear, he said, that 'the scheme [wa]s deeply flawed, operating in secret without proper consideration of the public interest, and allowing the pursuit of whistle-blowers by using journalists' relationships with confidential sources to hunt them down'.[64]

Six months earlier – in response to the Snowden disclosures – Parliament had passed a law which gave ASIO even more power, as the government responded to the Snowden leaks. The National Security Legislation Amendment Act (2014) introduced a three-year prison sentence for intelligence officers who removed or copied classified material without authorisation. If the information was given to a third party – for example a journalist – the officer could face ten years in prison. And to prevent any outside scrutiny of the intelligence organisation the government rushed through a law which made it extremely difficult for ASIO's actions to be investigated by journalists. Section 35P of the Act created an offence which makes it a crime, with a possible sentence of five years, to disclose information about a 'special intelligence operation' – an SIO. If the disclosure endangered anyone's health or safety – or the effective conduct of an operation – then the maximum sentence increased from five to ten years. The all-encompassing nature of the law placed journalists in an impossible legal position. If they reported, even inadvertently, on an SIO, they could be charged. If they tried to check with ASIO, they would also potentially run them into trouble: even discussing an SIO would itself be illegal. There was no defence that the public had a right to know about botched ASIO operations. ASIO would only be answerable to the Inspector General of Intelligence, a government-appointed official.

After a strong campaign by newspapers and the electronic media, the government eventually amended the law, introducing a defence of 'prior publication'. That meant that if another publication had already reported the event, the journalist might be in the clear. As Mike Dobbie, the Australian journalists' union communications manager, pointed out, 'Being first with the news can get you up to 10 years in the slammer.'[65]

In early 2017 the Australian government began examining the possibility of including the cover of SIOs to the Australian Federal Police. Already a journalist could be imprisoned for between six months and seven years for 'receiving' any 'sketch, plan, photograph, model, cipher, note, document article or information' covered by the Official Secrets section of the Crimes Act (1914). Coupled with the Metadata Act and the ASIO Amendment Act it would make reporting on significant matters of national security, and holding the government and its agencies to account, that much more difficult for journalists, and make whistle-blowers that much more wary of speaking out. Australia, the nation that had passed more counter-terrorism legislation than any other place on earth, now had specific law targeting journalists, a knee-jerk reaction to the Snowden disclosures which had done so much to make the world aware of the dangers of mass surveillance. As the MEAA's Paul Murphy argues: 'In Australia, our Parliament has ruled that journalism is a crime [with] laws that can imprison journalists for up to 10 years simply for doing their job.'[66]

There is a conflict between the public's need to have information so it can make informed democratic decisions and the state's self-appointed responsibility to protect its citizens from external threat. Simon Longstaff, director of the St James Ethics Centre, Sydney points out:

> The Government's assumption is that the Australian people lack the courage and commitment to choose liberty over security; that we are not brave enough to defy the terrorists' threats and accept the cost of our freedom. Perhaps it is time that we sent our politicians a message: we are a courageous and free people wishing to live as equals under the rule of law. Defend this ideal and you defend us.[67]

In France, on the surface, it might have appeared that the nation stood out among the western liberal democracies, going against the tide of increased surveillance. In 2010 the French National Assembly updated, for the internet age, a law from 1881 [Loi du 29 juillet 1881 sur la liberté de la presse – Law of 29 July on Press Freedom] giving journalists and their sources legal protection in their role of informing the public ('Le secret des sources des journalistes est protégé dans l'exercice de leur mission d'information du public.')[68]

Based on the Declaration of the rights of Man and the Citizen [Declaration des droits de l'homme et du citoyen], the press law was first enshrined in legislation shortly after the French Revolution.

Despite the constitutional certainty of press protection, all was not what it seemed. In a secret order in 2008, the then president Nicholas Sarkozy had given the DGSE, the French equivalent of the NSA, the authority to tap the undersea cables carrying much of the telecommunications traffic into and out of France, recruiting the help of telecommunications operators Orange and Alcatel-Lucent to plug in 'black boxes' for the surveillance operation. The presidential decree authorised the interception of cable traffic from

40 countries including Algeria, Morocco, Tunisia, Iraq, Syria, Sub-Saharan Africa, Russia, China, India and the US.

Two years later, according to the French news magazine *L'Obs*, Sarkozy signed a deal with British Prime Minister David Cameron, allowing the data to be shared with the UK's GCHQ. France had joined the Anglo-Saxon information intelligence sharing system, becoming in effect its Sixth Eye. There was no judicial oversight of the surveillance – all communications in and out of France could be intercepted.

The secret spying on French international communications by the DGSE would probably have remained secret, but for the events of 2015.

Until then, apart from the bombings of the Paris metro in 1995 involving an Islamist group demanding independence for Algeria, the country had escaped a major terrorist assault on its metropolitan homeland. The attacks at satirical magazine *Charlie Hebdo*'s office near the centre of Paris and a kosher grocery by gunmen affiliated with al-Qaeda in the Arabian Peninsula in January 2015 which killed 17 people – eight of them journalists – ushered in the first significant anti-terrorist laws for more than two decades.

Like the Patriot Act, the French law required internet service providers to collect the metadata of everyone in France – a close copy of the system used by the NSA. Wrapped into the new laws, as part of the Code de la sécurité intérieure (Internal Security Code) the government inserted special powers which gave legal cover to the DGSE's secret operations which had been revealed just a few weeks earlier by *L'Obs*. It confirmed in greater detail what *Le Monde* disclosed in 2013: that the DGSE systematically collects electromagnetic signals from computers or telephones in France, as well as flows between French and foreign countries. All of our communications are spied on. All emails, SMS, phone calls, Facebook, Twitter, are then stored for years, *Le Monde* reported.

With the surveillance exposed, the government was not only desperate to get its new domestic data laws passed; it urgently needed legal cover for its international spying.

Not far from the palatial Senate building, where the bill had just been passed into law, France's Constitutional Council, close to the Palais Royale, now sat in judgement on the proposed new laws. Whereas the Council accepted most of the domestic legislation, with minor changes to oversight, it rejected sections of the DGSE's submarine cable surveillance program, which by now had been operating in questionable legal circumstances for seven years.

Under the French law, surveillance operations would be overseen by a new committee led by the prime minister, the National Commission for the Control of Intelligence [commission nationale de controle des techniques de resseignement (CNCTR) – but the committee was not legally able to overrule the prime minister, even if it completely disagreed with the acts of surveillance he demanded. Only one person would make the final decision: the prime minister.

The power invested in a single member of the French legislative executive, coupled with the loose language of the bill, alarmed many people: surveillance

could be conducted for 'the prevention of attacks on the Republican form of institutions,' or the protection of 'major scientific, industrial and economic interests'
or 'of major foreign policy interests.'[69]

So wide-ranging was the law that one of the senior members of the French
intelligence administration expressed his 'strong reservations'.[70, 71] Jean-Marie
Delarue, the president of the Commission nationale de controle des interceptions
de sécurité – the organisation then in charge of security intercepts – questioned
the wholesale collection of metadata. Delarue did not believe that the 'collection
and conservation of billions of data for five years' was a 'proportionate' response
'to the need to find, for example, a dozen suspected terrorists'.[72]

Though the then French prime minister, Manuel Valls, described claims of
similarities to the Patriot Act as 'a lie', his defence bore a marked similarity to
the argument put forward by the White House shortly after 9–11. The laws
which gave Valls great wiretapping powers were designed to protect France from
terrorism.[73]

The Constitutional Court eventually passed the amended laws, but they
pointedly created an exemption for journalists and publishers, stressing that anything that restricted the work of journalists – apart from the most extreme matters of national security – would be against the constitution of France. But as we
have seen before, intelligence agencies have spied on journalists at the direction
of the president before, when the same protective laws were in place. There were
other problems too. The limited protections that were included in the original
surveillance bill – including assurances that French journalists, judges and lawyers would be protected from dragnet surveillance – would be undermined by
their inevitable inclusion in the vacuuming up of all international traffic.

The law rules out the targeting of the 'professional information' of journalists
practising in France, but as the French advocacy group promoting digital rights,
La Quadrature du Net (Squaring of the Net) pointed out, French journalists
operating outside France could be targeted. More importantly, only the surveillance of individual journalists was illegal in France. If their information was gathered up in mass surveillance, according to La Quadrature du Net, their information
could be easily accessed. How the surveillance agency would sort out what was
professional information, and thus covered by the exemption protecting journalists, and what was private and thus potentially could be accessed, raised questions
about the effectiveness of that protection. And while journalists might receive
some safeguards, as Quadrature du Net pointed out 'The protection of journalists'
sources is totally violated.'[74] In other words, journalists may be protected from
giving up the name of their sources to the state, but that does not prevent the
state from piecing together other information to identify a journalist's sources.

On 13 November, 2015, six weeks after the legislation became law, France was
hit by its worst ever terrorist attack: in all 130 people were killed and 389 injured.

President Francois Hollande ordered troops onto the street as part of a state of
emergency which gave the government sweeping powers under section 16 of the
French Constitution: 'When the institutions of the Republic, the independence

of the nation, the integrity of its territory, or the fulfilment of its international commitments are under grave and immediate threat.'[75]

The state of emergency gave police hugely increased powers of search and arrest. It also gave the French authorities greater electronic surveillance powers. Warrantless searches of electronic devices were authorised. Data could be accessed and copied by the law enforcement agencies. Mediapart's editor Edwy Plenel accused the government of the 'politics of fear', in which the terrorist threat was used to 'establish a state of exception . . . in which the executive branch disproportionately extends its secret prerogatives by shielding itself from the procedures of justice and the investigations of the press'.[76]

By the following July, after the Bastille Day attack in Nice where a huge truck drove through celebrating crowds, killing 86 people, several members of the National Assembly attempted to roll back the 2010 law protecting journalists' sources, but they failed. It was a small win for French journalists, and their sources. But with the DGSE spying on international communications, the power of the prime minister to arbitrarily order wiretaps, and a state of emergency extended to the end of 2017, it was little wonder that France had slipped from 38 to 45 in the Press Freedom Index by the international journalism advocacy group, Reporters Sans Frontières (RSF) also known as Reporters Without Borders.

In the UK, the government passed the Investigatory Powers Act (2016), known as the Snoopers' Charter. Over the previous six years the government had repeatedly run into trouble with its data retention policies. The Data Retention Directive (2009) was overturned by the European Court of Justice, the European Data Protection Supervisor describing the directive as 'without doubt the most privacy invasive instrument ever adopted [in] the EU'.[77] As a stopgap the government rushed through the Data Retention and Investigatory Powers Act (DRIPA, 2014) DRIPA permitted the Secretary of State to issue notices to communications service providers mandating the retention of data for a year where 'necessary and proportionate'.[78] It too was later overturned by a court decision.

The original Regulatory Investigatory Powers Act (2000) gave the intelligence agencies the power to intercept data, but the Investigatory Powers Act (2016) handed them much more power. The telecommunications providers would be required to store the personal data of every person in the UK who used a phone or the internet. This mass of data would be stored for a year and be accessible to a vast number of UK organisations: everyone from the intelligence agencies to government authorities such as the Scottish Ambulance Service. Strong opposition from the National Union of Journalists and human rights organisations forced the government to include a provision which it said would help protect journalists and their sources; whereas most meta data could be easily accessed by government agencies without a warrant, the work of journalists, the government argued, would be protected. Any agency wishing to access the metadata of a journalist would need to argue their case before a judge, especially appointed to oversee cases involving media sources. There is reasonable scepticism as to whether these laws will do very much to protect either journalists or their sources.

It was Duncan Campbell whose work in the 1970s exposed the existence of a vast UK telephone interception operation run by the Post Office, and led to the establishment of the first accountability mechanism. In the wake of his revelations, the government appointed a judge to act as a commissioner overseeing some of the UK's domestic intelligence operations. Campbell is sanguine about how effective the commissioners have been. For 30 years there have been such commissioners, he points out, but 'only in the last two years since Snowden have the commissioners actually learned that they have to have teeth'.[79]

Campbell believed that the 'protection' granted to journalists did not 'strike the balance' in the public interest. What appears to have been forgotten in the laws, he said, is the lack of protection afforded to whistle-blowers, 'the people who are vulnerable but whose information is needed in the public interest will never feel safe with a law like this'.[80]

Campbell points out that much of the new law is merely legalising what had been accepted practice for decades in the intelligence communities. 'Every sort of new method including hacking phones, mass automated hacking of phones without regard to who is targeted are now to be authorized by this law,'[81] Campbell said. All that stands in the way of a journalist's communications with a source being intercepted is a judge selected by the government.

> Many judges are very good, very distinguished and very independent; they just would go to the judge who is subservient and sympathetic. They can spin them any kind of story about fears about this or that. There is no safety there. For the reason, it is a farrago.[82]

The role of the media in its reporting leading up to the introduction of these new laws bears some examination. In the wake of the Murdoch phone-hacking revelations, as the public called for greater control of the press, the British media fell into two camps. Murdoch's newspapers, *The Sun* and *The Times*, perhaps self-servingly, launched strong campaigns against any restrictions. They were joined by the *Daily Mail* and the *Daily Telegraph*, which argued against any control, invoking the role of the media in exposing the excesses of government. On the other side, *The Guardian* and *The Independent* took a more nuanced view, supporting the right to privacy for individuals in most cases.

The Snowden revelations changed all that. The press was once again divided but this time, those who formerly stood against any control of the print media – in particular the Murdoch press, *The Daily Telegraph* and the *Daily Mail* – now wanted the media not only controlled but prosecuted.

'Prosecute *The Guardian* for Aiding Terrorists Via Leaks',[83] screamed *The Sun*, 'Leftwing Paper's Leaks Caused "'Greatest Damage to Western Security in History", say Whitehall Insiders',[84] exclaimed the *Daily Mail*. It was a perfect cue for the government.

Seemingly motivated by the Snowden leaks, the Cabinet Office asked the Law Commission for 'an effective and coherent legal response to unauthorised disclosures'.[85] Given the strident support of sections of the media, it would have suited the Conservative government that the Law Commission, established as an independent body, proposed even more draconian legislation to clamp down on free speech. In a 326-page consultation paper, *Protection of Official Data*, the commission proposed that the 'redrafted offence'[86] of espionage would 'be capable of being committed by someone who not only communicates information, but also by someone who obtains or gathers it'.[87] There should be 'no restriction on who can commit the offence',[88] including hackers, leakers, elected politicians, journalists and NGOs. Former guardian editor Alan Rusbridger described it as alarming that 'such a far–reaching proposed reform of laws which could be used to jail whistle-blowers and journalists should have been drafted without any adequate consultation with free speech organisations'.[89] Under the proposals Rusbridger would have almost certainly been imprisoned for handling the Snowden documents. In mid-2017 the Law Commission was preparing to make its final recommendations.

In their championing being tough on terrorism and stoking fear in the community, many in the right-wing media had handed the government a legal stick with which to beat them. And in the poetry that sometimes passes for justice, beat them they did.

Notes

1 Brokaw, T. 11th September, 2001. *Breaking News*. NBC [online]. Available at https://archives.nbclearn.com/portal/site/k-12/flatview?cuecard=1419 [Accessed 5 January, 2017].
2 American Civil Liberties Union. 2017. Surveillance Under the Patriot Act [online]. Available at www.aclu.org/infographic/surveillance-under-patriot-act [Accessed July, 2016].
3 National Commission on Terrorist Attacks Upon the United States. 2004. The 9-11 Commission Report [online]. Available at http://govinfo.library.unt.edu/911/report/911Report_Exec.htm [Accessed 5 September, 2016].
4 Zelizer, B. and Allan, S. [editors]. 2002. *Journalism After September 11*. Routledge, UK.
5 Gans, H. 2004. *Deciding What's News: A Study of CBS Evening News, NBC Nightly News, Newsweek and Time*. Random House, USA.
6 American Civil Liberties Union. 2017. Surveillance Under the Patriot Act [online]. Available at www.aclu.org/infographic/surveillance-under-patriot-act [Accessed July, 2016].
7 American Civil Liberties Union. 2017. Surveillance Under the Patriot Act [online]. Available at www.aclu.org/infographic/surveillance-under-patriot-act [Accessed July, 2016].
8 American Civil Liberties Union. 2017. Surveillance Under the Patriot Act [online]. Available at www.aclu.org/infographic/surveillance-under-patriot-act [Accessed July, 2016].
9 Eggan, D. 27th September, 2007. *Patriot Act Provisions Voided*. The Washington Post [online]. Washington. Available at www.washingtonpost.com/wp-dyn/content/article/2007/09/26/AR2007092602084.html [Accessed October, 2016].
10 Eggan, D. 27th September, 2007. *Patriot Act Provisions Voided*. The Washington Post [online]. Washington. Available at www.washingtonpost.com/wp-dyn/content/article/2007/09/26/AR2007092602084.html [Accessed October, 2016].
11 US Ninth Circuit. 11th December, 2009. Mayfield v. US No. 07-35865 [online]. Available at http://blogs.findlaw.com/ninth_circuit/2009/12/mayfield-v-us-no-07-35865.html#sthash.FAW16Ihm.dpuf [Accessed August, 2016].

12 American Civil Liberties Union. 2017. Surveillance Under the Patriot Act [online]. Available at www.aclu.org/infographic/surveillance-under-patriot-act [Accessed July, 2016].

13 Bonner, R. 9th September, 2011. The Media and 9/9: How We Did [online]. *The Atlantic*. Available at www.theatlantic.com/national/archive/2011/09/the-media-and-9-11-how-we-did/244818/ [Accessed 3 July, 2016].

14 BBC News. 23rd April, 2010. 9/11 arrest pilot Lotfi Raissi wins compensation battle [online]. Available at http://news.bbc.co.uk/2/hi/uk_news/8640659.stm [Accessed 12 June, 2016].

15 Bonner, R. 9th September, 2011. *The Media and 9/9: How We Did* [online]. The Atlantic. Available at www.theatlantic.com/national/archive/2011/09/the-media-and-9-11-how-we-did/244818/ [Accessed 3 July, 2016].

16 Bowden, C. 2002. *Closed Circuit Television for Inside Your Head: Blanket Traffic Data Rention and the Emergency Anti-Terrorism Legislation*. Duke Law & Technology Review [online]. Available at http://scholarship.law.duke.edu/dltr/vol1/iss1/47/ [Accessed 18 July, 2017].

17 Bowden, C. 2002. *Closed Circuit Television for Inside Your Head: Blanket Traffic Data Rention and the Emergency Anti-Terrorism Legislation*. Duke Law & Technology Review [online]. Available at http://scholarship.law.duke.edu/dltr/vol1/iss1/47/ [Accessed 18 July, 2017].

18 Bowden, C. 2002. *Closed Circuit Television for Inside Your Head: Blanket Traffic Data Rention and the Emergency Anti-Terrorism Legislation*. Duke Law & Technology Review [online]. Available at http://scholarship.law.duke.edu/dltr/vol1/iss1/47/ [Accessed 18 July, 2017].

19 Abbott, J. 15th June, 2000. *We Won't Read Your Emails*. The Guardian [online]. Available at www.theguardian.com/technology/2000/jun/15/security.internet [Accessed 17 July, 2017].

20 Gaspar, R. 21st August, 2000. *Looking to the Future*. NCIS Submission on Communications Data Retention Law [online]. Available at https://cryptome.org/ncis-carnivore.htm [Accessed 17 July, 2017].

21 Schmitt, G. 2010. *Safety, Liberty and Islamist Terrorism: American, and European Approaches to Domestic Counterterrorism*. American Enterprise Institute, Washington DC.

22 Hocking, J. 2004. *Terror Laws: ASIO, Counter-Terrorism and the Threat to Democracy*. UNSW Press.

23 Review Mania. 6th February 2011. Anti-Terrorism Laws and the Implications for Australian Publishing [online]. Available at https://ausink.wordpress.com/2011/02/06/anti-terrorism-laws-and-the-implications-for-australian-publishing/ [Accessed 20 July, 2017].

24 Review Mania. 6th February 2011. Anti-Terrorism Laws and the Implications for Australian Publishing [online]. Available at https://ausink.wordpress.com/2011/02/06/anti-terrorism-laws-and-the-implications-for-australian-publishing/ [Accessed 20 July, 2017].

25 Review Mania. 6th February, 2011. Anti-Terrorism Laws and the Implications for Australian Publishing [online]. Available at https://ausink.wordpress.com/2011/02/06/anti-terrorism-laws-and-the-implications-for-australian-publishing/ [Accessed 20 July, 2017].

26 Media Entertainment and Arts Alliance. 2006. Criminalising the Truth Supressing the Right to Know [online]. Available at www.meaa.org/wp-content/uploads/2016/05/PF_report_2016_HiRes_eBook.pdf [Accessed 20 July, 2017].

27 United Nations. 1948. Universal Declaration of Human Rights [online]. Available at www.un.org/en/universal-declaration-human-rights/index.html [Accessed 20 July, 2017].

28 Williams, G. 2011. *A Decade of Australian Anti-Terror Laws*. Melbourne University Law Review, Melbourne [online]. Available at www.austlii.edu.au/au/journals/MelbULawRw/2011/38.html [Accessed 20 July, 2017].

29 Roach, K. 2011. *The 9/11 Effect: Comparative Counter-Terrorism*. Cambridge University Press.
30 US Office of the Inspector General. 24th March, 2009. Review of President's Surveillance Program [PSP] [online]. Working Draft. Available at https://stanford.edu/~jmayer/law696/week9/NSA%20Inspector%20General%20Draft%20Report.pdf [Accessed 20 July, 2017].
31 US Office of the Inspector General. 24th March, 2009. Review of President's Surveillance Program [PSP] [online]. Working Draft. Available at https://stanford.edu/~jmayer/law696/week9/NSA%20Inspector%20General%20Draft%20Report.pdf
32 Snowden, E. 2017. *Interview*.
33 Snowden, E. 2017. *Interview*.
34 US Office of the Inspector General. 24th March, 2009. Review of President's Surveillance Program [PSP] [online]. Working Draft. Available at https://stanford.edu/~jmayer/law696/week9/NSA%20Inspector%20General%20Draft%20Report.pdf
35 Bamford, J. 15th March, 2012. *The NSA Is Building the Country's Biggest Spy Center (Watch What You Say)*. Wired [online]. Available at www.wired.com/2012/03/ff_nsadatacenter/ [Accessed 20 July, 2017].
36 Snowden, E. 2017. *Interview*.
37 Snowden, E. 2017. *Interview*.
38 US Office of the Inspector General. 24th March, 2009. Review of President's Surveillance Program [PSP] [online]. Working Draft. Available at https://stanford.edu/~jmayer/law696/week9/NSA%20Inspector%20General%20Draft%20Report.pdf.
39 US Office of the Inspector General. 24th March, 2009. Review of President's Surveillance Program [PSP] [online]. Working Draft. Available at https://stanford.edu/~jmayer/law696/week9/NSA%20Inspector%20General%20Draft%20Report.pdf.
40 US Office of the Inspector General. 24th March, 2009. Review of President's Surveillance Program [PSP] [online]. Working Draft. Available at https://stanford.edu/~jmayer/law696/week9/NSA%20Inspector%20General%20Draft%20Report.pdf.
41 Snowden, E. 2017. *Interview*.
42 Obama, B. 17th June, 2013. *President Barack Obama*. Charlie Rose, PBS TV [online]. Available at https://charlierose.com/videos/17754 [Accessed 10 February, 2017].
43 Obama, B. 17th January, 2014. *Obama's Speech on NSA Phone Surveillance*. The New York Times [online]. Available at www.nytimes.com/2014/01/18/us/politics/obamas-speech-on-nsa-phone-surveillance.html?_r=0 [Accessed 20 July, 2017].
44 Obama, B. 17th January, 2014. *Obama's Speech on NSA Phone Surveillance*. The New York Times [online]. Available at www.nytimes.com/2014/01/18/us/politics/obamas-speech-on-nsa-phone-surveillance.html?_r=0 [Accessed 20 July, 2017].
45 Roberts, D and Ackerman S. 18th December 2013. *Obama Review Panel: Strip NSA of Power to Collect Phone Data Records*. The Guardian [online]. Available at www.theguardian.com/world/2013/dec/18/nsa-bulk-collection-phone-date-obama-review-panel [Accessed 16 July, 2017].
46 Nakashima, E and Soltani, A. 18th December, 2013. *NSA Shouldn't Keep Phone Database Review Board Recommends*. The Washington Post [online]. Available at www.washingtonpost.com/world/national-security/nsa-shouldnt-keep-phone-database-review-board-recommends/2013/12/18/f44fe7c0-67fd-11e3-a0b9-249bbb34602c_story.html?tid=a_inl&utm_term=.34d5a4e7e401 [Accessed 20 July, 2017].
47 McGregor, R. 19th December, 2013. *NSA Panel Looks for Surveillance Overhaul*. The Financial Times [online]. London. Available at www.ft.com/content/e49e45ae-682c-11e3-a905-00144feabdc0?mhq5j=e2 [Accessed 29 July, 2017].
48 Foreign Intelligence Security Court. October 2011. *Judge's Opinion on NSA Program*. New York Times [online]. New York. Available at www.nytimes.com/interactive/2013/08/22/us/22nsa-opinion-document.html [Accessed 20 July, 2017].
49 Foreign Intelligence Security Court. October 2011. *Judge's Opinion on NSA Program*. New York Times [online]. New York. Available at www.nytimes.com/interactive/2013/08/22/us/22nsa-opinion-document.html [Accessed 20 July, 2017].

50 Foreign Intelligence Security Court. October 2011. *Judge's Opinion on NSA Program*. New York Times [online]. New York. Available at www.nytimes.com/interactive/2013/08/22/us/22nsa-opinion-document.html [Accessed 20 July, 2017].

51 Foreign Intelligence Security Court. October 2011. *Judge's Opinion on NSA Program*. New York Times [online]. New York. Available at www.nytimes.com/interactive/2013/08/22/us/22nsa-opinion-document.html [Accessed 20 July, 2017].

52 Foreign Intelligence Security Court. October 2011. *Judge's Opinion on NSA Program*. New York Times [online]. New York. Available at www.nytimes.com/interactive/2013/08/22/us/22nsa-opinion-document.html [Accessed 20 July, 2017].

53 Foreign Intelligence Security Court. October 2011. *Judge's Opinion on NSA Program*. New York Times [online]. New York. Available at www.nytimes.com/interactive/2013/08/22/us/22nsa-opinion-document.html [Accessed 20 July, 2017].

54 Foreign Intelligence Security Court. October 2011. *Judge's Opinion on NSA Program*. New York Times [online]. New York. Available at www.nytimes.com/interactive/2013/08/22/us/22nsa-opinion-document.html [Accessed 20 July, 2017].

55 Foreign Intelligence Security Court. October 2011. *Judge's Opinion on NSA Program*. New York Times [online]. New York. Available at www.nytimes.com/interactive/2013/08/22/us/22nsa-opinion-document.html [Accessed 20 July, 2017].

56 Foreign Intelligence Security Court. October 2011. *Judge's Opinion on NSA Program*. New York Times [online]. New York. Available at www.nytimes.com/interactive/2013/08/22/us/22nsa-opinion-document.html [Accessed 20 July, 2017].

57 Foreign Intelligence Security Court. 2017. *Judge's Opinion on NSA Program*. Office of the Director of National Intelligence [online]. Available at www.dni.gov/files/documents/icotr/51117/2016_Cert_FISC_Memo_Opin_Order_Apr_2017.pdf.

58 Foreign Intelligence Security Court. 2017. *Judge's Opinion on NSA Program*. Office of the Director of National Intelligence [online]. Available at www.dni.gov/files/documents/icotr/51117/2016_Cert_FISC_Memo_Opin_Order_Apr_2017.pdf [Accessed April, 2017].

59 Savage, C. and Poitras, L. 11th March, 2014. *How a Court Secretly Evolved, Extending US Spies' Reach*. New York Times [online]. Available at www.nytimes.com/2014/03/12/us/how-a-courts-secret-evolution-extended-spies-reach.html [Accessed 20 July, 2017].

60 NSA. 28th April, 2017. NSA Stops Certain Foreign Intelligence Collection Activities Under Section 702 [online]. Available at www.nsa.gov/news-features/press-room/press-releases/2017/nsa-stops-certain-702-activites.shtml [Accessed 20 July, 2017].

61 Greenberg, A. 28th, April, 2017. *A Big Change in NSA Spying Marks a Win for American Privacy*. Wired [online]. Available at www.wired.com/2017/04/big-change-nsa-spying-marks-win-american-privacy/ [Accessed 20 July, 2017].

62 O'Brien, D. 30th September, 2015. *France's Government Aims to Give Itself – and the NSA – Carte Blanche to Spy on the World*. Electronic Frontier Foundation [online]. Available at www.eff.org/deeplinks/2015/09/frances-government-aims-give-itself-and-nsa-carte-blanche-spy-world [Accessed 20 July, 2017].

63 Foucault. 2017. *The Birth of Power*. Polity Press, Cambridge, UK.

64 Media Entertainment and Arts Alliance. 2017. ASIO Confirms it is Spying on Journalists [online]. Available at www.meaa.org/mediaroom/asio-confirms-it-is-spying-on-journalists/ [Accessed 20 July, 2017].

65 Dobbie, M. 29th March, 2017. *Press Freedom is Under Attack, Not Least in Australia*. The Walkley Foundation [online]. Available at www.walkleys.com/press-freedom-is-under-attack-not-least-in-australia/ [Accessed 20 July, 2017].

66 Media Entertainment and Arts Alliance. 2006. Criminalising the Truth Supressing the Right to Know [online]. Available at www.meaa.org/wp-content/uploads/2016/05/PF_report_2016_HiRes_eBook.pdf [Accessed 20 July, 2017].

67 Media Entertainment and Arts Alliance. 22nd April, 2015. Joint Submission to the Independent National Security Legislation Monitor [online]. Available at www.meaa.org/mediaroom/submission-to-inslm-on-s35p/ [Accessed 20 July, 2017].

68 L'Assemblee nationale et le Senat. 1st April, 2010. LOI n° 2010-1 du 4 janvier 2010 relative à la protection du secret des sources des journalistes [online]. Available at www. legifrance.gouv.fr/affichTexte.do?cidTexte=JORFTEXT000021601325&categorieLien =id [Accessed 20 July, 2017].

69 Marthoz, J. 7th May, 2015. *French Surveillance Law Passes National Assembly, But It's Not the Last Word.* Committee to Protect Journalists [online]. Available at https://cpj. org/blog/2015/05/french-surveillance-law-passes-national-assembly-b.php [Accessed 20 July, 2017].

70 Frandin, A. 31st March, 2015. Loi sur le reseignement: le gardien des ecoutes degormme le project. L'Obs avec Rue89 [online]. Available at http://tempsreel. nouvelobs.com/rue89/rue89-internet/20150331.RUE8503/loi-sur-le-renseignement-le-gardien-des-ecoutes-degomme-le-projet.html [Accessed 20 July, 2017].

71 Frandin, A. 31st March, 2015. Loi sur le reseignement: le gardien des ecoutes degormme le project. L'Obs avec Rue89 [online]. Available at http://tempsreel. nouvelobs.com/rue89/rue89-internet/20150331.RUE8503/loi-sur-le-renseignement-le-gardien-des-ecoutes-degomme-le-projet.html [Accessed 20 July, 2017].

72 Frandin, A. 31st March, 2015. Loi sur le reseignement: le gardien des ecoutes degormme le project. L'Obs avec Rue89 [online]. Available at http://tempsreel. nouvelobs.com/rue89/rue89-internet/20150331.RUE8503/loi-sur-le-renseignement-le-gardien-des-ecoutes-degomme-le-projet.html [Accessed 20 July, 2017].

73 Chrisafis, A. 5th May, 2015. *France Passes New Surveillance Law in Wake of Charlie Hebdo Attack.* The Guardian [online]. London. Available at www.theguardian.com/ world/2015/may/05/france-passes-new-surveillance-law-in-wake-of-charlie-hebdo-attack [Accessed 20 July, 2017].

74 La Quadrature Du Net. 2017. French International Surveillance Law/Analysis [online]. Available at https://wiki.laquadrature.net/PPL_Surveillance_internationale/ Analyse/en [Accessed 20 July, 2017].

75 Legifrance. 2017. Constitution du 4 octobre 1958 [online]. Available at www.legifrance. gouv.fr/Droit-francais/Constitution/Constitution-du-4-octobre-1958# ancre2178_0_3_16 [Accessed 10 October, 2016].

76 Plenel, E. 18th April, 2015. *Loi sur le renseignement: un attentat aux libertes.* Mediapart [online]. Available at www.mediapart.fr/journal/france/180415/loi-sur-le-renseignement-un-attentat-aux-libertes [Accessed 3 August, 2016].

77 Media Policy Project Blog. [Undated]. *Surveillance and Civil Liberties: Interview with David Davis MP.* London School of Economics and Political Science [online]. London. Available at http://blogs.lse.ac.uk/mediapolicyproject/2015/11/05/surveillance-and-civil-liberties-interview-with-david-davis-mp/ [Accessed 21 June, 2016].

78 Media Policy Project Blog. [Undated]. *Surveillance and Civil Liberties: Interview with David Davis MP.* London School of Economics and Political Science [online]. London. Available at http://blogs.lse.ac.uk/mediapolicyproject/2015/11/05/surveillance-and-civil-liberties-interview-with-david-davis-mp/ [Accessed 21 June, 2016].

79 Campbell, D. October, 2016. *Interview.*

80 Campbell, D. October, 2016. *Interview.*

81 Campbell, D. October, 2016. *Interview.*

82 Campbell, D. October, 2016. *Interview.*

83 Dunn, T. 10th October, 2013. *Prosecute the Guardian for Aiding Terrorists.* The Sun [online]. Available at www.thesun.co.uk/archives/politics/1058722/prosecute-guardian-for-aiding-terrorists/ [Accessed 20 July, 2017].

84 Slack, J. 9th October, 2013. *Guardian has Handed a Gift to Terrorists.* The Daily Mail[online]. Available at www.dailymail.co.uk/news/article-2450237/MI5-chief-Andrew-Parke-The-Guardian-handed-gift-terrorists.html.

85 Campbell, D. 10th February, 2017. *Planned Espionage Act Could Jail Journos and Whistleblowers as Spies.* The Register [online]. Available at www.theregister.co.uk/ 2017/02/10/espionage_law_jail_journalists_as_spies/ [Accessed 1 August, 2017].

86 Law Commission. February, 2017. Protection of Official Data [online]. Available at www.lawcom.gov.uk/project/protection-of-official-data/ [Accessed 1 August, 2017].
87 Law Commission. February, 2017. Protection of Official Data [online]. Available at www.lawcom.gov.uk/project/protection-of-official-data/ [Accessed 1 August, 2017].
88 Law Commission. February, 2017. Protection of Official Data [online]. Available at www.lawcom.gov.uk/project/protection-of-official-data/ [Accessed 1 August, 2017].
89 Campbell, D. 10th February, 2017. *Planned Espionage Act Could Jail Journos and Whistleblowers as Spies*. The Register [online]. Available at www.theregister.co.uk/2017/02/10/espionage_law_jail_journalists_as_spies/ [Accessed 1 August, 2017].

10

THE CHILLING EFFECT

The freezing fog and rain forecast for London on Wednesday, 19 September, 2012 may well have been an omen. Late in the evening that day an officer of the UK's armed Diplomatic Protection Group (DPG), on duty outside the British prime minister's Downing Street home telephoned *The Sun*'s news desk to tip them off on a story he was sure they would be interested in publishing. What unfolded over the next few months would see a cabinet minister resign, police jailed, and expose the fragile, and at times non-existent application of a law designed to protect journalists. Just as importantly, it would expose what might be called the lazy hypocrisy of *The Sun* and other newspapers who did the government's bidding in attacking Snowden, while he was warning them of the real surveillance dangers they faced as journalists. In *The Sun*'s case in particular, the newspaper which would campaign so strongly for Brexit with questionable stories about the failings of the European Union shamelessly used the EU's European Convention of Human Rights, mirrored in the UK's Human Rights Act (2000), to argue that its reporters had been illegally spied on by the police.

For a story of such magnitude, it had humble beginnings.

It started innocently enough at about 7.30 p.m. when the Conservative government chief whip, Andrew Mitchell, MP, asked a member of the DPG charged with guarding the large black wrought iron gates that blockade Central London's Downing Street, where the prime minister and chancellor live, to open them up. It was a reasonable request for anyone driving a car, but Mitchell was riding a bike. He was in a hurry to get to the Carlton Club, the 'oldest, most elite, and most important of all Conservative clubs',[1] a five-minute ride away near St James's Palace.

The DPG officer directed him to use a side gate instead. Exactly what happened next is not clear but according to the police log of the affair Mitchell was not impressed. Police constable Toby Rowland wrote in the log that he explained to Mitchell that he was happy to open the side pedestrian gates for him, but that 'no officer present would be opening the main gates as this was the policy we were directed to follow'.[2]

According to the police log, Mitchell refused, repeatedly reiterating he was the chief whip. Rowland said his exact explanation to 'Mr Mitchell' was 'I am more than happy to open the side pedestrian gate for you Sir, but it is policy that we are not to allow cycles through the main vehicle entrance.'[3]

After several refusals Mitchell got off his bike and walked to the pedestrian gate with PC Rowland, who again offered to open it for him.

There were several members of public present as was 'the norm opposite the pedestrian gate'. As the pair neared it Mitchell said 'Best you learn your fucking place . . . you don't run this fucking government . . . You're fucking plebs.'[4]

PC Rowland said he was unsure whether the statement was aimed at him personally, the officers present, or the police service in general. Rowland said he was 'somewhat taken aback by the language used and the view expressed by a senior government official'.[5]

Rowland then warned Mitchell about his language, telling him: 'Please don't swear at me Sir. If you continue to I will have no option but to arrest you under the public order act.'[6] As he cycled away, Mitchell issued a threat over his shoulder: 'You haven't heard the last of this'[7] he said.

Other police were clearly incensed at Mitchell's behaviour. When PC James Glanville decided to call *The Sun*'s news desk he found a willing listener in its chief political correspondent, Tom Newton Dunn. Two days later *The Sun* splashed the 'Plebgate' story on its front page with the headline 'Cabinet Minister: Police are Plebs'. And there the matter might have rested, if *The Sun* hadn't decided to pursue the story further. When one of the journalists from *The Sun* contacted the Police Federation for comment on the affair, he suggested that the newspaper had a copy of the full police log. It seemed there was a closer relationship between *The Sun* and the police informants than a simple tip-off. Within hours the Department of Professional Standards (DPS) – the organisation responsible for internal police investigations – launched an inquiry, code-named Operation Alice, 'for the purpose of investigating the source of the leaked Police Log'.[8]

On 2 October, 12 days after *The Sun* had published its first story, an officer from the DPS wrote to News Corp asking to discuss the police log. News Corp replied that 'having spoken to the editor of *The Sun* . . . the journalists had a professional and moral obligation to protect their sources and therefore did not wish to discuss where the information had come from'.[9] They believed they had a sound public interest defence, and the police seemed to agree.

The DPS senior investigating officers, Detective Superintendent Philip Williams and Detective Chief Inspector Tim Neligan decided that the 'evidential threshold for a criminal offence' had not been met.[10] Detective Chief Inspector Neligan believed that the leak of a restricted document to the press, although amounting to gross misconduct by a police officer, would arguably not amount to a criminal offence. Having failed to discover the source of the leak the Operation Alice investigation was closed in October, 2012.

But that was not the end of the story. Exactly one month after the altercation at the Downing Street gates Andrew Mitchell resigned from the government. The Conservative Party's deputy whip told Prime Minister David Cameron that he had received a complaint from one of his constituents, saying he had witnessed what had gone on between the DPG officer and Mitchell. When police reopened the case, they quickly discovered that that the 'constituent' was in fact another DPG officer. When the news leaked out that at least one police officer was playing dirty tricks, Mitchell seized his chance. He appeared on *News at Ten* to 'reiterate once again that . . . the contents of the alleged Police Log . . . are false, they are false and I want to make that very clear'.[11]

The fact that they were not false would not come out until later but in the meantime, with Mitchell protesting his innocence, there was the possibility that a government minister had been forced to stand down because of fabricated evidence. As Detective Chief Inspector Neligan put it, the police were unable to rule out the very serious allegation that police officers had 'fitted up Andrew Mitchell and leaked the story to the press'.[12]

It is understandable that the Metropolitan Police were concerned; the matter was getting huge media coverage and Andrew Mitchell, well known for his demanding attitude as Chief Whip, wanted action.

But what the DPS did next took them on a course which revealed how flimsy were the laws protecting journalists' sources. Just before Christmas 2012 a request under RIPA was made for the phone data of three *Sun* journalists including Newton Dunn. The phone records of one of the police officers showed that he had been in contact based on analysis of the officers' 'mobile phone records and of the mobile phone records of Newton Dunn.'[13]

Just why it was necessary to examine the journalist's mobile phone to discover that he had been contacted by the police officer has not been disclosed. The mobile phone record of the officer himself would have revealed the numbers he had called and since Newton Dunn had contacted the Metropolitan police on several occasions it is most likely they would already have had a copy of his mobile phone number as an incoming call.

Yet since there was no specific provision 'protecting communications data involving information relating to journalists'[14] the Metropolitan police were quite within their legal rights to collect the *Sun* reporter's data. In the application, the police said that 'full consideration has been given to the Human Rights Act, in particular Article 8 (Right to a Private Life) and Article 10 (Freedom of expression)'. It added that the 'intrusion into privacy of potential subjects identified has been considered but deemed justified when balanced against the seriousness of the allegation . . . of misconduct in a public office', and 'full consideration has been given to the examination of a journalist['s] mobile phone'.[15]

Later the case would become more complicated by a supposed call to *The Sun's* hotline in which a woman apparently overheard the Downing Street conversation and said Mitchell had called the police 'fucking morons'.

For the police this was either further evidence of possible conspiracy against Mitchell, or the 'fabricating of defence by *The Sun*' for a civil claim. The newspaper was being sued by Mitchell for defamation for publishing his unsavoury words at the gates of Downing Street.[16] The police had a choice about how to gain access to the numbers that had called *The Sun*'s hotline. They could have chosen to make an application under the Police and Criminal Evidence Act 1984 (PACE) which would require them to make an application to a communications service provider (CSP), in this case *The Sun*'s telephone company. If the case involved 'journalistic material' a judge would be likely to require 'notice to be given to the newspaper'[17] to allow it to argue its case.

In other words, the police would have had to persuade a judge that the only way to effectively complete the investigation was to seize the journalist's phone records, and disregard the fact that confidential sources might be exposed.

Instead the Met went around the restrictive PACE law. Under RIPA there was no necessity to appear before a judge to argue the case. The order could be signed off by anyone not directly connected with the investigation. And as long as the decision was not arbitrary, everything would be in order.

The Metropolitan Police had just used a large loophole to destroy the protection that the news organisations believed they had under the European Convention of Human Rights and the laws it underpinned in the UK. The Met were checking journalists' phone records solely on the say-so of someone a couple of ranks higher in the police force.

The action taken by the Metropolitan Police would have remained secret, but for the fact that they disclosed what they had done in a report dealing with the Andrew Mitchell affair. Without that admission, *The Sun* would not have known how the police discovered their sources. The newspaper's only recourse in seeking an investigation into what they believed was a breach of the law protecting journalists' sources was to appeal to the most secretive legal organisation in the UK for help. Even its address, close to the MI6 building on the banks of the Thames, is secret. It uses a PO box for any correspondence.

The Investigatory Powers Tribunal (IPT), the only judicial body in the UK with the authority to investigate complaints against the intelligence services, had untrammelled power. It could decide which cases could be heard, whether a case could be heard at all, and there was no appeal against a decision of the tribunal. It also decided whether or not to make its decisions public.

When the IPT handed down its ruling *The Sun* focussed on its one victory in the case. One of the applications to collect information on one journalist's phone was ruled illegal on the grounds that it was not necessary; the police had already gathered enough evidence to prove the case, the tribunal ruled. A *Sun* spokesperson was quoted as saying that the tribunal had ruled the police's action in secretly accessing the telephone data of *The Sun* and three of its journalists was 'in breach of our rights to protect our confidential sources.'[18] Despite the exuberance of *The Sun* crowing its victory, the tribunal had done nothing of the sort. It had in fact ruled that RIPA gave the police every right to access the journalists' telephone numbers in the way they did. And the Human Rights Act (HRA, 2000) which guaranteed journalists rights, was only effective in one case. *The Sun's* headline 'Met police illegally seized Sun journalist's phone records, court rules'[19] could have more accurately have read: Police 2, *The Sun* 1.

Although the newspaper was right to point out that the tribunal ruled that under Article 10 of the European Convention of Human Rights, all three journalists and the newspaper should have been able to protect their confidential sources, the blame for the weak laws lay with newspapers like *The Sun*, along with the *Daily Mail* and the *Daily Telegraph* who whipped up such fear in the community, creating a demand for counter-terrorism measures including tough surveillance laws to be implemented.

Yet conversely, *The Sun* had in this case operated at the highest levels of journalistic principle: though the police involved in the leak had been fired from the force, only one of them had been charged with any criminal offence. *The Sun* and the police who leaked the information had both been doing their duty. As the Crown Prosecution Service argued, no jury would convict them because the information they had leaked to *The Sun* was in the 'public interest'.[20] Stung into action after one of its most ardent media supporters, News Corp, had felt the full force of the new surveillance laws, in 2015 the Conservative government refined the legislation. It wrapped aspects of PACE which gave journalists more rights into the RIPA law, forcing police in future to go through a court process before they sought a journalist's phone records, unless there was an immediate danger to life.

But the Investigatory Powers Act (IPA) would later strip away those protections. News organisations and journalists would not be able to argue their case in court against the release of digital material. Police could make their requests to view journalists' phone call data in secret to telecommunications providers and would only need approval from a judicial commissioner.

As late as June 2017 the IPA was still mired in doubt. Its basic provisions which allowed the indiscriminate wholesale collection and retention of meta data had been rejected by the UK Court of Appeal, and referred to the European Court of Justice. There was bad news there too for the government. The court ruled that the Charter of Fundamental Rights of the European Union outlawed 'general and indiscriminate retention'[21] of all communications including location and subscriber data. Only targeted interception of traffic and the collection of location data in order to combat serious crime – including terrorism – was justified.

But all these concerns are likely to be swept aside. As Britain exits the European Union the government has repeatedly stated it will also leave the authority of the European Court of Justice, whose rulings have helped shape the UK laws which gave journalists a form of limited protection.

Newspapers like *The Sun*, who were seeking special protection for their journalists, seemed not to understand that the mass surveillance they championed in the so-called war on terrorism was part of the problem exposed in Plebgate: the right of the state to pry into private or professional lives, yet keep its actions secret.

If *The Sun* had been fighting for greater privacy they might have had an argument. But they weren't. They were often championing mass state spying and, more importantly, attacking newspapers and journalists who had revealed just how all-pervasive surveillance had become, and how protections were slowly being whittled away, nearly always in the name of protecting the state. It was a similar situation in the US, where the Attorney General Eric Holder invoked national security concerns when he took the legally unprecedented step of seeking a FISA court order to force the US telecommunications giant Verizon to hand over the phone records of several Associated Press (AP) journalists. They had been involved in producing a report which detailed 'an ambitious plot by Al-Qaeda's affiliate in Yemen to destroy a U.S.-bound airliner using a bomb with a sophisticated new design'.[22]

One year later, in June 2013, Edward Snowden would reveal that Verizon was part of a massive NSA collection program which swept up millions of US customers in a dragnet surveillance of its digital metadata. But at the time no one knew about the secret court ruling affecting the home and mobile telephone records of individual reporters and an editor; AP general office numbers in Washington, New York and Hartford, and the main number for AP reporters covering Congress.

The plot involved an upgrade of the so-called 'underwear bomb' that failed to detonate on board a jetliner over Detroit at Christmas, 2009. This new bomb was also designed to be used in a passenger's underwear, but this time al-Qaeda developed a more refined detonation system.

The AP reported US officials as saying that the FBI was examining the bomb to see whether it could have passed through airport security and brought down an aircraft. The device did not contain metal, meaning it probably could have passed through an airport metal detector. But it was not clear whether new body scanners used in many airports would have detected it.

There seemed to be nothing unusual in the report, which showed the US intelligence agencies simply doing their job. AP had even played by Washington's rules of journalism.

'We held that story until the government assured us that the national security concerns had passed,' said Gary B Pruitt, president and CEO of AP.[23] But AP's agreement to hold the story for 24 hours was apparently not sufficient for the Department of Justice. Holder described the AP report as among 'the top two or three most serious leaks that I've ever seen' in a 35-year career.[24]

Whether or not that was hyperbole, for the next year the Justice Department and the FBI carried out what they called a 'comprehensive investigation', including 550 interviews and a review of 'tens of thousands of documents' in an attempt to find the leak.[25]

According to AP at least two of the journalists' personal cellphone records were provided to the government by Verizon Wireless without any attempt to either challenge the subpoenas or give the reporters a chance to argue their cases against disclosure. Verizon simply said the company 'complies with legal processes for requests for information by law enforcement'.[26] Though Verizon appeared to have given in without a fight, not all communications companies have been so compliant. In 2010 Twitter challenged a US Department of Justice subpoena demanding the company hand over of the accounts belonging to WikiLeaks, and after winning a court order, the company warned those who had been targeted. Others, though, who were plugged directly into the NSA information dragnet like Verizon were apparently more obliging to the government's demands.

In the AP investigation, the Department of Justice and the FBI even went against their normal procedures which governed how they dealt with the media. The regulation requires subpoenas for reporters' phone records – logs of calls made and received – to be narrowly focused and undertaken only after other ways of obtaining information are exhausted. Under normal circumstances, news organisations are to be notified ahead of time so they can negotiate or ask a judge to quash the subpoena, but the regulation allows exceptions, in which case journalists must be notified no more than 90 days later.

But AP was not told until a year had passed and even then the information was passed on in a cursory way. A letter, from a federal prosecutor, consisted of a single sentence saying that AP 'is hereby notified that the United States Department of Justice has received toll [phone] records from April and May 2012 in response to subpoenas issued'[27] for 20 phone numbers in five area codes and three states'.

The Attorney General's department made one concession, that the subpoenas 'should have been more narrowly drawn', but emphasized 'there was a basis to believe the [phone] numbers were associated with A.P. personnel involved in the reporting of classified information'.[28]

The delay in telling AP their phones had been subject to surveillance was not the only issue. Under the US Code of Federal Regulations [50.10] the Department supposedly viewed the use of subpoenas, court orders and search warrants to seek information from what it called 'non-consenting members of the news media' as 'extraordinary measures',[29] not standard investigatory practices.

The code states that if the department decided to target journalists they would receive 'appropriate notice'[30] unless the Attorney General determined that, 'for compelling reasons', any discussion 'would pose a clear and substantial threat to the integrity of the investigation, risk grave harm to national security, or present an imminent risk of death or serious bodily harm'.[31]

There may well have been a simpler explanation for why the Attorney General's department decided the case was so important and it had more to do with political embarrassment than the security of the state. Two weeks before the AP story was published, with the anniversary of the bin Laden killing approaching, the White House press secretary Jay Carney told reporters: 'We have no credible information that terrorist organizations, including Al-Qaida, are plotting attacks in the U.S. to coincide with the anniversary of bin Laden's death.'[32] One week later, on 1 May, a spokesperson for the Department of Homeland Security said, 'We have no indication of any specific, credible threats or plots against the U.S. tied to the one-year anniversary of bin Laden's death.'[33]

AP had learned about the thwarted plot a week earlier but agreed to White House and CIA requests not to publish it immediately because the sensitive intelligence operation was still under way. Once officials confirmed those concerns were allayed, AP said, it decided to disclose the plot on 7 May, 2012 despite requests from the Obama administration to wait for an official announcement the following day, 6 May.[34]

What undermines the fragile argument that the AP story threatened national security is the fact that at the time of publication the then presidential counter-terrorism advisor, John Brennan hosted a conference call with a number of terrorism experts working for US TV networks. In the high-level briefing, Brenan discussed details of the new aircraft bomb discovery, revealing a crucial piece of information: the bomb plot was never a threat to the American public or aviation safety because intelligence officials had 'inside control'[35] over it. Brenan's statement went further than the AP story, suggesting the US had an operative working with the bomb makers. 'It complicates considerably the force of the argument that this disclosure seriously compromised national security,'[36] said Floyd Abrams, a leading First Amendment lawyer who represented the *New York Times* in a historic legal battle over its publication of the Pentagon Papers in 1971.

One plausible reason for the Department of Justice's action against AP, described by AP president Pruitt as 'a serious interference with A.P.'s constitutional rights to gather and report the news',[37] was that the article refuted White House claims that there had been no al-Qaeda plots at the time of the anniversary of the killing of Osama bin Laden. The White House was extremely sensitive about the details surrounding bin Laden's death – although at the time of the AP story few outside knew why. What we now know is that the official version of how he was killed by US Navy Seals in an operation immortalised by the film *Zero Dark Thirty* bore a questionable resemblance to the truth. Investigative journalist Seymour Hersh almost certainly got closer to what had happened when he revealed in an article, rejected by the *New Yorker* and eventually published in the *London Review of Books*, details he had discovered about the operation. It had not been clever CIA operatives who tracked bin Laden down; the al-Qaeda leader had been turned in by an informer who walked in to the US Embassy in Islamabad to pick up a slice of the reward for information about his whereabouts. The Obama administration, for all its early concern about the problems of a surveillance state, had developed a bad record on press freedom.

The AP subpoena came against the backdrop of six prosecutions of officials in leak-related cases under President Obama – twice the number prosecuted under all previous presidents combined. It also appears to be the first administration to have considered prosecuting a journalist. As we saw earlier, reporter James Risen of the *New York Times* was easily tracked by the digital fingerprints he left behind while communicating with his CIA informant Jeffrey Sterling. It was accepted that the case against Stirling was already very strong, but Attorney General Holder was looking for a confession from Risen that Sterling was his source. Forcing Risen to attend court would send a strong message to journalists that they might have constitutional protections in some areas, but they were not totally immune from prosecution. These actions were seen as part of a strategy by the Obama administration to influence press coverage. In Risen's case he would be confronted with a stark choice under questioning: reveal your source, or face the possibility of jail for contempt of court.

The case against Stirling had been on hold for years, awaiting Risen's testimony – something the *New York Times* reporter, had fought to withhold. The prosecutors thought they had won their battle in June 2014 when the US Supreme Court rejected Risen's appeal against appearing. But just weeks before a pre-trial hearing, where Risen was due to give evidence, Holder stepped back from the brink. He failed to authorise the prosecution to pursue Risen to force him to identify his confidential sources.

Later that year, Holder approved a subpoena of another journalist, US 60 *Minutes* producer Richard Bonin, to testify at a terrorism trial. Prosecutors wanted Bonin to discuss his dealings with al-Qaeda's media office during an unsuccessful attempt to interview Osama bin Laden in 1998. Holder only rescinded his approval when Bonin notified the Attorney General's office that he would challenge the subpoena. Fox News James Rosen was also threatened with prosecution under the Espionage Act (1917) for being a co-conspirator with his informant, State Department nuclear arms expert Stephen Jin-Woo Kim, who had given him the story about North Korea's nuclear weapons development. Whether it was the strong opposition from other members of the media, or there was never the intention to prosecute journalists as spies, or jail them for refusing to reveal their sources, the US administration's action were part of an identifiable global pushback by executive government against disclosure of uncomfortable truths – particularly relating to national security.

In Australia, where journalists have limited defences to protect their metadata, ASIO director-general Duncan Lewis confirmed in 2017 that the first Journalist Information Warrants had been issued under new metadata retention laws. Whereas police agencies have to appear before a judge to argue their case – even though the journalist will not be told – ASIO only needs the Attorney General to sign off on the warrant. Just how many warrants had been issued the director-general refused to reveal. Lewis said because of the 'small nature of the number it would be very easy to start identifying what cases were involved' and it could 'clearly point to an investigation that is underway'.[38]

Even before the data retention legislation became law security agencies gained comparatively easy access to reporters' meta data. The Australian Federal Police (AFP) confirmed that it had sought 'subscriber checks'[39] and email records relating to the Guardian Australia journalist Paul Farrell.

In 2016 Guardian Australia reported that the AFP had accrued a file of at least 200 pages on Farrell in an attempt to discover sources of his revelatory reports about Australia's secret operations which used the Australian Navy to turn back refugee boats. The government had passed a special law, the Australian Border Force Act (2015) – section 42[40] to make it a criminal offence for anyone involved to talk about what the government called 'on water matters': the implementation of a refugee policy which has seen shootings, children sexually assaulted and suicides in Australia's off-shore detention centres on the remote islands of Manus, 400 kilometres off the north coast of Papua New Guinea, and Naru, more than 2000 kilometres east.

The file contained a heavily redacted dossier of operational minutes, file notes, interview records and a plan for an investigation the AFP undertook into one of Farrell's reports.

The correspondence was sent to Farrell after he lodged a complaint under the Privacy Act (1988) to gain access to parts of the AFP files that had been redacted.

In the course of the investigation, the AFP provided submissions to the Privacy Commissioner that were passed to Farrell, including an admission that the AFP had sought 'subscriber checks' relating to him.

The AFP's submission said: 'You will see that exemptions have been claimed under s47E(d) and s37(2)(b) on some folios. These exemptions primarily relate to e-mail and other subscriber checks relating to Mr Farrell, and examination of meta data associated with some electronic files.'[41]

The CEO of the journalists' union, the Media Entertainment and Arts Alliance, Paul Murphy, said he was appalled by news that the AFP had sought access to Farrell's metadata. 'It comes down to this: journalists writing legitimate news stories in the public interest now have police trawling through their private metadata all because a government agency is embarrassed about a leak,'[42] Murphy said.

Though the demands to access Farrell's metadata were made in 2014 – before changes to the law which introduced extremely limited protection for journalists – they are evidence that the police have no compunction in rifling through a journalist's professional communications at the government's instruction. It seems unlikely that the new laws, which will see a government-selected lawyer representing the interests of a journalist – who will know nothing about the secret hearing before a judge selected by the government – will stop the police and the government from attempting to get what they want. The use of surveillance directly targeting journalists appears to be an increasing trend, often using provisions of the newly-introduced anti-terrorism laws. The UK Government openly cites what it seems as the threat of revelatory investigative journalism.

Every year the government issues an Annual Threat Assessment to all Whitehall departments. The assessment includes personnel who may be from or influenced by foreign intelligence services (FIS), authorised users who 'for whatever motive'[43] may seek to gain access to official information they have no 'need to know'.[44] Listed among the others which the government sees as a threat to the state are 'subversive or terrorist organisations, and investigative journalists'.[45]

Further evidence of how governments perceive journalists as a potential enemy can be found in another Five-Eyes country. A leaked New Zealand Defence Force security manual assessed three main 'subversion' threats it needed to protect itself against: FIS, organisations with extreme ideologies and 'certain investigative journalists'.[46] New Zealand Investigative journalist Nicky Hager, who first revealed the manual, says that in the minds of New Zealand defence chiefs, probing journalists apparently belonged in the same category as al-Qaeda.

The manual, which was issued as an order by the Chief of Defence Force, defined 'the threat' as espionage, sabotage, subversion and terrorism, and included investigative journalists under the heading 'subversion'. Hager, whose home was illegally raided by police after he wrote a book exposing how the prime minister had been involved in a dirty tricks campaign to discredit a political opponent, also revealed how state intelligence targeted the phone of a New Zealand journalist working in Afghanistan. He believed that the journalist Jon Stephenson had been targeted as being 'subversive'[47] because the New Zealand Defence Force was unhappy at Stephenson's reporting of its handling of Afghan prisoners and was trying to find out who was giving him confidential information. According to Hager, classifying Stephenson's work as subversion was an attempt to give the intelligence agencies legal cover to act against him.

The monitoring occurred in the second half of 2012 when Stephenson was working as Kabul correspondent for the US McClatchy news service and for various New Zealand news organisations. According to Hager, New Zealand SAS troops in Kabul had access to the reports and were using them in active investigations into Stephenson. New Zealand Defence Force personnel had copies of intercepted phones' metadata which helped the military create a 'tree'[48] of Stephenson's associates including contacts in the Afghan government and military.

To reinforce its concern, the defence security manual mentioned investigative journalists a second time under the category 'non-traditional threats'. The threat of investigative journalists, it says, is that they may attempt to obtain 'politically sensitive information'.[49]

Metro magazine editor Simon Wilson, who has published a number of Stephenson's Afghan prisoner reports, said the Defence Force seemed to see Stephenson as the 'enemy . . . confusing national security with its own desire not to be embarrassed by disclosures that reveal it has broken the rules'.[50]

Stephenson was not alone in having his phone targeted in Afghanistan. The news magazine *Der Spiegel*, reported that the *Federal Intelligence Service* (BND), Germany's foreign intelligence agency, conducted surveillance on 'dozens of connections belonging to the BBC in Afghanistan.'[51] Since 1999, it also eavesdropped on 'at least 50 additional telephone numbers, fax numbers and email addresses belonging to journalists or newsrooms around the world',[52] including more than a dozen connections belonging to the offices of the BBC World Service. The documents indicate that the German intelligence agency did not just tap into the phones of BBC correspondents in Afghanistan, but also targeted telephone and fax numbers at BBC headquarters in London.

A phone number belonging to the *New York Times* in Afghanistan was also on the BND list, as were several mobile and satellite numbers belonging to the news agency Reuters in Afghanistan, Pakistan and Nigeria. The German spies also conducted surveillance on other numbers belonging to news agencies from Kuwait, Lebanon and India in addition to journalist associations in Nepal and Indonesia.

Less than two kilometres from the event which accelerated the introduction of surveillance laws, the attack on the Twin Towers in Manhattan, the PEN American Center – a literary and human rights organisation – published extensive research into the effect of surveillance on writers four months after Snowden's exposures. Titled: 'Chilling Effects: NSA surveillance drives writers to self-censor'[53] the report said that in human rights and free expression communities it was a widely shared assumption that the 'explosive growth and proliferating'[54] of surveillance technologies must be harmful – to intellectual freedom, to creativity and to social discourse. But, PEN asked,

> how exactly do we know, and how can we demonstrate, that pervasive surveillance is harming freedom of expression and creative freedom? We know – historically, from writers and intellectuals in the Soviet Bloc, and contemporaneously from writers, thinkers, and artists in China, Iran, and elsewhere – that aggressive surveillance regimes limit discourse and distort the flow of information and ideas. But what about the new democratic surveillance states?[55]

PEN partnered with independent researchers at the FDR Group – which describes itself as a non-profit, non-partisan research organisation – to conduct a survey of over 520 American writers to better understand the specific ways in which awareness of far-reaching surveillance programs influences writers' thinking, research and writing.

The initial survey results showed that writers were significantly more likely than the general public to *disapprove* of 'the government's collection of telephone and Internet data as part of anti-terrorism efforts'[56] – 66% of writers vs. 44% of the general public. Only 12% of writers approve, compared with 50% of the general public.

About two-thirds of investigative journalists surveyed (64%) believed that the U.S. government had probably collected data about their phone calls, emails or online communications, and eight in ten believe that being a journalist increased the likelihood that their data will be collected. Those who report on national security, foreign affairs or the federal government are particularly likely to believe the government has already collected data about their electronic communications (71% say this is the case), according to a survey of members of Investigative Reporters and Editors (IRE) – a non-profit member organisation for journalists – by the Pew Research Center in association with Columbia University's Tow Center for Digital Journalism.

Fourteen per cent of journalists said that in the previous 12 months, concerns about being under surveillance had kept them from pursuing a story or reaching out to a particular source, or had led them to consider leaving investigative journalism altogether.

Freedom of expression was under threat and, as a result, freedom of information was imperilled as well. PEN found that 85% of writers responding to the survey were worried about government surveillance of Americans, and 73% of writers 'have never been as worried about privacy rights and freedom of the press as they are today.'[57]

PEN stated that 'writers are not only overwhelmingly worried about government surveillance, but are engaging in self-censorship as a result.'[58] As Steve Coll, staff writer for *The New Yorker* and Dean of the Graduate School of Journalism at Columbia University, explained: 'Every national security reporter I know would say that the atmosphere in which professional reporters seek insight into policy failures [and] bad military decisions is just much tougher and much chillier.'[59]

In 2014 Human Rights Watch (HRW) produced a 90-page research report 'With Liberty to Monitor All: How Large-Scale US surveillance is Harming Journalism, Law and American Democracy'. Several journalists HRW spoke with asserted that the new challenges they faced significantly impeded news coverage of 'matters of great public concern'.[60] Many journalists emphasised the extra time entailed by the new techniques they employed to protect their sources and communications. 'It's a tax on my time,' noted *New York Times* reporter Bart Gellman. 'I could do double the work if I weren't spending so much effort on encryption and a secure workflow between networked and air-gapped machines.'[61] Part of the delay results from using more advanced privacy and security technologies, which may involve trade-offs with convenience, and ensuring that sources do the same. Part of the delay also comes from the scaled-back use of digital technology, opting for pre-internet forms of communication. 'Mail is slow,'[62] observed Martin Knobbe, a New York-based correspondent for Stern Magazine. 'It can take two weeks to get an okay to meet someone [using mail].'[63] All things considered, '[i]t absolutely slows down coverage,' claimed investigative reporter Marisa Taylor[64]

With newspapers running on lower levels of staff it was not always possible to begin an investigation simply because a story looks interesting or promising. According to Stephen Engelberg, founding managing editor of ProPublica, 'We have to pick our spots. It takes thought.'[65] Additionally, many journalists said the amount of information provided or confirmed by sources is diminishing. Sources were becoming less candid over email and phone. 'I definitely see a trend of sources speaking at a different level of candour face to face [as compared to over the phone],'[66] noted a national security reporter. As a result, he acknowledged spending more time physically near where his sources work. Others also confirmed travelling more (and spending the money that goes with that), or facing the difficult choice of how to pursue information if travel is not an option. As Peter Maass, a senior writer for *The Intercept*, noted, 'The government doesn't need to know what people are talking about – just *that* they're talking.'[67] Maass described being approached by a would-be source, and urging that person to mail him information rather than sending it electronically. He never heard from the person again, and Maas suspects the reason is that 'I made him aware of the danger of being connected to me. As a result, I lost that story.'[68]

This situation has a direct effect on the public's ability to obtain important information about government activities, and on the ability of the media to serve as a check on government. Many journalists said it is taking them significantly longer to gather information (when they can get it at all), and they are ultimately able to publish fewer stories for public consumption. The report found that the chilling effects stand out most starkly in the case of reporting on the intelligence community, national security and law enforcement – 'all areas of legitimate – indeed, extremely important – public concern.'[69]

In turn, journalists increasingly feel the need to adopt elaborate steps to protect sources and information, and eliminate any digital trail of their investigations – from using high-end encryption, to resorting to burner phones – used once and thrown away – to abandoning all online communication and trying exclusively to meet sources in person.

Journalists expressed concern that, rather than being treated as essential checks on government and partners in ensuring a healthy democratic debate, they now feel they may be viewed as suspect for doing their jobs. One prominent journalist summed up what many seemed to be feeling as follows: 'I don't want the government to force me to act like a spy. I'm not a spy; I'm a journalist.'[70]

Two years later the disruptive effect of surveillance was still being felt. In 2016 Dr Paul Lashmar from Sussex University carried out a post-Snowden study on the effect of surveillance on journalists' work. Lashmar's detailed assessment concluded that 'In a sense it does not matter whether intelligence agencies do use data to track down confidential sources, it is the fact that they can do so much more easily than ever before that is significant.'[71] The negative effect of 'chilling' the flow of information from confidential sources was recognised, Lashmar argues, at least as far back as the Watergate scandal in the early 1970s. In recent years governments had chosen to 'turn the temperature control down further'.[72] What Snowden disclosed may freeze the flow. The current situation would prevent all but the most determined from speaking to journalists. In effect, the threat of mass surveillance may all but 'eliminate confidential sources'.[73] Given that many experienced journalists believed confidential sources were once an effective accountability mechanism, few thought that internal accountability remedies worked, and that much of government and related private-sector organisations will 'no longer be subject to effective scrutiny by the fourth estate'.[74]

Given that for journalists, particularly those working in intelligence and investigative areas, to operate freely has become much more difficult with the rise of mass surveillance, one of the as yet unanswered questions is: has the surveillance been worth it? Does surveillance do anything more than subdue those who dissent, or inhibit journalists whose job it is to hold executive government to account, particularly in important areas of national security? The argument has been vigorously put that to be safer we must sacrifice some freedom. Increased surveillance powers will help stop terrorism. The attacks could be prevented. But is that right?

Notes

1 Tory Diary. 19th May, 2007. *Women to Remain Half-Members at the Carlton Club*. Conservativehome [online]. Available at http://conservativehome.blogs.com/torydiary/2007/05/women_to_remain.html [Accessed 4 December, 2016].
2 Winnett, R. 24th September, 2012. *In Full: Police Log Detailing Andrew Mitchell's 'Pleb' Rant*. Daily Telegraph [online]. London. Available at www.telegraph.co.uk/news/politics/conservative/9564006/In-full-Police-log-detailing-Andrew-Mitchells-pleb-rant.html [Accessed 4 December, 2016].
3 Winnett, R. 24th September, 2012. *In Full: Police Log Detailing Andrew Mitchell's 'Pleb' Rant*. Daily Telegraph [online]. London. Available at www.telegraph.co.uk/news/politics/conservative/9564006/In-full-Police-log-detailing-Andrew-Mitchells-pleb-rant.html [Accessed 4 December, 2016].
4 Winnett, R. 24th September, 2012. *In Full: Police Log Detailing Andrew Mitchell's 'Pleb' Rant*. Daily Telegraph [online]. London. Available at www.telegraph.co.uk/news/politics/conservative/9564006/In-full-Police-log-detailing-Andrew-Mitchells-pleb-rant.html [Accessed 4 December, 2016].
5 Winnett, R. 24th September, 2012. *In Full: Police Log Detailing Andrew Mitchell's 'Pleb' Rant*. Daily Telegraph [online]. London. Available at www.telegraph.co.uk/news/politics/conservative/9564006/In-full-Police-log-detailing-Andrew-Mitchells-pleb-rant.html [Accessed 4 December, 2016].
6 Winnett, R. 24th September, 2012. *In Full: Police Log Detailing Andrew Mitchell's 'Pleb' Rant*. Daily Telegraph [online]. London. Available at www.telegraph.co.uk/news/politics/conservative/9564006/In-full-Police-log-detailing-Andrew-Mitchells-pleb-rant.html [Accessed 4 December, 2016].
7 Winnett, R. 24th September, 2012. *In Full: Police Log Detailing Andrew Mitchell's 'Pleb' Rant*. Daily Telegraph [online]. London. Available at www.telegraph.co.uk/news/politics/conservative/9564006/In-full-Police-log-detailing-Andrew-Mitchells-pleb-rant.html [Accessed 4 December, 2016].
8 Investigatory Powers Tribunal. 4th February, 2016. *News Group Newspapers Limited and Others v.v. The Commissioner of Police of the Metropolis* [online]. Available at www.ipt-uk.com/judgments.asp?id=31 [Accessed 20 July, 2017].
9 Investigatory Powers Tribunal. 4th February, 2016. News Group Newspapers Limited and Others v.v. The Commissioner of Police of the Metropolis [online]. Available at www.ipt-uk.com/judgments.asp?id=31 [Accessed 20 July, 2017].
10 Investigatory Powers Tribunal. 4th February, 2016. News Group Newspapers Limited and Others v.v. The Commissioner of Police of the Metropolis [online]. Available at www.ipt-uk.com/judgments.asp?id=31 [Accessed 20 July, 2017].
11 Investigatory Powers Tribunal. 4th February, 2016. News Group Newspapers Limited and Others v.v. The Commissioner of Police of the Metropolis [online]. Available at www.ipt-uk.com/judgments.asp?id=31 [Accessed 20 July, 2017].
12 Investigatory Powers Tribunal. 4th February, 2016. News Group Newspapers Limited and Others v.v. The Commissioner of Police of the Metropolis [online]. Available at www.ipt-uk.com/judgments.asp?id=31 [Accessed 20 July, 2017].
13 Investigatory Powers Tribunal. 4th February, 2016. News Group Newspapers Limited and Others v.v. The Commissioner of Police of the Metropolis [online]. Available at www.ipt-uk.com/judgments.asp?id=31 [Accessed 20 July, 2017].
14 Investigatory Powers Tribunal. 4th February, 2016. News Group Newspapers Limited and Others v.v. The Commissioner of Police of the Metropolis [online]. Available at www.ipt-uk.com/judgments.asp?id=31 [Accessed 20 July, 2017].

15 Investigatory Powers Tribunal. 4th February, 2016. News Group Newspapers Limited and Others v.v. The Commissioner of Police of the Metropolis [online]. Available at www.ipt-uk.com/judgments.asp?id=31 [Accessed 20 July, 2017].

16 Investigatory Powers Tribunal. 4th February, 2016. News Group Newspapers Limited and Others v.v. The Commissioner of Police of the Metropolis [online]. Available at www.ipt-uk.com/judgments.asp?id=31 [Accessed 20 July, 2017].

17 Investigatory Powers Tribunal. 4th February, 2016. News Group Newspapers Limited and Others v.v. The Commissioner of Police of the Metropolis [online]. Available at www.ipt-uk.com/judgments.asp?id=31 [Accessed 20 July, 2017].

18 Dunn, T. 17th December, 2015. Met Police Illegally Seized Sun Journalist's Phone Records, Court Rules [online]. Available at www.thesun.co.uk/archives/news/882152/met-police-illegally-seized-sun-journalists-phone-records-court-rules/ [Accessed 20 July, 2017].

19 Dunn, T. 17th December, 2015. Met Police Illegally Seized Sun Journalist's Phone Records, Court Rules [online]. Available at www.thesun.co.uk/archives/news/882152/met-police-illegally-seized-sun-journalists-phone-records-court-rules/ [Accessed 20 July, 2017].

20 Investigatory Powers Tribunal. 4th February, 2016. News Group Newspapers Limited and Others v.v. The Commissioner of Police of the Metropolis [online]. Available at www.ipt-uk.com/judgments.asp?id=31 [Accessed 20 July, 2017].

21 European Court of Justice. 21st December, 2016. Judgement of the Court [online]. Available at http://curia.europa.eu/juris/document/document.jsf?text=&docid=186492&pageIndex=0&doclang=en&mode=lst&dir=&occ=first&part=1&cid=424799 [Accessed 4 September, 2016].

22 Savage, C. and Shane, S. 14th May, 2013. *Justice Dept. Defends Seizure of Phone Records*. The New York Times [online]. New York. Available at www.nytimes.com/2013/05/15/us/politics/attorney-general-defends-seizure-of-journalists-phone-records.html [Accessed 12 July, 2016].

23 Savage, C. and Shane, S. 14th May, 2013. *Justice Dept. Defends Seizure of Phone Records*. The New York Times [online]. New York. Available at www.nytimes.com/2013/05/15/us/politics/attorney-general-defends-seizure-of-journalists-phone-records.html [Accessed 12 July, 2016].

24 Savage, C. and Shane, S. 14th May, 2013. *Justice Dept. Defends Seizure of Phone Records*. The New York Times [online]. New York. Available at www.nytimes.com/2013/05/15/us/politics/attorney-general-defends-seizure-of-journalists-phone-records.html [Accessed 12 July, 2016].

25 Cole, J. 14th May, 2013. Letter from Office of the Attorney General, Washington DC [online]. Available at https://fas.org/sgp/news/2013/05/dag-ap.pdf [Accessed 20 July, 2017].

26 Savage, C. and Shane, S. 14th May, 2013. *Justice Dept. Defends Seizure of Phone Records*. The New York Times [online]. New York. Available at www.nytimes.com/2013/05/15/us/politics/attorney-general-defends-seizure-of-journalists-phone-records.html [Accessed 12 July, 2016].

27 Savage, C. and Shane, S. 14th May, 2013. *Justice Dept. Defends Seizure of Phone Records*. The New York Times [online]. New York. Available at www.nytimes.com/2013/05/15/us/politics/attorney-general-defends-seizure-of-journalists-phone-records.html [Accessed 12 July, 2016].

28 Savage, C. and Shane, S. 14th May, 2013. *Justice Dept. Defends Seizure of Phone Records*. The New York Times [online]. New York. Available at www.nytimes.com/2013/05/15/us/politics/attorney-general-defends-seizure-of-journalists-phone-records.html [Accessed 12 July, 2016].

29 Legal Information Institute. [No date]. *Policy Regarding Obtaining Information from, or Records of, Members of the News Media; and Regarding Questioning, Arresting, or Charging Members of the News Media*. Cornell Law School [online]. Available at www.law.cornell.edu/cfr/text/28/50.10 [Accessed 20 July, 2017].

30 Legal Information Institute. [No date]. *Policy Regarding Obtaining Information from, or Records of, Members of the News Media; and Regarding Questioning, Arresting, or Charging Members of the News Media.* Cornell Law School [online]. Available at www.law.cornell.edu/cfr/text/28/50.10 [Accessed 20 July, 2017].

31 Legal Information Institute. [No date]. *Policy Regarding Obtaining Information from, or Records of, Members of the News Media; and Regarding Questioning, Arresting, or Charging Members of the News Media.* Cornell Law School [online]. Available at www.law.cornell.edu/cfr/text/28/50.10 [Accessed 20 July, 2017].

32 Bull, A. and Hosenball, M. 27th April, 2012. *US on Guard for Attacks Ahead of Bin Laden Anniversary.* Reuters [online]. Available at www.reuters.com/article/us-obama-binladen-idUSBRE83P15420120426 [Accessed 20 July, 2017].

33 Associated Press. 8th May, 2012. CIA Thwarts New Al-Qaeda Underwear Bomb Plot [online]. Available at https://usatoday30.usatoday.com/news/washington/story/2012-05-07/al-qaeda-bomb-plot-foiled/54811054/1 [Accessed 14 December, 2016].

34 Associated Press. 8th May, 2012. CIA Thwarts New Al-Qaeda Underwear Bomb Plot [online]. Available at https://usatoday30.usatoday.com/news/washington/story/2012-05-07/al-qaeda-bomb-plot-foiled/54811054/1 [Accessed 14 December, 2016].

35 Isikoff, M. 15th May, 2013. *Bomb Plot Briefing May Undercut DOJ's Case for AP Records Seizure.* NBC News [online]. Available at http://investigations.nbcnews.com/_news/2013/05/15/18280953-bomb-plot-briefing-may-undercut-dojs-case-for-ap-records-seizure?lite [Accessed 8 June, 2016].

36 Isikoff, M. 15th May, 2013. *Bomb Plot Briefing May Undercut DOJ's Case for AP Records Seizure.* NBC News [online]. Available at http://investigations.nbcnews.com/_news/2013/05/15/18280953-bomb-plot-briefing-may-undercut-dojs-case-for-ap-records-seizure?lite [Accessed 8 June, 2016].

37 Savage, C. and Kaufman, L. 13th May, 2013. *Phone Records of Journalists Seized by US.* The New York Times [online]. New York. Available at www.nytimes.com/2013/05/14/us/phone-records-of-journalists-of-the-associated-press-seized-by-us.html [Accessed 23 May, 2016].

38 Farrell, P. 28th February, 2017. *Asio Given Access to Journalists' Phone and Web Records.* The Guardian [online]. Available at www.theguardian.com/australia-news/2017/feb/28/asio-spy-agency-access-to-journalists-phone-web-records-metadata [Accessed 21 March, 2017].

39 Farrell, P. 28th February, 2017. *Asio Given Access to Journalists' Phone and Web Records.* The Guardian [online]. Available at www.theguardian.com/australia-news/2017/feb/28/asio-spy-agency-access-to-journalists-phone-web-records-metadata [Accessed 21 March, 2017].

40 Commonwealth Consolidated Acts. 2015. *Australian Border Force Act 2015 – Sect 42* [online]. Available at www.austlii.edu.au/au/legis/cth/consol_act/abfa2015225/s42.html [Accessed 3 January, 2017].

41 Meade, A. 14th April, 2016. *Federal Police Admit Seeking Access to Reporter's Metadata Without Warrant.* The Guardian [online]. Available at www.theguardian.com/world/2016/apr/14/federal-police-admit-seeking-access-to-reporters-metadata-without-warrant [Accessed 28 October, 2016].

42 Meade, A. 14th April, 2016. *Federal Police Admit Seeking Access to Reporter's Metadata Without Warrant.* The Guardian [online]. Available at www.theguardian.com/world/2016/apr/14/federal-police-admit-seeking-access-to-reporters-metadata-without-warrant [Accessed 28 October, 2016].

43 WikiLeaks. October, 2001. The Defence Manual of Security Volumes 1, 2 and 3 Issue 2 [online]. Available at https://file.wikileaks.org/file/uk-mod-jsp-440-2001.pdf [Accessed 26 August, 2016].

44 WikiLeaks. October, 2001. The Defence Manual of Security Volumes 1, 2 and 3 Issue 2 [online]. Available at https://file.wikileaks.org/file/uk-mod-jsp-440-2001.pdf [Accessed 26 August, 2016].

45 WikiLeaks. October, 2001. The Defence Manual of Security Volumes 1, 2 and 3 Issue 2 [online]. Available at https://file.wikileaks.org/file/uk-mod-jsp-440-2001.pdf [Accessed 26 August, 2016].
46 Hager, N. 27th July, 2013. *US Spy Agencies Eavesdrop on Kiwi*. Stuff.co.nz [online]. Available at www.stuff.co.nz/national/8972743/US-spy-agencies-eavesdrop-on-Kiwi [Accessed 20 July, 2017].
47 Hager, N. 27th July, 2013. *US Spy Agencies Eavesdrop on Kiwi*. Stuff.co.nz [online]. Available at www.stuff.co.nz/national/8972743/US-spy-agencies-eavesdrop-on-Kiwi [Accessed 20 July, 2017].
48 Hager, N. 27th July, 2013. *US Spy Agencies Eavesdrop on Kiwi*. Stuff.co.nz [online]. Available at www.stuff.co.nz/national/8972743/US-spy-agencies-eavesdrop-on-Kiwi [Accessed 20 July, 2017].
49 Hager, N. 27th July, 2013. *US Spy Agencies Eavesdrop on Kiwi*. Stuff.co.nz [online]. Available at www.stuff.co.nz/national/8972743/US-spy-agencies-eavesdrop-on-Kiwi [Accessed 20 July, 2017].
50 Hager, N. 27th July, 2013. *US Spy Agencies Eavesdrop on Kiwi*. Stuff.co.nz [online]. Available at www.stuff.co.nz/national/8972743/US-spy-agencies-eavesdrop-on-Kiwi [Accessed 20 July, 2017].
51 Baumgartner, M., Knobbe, M. and Schindler, J. 24th February, 2017. *Documents Indicate Germany Spied on Foreign Journalists*. Der Spiegel [online]. Available at www.spiegel.de/international/germany/german-intelligence-spied-on-foreign-journalists-for-years-a-1136188.html [Accessed 2 March, 2017].
52 Baumgartner, M., Knobbe, M. and Schindler, J. 24th February, 2017. *Documents Indicate Germany Spied on Foreign Journalists*. Der Spiegel [online]. Available at www.spiegel.de/international/germany/german-intelligence-spied-on-foreign-journalists-for-years-a-1136188.html [Accessed 2 March, 2017].
53 Pen America. 12th November, 2013. Chilling Effects: NSA Surveillance Drives US Writers to Self-Censor [online]. Available at https://pen.org/sites/default/files/Chilling%20Effects_PEN%20American.pdf [Accessed 18 November, 2016].
54 Pen America. 12th November, 2013. Chilling Effects: NSA Surveillance Drives US Writers to Self-Censor [online]. Available at https://pen.org/sites/default/files/Chilling%20Effects_PEN%20American.pdf [Accessed 18 November, 2016].
55 Pen America. 12th November, 2013. Chilling Effects: NSA Surveillance Drives US Writers to Self-Censor [online]. Available at https://pen.org/sites/default/files/Chilling%20Effects_PEN%20American.pdf [Accessed 18 November, 2016].
56 Pen America. 12th November, 2013. Chilling Effects: NSA Surveillance Drives US Writers to Self-Censor [online]. Available at https://pen.org/sites/default/files/Chilling%20Effects_PEN%20American.pdf [Accessed 18 November, 2016].
57 Pen America. 12th November, 2013. Chilling Effects: NSA Surveillance Drives US Writers to Self-Censor [online]. Available at https://pen.org/sites/default/files/Chilling%20Effects_PEN%20American.pdf [Accessed 18 November, 2016].
58 Pen America. 12th November, 2013. Chilling Effects: NSA Surveillance Drives US Writers to Self-Censor [online]. Available at https://pen.org/sites/default/files/Chilling%20Effects_PEN%20American.pdf [Accessed 18 November, 2016].
59 Human Rights Watch. 28th July, 2014. Surveillance Harming Journalism, Law, Democracy [online]. Available at www.hrw.org/report/2014/07/28/liberty-monitor-all/how-large-scale-us-surveillance-harming-journalism-law-and [Accessed 20 July, 2017].
60 Human Rights Watch. 28th July, 2014. Surveillance Harming Journalism, Law, Democracy [online]. Available at www.hrw.org/report/2014/07/28/liberty-monitor-all/how-large-scale-us-surveillance-harming-journalism-law-and [Accessed 20 July, 2017].
61 Human Rights Watch. 28th July, 2014. Surveillance Harming Journalism, Law, Democracy [online]. Available at www.hrw.org/report/2014/07/28/liberty-monitor-all/how-large-scale-us-surveillance-harming-journalism-law-and [Accessed 20 July, 2017].

62 Human Rights Watch. 28th July, 2014. Surveillance Harming Journalism, Law, Democracy [online]. Available at www.hrw.org/report/2014/07/28/liberty-monitor-all/how-large-scale-us-surveillance-harming-journalism-law-and [Accessed 20 July, 2017].

63 Human Rights Watch. 28th July, 2014. Surveillance Harming Journalism, Law, Democracy [online]. Available at www.hrw.org/report/2014/07/28/liberty-monitor-all/how-large-scale-us-surveillance-harming-journalism-law-and [Accessed 20 July, 2017].

64 Human Rights Watch. 28th July, 2014. Surveillance Harming Journalism, Law, Democracy [online]. Available at www.hrw.org/report/2014/07/28/liberty-monitor-all/how-large-scale-us-surveillance-harming-journalism-law-and [Accessed 20 July, 2017].

65 Human Rights Watch. 28th July, 2014. Surveillance Harming Journalism, Law, Democracy [online]. Available at www.hrw.org/report/2014/07/28/liberty-monitor-all/how-large-scale-us-surveillance-harming-journalism-law-and [Accessed 20 July, 2017].

66 Human Rights Watch. 28th July, 2014. Surveillance Harming Journalism, Law, Democracy [online]. Available at www.hrw.org/report/2014/07/28/liberty-monitor-all/how-large-scale-us-surveillance-harming-journalism-law-and [Accessed 20 July, 2017].

67 Human Rights Watch. 28th July, 2014. Surveillance Harming Journalism, Law, Democracy [online]. Available at www.hrw.org/report/2014/07/28/liberty-monitor-all/how-large-scale-us-surveillance-harming-journalism-law-and [Accessed 20 July, 2017].

68 Human Rights Watch. 28th July, 2014. Surveillance Harming Journalism, Law, Democracy [online]. Available at www.hrw.org/report/2014/07/28/liberty-monitor-all/how-large-scale-us-surveillance-harming-journalism-law-and [Accessed 20 July, 2017].

69 Human Rights Watch. 28th July, 2014. Surveillance Harming Journalism, Law, Democracy [online]. Available at www.hrw.org/report/2014/07/28/liberty-monitor-all/how-large-scale-us-surveillance-harming-journalism-law-and [Accessed 20 July, 2017].

70 Human Rights Watch. 28th July, 2014. Surveillance Harming Journalism, Law, Democracy [online]. Available at www.hrw.org/report/2014/07/28/liberty-monitor-all/how-large-scale-us-surveillance-harming-journalism-law-and [Accessed 20 July, 2017].

71 Lashmar, P. 24th May, 2016. *No More Sources? The Impact of Snowden's Revelations on Journalists and Their Confidential Sources*. Taylor & Francis Online. Available at www.tandfonline.com/doi/full/10.1080/17512786.2016.1179587 [Accessed 28 August, 2016].

72 Lashmar, P. 24th May, 2016. *No More Sources? The Impact of Snowden's Revelations on Journalists and Their Confidential Sources*. Taylor & Francis Online. Available at www.tandfonline.com/doi/full/10.1080/17512786.2016.1179587 [Accessed 28 August, 2016].

73 Lashmar, P. 24th May, 2016. *No More Sources? The Impact of Snowden's Revelations on Journalists and Their Confidential Sources*. Taylor & Francis Online. Available at www.tandfonline.com/doi/full/10.1080/17512786.2016.1179587 [Accessed 28 August, 2016].

74 Lashmar, P. 24th May, 2016. *No More Sources? The Impact of Snowden's Revelations on Journalists and Their Confidential Sources*. Taylor & Francis Online. Available at www.tandfonline.com/doi/full/10.1080/17512786.2016.1179587 [Accessed 28 August, 2016].

11

TOO MUCH INFORMATION

The pattern of surveillance laws enacted by Western liberal democracies during the past one and a half decades has an eerie symmetry about it. Nearly every new law has been introduced following a terrorist attack. And nearly every law has increased the power of state authorities to intercept or gather information on its citizens, including journalists.

From the moment the US mainland was attacked by al-Qaeda in September 2001, the so-called War on Terror unleashed a terrifying increase in surveillance, with no end in sight. The fact that in some cases terrorist plots are disrupted, or arrests are made, is repeatedly asserted by government, politicians and much of the media as the reason why more intrusive laws are needed. Sixteen years after the US attacks the same rhetoric was being rolled out. After eight people were killed in central London on 3 June, 2017, the British prime minister, Theresa May, promised tougher anti-terrorism laws. In France, where the nation was placed under a State of Emergency in November 2015, it was a similar story. Not all these changes were related directly to increased surveillance but they were part of the erosion of civil liberties, the trade-off that promises the population greater security in exchange for limitations on their liberty. Yet there is ample proof that the wide-ranging surveillance dragnets which are so disrupting the work of many journalists – particularly those whose job it is to hold governments and their intelligence services to account – are not the answer to combating terrorism. A more focused approach on the state's enemies could well provide better outcomes. The NSA's argument that it was necessary to 'collect it all' so that the information could then be sifted to find the 'needle in the haystack' is well countered by Edward Snowden's view that 'When you are searching for a needle in a haystack the one thing you don't do is pour hay on top of it. And that is what bulk collection mass surveillance does.'[1] Snowden paints a graphic picture of the failings of mass surveillance:

> You take all of the communications from all the people in the world that you have no reason to believe are valuable, yet you keep throwing them into your data set which you are trying to narrow down to things that are actually valuable. This is the difference between indiscriminate surveillance and targeted surveillance.[2]

Snowden pointed out that targeted surveillance had always been used by intelligence services, law enforcement services and for 'good old fashioned police work throughout history'.[3] If the police or intelligence agencies had a suspect who they thought had perpetrated a crime, they started to look at everything the perpetrator did. The authorities would go to court, get a warrant and 'show that you have probable cause to violate the persons privacy rights'.[4]

If the court authorised the surveillance after providing evidence that the suspect was probably up to no good, then the authorities stopped looking at everything else. 'You are not looking at what grandma did when she went to the local strip mall, because that is going to waste your time, waste your resources.'[5] Problems with the efficiency of intelligence and security agencies are littered through the history of anti-terrorism activity, but never more so than in the methods they have employed to stop terrorism since 2001.

Late in December, 1999, the NSA intercepted an alarming call to a house in Yemen, instructing two low level al-Qaeda operatives – Khalid al-Mihdhar and Nawaf al-Hazmi – to fly to Kuala Lumpur, Malaysia, for what appeared to be a terrorist summit.

In an insightful reconstruction of what happened, the US national public broadcaster PBS reported: 'This is the phone [call] that sets in motion the 9/11 attacks.'

James Bamford, a recognised expert on US intelligence and the author of 'Puzzle Palace' [Houghton Mifflin Company, 1982, USA], the first expose of the NSA's inner working, explained in his PBS documentary 'The Spy Factory':

> After picking up this critical call, NSA passed on their first names to the FBI and the CIA but not their last names. Nawaf's last name had been in the NSA's database for over a year, because of his association with bin Laden's operations center in Yemen, but apparently the NSA never looked it up.[6]

As the programme's narrator explains, 'the CIA does find al-Mihdhar's name in its database':

NARRATOR: They ask security agents to make a copy of his passport as he passes through a checkpoint in Dubai. When analysts at CIA headquarters see it, they are astonished to find a valid U.S. visa inside. The CIA's bin Laden unit, code named Alec Station, now has two FBI agents detailed to it, Doug Miller and Mark Rossini.

CIA OFFICER MARK ROSSINI: Once they arrived in Kuala Lumpur, of course, the CIA requested the intelligence service over there in Malaysia to conduct surveillance of these subjects and find out as much as they can. They took photographs, followed them. And you read from that one of the individuals had a visa to come to the U.S.

NARRATOR: Fearing an Al Qaeda terrorist may be headed to the U.S., the agents are determined to tell the FBI, but a CIA official will not allow it.

CIA OFFICER ROSSINI: I guess I was the more senior agent. So, I went up to the individual that had the ticket on the Yemeni cell, the Yemeni operatives. And I said to her, I said, 'What's going on? You know, we've got to tell the Bureau [FBI] about this. These guys clearly are bad. One of them, at least, has a multiple-entry visa to the U.S. We've got to tell the FBI.'

And then she said to me, 'No, it's not the FBI's case, not the FBI's jurisdiction.'

So, I go tell Doug. And I'm like, 'Doug, what can we do?' If we had picked up the phone and called the Bureau [FBI], I would have been violating the law. I would have broken the law. I would have been removed from the building that day. I would have had my clearances suspended, and I would be gone.

JAMES BAMFORD: This is one of the most astonishing parts of the story. The CIA had FBI operatives working within their bin Laden unit, but when the FBI operatives found out that one, and possibly two, of the terrorists had visas to the United States, were heading for the United States, the CIA wouldn't let them tell their headquarters that they were coming.[7]

Yet only the FBI was authorised to put out alerts to stop Khalid al-Mihdhar and Nawaf al-Hazmi from entering the US.

On January15, 2000 United Airlines Flight 2 arrived at Los Angeles International Airport from Bangkok, where the CIA lost al-Mihdhar and al-Hazmi's trail. They passed through U.S. Immigration undetected. Within two weeks they moved into the anonymity of a San Diego suburb, where some of the planning for the New York and Washington attacks took place.

These errors in processing information already held by intelligence agencies have been well documented. The 9/11 Commission of Inquiry placed 'not watching Hazmi and Mihkhar'[8] at No 1 on the list of operational failures, coupled with the decision not to share information about al-Qaeda between intelligence agencies.

However, it seems that the lessons of 9/11 have not been learnt.

Thirteen years later an attack on a Sydney cafe by a self-styled Islamic cleric, Man Haron Monis, which left three people including the gunmen dead, threw up similar problems. A report by Australia's counter-intelligence agency ASIO detailing Monis's online activities was withheld from the police as they tried to negotiate with Monis to free hostages he was holding. The coroner's report was severely critical of ASIO citing an internal email sent in the middle of the siege entitled 'Haron – brief [. . .] summary on possible motivation'. The coroner believed the document 'should have been shared' and, importantly, would have assisted the police in 'responding to Monis'.[9]

What is so telling is that more than a decade after 9/11, an intelligence agency whose job it is to protect the public from acts of political violence not only held back information at a critical time, but later resisted demands from the coroner that some of its officers give evidence at the inquiry. Only when they were subpoenaed did they make statements. ASIO held a huge file on Man Monis, who was wanted in his home country of Iran for fraud, but the extent of their involvement in what transpired during the siege may never be known. The coroner made separate findings about the security agency in a chapter, marked Secret. What little the coroner revealed indicated there were still problems in the way ASIO alerted other agencies – issues similar to those identified more than a decade ago in the 9/11 Commission of Inquiry.

In the UK, it took the public killing of a British soldier on the streets of London to force an inquiry into the way information was handled inside the UK's intelligence establishment. If there was an element of openness by government authorities anywhere relating to surveillance and counter-terrorism it emerged during the investigation into the killing of British Fusilier Lee Rigby by two men who claimed inspiration from extremist Islam. The UK's Intelligence Security Committee of Parliament produced a critical assessment of the flaws in the UK's counter-terrorism efforts pointing out that GCHQ had failed to report 'an item of intelligence'[10] which revealed contact between one of the killers and an al-Qaeda extremist which was 'significant'. If MI5 had known about this contact it would have led to different investigative decisions. There were other blunders, this time by MI5. They only asked for billing data on mobile phones, because most people did not use landlines. This decision meant they missed data on a call made by one of the killers from a home phone to an al-Qaeda number in Yemen. On another occasion when one of the killers, Michael Adebolajo was arrested in Kenya, the committee found that MI6's actions were 'deeply unsatisfactory'.[11] MI6's role in countering 'jihadi tourism'[12] the committee said, did not appear to have extended to any practical action being taken, warning MI6 that it must ensure that their procedures are improved so that 'this does not happen again'.[13]

Though the committee, chaired by Sir Malcolm Rifkind, was severely criticised for not adequately explaining whether MI6 had tried to recruit Adebolajo to work as an agent, something which might have played a part in his radicalisation, the most significant part of the report lay in explaining the difficulties involved in apportioning resources to deal with 'subjects of interest who occur on the periphery of several investigations'.[14] The committee describes this fact as 'a key issue which has arisen during the course of our Inquiry'.[15]

In what could be interpreted as MI5's ability to disrupt some attacks, the committee accepted that 'MI5 must focus primarily on the highest priority individuals',[16] but it specifically identified 'a large group of individuals who may also pose a risk to national security, but who are not under active investigation'.[17] It is this group which causes the security organisations so many potential problems. The committee pointed out: 'Previous attempts by MI5 and the police to manage this group have failed: we have not yet seen any evidence that the new programme, established in late 2013, will be any better.'[18]

Failures of this kind have had wide-ranging repercussions around the world, but Rigby's case was a glaring example. As Duncan Campbell told me,

> What is unambiguously clear is . . . these guys were on the radar, they had been approached, they had possibly been mishandled, but there was not the resource to allocate intensive surveillance to a level 3 target or whatever they call it. As a result, the guy got killed.[19]

It is perhaps a mark of how confrontational this report by Rifkind's committee was that in response to its publication the Home Office largely avoided the substantial and critical points raised and instead spun the story that Facebook was to blame. A Facebook comment by Adebolajo which was picked up later stated that he wanted to kill a British soldier.

While it was important to consider the role of social media, the main issue centred on the fact that 'MI5 does not currently have a strategy for dealing with Subjects of Interest who occur on the periphery of several investigations.'[20] The committee described this fact as a 'key issue' which had arisen during the course of its inquiry which 'must be addressed by MI5'.[21] The Committee recommended that where individuals repeatedly came to MI5's attention, through their connections with a 'wide range of Subjects of Interest',[22] MI5 'must take this "cumulative effect" into account'.[23]

The report suggested that to counter terrorism threats MI5 would have to shift away from relying on dragnet surveillance. It said that that given the challenge of identifying 'self-starting terrorists',[24] particularly those who were security conscious, and took counter-measures to keep their activities secret, 'MI5 would become increasingly reliant on intelligence from local communities'.[25]

Yet what had happened around the world appeared to be exactly the opposite as governments poured more and more money into internet and digital surveillance systems, and shifted away from more traditional policing and security methods. In addition, security agencies had been relying too much on the mass surveillance of entire populations instead of targeting those who posed a real risk. It was a problem as long ago as 2004 when mass surveillance was in its infancy. A detailed assessment of major terrorist attacks in Western countries over the following 13 years reveals that of the 36 cases, 26 involved people known to the security agencies as potential terrorists. Only ten came as a complete surprise to the authorities.

On March, 11, 2004 three bombs exploded on trains in Madrid, killing 192 people and injurng more than 2000. Spanish Security agencies had received information from the imam of the Villaverde mosque near Madrid Mosque, who, using the code name Cartagena – between October 2002 and February 2004 – warned about the activities of the Islamists who he believed were planning attacks. 'Cartagena'[26] specifically named Rabei Osman Sayed Ahmed, an Egyptian citizen, later detained in Italy as the mastermind behind the bombings. But Cartagena's information was never followed up.

The following year on 7 July, 2005, terrorists killed 52 people, planting bombs on London Underground trains and a London bus. A commission of inquiry raised serious concerns about how MI5 prioritised suspects, warning that poor record-keeping could allow flawed decisions to slip through with 'dire consequences'.[27] The inquiry singled out MI5's 'dreadful'[28] editing of a sharp colour photograph of 7/7 ringleader Mohammad Sidique Khan and his number two, Shehzad Tanweer, taken by an undercover surveillance team at a motorway service station in February 2004. At the time the security services did not know who the pair were, although they had been seen meeting a known terrorist who was plotting a fertiliser bomb atrocity.

Surveillance teams watched, followed and photographed Mohammed Sidique Khan and Shehzad Tanweer as they travelled from their homes in Leeds to meet a known terrorist, Omar Khyam, who authorities suspected was in the early stages of constructing a fertiliser bomb. But intelligence officials concluded that the pair were only small-time fraudsters and therefore not a top priority for further inquiries.

The inquiry recommended that MI5 should examine its procedures 'to establish if there is room for further improvement in the recording of decisions relating to the assessment of targets'.[29] Eight years later a similar issue would arise again with MI5's handling of the Rigby attackers.

Yet not all the killers were known to the security authorities. On 2 March, 2011 Arid Uka, a postal worker, who shot dead two US airmen at Frankfurt airport had no police record, but had become radicalised in the weeks before the attack.

Between 11 and 19 March, 2012 Mohammed Merah, who was known to have jihadist sympathies and had been interviewed by intelligence agencies four months earlier after returning from Afghanistan and Pakistan, killed seven people, including three soldiers and three children at a Jewish school in the south of France. Merah, a Frenchman of Algerian descent, told one of his military victims: 'You kill my brothers; I'm killing you.'[30] Merah was known for his jihadi sympathies. He was on a US 'no-fly' list.

On 15 April, 2013 two homemade bombs exploded near the finish line of the Boston Marathon killing three people and injuring several hundred. Two years earlier, in March 2011, the Russian FSB security service had warned the FBI that Tamerlan Tsarnaev, who planted the bombs, had 'become radicalized'.[31] A Homeland Security Committee which investigated the attack criticised the FBI for allowing him to later travel to Russia, without informing the FSB as they had requested. It is believed that during this trip he was further radicalised, before returning to New York to carry out the attack. The committee found that though Tsarnaev was on a watch list, there were 'insufficient resources to examine all individuals of concern'[32] at JFK International Airport.

On 24 May, 2014 Mehdi, Nemmouche gunned down four people at a Jewish Museum in Brussels. Nemmouche was known to French counter-terrorism police, who had placed him under surveillance after his return from Syria last year, where he was suspected of having joined Islamist fighters.

In September 2014 Abdul Numan Haider, aged 18, was shot dead after he stabbed two counter-terrorism officers in Melbourne. Haider, originally from Afghanistan, had been under investigation as a 'person of interest'.[33] by anti-terrorism officials and had had his passport cancelled.

Canadian Police became aware of Martin Couture-Rouleau after a relative alerted them to his 'terrorist leanings'.[34] On 20 October, 2014, after authorities revoked his passport to stop him travelling to Turkey, he ran down two soldiers in his car, killing one of them.

On 20 December, 2014, a man yelling 'Allah Akbar'[35] attacked a police station in Joue-les-Tours, France, injuring three officers. Though the attacker, Nertrand Nzohabonayo, had a history of petty criminal convictions, he was apparently not on any watch list. In the week of the attack Nzohabonayo, 20, updated his Facebook profile page with the black flag of the Islamic State. His brother was known to security agencies for his radical convictions and had planned to travel to Syria.

On 7 January, 2015 two brothers Said and Cherif Kouachi, armed with assault rifles stormed the offices of the satirical magazine *Charlie Hebdo* in Paris, killing 12 people and injuring 11 others. According to the *New York Times* the brothers were on a US database as terror suspects and named on a US no-fly list. Cherif Kouachi came to the notice of the intelligence agencies in 2005 when he was arrested as he prepared to leave for Syria on his way to fight in Iraq against the US coalition. He had been sentenced to three years in prison.

Two days after the *Charlie Hebdo* attack Amedy Coulibaly took hostages in a Jewish supermarket, killing four of them before police stormed the building. Coulibably was also known to French security for his radical beliefs.

On 11 January, 2015 a 15-year-old who slashed a Jewish teacher with a machete in Marseille told investigators he was proud of the attack which he had committed 'in the name of Allah and Islamic State'.[36] He was not known to the authorities.

On 26 June, 2015, a truck driver beheaded his boss in an attack in Saint-Quentin-Fallavier near Lyon. He photographed the act before sending a photo to a friend where it ended up on an ISIS website. The killing apparently had nothing to do with terrorism, police said, but more to do with a bad family life and trouble at work.

In the following month, on 16 July, 2015, Mahammad Youssef Abdulazeez's killing of four US Marines at Chatanooga, Tennessee, also came as a surprise to law enforcement and security agencies. They were unclear about his motives, except for a post on his blog which said that 'the life we are living is nothing more than a test of our faith and patience . . . designed to separate the inhabitants of Paradise from the inhabitants of Hellfire'.[37]

On 21 August, 2015, Ayoub El Khazzani, aged 25, opened fire on passengers on board a high speed train from Amsterdam to Paris. He was the subject of a

'Fiche S', or 'S notice',[38] which signalled to security organisations across Europe that he was a person who merited special surveillance.

Two months later, on 2 October, a 15-year-old boy shot dead an unarmed police accountant as he left work in Parramatta, western Sydney. Farhad Khalil Mohammad Jaba was not known to police.

On 13 November, 2015 terrorists attacked the Stade de France, the Bataclan Theatre and cafes and bars lining the boulevard Voltaire in north eastern Paris, killing 130 people and wounding hundreds of others. Abdelhamid Abaaoud, who French authorities said masterminded the attack, had already been identified as an accomplice of two jihadis who were killed in a shootout at a house in the eastern Belgian town of Verviers earlier in the year. Abaaoud boasted in an interview with *Dabiq,* an online magazine published by Islamic State of Iraq and the Levant (ISIL), that they had travelled back from Syria with him the previous year and set up a safe house there.

After the raid on the house, the authorities 'figured out that I had been with the brothers and that we had been planning operations together',[39] he said. At one point, Abaaoud said he was stopped by police who checked him against the picture in his wanted notice but still failed to recognise him and let him go.

According to Le Monde, Abaaoud was also in contact with Mehdi Nemmouche, who had carried out the attack on the Jewish Museum in Brussels on 24 May, 2014, killing four people. Analysis of telephone calls is said to have shown the two men spoke in January 2014.

One of the attackers at the Stade de France, Omar Ismaïl Mostefai, had had a French police 'S' file since 2010. He had gone to Syria in 2013 and returned to France in the spring of 2014. Turkish authorities claim they twice tried to alert their French counterparts in December 2014 and in June 2015 to the threat he represented.

Sami Amimour, one of the Bataclan gunmen, had been detained in October 2012 on suspicion of terrorist links. He was the subject of an international arrest warrant after he broke his parole and travelled to Syria. He returned in mid-October 2014, and was able to remain at large until the attacks.

Salah Abdeslam, who hired one of the cars used by the attackers and is the brother of one of the terrorists who blew himself up outside the Comptoir Voltaire cafe, was stopped in a vehicle with two other men on the French-Belgian border a few hours after the attack and questioned, but then released.

The then CIA director, John Brennan, blamed the intelligence gaps leading up to the Paris attacks on the increased ability of terrorist networks to communicate without being intercepted by the security services.

However, given the facts that were unfolding, François Heisbourg, a former member of a French presidential commission on defence and security, made the perhaps more relevant assertion that the biggest problem was not a shortage of information about suspects but a lack of capacity to process that information.

'It is less a failure of intelligence than the ability to follow through on the intelligence data,'[40] said Heisbourg, then chairman of the International Institute for Strategic Studies and the Geneva Centre for Security Studies. 'The domestic security service was revamped in 2013 but it is still underfunded and under-manned. It is the process of being reformed but reform only produces fruit over four or five years.'[41]

On 2 December, 2015 a married couple, Rizwan Farook and Tashfeen Malik, shot and killed 14 people and injured 14 others at a Christmas Party in San Bernardino, California. The FBI said the husband and wife team had self-radicalised, but were not on any terrorism watch list.

On 7 January, 2016 Tarek Belgacem, a Tunisian refugee, was shot dead by police when he walked into a Paris police station wearing a fake explosives belt. German officials said he had been 'under surveillance'[42] because he displayed an ISIS poster in his room at a refuge where he had lived in in Reklinghausen in North Rhine-Westphalia.

22 March, 2016 – Attacks at Brussels Airport and the city's metro killed 35 people, including the attackers. One week earlier, on 16 March, the FBI informed Dutch police that two of the airport bombers were being sought by Belgian authorities. Ard van der Steur, the Dutch Interior Minister, wrote that Ibrahim El Bakraoui was sought by the Belgian authorities for 'his criminal background', while his brother Khaled was wanted for 'terrorism, extremism and recruitment'.[43]

Omar Mateen, who shot dead 49 people in an Orlando Florida nightclub on 12 June, 2016, was on a 'terror watch list'.[44] He had expressed sympathies for al-Qaeda affiliate Jabhat al-Nusra and Shia militant group Hezbollah. In 2013, he was investigated because of the inflammatory comments he made to co-workers alleging possible terrorist ties. In 2014 the FBI investigated him for possible links to Moner Mohammad Abu Salha, who was also from Florida.

Abu Salha travelled to Syria where he killed himself and several American troops with a truck bomb in the name of the Al-Nusra Front.

On 13 June, 2016, a police officer and his partner, a police secretary, were stabbed to death in their home in Magnanville, France, near Paris, by a man convicted in 2013 of associating with a group planning terrorist acts. French prosecutor François Molins said the attacker, Larossi Abballa, appeared to be acting on a recent general order from Abu Bakr al-Baghdadi to 'kill miscreants at home with their families'[45] during the month of Ramadan.

On 14 July, 2016 Mohamed Lahouaiej-Bouhlel drove a truck through revellers celebrating the French national day on the Promenade des Anglais in Nice, killing 86 people. Lahouaiej-Bouhlel, born in Tunisia, fitted none of the Islamic profiles. Though ISIL claimed credit for the attack, Lahouaiej-Bouhlel did not pray and apparently never observed the holy month of Ramadan. He seemed to be suffering from depression and had been seeing psychologists for several years.

On 18 July, 2016 a 17-year-old Afghan refugee injured five people with a knife and a hatchet on a train near the German town of Wurzburg. The attacker, who had written to his father saying 'now I can take revenge on these infidels',[46] was shot dead by police.

Three days later, Mohammad Daleel detonated a bomb outside a wine bar in Ansbach Germany which killed him and injured 15 others. A message on his mobile phone said the attack was an 'act of revenge against Germans, because they obstructed Islam'[47] There were clear signs Daleel, from Pakistan, was a risk. Police said he had twice attempted suicide, and had twice had his application for asylum rejected.

On 26 July, 2016 attackers interrupted a church service, in Saint-Etienne-du-Rouvray, northern France, forced the priest to his knees and slit his throat.

One of the attackers, 19-year-old Adel Kermiche, was known to intelligence services for his failed bids to reach Syria to wage jihad. Kermiche first tried to travel to Syria in March 2015 but was arrested in Germany. Returned to France, he was placed under surveillance and barred from leaving his local area. But less than two months later he was intercepted in Turkey making his way towards Syria again. He was sent back to France and detained until March, 2016, when he was released on bail. He had to wear an electronic tag, surrender his passport and was only allowed to leave his parents'[48] home for a few hours a day.

On 28 November, 2016, Abdul Razak Ali Artan, an 18-year-old Somali refugee, with no history of violence or support for radical jihad, rammed his car into a crowd at Ohio State university where he was studying, injuring 11 people including a number of people he subsequently stabbed. He had earlier made a statement to the local student newspaper that he was 'scared'[49] to pray in public because of the way people looked at him.

On 19 December, 2016 Anis Amri drove a stolen truck into the Christmas Market at Breitscheidplatz in Berlin, killing 12 people and injuring 56 others. In a document marked Secret seen by the German newspaper Zeit, regional security police revealed that Amri, a 24-year-old asylum seeker from Tunisia, had spoken of 'launching Islamic attacks'[50] and said he planned to procure 'large-calibre automatic weapons'[51] in France. Citing these statements, an undercover officer from North Rhine-Westphalia had warned investigators a few days earlier Amri had also said: 'They kill Muslims every day, so I have to kill them.'[52] 'On the basis of the available findings, it can presently be assumed that Amri will carry out his attack plans on a persistent and long-term basis,[53] 'the police noted. But their more senior colleagues from the Federal Criminal Police Office (BKA), concluded: 'The occurrence of a dangerous event in the form of an attack by Amri' was 'rather unlikely'. He was not placed on a watch list.

On 17 March, 2017 Ziyed ben Belgarcem, aged 39, who was on a French terrorism watch list, was shot dead at Orly Airport. Belgarcem, who shouted: 'I'm there to die for Allah',[54] grabbed an assault rifle from a police officer before he was killed.

On 7 April, 2017 a hijacked truck was deliberately driven into crowds in Drottninggatan in Stockholm, Sweden before crashing into a department store. Police said that 39-year-old Rakhmat Akilov had 'shown sympathies for extremist organizations',[55] such as ISIS, before the attack. He had shared ISIS propaganda productions on his Facebook account, according to Swedish newspaper *Aftonbladet*. Akilov had liked images of dead bodies after atrocities such as the

Boston Marathon bombing and had Facebook connections linked to the Islamic Hizb ut-Tahrir group. He was also a member of a group called 'Friends of Libya and Syria',[56] which has shared pro-ISIS propaganda.

On 20 April, 2017 three police officers and a bystander were shot by an attacker wielding an AK-47 on the Champs-Elysees. Kaarim Cheurfi's neighbours said that he nourished a 'hatred'[57] of the police, and that he was 'suffering psychologically'.[58] French anti-terrorism researchers knew as early as the beginning of 2016 that Cheurfi was trying to buy weapons, and that he wanted to kill police in revenge for children killed in Syria, according to *France 24 TV*.

22 March, 2017 – Khalid Masoon, a 52-year-old ex-convict who used a string of aliases and reportedly converted to Islam only in later life, drove a car into pedestrians on London's Westminster Bridge, killing four people and injuring 50.

Prime Minister Theresa May told MPs Masood had been previously known to MI5: 'Some years ago, he was once investigated in relation to concerns about violent extremism. He was a peripheral figure. The case is historic – he was not part of the current intelligence picture.'[59] May's comments were an eerie reminder of the scathing comments from Sir Malcolm Rifkind's committee investigating the killing of fusilier Lee Rigby. MI5 should keep watch on the large group of individuals which 'pose a risk to national security, but who are not under active investigation'.[60] The committee was not convinced that MI5's programme established in 2013 would be better than the ones that had failed before. It seems Rifkind was right. The suicide bomber Salman Abedi, who attacked a Manchester pop concert on 22 May, 2017, killing 22 people, including children, was known to police and MI5. In 2016 the FBI reportedly placed Abedi on a 'terrorist watch list'[61] and warned MI5 that his group was looking for a 'political target'[62] in Britain.

3 June, 2017. The leader of the attack on London Bridge, and on nearby Borough Market which left eight people dead, was known to MI5 and the police. Khuram Butt, 27, a British national who was born in Pakistan, was filmed praying in front of an ISIL flag in London's Regent's Park as part of a controversial Channel 4 programme that was broadcast in January 2016. British counter-terrorism police said Butt had been 'prioritised in the lower echelons of our investigative work'.[63]

6 June, 2017 – Farid Ikken, an Algeria, who was in France as a PhD student writing a doctoral thesis on media in North Africa, was shot after he attacked a police officer with a hammer outside Notre Dame Cathedral in central Paris. Ikken, who shouted 'this is for Syria'[64] before the attack, was not known to the police or intelligence services.

19 June, 2017. An attempted terrorism attack on the Champs Elysee in central Paris was thwarted when a would-be assailant – known to authorities and apparently on a watch list – died after ramming his car containing gas canisters and guns into a police van.

Analysis of the Islamist-related terror attacks throughout the Western countries raises some intriguing questions. Why were so many attackers known to the security agencies? In the case of the Manchester bomber, he had been to Libya as a member of a resistance group and been allowed to travel backwards and forwards throughout Europe though MI5 must have known he was a terrorist threat. When Lee Rigby was killed, those who did it were known to the intelligence agencies. They had already been warned not to let those who were not under intensive surveillance slip under the radar, but they have done so time and time again. The London Bridge attacker was another example. It was the same elsewhere. Did the intelligence agencies and police lose control of some of these intelligence 'assets'? Or was it simply incompetence, or as in the case of the Boston bomber, not enough staff to operate the terrorist screening system effectively? The security agencies argue that they have prevented many attacks, without, in most cases, providing any verifiable details. What we do know is that the vast majority of terrorists attacks on the West – 29 out of 37 since 2001 – involved people who had already been identified as posing a possible threat. Those figures alone – three quarters known to authorities – raise questions about the effectiveness of mass surveillance, which employs tens of thousands of people and costs billions of dollars each year to operate. With spending so heavily skewed towards electronic information gathering, working with existing information to develop threat analysis and keeping track of known possible suspects is greatly reduced. By using mainly publicly available information it is possible to reach some conclusions which shed light in this murky area. A declassified, heavily redacted US Government report entitled 'Review of the Department of Justice's Involvement in the President's Surveillance Program'[65] originally marked Top Secret/No For (No Foreigners) gives some insight.

The report cites the example of an apparently significant counter-terrorism case where a telephone number provided by the NSA, according to the FBI, would have been discovered in the 'natural course of the investigation'[66] by accessing information 'including toll records, open source information or physical surveillance' (p.289). The report said the NSA professed to be sending out high value information about known links to terrorism and was 'uncomfortable' to receive little feedback from FBI field offices other than 'You're sending us garbage' (p.300). Whereas the NSA believed the system of 'tippers' – alerts based on metadata – 'contributed significantly' to international terrorism investigations, none of the FBI officials and agents from the International Terrorism and Operations Section 'could identify significant investigations to which Stellar Wind substantially contributed' (p.305). The FBI considered information 'significant' if it led to 'the identification of a terrorist, the deportation from the US of a suspected terrorist, or the development of an asset that can report about the activities of terrorists' (p.327). Although the people the Justice Department interviewed for the review 'generally were supportive' of Stellar Wind, the report cited two FBI studies which raised questions about its effectiveness in helping the FBI stop a terrorist attack. The first, from October 2001 to December 2005, found only 1.2 percent of the NSA leads made 'significant' contributions. The second statistical study, from August 2004 to January 2006, provided 'no examples' of 'significant' contributions to FBI counter-terrorism efforts (p.327). The report agreed with the FBI that 'although the information produced under the Stellar Wind program had value in some counter-terrorism investigations, it played a limited role in the FBI's overall counter terrorism efforts' (p 326). As the UN Special Rapporteur on the Right to Privacy (SRP) wrote in February 2017,

> There is little or no evidence to persuade the SRP of either the efficacy or the proportionality of some of the extremely privacy-intrusive measures that have been introduced by new surveillance laws in France, Germany, the UK and the USA.[67]

He asked if it might be less privacy-intrusive if

> more money was spent on the human resources to carry out targeted surveillance infiltration and if less effort were expended on electronic surveillance. This, in a time when the vast majority of terrorist attacks were carried out by suspects already known to the authorities prior to the attacks.[68]

The UN report argued that

> long-term targeted surveillance and cell infiltration would seem to be far more effective than indulging in gesture politics. Trying to appear tough on security by legitimizing largely useless, hugely expensive and totally disproportionate measures which are intrusive to so many people's privacy – and other rights – is patently not the way governments should go.[69]

Or as Edward Snowden put it more succinctly in answer to the question: why does the NSA capture all this material? 'Forget about terrorism completely,' he said '. . . this is not effective for [counter] terrorism. . .'[70] these programs never save lives.' Stirring up the fear of terrorism simply made it easier to get funding by arguing, 'if you don't do this your children will die'.[71]

It appears that the use of mass surveillance has at best a limited benefit in preventing terrorism. But it does arm the state with a formidable tool nevertheless, part of the armoury which has such a chilling effect on journalism. Other countries which have no check on government executive power, have embraced the idea of tough anti-terror laws and mass surveillance, using them to gather 'evidence' against their political opponents and those who report their comments, newspaper editors and the journalists who work for them. The West's answers to the problem of global terrorism is in danger of creating a bigger problem than it supposedly set out to solve.

Notes

1 Snowden, E. May, 2017. *Interview.*
2 Snowden, E. May, 2017. *Interview.*
3 Snowden, E. May, 2017. *Interview.*

4 Snowden, E. May, 2017. *Interview*.

5 Snowden, E. May, 2017. *Interview*.

6 PBS. 3rd February, 2009. The Spy Factory [online]. Available at www.pbs.org/wgbh/nova/military/spy-factory.html [Accessed 10 November, 2016].

7 PBS. 3rd February, 2009. The Spy Factory [online]. Available at www.pbs.org/wgbh/nova/military/spy-factory.html [Accessed 10 November, 2016].

8 9/11 Commission Report. 2004. Final Report of the National Commission on Terrorist Attacks Upon the United States [online]. Available at http://govinfo.library.unt.edu/911/report/911Report_Exec.htm [Accessed 25 October, 2016].

9 State Coroner of New South Wales. May, 2017. Inquest into the Deaths Arising from the Lindt Café Siege [online]. Available at www.lindtinquest.justice.nsw.gov.au/Documents/findings-and-recommendations.pdf [Accessed 30 May, 2017].

10 UK Intelligence and Security Committee of Parliament. 2014. Report on the Intelligence Relating to the Murder of Fusilier Lee Rigby [online]. Available at https://b1cba9b3-a-5e6631fd-s-sites.googlegroups.com/a/independent.gov.uk/isc/files/20141125_ISC_Woolwich_Report%28website%29.pdf?attachauth=ANoY7con8vRFdQ_tItYF2bYknB1eeG7uxzKdSfu4-AqfNpzZMaZQFw5xVNWD2-I6Pr0IgcjzEbzd3rnFyO0lHqOgBC4rNbvwN2kl-5wB16NT19t7Jp6TlFN2-zw5hxEOybVdx0SgSyVGcKUVl1-TKRq8BkUMht3lWRNsiGjgUNMSq9Hz38rM0bX1JCV7BksjLZtuh2k4BBZFwjkj9s28U8RhKlBKpNQbKVqgBkVmtTBt9H7Q6yXryldNnyXfTsKB0RzfK8T8vtlG&attredirects=0 [Accessed 22 August, 2016].

11 UK Intelligence and Security Committee of Parliament. 2014. Report on the Intelligence Relating to the Murder of Fusilier Lee Rigby [online]. Available at https://b1cba9b3-a-5e6631fd-s-sites.googlegroups.com/a/independent.gov.uk/isc/files/20141125_ISC_Woolwich_Report%28website%29.pdf?attachauth=ANoY7con8vRFdQ_tItYF2bYknB1eeG7uxzKdSfu4-AqfNpzZMaZQFw5xVNWD2-I6Pr0IgcjzEbzd3rnFyO0lHqOgBC4rNbvwN2kl-5wB16NT19t7Jp6TlFN2-zw5hxEOybVdx0SgSyVGcKUVl1-TKRq8BkUMht3lWRNsiGjgUNMSq9Hz38rM0bX1JCV7BksjLZtuh2k4BBZFwjkj9s28U8RhKlBKpNQbKVqgBkVmtTBt9H7Q6yXryldNnyXfTsKB0RzfK8T8vtlG&attredirects=0 [Accessed 22 August, 2016].

12 UK Intelligence and Security Committee of Parliament. 2014. Report on the Intelligence Relating to the Murder of Fusilier Lee Rigby [online]. Available at https://b1cba9b3-a-5e6631fd-s-sites.googlegroups.com/a/independent.gov.uk/isc/files/20141125_ISC_Woolwich_Report%28website%29.pdf?attachauth=ANoY7con8vRFdQ_tItYF2bYknB1eeG7uxzKdSfu4-AqfNpzZMaZQFw5xVNWD2-I6Pr0IgcjzEbzd3rnFyO0lHqOgBC4rNbvwN2kl-5wB16NT19t7Jp6TlFN2-zw5hxEOybVdx0SgSyVGcKUVl1-TKRq8BkUMht3lWRNsiGjgUNMSq9Hz38rM0bX1JCV7BksjLZtuh2k4BBZFwjkj9s28U8RhKlBKpNQbKVqgBkVmtTBt9H7Q6yXryldNnyXfTsKB0RzfK8T8vtlG&attredirects=0 [Accessed 22 August, 2016].

13 UK Intelligence and Security Committee of Parliament. 2014. Report on the intelligence relating to the murder of Fusilier Lee Rigby [online]. Available at https://b1cba9b3-a-5e6631fd-s-sites.googlegroups.com/a/independent.gov.uk/isc/files/20141125_ISC_Woolwich_Report%28website%29.pdf?attachauth=ANoY7con8vRFdQ_tItYF2bYknB1eeG7uxzKdSfu4-AqfNpzZMaZQFw5xVNWD2-I6Pr0IgcjzEbzd3rnFyO0lHqOgBC4rNbvwN2kl-5wB16NT19t7Jp6TlFN2-zw5hxEOybVdx0SgSyVGcKUVl1-TKRq8BkUMht3lWRNsiGjgUNMSq9Hz38rM0bX1JCV7BksjLZtuh2k4BBZFwjkj9s28U8RhKlBKpNQbKVqgBkVmtTBt9H7Q6yXryldNnyXfTsKB0RzfK8T8vtlG&attredirects=0 [Accessed 22 August, 2016].

14 UK Intelligence and Security Committee of Parliament. 2014. Report on the Intelligence Relating to the Murder of Fusilier Lee Rigby [online]. Available at https://b1cba9b3-a-5e6631fd-s-sites.googlegroups.com/a/independent.gov.uk/isc/files/20141125_ISC_Woolwich_Report%28website%29.pdf?attachauth=ANoY7con8vRFdQ_tItYF2bYknB1eeG7uxzKdSfu4-AqfNpzZMaZQFw5xVNWD2-I6Pr0IgcjzEbzd3rnFyO0lHqOgBC4rNbvwN2kl-5wB16NT19t7Jp6TlFN2-zw5hxEOybVdx0SgSyVGcKUVl1-TKRq8BkUMht3lWRNsiGjgUNMSq9Hz38

rM0bX1JCV7BksjLZtuh2k4BBZFwjkj9s28U8RhKlBKpNQbKVqgBkVmtTBt9H7Q6y
XryldNnyXfTsKB0RzfK8T8vtlG&attredirects=0 [Accessed 22 August, 2016].

15 UK Intelligence and Security Committee of Parliament. 2014. Report on the Intelli-
gence Relating to the Murder of Fusilier Lee Rigby [online]. Available at https://b1cba9b3-
a-5e6631fd-s-sites.googlegroups.com/a/independent.gov.uk/isc/files/20141125_ISC_
Woolwich_Report%28website%29.pdf?attachauth=ANoY7con8vRFdQ_tItYF2bYkn
B1eeG7uxzKdSfu4-AqfNpzZMaZQFw5xVNWD2-I6Pr0IgcjzEbzd3rnFyO0lHq
OgBC4rNbvwN2kl-5wB16NTl9t7Jp6TlFN2-zw5hxEOybVdx0SgSyVGcKUVl1-
TKRq8BkUMht3lWRNsiGjgUNMSq9Hz38rM0bX1JCV7BksjLZtuh2k4
BBZFwjkj9s28U8RhKlBKpNQbKVqgBkVmtTBt9H7Q6yXryldNnyXfTsKB0RzfK
8T8vtlG&attredirects=0 [Accessed 22 August, 2016].

16 UK Intelligence and Security Committee of Parliament. 2014. Report on the Intelligence
Relating to the Murder of Fusilier Lee Rigby [online]. Available at https://b1cba9b3-
a-5e6631fd-s-sites.googlegroups.com/a/independent.gov.uk/isc/files/20141125_ISC_
Woolwich_Report%28website%29.pdf?attachauth=ANoY7con8vRFdQ_tItYF2bYknB1
eeG7uxzKdSfu4-AqfNpzZMaZQFw5xVNWD2-I6Pr0IgcjzEbzd3rnFyO0
lHqOgBC4rNbvwN2kl-5wB16NTl9t7Jp6TlFN2-zw5hxEOybVdx0SgSyVG
cKUVl1-TKRq8BkUMht3lWRNsiGjgUNMSq9Hz38rM0bX1JCV7Bksj
LZtuh2k4BBZFwjkj9s28U8RhKlBKpNQbKVqgBkVmtTBt9H7Q6yXryld
NnyXfTsKB0RzfK8T8vtlG&attredirects=0 [Accessed 22 August, 2016].

17 UK Intelligence and Security Committee of Parliament. 2014. Report on the Intelligence
Relating to the Murder of Fusilier Lee Rigby [online]. Available at https://b1cba9b3-
a-5e6631fd-s-sites.googlegroups.com/a/independent.gov.uk/isc/files/20141125_ISC_
Woolwich_Report%28website%29.pdf?attachauth=ANoY7con8vRFdQ_tItYF2bYknB1
eeG7uxzKdSfu4-AqfNpzZMaZQFw5xVNWD2-I6Pr0IgcjzEbzd3rnFyO0
lHqOgBC4rNbvwN2kl-5wB16NTl9t7Jp6TlFN2-zw5hxEOybVdx0SgSyVG
cKUVl1-TKRq8BkUMht3lWRNsiGjgUNMSq9Hz38rM0bX1JCV7Bksj
LZtuh2k4BBZFwjkj9s28U8RhKlBKpNQbKVqgBkVmtTBt9H7Q6yXryld
NnyXfTsKB0RzfK8T8vtlG&attredirects=0 [Accessed 22 August, 2016].

18 UK Intelligence and Security Committee of Parliament. 2014. Report on the Intelligence
Relating to the Murder of Fusilier Lee Rigby [online]. Available at https://b1cba9b3-
a-5e6631fd-s-sites.googlegroups.com/a/independent.gov.uk/isc/files/20141125_ISC_
Woolwich_Report%28website%29.pdf?attachauth=ANoY7con8vRFdQ_tItYF2bYknB1
eeG7uxzKdSfu4-AqfNpzZMaZQFw5xVNWD2-I6Pr0IgcjzEbzd3rnFyO0
lHqOgBC4rNbvwN2kl-5wB16NTl9t7Jp6TlFN2-zw5hxEOybVdx0Sg
SyVGcKUVl1-TKRq8BkUMht3lWRNsiGjgUNMSq9Hz38rM0bX1JCV7Bksj
LZtuh2k4BBZFwjkj9s28U8RhKlBKpNQbKVqgBkVmtTBt9H7Q6yXryld
NnyXfTsKB0RzfK8T8vtlG&attredirects=0 [Accessed 22 August, 2016].

19 Campbell, D. August, 2016. *Interview*.

20 UK Intelligence and Security Committee of Parliament. 2014. Report on the Intelligence
Relating to the Murder of Fusilier Lee Rigby [online]. Available at https://b1cba9b3-
a-5e6631fd-s-sites.googlegroups.com/a/independent.gov.uk/isc/files/20141125_ISC_
Woolwich_Report%28website%29.pdf?attachauth=ANoY7con8vRFdQ_tItYF2bYknB1
eeG7uxzKdSfu4-AqfNpzZMaZQFw5xVNWD2-I6Pr0IgcjzEbzd3rnFyO0
lHqOgBC4rNbvwN2kl-5wB16NTl9t7Jp6TlFN2-zw5hxEOybVdx0Sg
SyVGcKUVl1-TKRq8BkUMht3lWRNsiGjgUNMSq9Hz38rM0bX1JCV7Bksj
LZtuh2k4BBZFwjkj9s28U8RhKlBKpNQbKVqgBkVmtTBt9H7Q6yXryld
NnyXfTsKB0RzfK8T8vtlG&attredirects=0 [Accessed 22 August, 2016].

21 UK Intelligence and Security Committee of Parliament. 2014. Report on the Intelligence Relating to the Murder of Fusilier Lee Rigby [online]. Available at https://
b1cba9b3-a-5e6631fd-s-sites.googlegroups.com/a/independent.gov.uk/isc/
files/20141125_ISC_Woolwich_Report%28website%29.pdf?attachauth=
ANoY7con8vRFdQ_tItYF2bYknB1eeG7uxzKdSfu4-AqfNpzZMaZQFw5xVNWD2-
I6Pr0IgcjzEbzd3rnFyO0lHqOgBC4rNbvwN2kl-5wB16NTl9t7Jp6TlFN2-zw5hxEOyb
Vdx0SgSyVGcKUVl1-TKRq8BkUMht3lWRNsiGjgUNMSq9Hz38rM0

bX1JCV7BksjLZtuh2k4BBZFwjkj9s28U8RhKlBKpNQbKVqgBkVmtTBt9H7Q6yXryl
dNnyXfTsKB0RzfK8T8vtlG&attredirects=0 [Accessed 22 August, 2016].

22 UK Intelligence and Security Committee of Parliament. 2014. Report on the Intelligence
Relating to the Murder of Fusilier Lee Rigby [online]. Available at https://b1cba9b3-
a-5e6631fd-s-sites.googlegroups.com/a/independent.gov.uk/isc/files/20141125_ISC_
Woolwich_Report%28website%29.pdf?attachauth=ANoY7con8vRFdQ_tItYF2bYkn
B1eeG7uxzKdSfu4-AqfNpzZMaZQFw5xVNWD2-I6Pr0IgcjzEbzd3rnFyO0lHq
OgBC4rNbvwN2kl-5wB16NTl9t7Jp6TlFN2-zw5hxEOybVdx0SgSyVGcKUVl1-
TKRq8BkUMht3lWRNsiGjgUNMSq9Hz38rM0bX1JCV7BksjLZtuh2k4
BBZFwjkj9s28U8RhKlBKpNQbKVqgBkVmtTBt9H7Q6yXryldNnyXfTsKB0RzfK
8T8vtlG&attredirects=0 [Accessed 22 August, 2016].

23 UK Intelligence and Security Committee of Parliament. 2014. Report on the Intelligence
Relating to the Murder of Fusilier Lee Rigby [online]. Available at https://b1cba9b3-
a-5e6631fd-s-sites.googlegroups.com/a/independent.gov.uk/isc/files/20141125_ISC_
Woolwich_Report%28website%29.pdf?attachauth=ANoY7con8vRFdQ_tItYF2bYkn
B1eeG7uxzKdSfu4-AqfNpzZMaZQFw5xVNWD2-I6Pr0IgcjzEbzd3rnFyO0lHq
OgBC4rNbvwN2kl-5wB16NTl9t7Jp6TlFN2-zw5hxEOybVdx0SgSyVGcKUVl1-
TKRq8BkUMht3lWRNsiGjgUNMSq9Hz38rM0bX1JCV7BksjLZtuh2k4
BBZFwjkj9s28U8RhKlBKpNQbKVqgBkVmtTBt9H7Q6yXryldNnyXfTsKB0RzfK
8T8vtlG&attredirects=0 [Accessed 22 August, 2016].

24 UK Intelligence and Security Committee of Parliament. 2014. Report on the Intelligence
Relating to the Murder of Fusilier Lee Rigby [online]. Available at https://b1cba9b3-
a-5e6631fd-s-sites.googlegroups.com/a/independent.gov.uk/isc/files/20141125_ISC_
Woolwich_Report%28website%29.pdf?attachauth=ANoY7con8vRFdQ_tItYF2bYkn
B1eeG7uxzKdSfu4-AqfNpzZMaZQFw5xVNWD2-I6Pr0IgcjzEbzd3rnFyO0lHq
OgBC4rNbvwN2kl-5wB16NTl9t7Jp6TlFN2-zw5hxEOybVdx0SgSyVGcKUVl1-
TKRq8BkUMht3lWRNsiGjgUNMSq9Hz38rM0bX1JCV7BksjLZtuh2k4
BBZFwjkj9s28U8RhKlBKpNQbKVqgBkVmtTBt9H7Q6yXryldNnyXfTsKB0RzfK
8T8vtlG&attredirects=0 [Accessed 22 August, 2016].

25 UK Intelligence and Security Committee of Parliament. 2014. Report on the Intelligence
Relating to the Murder of Fusilier Lee Rigby [online]. Available at https://b1cba9b3-
a-5e6631fd-s-sites.googlegroups.com/a/independent.gov.uk/isc/files/20141125_ISC_
Woolwich_Report%28website%29.pdf?attachauth=ANoY7con8vRFdQ_tItYF2bYkn
B1eeG7uxzKdSfu4-AqfNpzZMaZQFw5xVNWD2-I6Pr0IgcjzEbzd3rnFyO0lHq
OgBC4rNbvwN2kl-5wB16NTl9t7Jp6TlFN2-zw5hxEOybVdx0SgSyVGcKUVl1-
TKRq8BkUMht3lWRNsiGjgUNMSq9Hz38rM0bX1JCV7BksjLZtuh2k4
BBZFwjkj9s28U8RhKlBKpNQbKVqgBkVmtTBt9H7Q6yXryldNnyXfTsKB0RzfK
8T8vtlG&attredirects=0 [Accessed 22 August, 2016].

26 Elmundo.es. 21st June, 2005. Las notas del confidente marroquí 'Cartagena' prueban que
la Policía controlaba a la cúpula del 11-M 9 [online]. Available at www.elmundo.es/
elmundo/2005/05/31/espana/1117506519.html [Accessed 20 March, 2017].

27 Gardham, D. 6th May, 2011. *MI5 Could Have Run More Thorough Investigation into July
7 Bomber* [online]. Available at www.telegraph.co.uk/news/uknews/terrorism-in-the-
uk/8499012/MI5-could-have-run-more-thorough-investigation-into-July-7-bomber.
html [Accessed 14 December, 2016].

28 Gardham, D. 6th May, 2011. *MI5 Could Have Run More Thorough Investigation into
July 7 Bomber* [online]. Available at www.telegraph.co.uk/news/uknews/terrorism-in-
the-uk/8499012/MI5-could-have-run-more-thorough-investigation-into-July-7-bomber.
html [Accessed 14 December, 2016].

29 Gardham, D. 6th May, 2011. *MI5 Could Have Run More Thorough Investigation into
July 7 Bomber* [online]. Available at www.telegraph.co.uk/news/uknews/terrorism-in-
the-uk/8499012/MI5-could-have-run-more-thorough-investigation-into-July-7-
bomber.html [Accessed 14 December, 2016].

30 Sayare, S. 22nd March, 2012. *Suspect in French Killings Slain as Police Storm Apartment
After 30-Hour Siege.* The New York Times [online]. Available at www.nytimes.com/

2012/03/23/world/europe/mohammed-merah-toulouse-shooting-suspect-french-police-standoff.html [Accessed 15 May, 2017].

31 US House of Representatives Committee on Homeland Security. March, 2014. The Road to Boston: Counterterrorism Challenges and Lessons from the Marathon Bombings [online]. Available at https://homeland.house.gov/files/documents/Boston-Bombings-Report.pdf [Accessed 1 April, 2017].

32 US House of Representatives Committee on Homeland Security. March, 2014. The Road to Boston: Counterterrorism Challenges and Lessons from the Marathon Bombings [online]. Available at https://homeland.house.gov/files/documents/Boston-Bombings-Report.pdf [Accessed 1 April, 2017].

33 Oakes, D. *Melbourne Shooting: What We Know About Abdul Numan Haider, Shot Dead After Stabbing Anti-Terrorism Officers at Endeavour Hills.* ABC Australia [online]. Available at www.abc.net.au/news/2014-09-24/what-we-know-about-abdul-numan-haider/5767044 [Accessed 12 February, 2017].

34 Deland, M. 20th October, 2014. *'Radicalized' Quebecer Shot Dead After Running Down 2 Soldiers in Suspected Terrorist Attack.* Toronto Sun, Canada [online]. Available at www.torontosun.com/2014/10/20/possible-terror-attack-as-soldiers-run-down-in-quebec-parking-lot [Accesssed 20 July, 2017].

35 Agence France Presse. 21st December, 2014. *Suspected Islamic Fanatic Shot Dead After Stabbing Three Police Officers.* News.com.au [online]. Available at www.news.com.au/world/europe/suspected-islamic-fanatic-shot-dead-after-stabbing-three-police-officers/news-story/7f44754c900f6700135d905d023148f2 [Accessed 19 February, 2017].

36 Chrisafis, A. 13th January, 2016. Teenager Faces Terror Charges Over Marseille Jewish Teacher Attack. The Guardian [online]. London. Available at www.theguardian.com/world/2016/jan/13/teenager-to-appear-in-court-over-marseille-jewish-teacher-attack [Accessed 20 February, 2017].

37 Armstrong, J. 17th July, 2015. *Chattanooga Shooting: Who is Mohammad Youssef Abdulazeez?* Global News [online]. Available at http://globalnews.ca/news/2116990/chattanooga-shooting-who-is-mohammad-youssef-abdulazeez/ [Accessed 20 July, 2017].

38 Musseau, F and Le Devin, W. 23rd August, 2015. *Ayoub El Khazzani, braqueur fauche et salafiste fiche.* Liberation [online]. Available at www.liberation.fr/societe/2015/08/23/ayoub-el-khazzani-braqueur-fauche-et-salafiste-fiche_1368325 [Accessed 12 January, 2017].

39 Dabiq. [Undated]. Interview with Abu Umar Al-Baljiki (Abdelhamid Abaaoud) [online]. Available at https://azelin.files.wordpress.com/2015/02/the-islamic-state-e2809cdc481biq-magazine-722.pdf [Accessed 14 April, 2017].

40 Borger, J. 16th November, 2015. *French and Belgian Intelligence Knew Paris Attackers Had Jihadi Backgrounds.* The Guardian [online]. London. Available at www.theguardian.com/world/2015/nov/16/french-and-belgian-intelligence-knew-paris-attackers-had-jihadi-backgrounds [Accessed 12 February, 2017].

41 Borger, J. 16th November, 2015. *French and Belgian Intelligence Knew Paris Attackers Had Jihadi Backgrounds.* The Guardian [online]. London. Available at www.theguardian.com/world/2015/nov/16/french-and-belgian-intelligence-knew-paris-attackers-had-jihadi-backgrounds [Accessed 12 February, 2017].

42 Lichfield, J. 10th January, 2016. *Paris Shooting: Man Killed by Police Had Lived in German Refugee Camp.* Independent [online]. Available at www.independent.co.uk/news/world/europe/paris-shooting-man-killed-by-police-had-lived-in-german-refugee-camp-a6805076.html [Accessed 12 February, 2017].

43 Reuters. 30th March, 2016. FBI Warned Dutch about El Bakraoui Brothers Week Before Brussels Attacks [online]. Available at www.reuters.com/article/us-belgium-blast-netherlands-idUSKCN0WV1ZY [Accessed 10 February, 2017].

44 Engel, P. 17th June, 2016. *Here Are the Pro-ISIS Messages the Orlando Shooter Posted on Facebook During the Attack.* Business Insider [online]. Available at www.businessinsider.com.au/orlando-shooter-facebook-omar-mateen-2016-6?r=US&IR=T [Accessed 21 July, 2017].

45 BBC.14th June, 2016. French Jihadist Police Killer 'Obeyed Islamic State Call' [online]. Available at www.bbc.com/news/world-europe-36530710 [Accessed 12 February, 2017].

46 Eddy, M. 19th July, 2016. *Afghan Teenager Spoke of Friend's Death Before Ax Attack in Germany.* The New York Times [online]. Available at www.nytimes.com/2016/07/20/world/europe/germany-train-ax-attack.html?_r=0 [Accessed 14 February, 2017].

47 Pleitgen, F., Hume, T., and McKirdy, E. 26th July 2016. *Suicide Bomber in Germany Pledged Allegiance to ISIS Leader.* CNN [online]. Available at http://edition.cnn.com/2016/07/24/world/ansbach-germany-blast/index.html [Accessed 15 February, 2017].

48 Olive, N. 26th July, 2016. *Islamists Attack French Church, Slit Priest's Throat.* Reuters [online]. Available at www.reuters.com/article/us-france-hostages-idUSKCN1060VA [Accessed 14 February, 2017].

49 Simon, S. 29th November, 2016. *Ohio State Attacker Said He Was 'Scared' to pray in Public.* CNN [online]. Available at http://edition.cnn.com/2016/11/28/us/ohio-state-attacker-abdul-razak-ali-artan/index.html [Accessed 27 February, 2017].

50 Amjahid, M., Muller, D., Musharbash, Y., Stark, H., and Zimmermann, F. 7th April, 2017. 'An Attack is Expected'. Ziet [online]. Available at www.zeit.de/politik/deutschland/2017-04/berlin-attack-christmas-market-breitscheidplatz-anis-amri [Accessed 8 April, 2017].

51 Amjahid, M., Muller, D., Musharbash, Y., Stark, H., and Zimmermann, F. 7th April, 2017. 'An Attack is Expected'. Ziet [online]. Available at www.zeit.de/politik/deutschland/2017-04/berlin-attack-christmas-market-breitscheidplatz-anis-amri [Accessed 8 April, 2017].

52 Amjahid, M., Muller, D., Musharbash, Y., Stark, H., and Zimmermann, F. 7th April, 2017. 'An Attack is Expected'. Ziet [online] Available at www.zeit.de/politik/deutschland/2017-04/berlin-attack-christmas-market-breitscheidplatz-anis-amri [Accessed 8 April, 2017].

53 Amjahid, M., Muller, D., Musharbash, Y., Stark, H., and Zimmermann, F. 7th April, 2017. 'An Attack is Expected'. Ziet [online]. Available at www.zeit.de/politik/deutschland/2017-04/berlin-attack-christmas-market-breitscheidplatz-anis-amri [Accessed 8 April, 2017].

54 Chazan, D. 18th March, 2017. *Radicalised Muslim Known to Security Agencies Shot Dead in Attack at Paris Airport—As Security Stepped Up at Stadium Where Duke and Dutchess Watch Rugby.* Daily Telegraph [online]. London. Available at www.telegraph.co.uk/news/2017/03/18/man-shot-killed-security-forces-paris-airport-attempting-seize/ [Accessed 23 February, 2017].

55 Moore, J. 10th April, 2017. *Stockholm Attack Suspect is 'ISIS Sympathizer' Who 'Partied and Drank'.* Newsweek [online]. Available at www.newsweek.com/stockholm-attack-suspect-isis-sympathizer-partied-and-drank-581419 [Accessed 11 May, 2017].

56 Moore, J. 10th April, 2017. *Stockholm Attack Suspect is 'ISIS Sympathizer' Who 'Partied and Drank'.* Newsweek [online]. Available at www.newsweek.com/stockholm-attack-suspect-isis-sympathizer-partied-and-drank-581419 [Accessed 11 May, 2017].

57 France24. 22nd April, 2017. Questions Remain Over Champs-Elysees Attacker's Links to IS Group [online]. Available at www.france24.com/en/20170422-questions-remain-champs-elysees-attacker-links-islamic-state-group [Accessed 10 May, 2017].

58 France24. 22nd April, 2017. Questions Remain Over Champs-Elysees Attacker's Links to IS Group [online]. Available at www.france24.com/en/20170422-questions-remain-champs-elysees-attacker-links-islamic-state-group [Accessed 10 May, 2017].

59 Dodd, V., Parveen, N., MacAskill, E., and Grierson, J. 24th March, 2017. Police Unravel Multiple Aliases of Westminster Terrorist Khalid Masood [online]. Available at www.theguardian.com/uk-news/2017/mar/23/westminster-attack-police-arrest-seven-people-in-raids-at-six-addresses [Accessed 1 April, 2017].

60 UK Intelligence and Security Committee of Parliament. 2014. Report on the Intelligence Relating to the Murder of Fusilier Lee Rigby [online]. Available at https://b1cba9b3-a-5e6631fd-s-sites.googlegroups.com/a/independent.gov.uk/isc/files/20141125_ISC_Woolwich_Report%28website%29.pdf?attachauth=

ANoY7con8vRFdQ_tItYF2bYknB1eeG7uxzKdSfu4-AqfNpzZMaZQFw5xVNWD2-I6Pr0IgcjzEbzd3rnFyO0lHqOgBC4rNbvwN2kl-5wB16NTl9t7Jp6TlFN2-zw5hxEOyb Vdx0SgSyVGcKUVl1-TKRq8BkUMht3lWRNsiGjgUNMSq9Hz38rM0 bX1JCV7BksjLZtuh2k4BBZFwjkj9s28U8RhKlBKpNQbKVqgBkVmtTBt9H7Q6yXr yldNnyXfTsKB0RzfK8T8vtlG&attredirects=0 [Accessed 22 August, 2016].
61 Nicol, M. 28th May, 2017. *FBI 'Warned MI5 in January that the Manchester Bomber Was Planning an Attack on Britain'*. Mail on Sunday [online]. Available at www.dailymail. co.uk/news/article-4548892/FBI-warned-MI5-Manchester-bomber-planning-attack. html [Accessed 1 June, 2017].
62 Nicol, M. 28th May, 2017. *FBI 'Warned MI5 in January that the Manchester Bomber Was Planning an Attack on Britain'*. Mail on Sunday [online]. Available at www.dailymail. co.uk/news/article-4548892/FBI-warned-MI5-Manchester-bomber-planning-attack. html [Accessed 1 June, 2017].
63 Watson, L., Horton, H., Jamieson, S., Henderson, B., Evans, M., and Graham, C. 6th June, 2017. *London Bridge Attack Latest: Terrorists Named as Police Say They Were Not Under Surveillance as They Posed 'Low Risk'*. Daily Telegraph [online]. London. Available at www.telegraph.co.uk/news/2017/06/05/london-bridge-attack-latest-gunshots-heard-police-launch-fresh/ [Accessed 7 June, 2017].
64 ABC Australia. 7th June, 2017. Notre Dame Attacker Shouted 'This is for Syria' Before Hitting Police Officer with Hammer [online]. Available at www.abc.net.au/ news/2017-06-07/notre-dame-attacker-shouted-this-is-for-syria-before-attack/8595326 [Accessed 8 June, 2017].
65 Savage, C. April 25, 2015. *Government Releases Once-Secret Report on Post-9/11 Surveillance*. The New York Times [online]. Available at www.nytimes.com/interactive/2015/04/25/ us/25stellarwind-ig-report.html [Accessed 20 July, 2017].
66 Savage, C. April 25, 2015. *Government Releases Once-Secret Report on Post-9/11 Surveillance*. The New York Times [online]. Available at www.nytimes.com/interactive/2015/04/25/ us/25stellarwind-ig-report.html [Accessed 20 July, 2017].
67 Cannataci, J. 24th February, 2017. *(Advanced Unedited Version) Report of the Special Rapporteur on the Right to Privacy*. [Copy held by author].
68 Cannataci, J. 24th February, 2017. *(Advanced Unedited Version) Report of the Special Rapporteur on the Right to Privacy*. [Copy held by author].
69 Cannataci, J. 24th February, 2017. *(Advanced Unedited Version) Report of the Special Rapporteur on the Right to Privacy*. [Copy held by author].
70 Snowden, E. 2017. *Interview*.
71 Snowden, E. 2017. *Interview*.

12

WHOSE SIDE ARE YOU ON?

It did not take long for the Chinese government to point out the obvious as they passed another law giving state surveillance agencies greater power: After all the West's moralising and complaining about human rights, China was simply following their example in acting to combat terrorism. It was the UK which provided some of the best examples of the worst laws that China had embraced. China closely copied the main thrust of the Investigatory Powers Act (2016), the 'Snoopers' Charter' which demanded telecommunications companies store the bulk metadata of UK citizens. Significantly, just as Britain at first wanted 'backdoor' access to telecommunications products, so did China. But both countries eventually dropped the plan, not for any human rights considerations but probably because forcing their technology companies to produce 'vulnerable' products would make them unsaleable in the rest of the world. No one would want to buy a British- or Chinese-made phone that could be so easily hacked into by the government (or anyone else). Instead both the UK and China have passed laws which give governments the right to force *communications* companies, which provide the means of transmission, to hand over the keys of encrypted material which can then potentially be used to unscramble stored messages. End-to-end encryption is offered by iMessage, WhatsApp and by other messaging systems including Telegram and Signal. Even the company that facilitates the communication cannot decipher messages encrypted in this way. But under the new laws a communications company could be forced to disable a user's end-to-end encryption, or weaken it, which would allow the messages to be read.

While in the UK in 2017 the European Court of Justice had expressed doubt over the legality of the entire Snooper's Charter, and the encryption breaking system appeared to be on hold at the Home Office, in China there was no such impediment: technology companies will still have to provide help with sensitive encryption information if law enforcement authorities demand it.

Britain had created the argument for such extraordinary intrusion, and the Chinese were keen to implement it. As Li Shouwei, deputy head of the Chinese parliament's criminal law division, said, 'This rule accords with the actual work need of fighting terrorism and is basically the same as what other major countries in the world do.'[1] China, he pointed out, was simply doing what other Western nations already do in asking technology to help fight terror.

In following Britain's legislative lead the Chinese government was now better equipped to deal with dissenting voices. Sixty-eight journalists were languishing in Chinese prisons in 2016, caught carrying out what the government determined were activities against the national interest. Many of them were charged under Article 103 of the penal code with 'undermining the unity of the country',[2] allowing the state to prosecute journalists covering minorities like Tibetans and Uighurs who have grievances with official policies.

For many years China maintained its world lead in jailing journalists but in 2017, Turkey, a country which had slipped down the ladder, surged into the lead with an estimated 159 editors and reporters in prison or facing trial.

As a symbol of how governments can invoke the threat of terrorism to silence the press, the treatment of Turkish journalist Erol Onderoglu is an outstanding example. Onderoglu, who represents Reporters Sans Frontieres (RSF) Reporters Without Borders in Turkey, was attending a newspaper editorial meeting in Istanbul when he was arrested in June 2016. Journalist Ahmet Nesin and the head of the Turkish Human Rights Foundation were also taken away. Giving a new meaning to the word irony, they were all arrested on World Press Freedom Day and charged with 'terrorism propaganda'.[3] Whatever case the Turkish government brings against Onderoglu and the others that they were in some way helping the Kurdish Workers Party (PKK), which has been involved in at times violent struggle for an independent homeland for the Kurds, they are in good company. An estimated 170 newspapers have been shut down, their editors and journalists variously charged with producing 'terrorism propaganda', or 'insulting the president'.[4] For Onderoglu, who faces the possibility of a 14-year prison term, the definition of 'the job that we do has been systematically eliminated from the Turkish dictionary'.[5] The early progressive liberalism of the government has slowly receded, as President Recep Tayyip Erdogan shifted the country's democratic centre away from its secular tradition to politicised Islam. After an abortive coup in July 2016 President Erdogan moved to silence independent voices, jailing a total of 50,000 people. Turkey's oldest mainstream newspaper, the secular *Cumhuriyet*, was raided by police and its editors arrested. The paper had published a report in 2015 revealing the Turkish intelligence service had been secretly arming Syrian rebels, a sensitive matter for Erdogan. Sentenced to 25 years in jail, the editor Can Dunbar, fled to Germany. Other critical voices also left the country or were jailed. As the BBC reported, freedom of expression was 'heavily squeezed'[6] and 'critical journalists, writers or artists were tarnished as "traitors."'[7]

In Mexico, attacks on journalists are promoted less through appeals to nationalism and the cult of the personality than the politics of power and money.

But the desire to silence them is the same. Using surveillance systems designed to prevent terrorism, Mexico is accused of turning them against those who unmask government wrongdoing.

An investigation by the press freedom organisation Article 19 and CitizenLab at the University of Toronto, Canada, revealed that investigative journalists in Mexico were being targeted with SMS texts including infected links which, if opened, compromised the phone. In one case, journalist Rafael Cabrero reported on a potential conflict of interest involving Mexican President Enrique Peña Nieto and his wife, Angélica Rivera. The story revealed that the first family's $7 million mansion was owned by a subsidiary of a Chinese company that had been awarded a multibillion-dollar high speed rail contract. The report forced the government to revoke the contract, and the presidential couple to sell their stake in the house and publicly declare their assets.

Taking on the Mexican president – who was cleared of wrongdoing or conflict of interest by a government inquiry in 2015 – might have made a name for Cabrera as an investigative journalist, but it also made him enemies – and a target. Infected SMS texts started arriving on his iPhone: 'Facebook reports efforts to access the account of: Rafael Cabrera. Avoid account blockage, Verify at: [MALICIOUS LINK]'[8]

TELCEL.COM/. DEAR CLIENT WE REMIND YOU THAT YOU HAVE AN OUTSTANDING DEBT OF $8,854.90 IN NATIONAL CURRENCY. TO VERIFY DETAILS [infected link][9]

Others too were targeted, including TV personality and investigative journalist Carmen Aristegui and journalists working with the group Mexicans Against Corruption and Impunity. Another journalist, Carlos Loret de Mola, received a message while reporting on the possible involvement of the government in the disappearance of 42 people in western Mexico. On 8 August, 2015, Loret revealed Mexican security forces had committed extrajudicial killings, with many of the victims shot in the back of the head at point blank range.

Twelve days later as Loret prepared for a trip to the US, he received an SMS text. Whoever sent it appeared very sure of themselves. The message read: 'US EMBASSY.GOV / WE DETECTED A PROBLEM WITH YOUR VISA PLEASE GO PROMPTLY TO THE EMBASSY. SEE DETAILS [infected link]'.[10]

Nine days later Loret received an SMS claiming he was being watched and including an infected link to a photograph: 'these people came asking for you they come in a van without license plates. I took a picture do you know them? look: [infected link]'.[11] Over the next few months he received other SMS messages including one that said: 'Dear Loret, look that tvnotas[Mexican TV] has photos of you in which you are dining with a chick. Look at them: [infected link]'.[12]

Once infected the phone became what CitizenLab called 'a digital spy in the pocket of the victim'.[13] The monitoring system that was installed by clicking on the infected link allowed messages to be intercepted, even those that were end-to-end encrypted. It could also record calls and send back photographs.

The manufacturer of the spying system, a highly secretive Israeli organisation named NSO, based in Tel Aviv, told CitizenLab that its mission was to 'help make the world a safer place'[14] to 'combat terror and crime'. It only provided its system, known as Pegasus, to 'authorised governments'[15] like Mexico. In an apparent attempt to distance itself from any wrongdoing, NSO said in a separate statement: 'the company does NOT operate any of its systems; it is strictly a technology company'.[16] But CitizenLab points out that although NSO's surveillance system might have a legitimate use against terrorists it was also being employed against journalists exposing criminal acts. In August 2016 CitizenLab revealed that NSO had sold its technology to the United Arab Emirates (UAE), a country accused by Amnesty International of using torture against political opponents. CitizenLab released a report revealing another example of how easy it had become to turn mobile phones into surveillance devices. Very often these spying techniques go undiscovered but when UAE activist Ahmed Mansoor was targeted by the NSO system to infect his iPhone 6 via a malicious link in an SMS text message, he passed on the information to CitizenLab, who traced it back to NSO. Journalists were also on the government's surveillance watch list. According to RSF, although the constitution allowed freedom of speech, journalists were often caught by a law which made it an offence for local or foreign publications 'to criticize domestic policies, the economy, the ruling families, religion'.[17] There was another area which it was forbidden to make adverse comments about: 'the UAE's relations with its allies'.[18] The UAE was clearly keen to remain on good terms with those it did not name: Saudi Arabia and in particular Egypt, who would call on it in years to come for help acquiring surveillance equipment. In 2016, it was first reported that a Danish subsidiary of the UK company BAE Systems had slipped through the net of European Union (EU) oversight to sell surveillance equipment to the UAE. Twelve months later in 2017 the BBC reported another surveillance export by BAE through the Danish company. The Danish government had approved the export partly because its own intelligence services and foreign affairs advisers had not objected, the BBC reported. Just why that was the case is not clear but what the BBC discovered, working with journalists from its Arabic section, revealed the dangers of selling high quality surveillance equipment to dictators and authoritarian regimes.

The BBC located two men who were employed to operate the BAE surveillance system, Evident, in Tunisia during the dictatorship of President Zine al-Abidine Ben Ali. Many opponents were locked up and tortured by his regime – one of the Arab world's most repressive – before he was overthrown in 2011 during the Arab Spring. One of the men told the BBC that his job was to monitor Tunisia's internet using the Evident system that had been installed in the basement of one of Ben Ali's houses. 'The tool works with keywords,' he told the BBC. 'You put in an opponent's name. You will see all the sites, blogs, social networks related to that user.'[19]

According to the BBC, the second man was part of a specialist intelligence unit that worked closely with Ben Ali. 'Sometimes they would ask me to get information about specific people . . . some information used to go directly to the president. Most of this was about his opponents.'[20]

Four years after the Arab Spring in 2015, an Italian company, Hacking Team, was exposed for allowing the Ethiopian Government to use its technology to spy on a journalist working for a Washington-based satellite TV channel. The discovery was made when the company itself was hacked and incriminating emails revealing the scope of its deception were spread on the web. Human Rights Watch reported that a comprehensive review of the internal company emails leaked revealed that the company trained 'Ethiopian intelligence agents to hack into computers . . . despite multiple reports that its services were being used to repress government critics and other independent voices.'[21]

Such is the lack of oversight in this crucial area, vital evidence is often only unearthed when what are known as 'virtual vigilantes' hack into companies' computer systems to produce evidence about breaches of the law. As the EU pointed out: 'Efforts to control arms exports from the EU have been marked by tensions between the economic interests of member states relating to their market shares.'[22] of the arms trade. Nonetheless, in 2008 the EU adopted rules which bound its member states not to sell weapons to countries where they might be used 'to commit serious violations of international humanitarian law'[23] and undermine regional peace and stability.

The EU particularly targeted Egypt, where an elected government had been removed from power in a military coup – and replaced by one that seemed intent on restoring all the authoritarianism of the past.

The role of Al Jazeera TV in reporting both the uprising against President Hosni Mubarak and the crushing removal of his elected successor, Mohammed Morsi, in a military coup in July 2013, in which hundreds were killed, would lead. It would lead to the arrest of Al Jazeera journalists including Australian Peter Greste, and a long public campaign by the network to free them. Al Jazeera received strong support from Europe. In August, 2013, EU Foreign Ministers decided' that member states [suspend] export licenses to Egypt for any equipment which could be used as a means of repression'.[24] The decision appeared to be a signal to Egypt and it developed a clever ploy to overcome the embargo. It called on its Gulf ally, the UAE, for help. According to the French magazine *Télérama*, in March 2014 the UAE bought a 10-million euro surveillance system from the French company Amesys, and promptly transferred it across the border to Egypt.

It was a deft move by the company, already under investigation in the French High Court for selling an earlier version of the surveillance system to the deposed Libyan leader Muammar Kaddafi.

The Libyan contract had been finalised through the intermediary companies Amesys created in 2012: the France-based Nexa Technologies and the Dubai-based Advanced Middle East Systems.

Amesys boasts that its surveillance technology, marketed as Cerebo, provides its end users with the potential for real-time surveillance of targets, due to what

Télérama describes as 'particularly intrusive sensors capable of tracking emails, text messages and accessing chat rooms and social media sites'.[25] It seemed that the Europeans had moved too slowly.

In January 2015, the European Parliament stepped up its restrictions, approving a resolution 'forbidding, on a European scale, the export to Egypt of surveillance technologies which could be used to spy on and suppress its citizens'.[26] Several months later the mutilated body of an Italian student from Cambridge University, was discovered in the suburbs of Cairo. Regeni, who was studying the politically sensitive area of independent trade unions in Egypt, appeared to have been the victim of an attack by government security agents: he had been tortured before being beaten to death. Following Regeni's death, the EU increased the pressure and broadened the restriction, demanding the suspension of all exports of 'surveillance systems which violate human rights'.[27]

But Egypt, already well armed with surveillance equipment, now moved against the Western countries who funded much of the NGO work in the country. On 29 May, 2017 the former Egyptian Army chief, General Abdel Fattah el-Sisi who seized power in the coup, enacted a law aimed at severely restricting the work of NGOs, and in particular, those defending human rights, effectively banning them from operating in Egypt. According to Le Monde the Egyptian government also had plans to restrict social media sites: 'The parliament intends to pass laws to control access to sites such as Twitter and Facebook.'[28] By July 2017 at least 63 online platforms, including 23 news websites had been blocked on the grounds that they were 'supporting terrorism and spreading lies'.[29]

One of the sites, Mada Masr, which publishes news and analysis deeply critical of the authorities was among the first to be blocked. On 11 June, 2017 the Egyptian news sites Albedaiah (run by independent journalist Khaled al Balshy), Elbadil and Bawabit Yanair were blocked. Access to the global online publishing platform Medium was also cut off on 10 June, 2017. But probably most significant was the decision taken by the Egyptian government to cut the international online service of Al Jazeera.

As the Egyptian government tightened the net on dissent they joined forces with one of the most repressive regimes in the Middle East, Saudi Arabia, to oppose one of the more liberal, Qatar. For cultural and strategic reasons Qatar is more closely aligned to Iran than its other Sunni neighbours, but what really sets it apart is its international satellite channel, Al Jazeera, staffed by many former BBC reporters and widely applauded for its professional high quality journalism. Yet while Al Jazeera shines a fierce light on what happens outside Qatar's borders, inside it's a different story. RSF points out that journalists in this small emirate are left little leeway by the 'oppressive legislative arsenal'[30] and the 'draconian system of censorship'.[31] Government, royal family and Islam are off limits, as in the rest of the Persian Gulf, and those who break the laws risk imprisonment. A cyber-crime law adopted in late 2014 imposed additional restrictions on journalists and criminalised posting 'false news'[32] online. What was false and what was true would be decided by the government.

Even so, Al Jazeera played an important role in challenging the hegemonic powers of dictators, from Tunisian president Ben Ali to Egypt's Hosni Mubarak, interviewing dissenting voices who had never been heard or seen before on TV. Its Arabic broadcasts, in particular, gained the channel a reputation for fearless journalism, a welcome change from the usual state sponsored propaganda which reported without question the decision of its rulers. But Al Jazeera's success, with an audience of 35 million in Arabic-speaking homes, came at a price. On 15 January, 2003, just two months before the invasion of Iraq, the US Ambassador to the UAE, Marcelee M Wahba, sent a secret cable to the CIA and DIA which gave a clear insight into how at least one Gulf country dealt with problems caused by the dissenting journalism of Al Jazeera. A secret cable released by WikiLeaks revealed that the US Ambassador reported that during a meeting with an embassy official, the Crown Prince of the UAE, Mohammed bin Zayed al Nahyan – referred to as MBZ – had emphasised 'the importance of reigning the Doha-based Al-Jazeera satellite network prior to any military action'.[33] According to the US Ambassador, the Crown Prince had 'laughingly recalled' a conversation between his father, Zayed bin Sultan al Nahyan, and the emir of Qatar, Hamad al-Thani.

Al-Thani complained al Nahyan had asked the then commander of the US Central Command General Tommy Franks to bomb the news channel. The Crown Prince then told former State Department official, Robert Haass, that his father had replied 'Do you blame him?'[34]

Al Jazeera's office was one of the first targets struck when US-backed Northern Alliance fighters drove the Taliban out of the Afghan capital, Kabul, in November, 2001, though the US denied deliberately targeting the network.

In March 2003 as the US-led invasion got underway, Al Jazeera reported on the carnage wrought on the Iraqi population. In the United States, there were calls for the station's American network to be taken off air. A few weeks later in April 2003, Al Jazeera's office in Baghdad was hit by a US missile which killed one of its reporters. The emergence of Qatar as a regional power – with its well-regarded Al Jazeera broadcaster – challenged Saudi Arabia's dominance of the Sunni world. In the aftermath of the disastrous US foray into Iraq, Saudi Arabia and Qatar would struggle for influence on the Syrian battlefield. WikiLeaks cables reveal the US believed both were courting the Sunni-aligned Islamic State of Iraq and the Levant (ISIL).

Hilary Clinton wrote in an email in September 2014:

> We need to use our diplomatic and more traditional intelligence assets to bring pressure on the governments of Qatar and Saudi Arabia, which are providing clandestine financial and logistic support to ISIL and other radical Sunni groups in the region.[35]

Whatever the truth of Clinton's assertion, by June 2017 the two leading Sunni nations had had a massive public falling out. What is intriguing is the reason Saudi Arabia gave for leading other Gulf States in an air, sea and road blockade of Qatar: it accused the Qatari government of funding terrorism. Critically one of the 13 conditions Saudi Arabia gave for lifting the blockade was to permanently shut down Al Jazeera. If Qatar backed down the voice of Saudi Arabia's greatest rival would be silenced.

The argument was not so much about terrorism, but control and influence, with a modern Arab nation embracing the modern world – outside its borders at least – and Saudi Arabia on the other hand struggling with modernity. Saudi is not alone in lacking an independent media, but its authoritarianism is of a particularly high level. The country does not tolerate political parties, unions or human rights groups, and self-censorship is the norm. As RSF pointed out, the internet was the only space where freely-reported information and views could circulate, albeit at great risk to its citizen journalists. Like professional journalists, they were watched closely, RSF reported, and critical comments were liable to lead to 'arrest and trial under the country's terrorism or cyber-crime laws'.[36] Blasphemy, insulting religion, inciting chaos, and defaming the king and the state were the most frequent charges brought against those who showed a desire to report the truth. They were also liable to be mistreated in prison or subjected to barbaric punishments such as flogging.

The West's response to the attack on free speech revealed how heavily compromised it had become to its stated position: the demand to shut Al Jazeera was met with silence from the West's political leadership. The BBC's World Affairs Editor, John Simpson, pointed out the hypocrisy:

> Imagine the rage if the EU's chief negotiator, Michel Barnier, demanded that Theresa May should close down the BBC as part of the Brexit deal. Well, of course it's not remotely conceivable: that isn't how modern democratic states do business.[37]

He said he seemed to have 'missed the huge wave of anger about this'.[38] President Trump, he noted, who was doing 'various deals'[39] with the Saudis, had not tweeted anything. Theresa May, in her desperate effort to find new markets for Britain, 'can't afford to upset them'.[40] Everyone else seemed to be looking away.

Simpson said that in its 21 years on air, Al Jazeera had become one of the world's major news channels, offering a 'different perspective'[41] from the major Western news organisations. Simpson identified Al Jazeera's only possible weakness that it may have been accused of being 'slanted in favour of the Islamist Muslim Brotherhood movement in Egypt and elsewhere but it employs talented ex-colleagues of mine from the BBC, and I've always felt its heart is in the right place'.[42]

Strangely it was not the Saudis who responded, but one of their close allies, the UAE, a country whose leader had made light of bombing Al Jazeera. Its constitution might guarantee free speech but the authorities could censor local or foreign publications if they criticised domestic policies, the economy, the ruling families, religion, or the UAE's relations with its allies.

The UAE dismissed Simpson's support of Al Jazeera, commenting that the station also broadcast in Arabic. 'Al-Jazeera Arabic has a history of inciting hatred and promoting terrorism, and has pushed dangerous ideologies across the Arabic-speaking world,'[43] the statement said.

Yet the shut-down was not demanded for just the Arabic part of the network. Saudi Arabia and other Gulf States wanted the entire station taken off air. What is so troubling, as Simpson points out, is that no one in any government in the world spoke up for Al Jazeera. Outrage from Western nations is reserved for causes which appear safer than offending a rich and powerful strategic ally. Clearly journalism's job is made that much more difficult when the countries with the world's worst human rights records are being supplied with surveillance equipment by those nations who supposedly uphold the ideals of free speech which are so clearly threatened. The question of how to resist the surveillance ideology that is increasingly afflicting the work of journalists, in the guise of combating terrorism, does not have a simple answer. It will be a vitally important yet grievously difficult fight.

Notes

1 Blanchard, B. 27th December, 2015. *China Passes Controversial Counter-Terrorism Law*. Reuters [online]. Available at www.reuters.com/article/us-china-security-idUSKBN0UA07220151227 [Accessed 30 November, 2016].

2 Campbell, M. 2012. *Under Cover of Security, Government's Jail Journalists*. Committee to Protect Journalists [online]. Available at https://cpj.org/2013/02/attacks-on-the-press-misusing-terror-laws.php [Accessed 12 July, 2016].

3 Lowen, M. 13th April, 2017. *Erdogan's Turkey*. BBC [online]. Available at www.bbc.co.uk/news/resources/idt-sh/Erdogans_Turkey [Accessed 1 May, 2017].

4 Lowen, M. 13th April, 2017. *Erdogan's Turkey*. BBC [online]. Available at www.bbc.co.uk/news/resources/idt-sh/Erdogans_Turkey [Accessed 1 May, 2017].

5 Lowen, M. 13th April, 2017. *Erdogan's Turkey*. BBC [online]. Available at www.bbc.co.uk/news/resources/idt-sh/Erdogans_Turkey [Accessed 1 May, 2017].

6 Lowen, M. 13th April, 2017. *Erdogan's Turkey*. BBC [online]. Available at www.bbc.co.uk/news/resources/idt-sh/Erdogans_Turkey [Accessed 1 May, 2017].

7 Lowen, M. 13th April, 2017. *Erdogan's Turkey*. BBC [online]. Available at www.bbc.co.uk/news/resources/idt-sh/Erdogans_Turkey [Accessed 1 May, 2017].

8 Scott-Railton, J., Marczak, B., Razzak, B., Crete-Nishihata, M., and Deibert, R. 19th June, 2017. *Mexican Journalists, Lawyers, and a Child Targeted with NSO Spyware*. The Citizen Lab [online]. Available at https://citizenlab.ca/2017/06/reckless-exploit-mexico-nso/#comment-287885 [Accessed 12 March, 2017].

9 Scott-Railton, J., Marczak, B., Razzak, B., Crete-Nishihata, M., and Deibert, R. 19th June, 2017. *Mexican Journalists, Lawyers, and a Child Targeted with NSO Spyware*. The Citizen Lab [online]. Available at https://citizenlab.ca/2017/06/reckless-exploit-mexico-nso/#comment-287885 [Accessed 12 March, 2017].

10 Scott-Railton, J., Marczak, B., Razzak, B., Crete-Nishihata, M., and Deibert, R. 19th June, 2017. *Mexican Journalists, Lawyers, and a Child Targeted with NSO Spyware*. The Citizen Lab [online]. Available at https://citizenlab.ca/2017/06/reckless-exploit-mexico-nso/#comment-287885 [Accessed 12 March, 2017].

11 Scott-Railton, J., Marczak, B., Razzak, B., Crete-Nishihata, M., and Deibert, R. 19th June, 2017. *Mexican Journalists, Lawyers, and a Child Targeted with NSO Spyware*. The Citizen Lab [online]. Available at https://citizenlab.ca/2017/06/reckless-exploit-mexico-nso/#comment-287885 [Accessed 12 March, 2017].

12 Scott-Railton, J., Marczak, B., Razzak, B., Crete-Nishihata, M., and Deibert, R. 19th June, 2017. *Mexican Journalists, Lawyers, and a Child Targeted with NSO Spyware*. The Citizen Lab [online]. Available at https://citizenlab.ca/2017/06/reckless-exploit-mexico-nso/#comment-287885 [Accessed 12 March, 2017].

13 Scott-Railton, J., Marczak, B., Razzak, B., Crete-Nishihata, M., and Deibert, R. 19th June, 2017. *Mexican Journalists, Lawyers, and a Child Targeted with NSO Spyware*. The Citizen Lab [online]. Available at https://citizenlab.ca/2017/06/reckless-exploit-mexico-nso/#comment-287885 [Accessed 12 March, 2017].

14 Scott-Railton, J., Marczak, B., Razzak, B., Crete-Nishihata, M. and Deibert, R. 19th June, 2017. *Mexican Journalists, Lawyers, and a Child Targeted with NSO Spyware*. The Citizen Lab [online]. Available at https://citizenlab.ca/2017/06/reckless-exploit-mexico-nso/#comment-287885 [Accessed 12 March, 2017].

15 Scott-Railton, J., Marczak, B., Razzak, B., Crete-Nishihata, M., and Deibert, R. 19th June, 2017. *Mexican Journalists, Lawyers, and a Child Targeted with NSO Spyware*. The Citizen Lab [online]. Available at https://citizenlab.ca/2017/06/reckless-exploit-mexico-nso/#comment-287885 [Accessed 12 March, 2017].

16 Fox-Brewster, T. 25th August, 2016. *Everything We Know About NSO Group: The Professional Spies Who Hacked iPhones With a Single Text*. Forbes [online]. Available at www.forbes.com/sites/thomasbrewster/2016/08/25/everything-we-know-about-nso-group-the-professional-spies-who-hacked-iphones-with-a-single-text/#696e94683997 [Accessed 16 March, 2016].

17 Reporters Without Borders. 2017. United Arab Emirates. Sophisticated Online Surveillance [online]. Available at https://rsf.org/en/united-arab-emirates [Accessed 15 May, 2017].

18 Reporters Without Borders. 2017. United Arab Emirates. Sophisticated Online Surveillance [online]. Available at https://rsf.org/en/united-arab-emirates [Accessed 15 May, 2017].

19 Evans, R. 15th June, 2017. *BAE Secretly Sold Mass Surveillance Technology to Repressive Regimes*. The Guardian [online]. Available at www.theguardian.com/business/2017/jun/15/bae-mass-surveillance-technology-repressive-regimes [Accessed 16 June, 2017].

20 Evans, R. 15th June, 2017. *BAE Secretly Sold Mass Surveillance Technology to Repressive Regimes*. The Guardian [online]. Available at www.theguardian.com/business/2017/jun/15/bae-mass-surveillance-technology-repressive-regimes [Accessed 16 June, 2017].

21 Human Rights Watch. 13th August, 2015. Ethiopia: Hacking Team Lax on Evidence of Abuse [online]. Available at www.hrw.org/news/2015/08/13/ethiopia-hacking-team-lax-evidence-abuse [Accessed 25 October, 2016].

22 EU. 20th January, 2013. EU Arms Exports [online]. Available at www.europarl.europa.eu/RegData/bibliotheque/briefing/2013/130454/LDM_BRI(2013)130454_REV1_EN.pdf [Accessed 16 September, 2016].

23 EU. 8th December, 2008. Acts Adopted Under Title V of the EU Treaty [online]. Available at http://eur-lex.europa.eu/LexUriServ/LexUriServ.do?uri=OJ:L:2008:335:0099:0103:EN:PDF [Accessed 31 August, 2016].

24 EU.10th September, 2013. Resolution du Parlement europeen sur l'Egypt [online]. Available at www.europarl.europa.eu/sides/getDoc.do?pubRef=-//EP//TEXT+MOTION+B7-2013-0420+0+DOC+XML+V0//FR [Accessed 25 April, 2017].

25 Mada Masr. 5th July, 2017. UAE Transfers Internet Surveillance System Bought from French Company to Egypt: Telerama [online]. Available at www.madamasr.com/en/2017/07/05/news/u/uae-transfers-internet-surveillance-system-bought-from-french-company-to-egypt-telerama/ [Accessed 7 July, 2017].

26 EU. 15th January, 2015. Resolution du Parlement europeen du 15 Janvier 2015 sur la situation Egypte [online]. Available at www.europarl.europa.eu/sides/getDoc.do?pubRef=-//EP//TEXT+TA+P8-TA-2015-0012+0+DOC+XML+V0//FR [Accessed 23 October, 2016].

27 EU. 9th March, 2016. Resolution du Parlement europeen sur l'Egypt, en particulier sur le cas de Giulio Regeni [online]. Available at www.europarl.europa.eu/sides/getDoc.do?pubRef=-//EP//TEXT+MOTION+P8-RC-2016-0338+0+DOC+XML+V0//FR [Accessed 23 October, 2016].

28 Sallon, H. 31st May, 2017. *En Egypte, le regime de Sissi porte un coup fatal a la societe civile* [online]. Available at www.lemonde.fr/afrique/article/2017/05/31/l-egypte-porte-un-coup-fatal-a-la-societe-civile_5136292_3212.html [Accessed 3 June, 2017].

29 Aboulenein, A. 25th May, 2017. *Egypt blocks 21 websites for 'terrorism' and 'fake news.'* Reuters [online]. Available at www.reuters.com/article/us-egypt-censorship-idUSKBN18K307 [Accessed 27 May, 2017].

30 Reporters Without Borders. 2017. Qatar [online]. Available at https://rsf.org/en/qatar [Accessed 1 June, 2017].

31 Reporters Without Borders. 2017. Qatar [online]. Available at https://rsf.org/en/qatar [Accessed 1 June, 2017].

32 Reporters Without Borders. 2017. Qatar [online]. Available at https://rsf.org/en/qatar [Accessed 1 June, 2017].

33 WikiLeaks. 15th January, 2003. Director Haass and Chief of Staff Huhammad Bin Zayid Discuss Iraq, Iran and Saudi-US Relations [online]. Available at https://wikileaks.org/plusd/cables/03ABUDHABI237_a.html [Accessed 8 September, 2016].

34 WikiLeaks. 15th January, 2003. Director Haass and Chief of Staff Huhammad Bin Zayid Discuss Iraq, Iran and Saudi-US Relations [online]. Available at https://wikileaks.org/plusd/cables/03ABUDHABI237_a.html [Accessed 8 September, 2016].

35 WikiLeaks. 27th September, 2016. Hilary Clinton Email [online]. Available at https://wikileaks.org/podesta-emails/emailid/3774 [Accessed 1 May, 2017].

36 RSF. 2017. Saudi Arabia No Independent Media [online]. Available at https://rsf.org/en/saudi-arabia. [Accessed 28 November, 2016].

37 Simpson, J. 29th June, 2017. *Western Silence Over the Threat to Al Jazeera Is Just Shameful* [online]. Available at www.standard.co.uk/comment/comment/western-silence-over-the-threat-to-al-jazeera-is-just-shameful-a3575681.html [Accessed 1 July, 2017].

38 Simpson, J. 29th June, 2017. *Western Silence Over the Threat to Al Jazeera Is Just Shameful* [online]. Available at www.standard.co.uk/comment/comment/western-silence-over-the-threat-to-al-jazeera-is-just-shameful-a3575681.html [Accessed 1 July, 2017].

39 Simpson, J. 29th June, 2017. *Western Silence Over the Threat to Al Jazeera Is Just Shameful* [online]. Available at www.standard.co.uk/comment/comment/western-silence-over-the-threat-to-al-jazeera-is-just-shameful-a3575681.html [Accessed 1 July, 2017].

40 Simpson, J. 29th June, 2017. *Western Silence Over the Threat to Al Jazeera Is Just Shameful* [online]. Available at www.standard.co.uk/comment/comment/western-silence-over-the-threat-to-al-jazeera-is-just-shameful-a3575681.html [Accessed 1 July, 2017].

41 Simpson, J. 29th June, 2017. *Western Silence Over the Threat to Al Jazeera Is Just Shameful* [online]. Available at www.standard.co.uk/comment/comment/western-silence-over-the-threat-to-al-jazeera-is-just-shameful-a3575681.html [Accessed 1 July, 2017].

42 Simpson, J. 29th June, 2017. *Western Silence Over the Threat to Al Jazeera Is Just Shameful* [online]. Available at www.standard.co.uk/comment/comment/western-silence-over-the-threat-to-al-jazeera-is-just-shameful-a3575681.html [Accessed 1 July, 2017].

43 Egypt Today. 3rd July, 2017. Closing Al Jazeera Not Against Free Speech: UAE Ambassador [online]. Available at www.egypttoday.com/Article/2/9900/Closing-Al-Jazeera-not-against-free-speech-UAE-amb [Accessed 5 July, 2017].

13

SHOOTING THE MESSENGER

At a time when journalists have never been more needed to explain the complexities of an increasingly integrated world, they have never been more under threat: jailed in increasing numbers by some of the more authoritarian administrations, threatened with prosecution in the countries which have democratic governments. There is a real possibility that the over-reach of national security laws in the West will damage the very commodity that heightened internet surveillance is supposedly designed to protect: security and liberty.

The ultimate absurdity is that the most extraordinarily liberating communications system invented since the printing press could bring the West down by being turned into a tool of oppression and censorship. Created originally as a way for signals between military commanders to withstand the destructive electromagnetic forces unleashed during a nuclear war, it became a beacon for democracy, encouraging an uninhibited flow of information around the planet. From a San Francisco newspaper which provided the first online version in the early 1980s, the internet eventually allowed readers to subscribe to just about any newspaper, anywhere in the world. Television went online, transmitting its programmes across international borders. Information stored in the world's libraries were available at the click of mouse. But now the internet, which couldn't be shut down by a nuclear attack, is subject to assault from within. The offices of government that played a role in its building want to take back the control they lost when the public gained access and embraced it as its own.

The internet is a dangerous place, we are told, where terrorists can freely roam, plotting to attack the West, using encryption to scramble their messages and blind security agencies. The problem is, nothing could be further from the truth. As was pointed out earlier, nearly three quarters of those people who committed terrorist acts in Western countries in the last one and a half decades were known to the authorities. Yet the clamour in the West is for more controls on those who use the internet for communications, but little control of the governments who use it for surveillance. The role of journalists is grudgingly accepted by Western nations as an inconvenient necessity, as a measure of democracy, but the fact is executive government has done all it can to manage the news, to restrict what journalists can reveal about the secret activities of state. One well-tried method of control is to 'shoot the messenger', or at least cripple his or her capability to reveal important and unpleasant truths. Which is why laws passed in so many jurisdictions around the world give little cover for journalists carrying out their important role of holding the powerful to account. Journalists and journalism are suffering from a 'chilling effect' where sources are afraid to speak for fear that surveillance will capture either their movements or their communications, and journalists are worried that they may inadvertently reveal the identities of their sources to the authorities. The fact that during the ten years he was in office, President Barack Obama prosecuted more whistle-blowers than all the presidents in US history combined is an indication of the increasing threat to journalism. And in 2017 the head of the CIA questioned the first amendment rights which protect free speech, while the US attorney-general threatened that Julian Assange would be prosecuted (for what he was not clear). Both are acts of intimidation designed to silence. In the UK and Australia there are fresh proposals that, if they ever become law, will see journalists jailed for simply possessing information the government has decided should be restricted.

It has been argued that governments are not that concerned about most of the work that journalists do, so for most, concerns about surveillance are not necessary. But the problem there is that generally speaking, if governments are not worried about what journalists are doing, the journalists are not doing their jobs. Reporting local news may be a useful social function, but the issues that arise where nations go to war, or where countries are involved in breaking the law, or plundering the treasure of other nations, are of great importance and need investigating. It is in these significant areas that journalists must be protected from the vested interests of the executive state; where the very people who make the decisions, as in the Iraq War, need to be exposed and held to account before the event, not after it. The invasion of Iraq, and the rise of global terrorism as a consequence, created huge pressure on governments to be seen to be taking action to protect the public.

What is so disturbing is that the media itself has often aided and abetted governments and the intelligence agencies – who always want more access to information – as they invoked the fear of terrorism as grounds for introducing tougher surveillance laws.

The most egregious exponents of this form of complicity in spreading the false hope of complete safety can be seen in the UK where right-wing newspapers, in league with a Conservative government, prosecuted a nationalist case: the state will guarantee security if the subjects give up their privacy. Journalists who expose unpalatable issues are faced with hysterical charges of treason for helping expose the blatant disregard for the laws, as revealed by Edward Snowden. Where does this leave journalists? Already in a weakened position because of the devastation wrought on the profitability of newspapers and other media by Facebook and other news aggregators, many have turned to collective action using the internet, to work co-operatively. Organisations like WikiLeaks led the way by providing documents and analysis, partnering with newspapers like *The Guardian*, the *Washington Post*, the *Sydney Morning Herald*, *Le Monde*, *Der Spiegel* and Spain's *El Pais*, to produce outstanding and revelatory journalism. Edward Snowden's disclosures came to light through the activities of a then online blogger, Glen Greenwald, who in turn teamed up with *The Guardian*. Along with the *Washington Post* they produced the greatest series of scoops in the history of journalism. The Panama Papers are another example of journalists working collectively to create outstanding results to the benefit of the public.

But even the International Consortium of Journalists, whose reports did not deal with matters of state security, needed to be extremely careful about protecting their information and their sources. They used encryption and apparently stored some of their information on computer systems in Iceland, making use of the friendly environment that exists in that country to protect data and privacy. It should not come as a surprise that Western governments increasingly vilify the use of secure encrypted communications, but it is a dangerous argument, both at home and among the less democratic nations that copy their every move to clamp down on dissent. Yet here the role of the journalist, with the need for confidentiality, comes into sharp conflict with the desire of the state for secrecy. States which should be publicly accountable demand privacy, while only allowing limited privacy to those who hold them to account. As we have seen in recent history, there is little new in this dilemma, from the prosecution of those like Duncan Campbell, who exposed the increasing surveillance powers of the UK government in the mid-1970s to the present-day hounding of journalists even in the United States, where free speech and the right to publish are enshrined in the Constitution. But since the days of fax machines and letters gave way to digital transmissions, communication now only has one highway. Since it is largely impractical to use an alternative method of delivering information, it is necessary to change the form that the message takes. A system of encryption is the simplest way for journalists to protect information, from a simple direct message system such as WhatsApp or Signal to the more complex Pretty Good Privacy (PGP). But even encryption, with its greatly increased use since the Snowden revelations, is not foolproof, and can expose the source to the attention of security agencies because their activities stand out from the crowd as, even now, all too few people use any form of encrypted technology.

What we do know is that information so far made public in the United States reveals that dragnet surveillance did not help the FBI to stop terrorists. The fact is that most terrorists are known to the authorities in the Western societies they attack, suggesting that the 'collect it all' process is both inefficient and does not work in protecting nations from attack.

Much of the evidence suggests that diverting money from surveillance systems that randomly collect information on everyone on the planet, to investigating known suspects would be a more efficient way to combat political violence. But as we have seen, the powerful industrialised countries, the most notable of which are the Five Eyes, use their unquestioned surveillance powers in cyber space for other reasons, to gather industrial information, and to potentially prepare for cyber war.

The argument that government oversight measures are effective is provably wrong, given what we know about what happened in the aftermath of the 2001 terrorist attacks. Even a great democracy like the United States can be subverted by wilful politicians and a sometimes compliant media.

Unless there is a concerted effort by the West to abandon the surveillance state into which we are all being drawn, it is highly likely that the journalism that relies on dissent to expose the great injustices perpetrated by governments, particularly when they hide behind the cloak of national security, will be journalism of the past. It won't disappear overnight, but will fade slowly over the years, like the democracy it defends.

INDEX